Praise for *Managing Diversity*

- Academy of Management's George R. Terry Book Award for the year's most outstanding contribution to the advancement of management knowledge
- *Choice* Award for Outstanding Academic Titles by the Association of Research and College Libraries

"*Managing Diversity* comprehensively addresses the corporate role for inclusiveness as part of workforce management as well as at community, state and federal, and international levels. Mor Barak has made a substantial contribution to the human resources and management literature."

—Gary Bess, *Profiles in Diversity Journal*

"The viewpoint of the book is truly global. By integrating established knowledge on diversity issues with contemporary perspectives on inclusion and globalization, this book pioneers the next generation of scholarship on issues of workforce diversity."

—Susan J. Lambert, *Journal of Sociology and Social Welfare*

"Authored by an extremely knowledgeable professor with a joint appointment in business and social work at the University of Southern California, this volume provides a thorough, well-written, and interesting resource on managing global workplace diversity that will be useful to both the practitioner and the conceptual researcher. All in all, this is a refreshing and compelling volume that will be useful to anyone in global business management. Highly recommended."

—T. Gutteridge, *CHOICE Magazine*

"This is a timely book. The book's subject, managing diversity in a global workplace, portends the future for a growing area of social work policy and practice. . . . A valuable resource for social work practice in a global context, the book is also highly recommended as a text in social work education programs."

—John J. Stretch, *Social Work Journal*

"*Managing Diversity* comprehensively addresses the importance of inclusiveness as part of workforce management, which is scalable from small community-based organizations to large multinational service agencies. . . . Practical relevance is threaded throughout the book. . . . This book is a must-read for social work management professionals and others committed to social justice in the workplace."

—*Administration in Social Work*

"[*Managing Diversity*] is thorough, well-written, and filled with interesting information and case examples. It deals with an important issue in a very complete manner, providing both theoretical and conceptual content and outstanding practical information. It should be valuable and useful to anyone studying international business management."

—**Sheila Akabas, Professor and Director, Center for Social Policy and Practice in the Workplace, Columbia University**

"The book will be helpful for students and scholars in international business management, international HRM, diversity management, and cross-cultural management. It is a useful resource for conceptualizing and implementing an inclusive workplace agenda. It reflects a global perspective and will interest readers across countries. The book has demonstrated well that when diversity and inclusion are being practiced as business strategies, they help in providing competitive advantage."

—**Debi S. Saini, *The Journal of Business Perspective***

"Over the last two decades organizations, government, and society have grappled with demands presented by increased diversity in nations and workplaces alike. . . . Mor Barak's book is one of the first to explore the synergies between international management and domestic diversity management."

—**Kate Hutchings, *Asia Pacific Journal of Human Relations***

"This book has been structured excellently and covers a vast number of diversity issues in just 16 chapters. . . . This book would be of value to anyone with research interests in diversity management or cross-cultural issues."

—**Sunil Kumar Singh, *IIMB Management Review***

"Professor Mor Barak's book provides a myriad of practical examples and case illustrations that bring the content to life. The concept of the Inclusive Workplace that she has originated and developed is particularly useful for managers and scholars alike. I highly recommend this book."

—**Nissan Pardo, PhD, CEO/CFO, *Dynamic Home Care & Nursing***

SECOND EDITION

MANAGING
DIVERSITY

For information:

SAGE Publications, Inc.
2455 Teller Road
Thousand Oaks, California 91320
E-mail: order@sagepub.com

SAGE Publications India Pvt. Ltd.
B 1/I 1 Mohan Cooperative
   Industrial Area
Mathura Road, New Delhi 110 044
India

SAGE Publications Ltd.
1 Oliver's Yard
55 City Road
London, EC1Y 1SP
United Kingdom

SAGE Publications Asia-Pacific Pte. Ltd.
33 Pekin Street #02–01
Far East Square
Singapore 048763

Printed in the United States of America

Library of Congress Cataloging-in-Publication Data

Mor Barak, Michàlle E.
Managing diversity : toward a globally inclusive workplace /
Michàlle E. Mor Barak.— 2nd ed.
    p. cm.
Includes bibliographical references and index.
ISBN 978-1-4129-7235-2 (pbk. : acid-free paper)
  1. Diversity in the workplace. I. Title.

HF5549.5.M5M662 2011
658.3008—dc22   2010015050

This book is printed on acid-free paper.

10   11   12   13   14   10   9   8   7   6   5   4   3   2   1

Acquisitions Editor:	Lisa Shaw
Editorial Assistant:	MaryAnn Vail
Production Editor:	Libby Larson
Typesetter:	C&M Digitals (P) Ltd.
Proofreader:	Cheryl Rivard
Indexer:	Wendy Allex
Cover Designer:	Candice Harman
Marketing Manager:	Helen Salmon

Contents

List of Boxes, Figures, and Tables   xi

Preface and Acknowledgments   xv

Chapter 1. Introduction and Conceptual Framework   **1**
    The Challenge of Managing Diversity in a Global Context   2
    Tensions Posed by Global Workforce Trends   4
    Diversity and Exclusion: A Critical Workforce Problem   6
    The Inclusive Workplace Model   8
    Conceptual Framework and Organization of the Book   12

**PART I: THE GLOBAL CONTEXT FOR
DIVERSITY MANAGEMENT**   **15**

**Chapter 2. Diversity Legislation in a Global
    Perspective: Equality and Fairness in Employment**   **16**
    The International Bill of Human Rights and
        Employment Rights   17
    Importance and Influence of the Declaration
        of Human Rights   21
    Implementation   23
    Diversity-Related Employment Legislation   25
    Broad-Based Antidiscrimination Legislation   26
    Practical Implications   36

    Appendix 2.1. Universal Declaration of Human Rights   **44**

    **Appendix 2.2. Global Antidiscrimination and
    Equal Rights Legislation Checklist of
    Protections Offered by Select Number of Countries**   **50**

Chapter 3. Discrimination, Equality, and Fairness in
   Employment: Social Policies and Affirmative/
   Positive Action Programs   59
     Discrimination and Equality in Employment   60
     Theoretical Perspectives of Discrimination and
       Affirmative Action   63
     Social Policies and Affirmative/Positive Action Programs   65
     Principles of Affirmative Action and Positive Action Programs   69
     The Public Debate Over Affirmative and
       Positive Action Policies   75

Chapter 4. Global Demographic Trends: Impact
   on Workforce Diversity   83
     Martha Farnsworth Riche and Michàlle E. Mor Barak
     International Population Trends   84
     National Trends   95

Chapter 5. Socioeconomic Transitions: The New
   Realities of the Global Workforce   107
     Martha Farnsworth Riche and Michàlle E. Mor Barak
     Worker Migration   110
     Occupational Diversity   112
     Migration of Employers   115
     Implications for Diversity of Gender, Disability,
       and Sexual Orientation   120
     Educational Trends and Workforce Diversity   121

PART II: SOCIAL PSYCHOLOGICAL PERSPECTIVES
OF WORKFORCE DIVERSITY   129

Chapter 6. Defining Diversity in a Global
   Context: Prejudice and Discrimination   130
     Workforce Diversity Defined   132
     Toward a Global Definition of Diversity   146
     Stereotypes and Prejudice   149
     Dehumanization and Oppression   155
     Employment-Related Discrimination   158

Chapter 7. Vive la Différence? Theoretical Perspectives
   on Diversity and Exclusion in the Workplace   164
     Diversity and Exclusion: A Critical Workforce Problem   165
     Theoretical Underpinnings of the
       Inclusion-Exclusion Construct   167
     Research on Organizational Demography Documenting Exclusion   170
     Social Psychological Theories on Diversity
       and Intergroup Relations   173

Chapter 8. Culture and Communication in the Global Workplace   **189**
    The Cultural Context for the Global Workplace   190
    Cross-Cultural Communication   201
    Effective Cross-Cultural Communication   203

Chapter 9. Interpersonal Relationships in a Global Work Context   **213**
    Jeffery Sanchez-Burks and Michàlle E. Mor Barak
    Cultural Styles and Relational Mental Models   215
    Diversity in Interpersonal Relationships   218
    Interpersonal Relationships and Cross-Cultural Communication   223
    Theoretical Perspectives on Interpersonal
       Cross-Cultural Communication   225

**PART III: MANAGING A DIVERSE WORKFORCE
IN THE GLOBAL CONTEXT—THE INCLUSIVE WORKPLACE**   **233**

**Chapter 10. Diversity Management: Paradigms,
Rationale, and Key Elements**   **234**
    Defining Diversity Management   235
    From Equal Rights Laws, to Affirmative/
       Positive Action, to Diversity Management   237
    Diversity Management Paradigms   240
    The Impetus for Implementing Diversity Management   246
    Characteristics and Limitations of Diversity Management   248

**Chapter 11. An Overview of the Inclusive Workplace
Model: Managing the Globalized Workforce Diversity**   **252**
    Diversity Management and the Inclusive Workplace   253

**Chapter 12. The Inclusive Workplace: Level I—Inclusion
Through Diversity Within the Work Organization**   **256**
    Inclusive Policies and Practices   257
    Barriers and Benefits of Implementing the
       Inclusive Approach at Level I   260
    Case Illustration: Level I—Inclusion Through Diversity
       Within Work Organizations—Denny's, Inc.   264
    Questions for Discussion and Further Analysis   272

**Chapter 13. The Inclusive Workplace: Level II—Inclusion
Through Corporate-Community Collaborations**   **274**
    Inclusive Policies and Practices   276
    Barriers and Benefits of Implementing the
       Inclusive Approach at Level II   279
    Case Illustration: Level II—Inclusion Through
       Corporate-Community Collaboration—Unilever   281
    Questions for Discussion and Further Analysis   288

**Chapter 14. The Inclusive Workplace: Level III—Inclusion
Through State/National Collaborations**   290
    Barriers and Benefits of Implementing the
        Inclusive Approach at Level III   293
    Case Illustration: Level III—Inclusion of
        Disadvantaged Groups at the National/State Level—Eurest   295
    Questions for Discussion and Further Analysis   301

**Chapter 15. The Inclusive Workplace: Level IV—Inclusion
Through International Collaborations**   303
    Barriers and Benefits to Implementing the
        Inclusive Approach at Level IV   307
    Case Illustration: Level IV—Inclusion Through
        Global Collaborations—The Fair Trade Company   308
    Fair Trade History   310
    Global Village and the Fair Trade Company   312
    Fair Trade Future   313
    Questions for Discussion and Further Analysis   314

**Chapter 16. Toward a Globally Inclusive
Workplace: Putting the Pieces Together**   317
    The Value Base for the Inclusive Workplace   317
    Implementation of the Inclusive Workplace   318

Appendix   324

References   333

Index   372

About the Author   389

List of Boxes, Figures, and Tables

Chapter 1   1

    Box 1.1 Hai Ha-Kotobuki Joint Venture (Vietnam):
       Programs for Inclusion Within the Company   9
    Box 1.2 The Port Authority of New York (USA):
       Programs for the Local Community   10
    Box 1.3 Delta Cafés (Portugal and East Timor):
       Programs for Disadvantaged Groups   10
    Box 1.4 La Siembra (Canada): International Inclusion Programs   11
    Figure 1.1 Conceptual Framework and Organization of the Book   13

Chapter 2   16

    Box 2.1 The Debate Over the Ban on the Wearing of
       Religious Attire and Religious Symbols in the Workplace   19
    Box 2.2 Equal Employment Legislation and
       De Facto Discrimination   24
    Figure 2.1 United Nations: The International
       Bill of Human Rights   18
    Figure 2.2 Worldwide Legislation Against Sexual
       Orientation Discrimination: Map of Countries   31
    Table 2.1 Worldwide Legislation Against Sexual Orientation
       Discrimination: Listing by Country   32
    Table 2.2 Comparison of the Legal Provision
       for Protection Against Sexual Harassment
       at the Workplace Among Selected Asian Countries   37

Chapter 3   59

    Box 3.1 Discrimination Categorization: Management
       Advice in 1943   61
    Box 3.2 Discrimination Categorization: Black Employees
       File a Discrimination Lawsuit Against Xerox   63

Box 3.3 Equal Employment Legislation and
   Religious Discrimination: The Case of Northern Ireland   72
Box 3.4 Making the Case Against and for Affirmative Action:
   The U.S. Supreme Court's Ruling in Favor of White Firefighters
   and the First Latina Supreme Court Justice   76
Table 3.1 Affirmative Action Legislation
   Worldwide (Select Countries)   66

Chapter 4   83

Box 4.1 The Women Who Leave, the Children
   Who Follow: Enrique's Story   93
Box 4.2 The Price of Migration for Women From the Philippines   95
Box 4.3 Ethnic Diversity in Malaysia   102
Figure 4.1 Worldwide Population Trends   85
Figure 4.2 Historic and Projected Age
   Composition, 1970 and 2050   88
Figure 4.3 International Demographic Trends   93
Table 4.1 World Population, Ages 15–64 (in 1,000s)   89
Table 4.2 Population Ages 15–64, Selected Countries (in 1,000s)   90
Table 4.3 Trends in the Population Under Age 15 (in 1,000s)   90
Table 4.4 Percentage of the Labor Force That Is
   Foreign-Born in Selected Countries   92
Table 4.5 Female Proportion of the Labor Force   97
Table 4.6 Women's and Men's Economic Activity Rates   99

Chapter 5   107

Box 5.1 Outsourcing: The Experience for the
   Displaced Workers and for Those Who Receive the Jobs   116
Box 5.2 The Bhopal Disaster: Economic Exploitation
   and Human Tragedy   119
Box 5.3 Sexual Harassment and the High-Tech Industry   121
Box 5.4 Barefoot College: Educating the Rural Poor   123
Table 5.1 Trends in Primary and Secondary Education   122
Table 5.2 Trends in Postsecondary Education   124

Chapter 6   130

Box 6.1 Ziauddin Sardar Statement on His
   Identity and Subsequent Stereotypes   150
Box 6.2 Documenting Employment Discrimination
   Against Migrant Workers   159
Figure 6.1 A Framework for Viewing Individuals
   Whose Culture Is Different From One's Own   157
Table 6.1 A Typology of Diversity Definitions   136

Chapter 7   164

Box 7.1 The Binocular Resolution Classical Experiments
   of Racial Categorization in South Africa:
   Prestige of Groups, Identification, and Exclusion   178
Box 7.2 The Classic Minimal Group Experiments   180

Chapter 8   189

Box 8.1 Leadership Through Effective Cross-Cultural
   Communication Saves the Day in Najaf   202
Box 8.2 How Can the Important Guest Sit at the
   Head of a Round Table? The Use of the Physical
   Setting to Convey Respect in Business Communication   207
Box 8.3 Are Members of a Cultural Group Interacting With a
   Member of Another Group More Likely to Change Their
   Original Communication Style or Reinforce It?   209
Figure 8.1 Barriers to Effective Cross-Cultural Communication   204
Table 8.1 Dimensions of Cultural Difference   192

Chapter 9   213

Box 9.1 Relational Mental Models About Time in Ecuador   216
Box 9.2 What Just Happened in That Meeting?   217
Box 9.3 Communicating Through the Exchange
   of Business Cards: Task-Oriented Versus
   Relationship/Task-Oriented Cultures   227
Figure 9.1 Combined Versus Differentiated
   Relational Styles   220
Figure 9.2 Beliefs About the Effects of Task and
   Relationship Conflict   224
Figure 9.3 "Keep Off the Grass," Stated Directly (U.S.), and the
   Same Message, Stated Indirectly, "Since We Have Broad
   Road, Why Should We Open Small Paths" (China)   230
Table 9.1 Cultural Context and Communication
   Orientation   226

Chapter 10   234

Box 10.1 A Diversity Training Gone Awry: The
   Texaco "Jelly Bean Jar" Incident   242
Table 10.1 The HR Approach to Diversity Management   242
Table 10.2 Motivation for Implementing
   Diversity Management   246

Chapter 11   252

Box 11.1 Definition of the Inclusive Workplace   253

Chapter 12   **256**

Box 12.1 A Company's Diversity Inclusion Programs (Level I):
    The Case of DCM Shriram Industries (India)   259
Figure 12.1 The Inclusive Workplace: The Value Base for Level I   257
Figure 12.2 The Inclusive Workplace: The Practice
    Model for Level I   261

Chapter 13   **274**

Box 13.1 A Company's Community Inclusion
    Programs (Level II)—The Case of Nestlé (Switzerland)   277
Figure 13.1 The Inclusive Workplace: The Value Base
    for Level II   276
Figure 13.2 The Inclusive Workplace Model: Obstacles
    and Benefits for Level II   280

Chapter 14   **290**

Box 14.1 A Company's Collaboration With Governmental
    Programs for Disadvantaged Populations (Level III):
    The Case of Hong Yip Service Company Ltd. (Hong Kong)   294
Figure 14.1 The Inclusive Workplace:
    The Value Base for Level III   292
Figure 14.2 The Inclusive Workplace Model:
    Obstacles and Benefits for Level III   294

Chapter 15   **303**

Box 15.1 A Company's International Inclusion Initiatives
    (Level IV): The Case of eShopAfrica (Ghana)   305
Figure 15.1 The Inclusive Workplace: The Value Base for
    Level IV Inclusion Through Global Collaborations   304
Figure 15.2 The Inclusive Workplace Model: Barriers
    and Benefits for Level IV Inclusion Through
    Global Collaborations   309
Table 15.1 Worldwide Fair Trade Market   000

Chapter 16   **317**

Figure 16.1 The Value Base for the Inclusive Workplace   319
Figure 16.2 Implementing the Inclusive Workplace Model   320

Preface and Acknowledgments

I have serious reasons to believe that the planet the little prince came from is Asteroid B-612. This asteroid has been sighted only once by telescope, in 1909 by a Turkish astronomer, who had then made a formal demonstration of his discovery at an International Astronomical Congress. But no one had believed him on account of the way he was dressed. Grown-ups are like that.

—*The Little Prince,* Antoine de Saint-Exupéry

In his beautiful account of the encounter between an aviator whose plane is forced down in the Sahara Desert and a little prince from a small planet, Antoine de Saint-Exupéry describes a process of seeking the secret to what is important in life. In the above excerpt, Saint-Exupéry illustrates in his unique and graceful style a key diversity experience that seems as relevant today as it was more than half a century ago when the book was first published: people who appear to be different may be discounted and overlooked regardless of how true or brilliant their ideas may be.

My quest to examine and understand key diversity experiences in today's global society has led to interviews with employees and managers around the globe, several research projects, and two international conferences—all culminating in this book. Over the years that I have been studying workforce diversity, many people have helped me gain insight into diversity experiences around the world. Although the responsibility for the contents of this book rests solely with me, I am deeply thankful to those who joined me on this exciting journey.

I am indebted to the many people who agreed to participate in my research projects over the years and who so generously shared their thoughts and their concerns regarding diversity. In fact, the realization that inclusion was key to understanding diversity in organizations came during the preliminary stages of a diversity research project that I conducted years ago. I was invited to carry out a study on diversity in a large high-tech company with headquarters in Southern California and business contracts all over the world. I approached the project with great trepidation because I felt that I lacked "a hook," a key construct or theme to provide the anchor for the study; I was wondering what was the common concern shared by people who were different from the organization's mainstream.

As a first step, I asked the company's management for permission to conduct some interviews. They agreed, and several interviews were scheduled with employees of diverse backgrounds at different levels of the organization. I was deeply touched by the interviewees' willingness to open up and tell me about their experiences, their thoughts, and their feelings. Some felt that they were an integral part of their work team and the organization, whereas others thought that their coworkers, their boss, or their subordinates could not get past a certain characteristic that made them different. Whether the interviewee was a woman manager, an African American supervisor, a Korean American engineer, or a Latina secretary, their statements were similar.

Invariably employees who were more included in the organization's decision making and information networks were more satisfied, more committed to the organization, and felt more productive than those who were not. After several interviews with women and members of ethnic and racial diverse groups repeatedly telling me how they felt, it finally dawned on me—*inclusion* was the key!

In the years that followed, I expanded my research to other countries and interviewed employees in several regions of the world. The theme of organizational inclusion guided my research and led to the development of the *inclusive workplace* model. I am thankful to the people who agreed to be interviewed and to the colleagues who collaborated with me on these projects.

I wish to thank the Rockefeller Foundation, particularly Susan Seckler and Susan Garfield, for their generosity in providing the Bellagio Award and inviting me to organize and lead a conference on Global Perspectives of Workforce Diversity. The discussions at the conference, held in the summer of 2001 at the Rockefeller Foundation's Villa Severloni in Bellagio, Italy, were inspiring. I wish to thank my dear colleagues who participated at the meetings: Manolo I. Abella, International Labour Organization, UN, Switzerland; Nancy J. Adler, McGill University, Canada; Cordula Barzantny, Groupe Ecole Supérieure de Commerce, Toulouse, France; Jae-Sung Choi, Yonsei University, South Korea; Philomena Essed, University of Amsterdam, The Netherlands; Brigida Garcia, El Colegio de Mexico, Mexico; Ellen Ernst Kossek, Michigan State University, U.S.; Alan D. Levy, Tishman International, U.K. and U.S.; Stella Nkomo, University of South Africa; Harriet Presser, University of Maryland; Martha Farnsworth Riche, Farnsworth Riche Associates, Maryland, U.S.; Maritta Soininen, University of Stockholm, Sweden; Hou Wenrou, Renmin University, China; and John Wrench, University of Southern Denmark, Denmark.

I am also grateful to the Borchard Foundation for generously providing funding for a colloquium on workforce diversity in the United States and Europe. I am particularly thankful to Dr. Beiling, the director of the Borchard Foundation, and his wife, Mrs. Beiling, for so graciously hosting the colloquium at the Foundation's Chateau de La Bretesche in Brittany, France, in the summer of 2003. Both Dr. and Mrs. Beiling have generously shared with the participants their wisdom, accumulated during their world travels and fascinating experiences, and enhanced the group's discussions. I am very grateful to Mr. Alan Levy, chairman and CEO of Tishman International, for his important contribution to both the Bellagio and the La Bretesche colloquia, for so generously sharing his unique perspective on diversity, and for keeping all of us honest with his real-world wisdom. I also wish to thank my dear colleagues who participated at the La Bretesche colloquium: Manolo I. Abella, International Labour Organization, UN, Switzerland; Sheila H. Akabas, Columbia University, U.S.; Cordula Barzantny, Groupe Ecole Supérieure de Commerce, Toulouse, France; Lena Domilelli, University of South Hampton, England; Paul Kurzman, Hunter College, City University of New York, U.S.; Lawrence Root, University of Michigan, U.S.; Jeffrey Sanchez-Burks, University of Michigan, U.S.; Abye Tasse, PhD, Institut du Developpement Social, France; and Gill Widell, Göteborg University, Sweden.

I wish to thank Dean Marilyn Flynn for her vision and support. I am especially thankful to Dnika Travis, who contributed to this project almost from its inception—for providing background research and helpful feedback. Her contribution was consistent and particularly valuable. I wish to thank Gary Bess for providing ongoing support and assistance with several of the diversity projects that led to this book and for assisting with various stages of the manuscript. I am thankful to Shunit Mor-Barak for initial edits of the manuscript and helpful comments on style and structure. Ralph Fertig and Jennifer Joseph provided helpful comments on the international legislation chapter. I am also thankful to doctoral students and research assistants who helped with various stages of the manuscript—Jan Nissly and Jim Fredo for their wonderful contribution to the various case studies; MinKyoung Rhee, Hsin-Yi 'Cindy' Hsiao, Erica Lizano, and Ahraemi Kim for their valuable assistance with the second edition of the book; and the students in my graduate seminars on global diversity management who cheerfully agreed to utilize drafts of the manuscript as the course textbook and provided helpful comments.

I wish to thank the editor of the first edition, Al Bruckner, who saw the value of this project from its inception and provided support and valuable assistance throughout my work on the book. Al has since tragically passed on and he is sorely missed. I am thankful to the wonderful team at Sage—Lisa Cuevas Shaw, the executive editor of the second edition for her support, astute input, and patience, and MaryAnn Vail, Diane Foster, Libby Larson, and Robert Holm.

My family has been supportive through the long hours of working on this manuscript, and for that I am deeply grateful. I wish to thank my parents for being their wonderful selves and for their continued support. I sorely miss my mother, who passed on recently—her wisdom, insightful perspective on human nature, and endless love.

To my beloved children, Tomer, Shunit, and her husband, Aaron, for engaging in interesting conversations that helped me think through some ideas I was struggling with and, together with Jennifer, Ori, Mikah, and Leah, for the insightful discussions around the dinner table during our Shabbat and holiday celebrations. To Tamar, Doron, Limor, Yoel, Shir, and Nir Inbal—I am so grateful that you are all in my life. And to Shay, Tzameret, Shir-Yam, Yinon, Yarden, Jonathan, Or, and Aviv and to the memory of our beloved Tali who continues to inspire us all. To my aunts, uncles, and cousins on four different continents who exemplify a *close-knit global* family. I feel fortunate to have them all in my life.

Most important, I wish to thank my husband, Ysrael Kanot, for helping me stay focused and on track—even at times when the task seemed overwhelming—and for his continued love and support as well as enthusiasm for this project.

To Ysrael—
the wind beneath my wings

CHAPTER 1

Introduction And Conceptual Framework

士	Shi	Scholars
農	Nong	Farmers
工	Gong	Artisans
商	Shang	Merchants

What makes a successful manager? The Chinese tradition divides human beings into four classes, each with its own unique qualities: the shi (scholars) are learned and contemplate vision and ethics; the nong (farmers) work the land and can provide for basic human needs; the gong (artisans) are creative and strive for beauty and excellence; and the shang (merchants) have strong ambition and a drive to succeed and to accumulate wealth. According to Chinese ancient wisdom, it is only when one can combine the qualities of all four classes—the vision and ethics of the scholars, the appreciation and respect for basic human needs of the farmers, the creativity and drive for excellence of the artisans, and the merchants' ambition to make a profit— that one can become a successful manager.

When I interviewed him for this book, Mr. Kyung-Young Park, the chief vision officer (CVO) of Harex,[1] relayed this wisdom, which had been imparted to him by the honorary chairman of his company, Mr. Seo. After a long discussion on diversity management and the outsider's misconception of the

1

homogeneity of both Korean and Chinese societies ("there are many differences among us that foreigners do not see—regional, for example"), he concluded that managers could learn a great deal about managing diversity from that Chinese teaching.

Indeed, effective diversity management should encompass these four principles: (a) like scholars, managers must adopt an ethical learned approach to diversity, always aiming to "do the right thing"; (b) like farmers, they must respect their employees' unique characteristics; and (c) like artisans, they must introduce creative solutions as they strive for excellence in diversity management. These qualities, combined with the last principle—ambition to utilize diversity to promote business goals and profitability for the organization—lay the groundwork for sound management. These interactive qualities—vision, ethics, respect, creativity, business goal orientation, and striving for excellence—are, in essence, *the heart and soul of this book.*

The Challenge of Managing Diversity in a Global Context

Successful management of today's increasingly diverse workforce is among the most important global challenges faced by corporate leaders, human resource managers, and management consultants. Workforce diversity is not a transient phenomenon; it is today's reality, and it is here to stay. Homogeneous societies have become heterogeneous, and this trend is irreversible. The problems of managing today's diverse workforce, however, do not stem from the heterogeneity of the workforce itself but from the unfortunate inability of corporate managers to fully comprehend its dynamics, divest themselves of their personal prejudicial attitudes, and creatively unleash the potential embedded in a multicultural workforce.

The global economy moves diversity to the top of the agenda. Immigration, worker migration (guest workers), and gender and ethnic differences continue to dramatically change the composition of the workforce. There is a growing demand for equal rights for these workers and for other groups like older workers, workers with disabilities, and gays and lesbians. Even without globalization, population projections suggest that the trend to a diverse workforce will be amplified in the coming decades. For example, due to consistently low birthrates and increased longevity, virtually all the industrial countries will need even larger waves of immigrants just to sustain their current ratio of workers to retirees. At the same time, developing countries are experiencing an unprecedented growth in the numbers of young people. The combination of push and pull factors is moving all countries toward the same outcome: a more diverse workforce (United Nations, 2000a, 2009).

Most large corporations in today's global economy are international or multinational, and even those that are not rely on vendors to sell to customers located outside their national boundaries. For example, Virgin Company, headquartered in the United Kingdom, provides services in the sectors of hotel/travel/tourism, media/entertainment, computer/IT/telecom, transportation, and services and has main offices in Australia, Japan, the United States, Singapore, and South Africa. With total revenues exceeding £4 billion (or $7.2 billion), Virgin employs more than 25,000 people in 200 subsidiaries around the world (Virgin Group, 2009).

In the context of the globalized economy, most large companies fall in the category of multinational companies (MNC). The literature on international management includes several typologies of MNC, which are useful for understanding, explaining, and conducting empirical studies about the functioning of multinational companies (Bartlett & Ghoshal 1998, 2002; Harzing, 2000; Hordes, Clancy, & Baddaley, 1995). Three categories are helpful for understanding the unique corporate culture that is relevant to global workforce diversity. The first is *international corporations* with headquarters in one country and operations in one or more other countries. Their strategy is based primarily on transferring and adapting the parent company's knowledge or expertise to foreign markets while retaining considerable influence and control (Bartlett & Ghoshal 1998, 2002). This category of companies is characterized by an organizational culture primarily influenced by the home country, particularly regarding human resource management.

The second category is *multinational companies,* in which the central corporate office still has the dominant decision-making power but each national or regional operation has some autonomy in business decisions. These companies develop strategic capabilities that allow them to be very sensitive and responsive to differences in national environments around the world. The company's culture is less unified and rigid, compared with those of international companies, and less dominated by one national culture.

The third form is the global company with headquarters that may be located in a specific geographic region but with a team composed of managers across the globe jointly making major business decisions. These companies are driven by their need for global efficiency and typically treat the world market as an integrated whole (Bartlett & Ghoshal, 1998, 2002). The corporate culture in this type of company is not dominated by any one national culture. There are few overarching universal policies, allowing for flexibility and diversity of processes, procedures, and technologies (Hordes et al., 1995).

In addition to strategic alliances and a wide-ranging business span, companies must be able to utilize the diversity of their human resources to become truly global. This means that they maximize human talents, regardless of where their employees are located or their national origin. As a first step, companies must learn the human side of the global company. The training, orientation, and cultural understanding needed for the management and employees of any company—national, international, multinational, or global—include the deep understanding of individuals who live in other national and cultural contexts, and the ability to work within a global team framework.

Tensions Posed by Global Workforce Trends

Global demographic trends create unprecedented workforce tensions. For example, Italy's population, currently almost 60 million, is projected to decrease to 56 million by 2050; over the same period, Germany's working-age population is expected to decrease from 82 million to 69 million (World Bank, 2009; Germany Federal Statistical Office, 2006; Population Reference Bureau, 2009a). To maintain their current working-age population levels to the year 2050, both countries will need a few hundred thousand immigrants every year. Historically, these relatively homogeneous societies have been resistant to immigration, yet their current practices, induced by workforce decline, indicate a tacit acceptance of it.

Developing countries, on the other hand, have seen a spurt in the size of young-adult populations in recent decades reflecting the widespread adoption of the public health knowledge and practices of the mid 20th century that have rapidly reduced mortality, especially for infants and youth. As a result, more than one half the population of developing countries is under age 30. Although many migrants are fleeing upheavals, even violence, in their native lands, most are seeking economic opportunities. With or without the transformation of economies in an increasingly global context, it would be difficult for these countries to accommodate such a surge of young adults into their labor force. For example, almost as many Mexicans as Americans reached age 15 each year during the first decade of the 21st century, yet the Mexicans faced an economy only one tenth the size of the U.S. economy. Can it be surprising, then, that there were not enough jobs in Mexico—let alone well-paying jobs—for such an exceptionally large generation of new workers?

Increasing numbers and shares of women in the workplace may be the most important component of diversity at the national level in most of the world. In particular, the gap between women's and men's rates has been narrowing in most regions (International Labour Office, 2009). Women's share in the workforce grew significantly in Latin America and in Western Europe as well as in other developed regions during the past several decades. Even in countries where women have traditionally been discouraged from working outside the home, they came to make up an increasing share of the measured labor force. As a result, women's economic activity rates are increasingly similar around the world, except in regions where society constrains women's roles outside the home.

A particularly relevant aspect of current workplace trends is that women increasingly migrate autonomously as workers, and women migrants equal or outnumber men in some parts of the world. They are even becoming common in Asia, largely as a result of more women workers migrating on their own. Rapid economic growth and structural changes in the labor market that began in the 1980s and continued into the 21st century have motivated women to independently migrate. Women migrants' earnings now represent an important source of income for their families at home. Contract labor migration is the most rapidly increasing type of international migration in Asia, and women migrants are concentrated in such female-dominated occupations as domestic helpers, entertainers, salespersons, hotel and restaurant employees, and assembly-line workers.

The global economic trends that generate increased or decreased demands for workers in different areas at different times create tremendous opportunities as well as hardships for work organizations, individuals, and families. For example, the technology industry's boom in the 1990s created increased demand for skilled workers, and the developed countries' generally strong economy during those years created a multinational, multicultural workforce that included many foreigners. Conversely, the global economy's downturn in the early 21st century has displaced many immigrants from their jobs and placed them in limbo. Unable to extend their legal stay in their host countries because their work visas were often linked to their original employer-sponsors, upon their return to their countries of origin, there were no jobs for them.

Global legislative trends banning discrimination against women, immigrants, minorities, and other diverse groups in the labor force have required employers in most democratic and quite a few nondemocratic countries to institute policies that ensure fair treatment of all employees. Some countries have introduced public policies stemming from the ideology of compensating population groups that have been discriminated against in the past. Employers are required to provide designated groups of applicants, such as racial and ethnic minorities and women, with a competitive advantage by actively recruiting them for open positions.

Disregarding these economic, demographic, and legislative trends can be devastating to companies, their employees, and the communities surrounding them. Companies unable or unwilling to change their policies and practices may suffer dire consequences. They may experience intergroup conflicts among their employees; they may limit their access to the pool of potentially talented employees; they may miss opportunities for creating alliances with business organizations; and they may be vulnerable to expensive lawsuits or government sanctions resulting in serious damage to their earnings, their public image, and their access to investment.

All signs point to increasing heterogeneity in the workforce, even as countries throughout the world struggle with hostile intergroup relations, prejudice, discrimination, and even violence. Gender, ethnicity, language, social class, religion, or other distinctions may define group membership, as each culture determines the context of social exchange and reward allocations. In Europe, for example, immigrants from North Africa and the former Soviet Union experience prejudice and discrimination in obtaining jobs. Worldwide, these group divisions contribute to exclusion of women and minorities from positions of power in the workplace and create barriers to job opportunities and promotion. They also stifle the economic growth that could come from these groups of workers and directly affect long-term corporate earnings.

As a result of the increasing heterogeneity in the workforce, countries throughout the world are struggling with a powder keg of hostile intergroup relations in the workplace. The impact of prejudice and discrimination can be more than just detrimental to businesses—it can even result in violence; but effective management of workforce diversity can create tremendous rewards for companies.

Diversity and Exclusion: A Critical Workforce Problem

One of the most significant problems facing today's diverse workforce is exclusion—both its overt practice, as a matter of formal or informal policy, and the perception by employees that they are not regarded as an integral part of the organization (Hitlan, Cliffton, & DeSoto, 2006; Insch et al., 2008; Kalev, 2009; Kanter, 1992; Mor Barak, 2000b; Wood, 2008). Though diversity groupings vary from one culture or country to the next, the common factor that seems to transcend national boundaries is the experience of social exclusion, particularly in the workplace (Mor Barak, Findler, & Wind, 2001). Individuals and groups are implicitly or explicitly excluded from job opportunities, information networks, team membership, human resource investments, and the decision-making process because of their actual or employer-perceived membership in a minority or disfavored identity group. Inclusion in organizational information networks and in decision-making processes has been linked to better job opportunities and career advancement in work organizations (Cunningham, 2007; O'Leary & Ickovics, 1992), as well as to job satisfaction and well-being (Mor Barak & Levin, 2002). Employees' experience of exclusion, therefore, may play a critical role in explaining the connection between the lack of opportunities for members of diverse groups and their discontent with their roles as employees in organizations. If leading organizations do not adapt to become multicultural and learn to remove barriers to full participation of minorities and women, social and economic tensions between majority and minority identity may only increase within employing organizations (Nkomo & Kossek, 2000). The implications are far-reaching, as work organizations represent opportunities to bridge understanding and tolerance among peoples from around the globe.

The unprecedented global demographic trends have created ethnically diverse work environments that are often the backdrop for hostile relations, discrimination, and even hate crimes (Stephan, Ybarra, & Martinez, 1998; Pettigrew & Tropp, 2006). In addition to race, gender, and social class that cut across different cultures as determinants of exclusion, other characteristics like ethnicity, language, or religion may define group membership, as each culture determines the context of social exchange and reward allocation (Hofstede & Hofstede, 2005; Smith & Fischer, 2003). Worldwide, these group divisions contribute to exclusion of group members from positions of power in the workplace and create barriers to job opportunities and promotion. The research on individual and intergroup differences in the workplace has been disjointed on a global scale. Although there are many similarities in areas of research (e.g., gender and intergroup relationships), they are often examined under different frameworks and using different terminology. Whereas U.S.-based scholars often identify their research under the title of "workforce diversity," European scholars and those from other countries who publish in this area usually identify their work under titles such as "gender studies," "demography of the workforce," "labor migration," and "guest workers." The difference is not only semantic, but stems from different historical perspectives and worldviews. U.S. researchers focus on diversity of the workforce (e.g., gender, racial, and ethnic differences) in the context of the country's historical role as an immigrant absorption nation. Their studies focus on the discrepancies between the ideals and realities of the traditional equal employment opportunities, antidiscrimination, and fairness paradigms in the dynamic and fast-changing American society. European researchers, on the other hand, examine immigration, worker migration, and gender work roles in the context of relatively long-term national racial and ethnic cohesion. Their studies focus on the social and emotional difficulties inherent in integrating immigrants and women into each country's relatively stable social fabric and gender roles. Beyond these two regions, little or no attention has been paid to issues of exclusion in the workplace, perhaps because jobs have been scarce for the dominant groups as well. There is clearly a need to bridge this gap and develop a comprehensive knowledge base.

Within the organizational context, the inclusion-exclusion construct is conceptualized as a continuum of the degree to which individuals feel a part of critical organizational processes, such as access to information, connectedness to coworkers, and ability to participate in and influence the decision-making process (Mor Barak & Cherin, 1998; Mor Barak, 2000b; Mor Barak, 2005; Mor Barak et al., 2006). The importance of the inclusion-exclusion experience has its historical roots in basic human needs, and thus the employee's experience is the measure of a work organization's success at becoming a truly global company. Because people have always depended on one another for their livelihood and needed to work together in order to acquire food, shelter, and clothing, social inclusion has had an important survival function through the ages and across cultures (Baumeister & Leary, 1995; Leary & Baumeister, 2000; MacDonald & Leary, 2005).

Research on organizational demography indicates that being in the minority has significant effects on individuals' affective experiences in the workplace, including feelings of isolation and lack of personal efficacy in team and in one-on-one relationships (Mor Barak et al., 2006; Lopez, Hodson, & Roscigno, 2009). Milliken and Martins (1996) indicate a strong and consistent relationship between diversity in gender, ethnicity, and age and exclusion from important workplace interactions. One of the most frequently reported problems faced by women and minorities in organizational settings is their limited access to, or exclusion from, informal interaction networks (Ely, & Thomas, 2001; Gray, Kurihara, Hommen, & Feldman, 2007; McDonald, Lin, & Ao, 2009). These networks allocate a variety of instrumental resources that are critical for job effectiveness and career advancement, as well as expressive benefits such as social support and friendship (Ibarra, 1993).

The Inclusive Workplace Model

This book presents the inclusive workplace model for managing diversity in a comprehensive way for the first time. Work organizations need to expand their notion of diversity to include, in addition to the organization itself, the larger systems that constitute its environment. Viewed from an ecological and systems perspective (Ashford, LeCroy, & Lortie, 2009), the notion of organizational inclusion is utilized as a focal point for understanding and managing workforce diversity (Mor Barak, 2000a). The concept of the inclusive workplace presented here and elaborated in later chapters refers to a work organization that accepts and utilizes the diversity of its own workforce—while also being active in the community, in state and federal programs that support immigrants, women, the working poor, and other disadvantaged groups—and that collaborates across cultural and national boundaries (Mor Barak, 2000b).

The inclusive workplace is defined as one that

- Values and utilizes individual and intergroup differences within its workforce
- Cooperates with, and contributes to, its surrounding community
- Alleviates the needs of disadvantaged groups in its wider environment
- Collaborates with individuals, groups, and organizations across national and cultural boundaries

Valuing and utilizing individual and intergroup differences within the organization's workforce refers to the organization's relations with its own employees. Whereas an exclusionary workplace is based on the perception that all workers need to conform to preestablished organizational values and norms (determined by its "mainstream"), the inclusive workplace is based on a pluralistic value frame that respects all cultural perspectives represented among its employees. It will strive to constantly modify its values and norms to accommodate its employees (see Box 1.1 for an example).

BOX 1.1
Hai Ha-Kotobuki Joint Venture (Vietnam):
Programs for Inclusion Within the Company

Hai Ha-Kotobuki Joint Venture Co., Ltd., is a food manufacturing company located in Hanoi, Vietnam. Hai Ha-Kotobuki produces candy, cookies, and fresh cakes for sale in Vietnam and other Asian countries, including Japan, Singapore, China, Russia, and Mongolia (Hai Ha-Kotobuki, 2003; United Nations Economic and Social Commission, 2003). The company was one of two businesses selected to partner with the Vietnam Chamber of Commerce and Industry, CARE International, and the National AIDS Committee in a joint project to promote HIV/AIDS prevention and control. With the support of top management and the involvement of a large number of company staff, Hai Ha-Kotobuki developed an HIV/AIDS workplace policy that included implementing prevention programs, confidential testing and nondisclosure of results, discrimination prevention, flexible work conditions for HIV staff, and care responsibility for HIV staff (Pramualratana & Rau, 2001). Employees were surveyed regarding their knowledge of HIV/AIDS; staff (including all supervisors and managers) was trained; and equal opportunity programs were implemented to ensure nondiscrimination of HIV staff, equal access to all company benefits, and flexible work conditions (Asian Business Coalition on AIDS, 2003).

Cooperating with, and contributing to, local community refers to the organization's sense of being an integral part of its surrounding community, regardless of whether it derives profits from local institutions and stakeholders. An exclusionary workplace misses the connection between profits and its community because it focuses solely on its responsibility to its financial stakeholders. An inclusive workplace, by contrast, maintains a dual focus, simultaneously intrinsic and extrinsic, that comes from acknowledging its responsibility to the wider community (see Box 1.2 for an example).

BOX 1.2
The Port Authority of New York (USA):
Programs for the Local Community

The Port Authority of New York and New Jersey is an agency that runs many diverse transportation-related facilities such as bus stations and the New York airports. The rising number of homeless people at the Port Authority's facilities caused increasing problems for the delivery of quality transportation services as well as for its image (Dutton & Dukerich, 1991; Port Authority of New York and New Jersey, 2004). The Port Authority took action in 1988 by forming a homeless project team and spending $2.5 million to fund homeless centers. Since 1997, the program has provided assessment and referral services to more than 500 people each month through a program located in the midtown bus terminal known as Operation Alternative. The agency, in partnership with Urban Pathways, created the Open Door Center located across from the Port Authority bus terminal to provide food, shelter, and social services to homeless people. The drop-in center provides comprehensive services to 130 homeless people daily and was the recipient of the 1999 Governor's Exemplary Community Service Award (Port Authority, 2000). As a result of this intervention, the homeless people in the community received much-needed food, clothing, and shelter, and the Port Authority of New York was able to provide better services to its customers and improve its image.

Alleviating the needs of disadvantaged groups in the organization's wider environment refers to the values that drive organizational policies with regard to the disenfranchised (e.g., the working poor and former welfare recipients). The exclusionary workplace views them as disposable labor, but the inclusive workplace perceives these groups as a potentially stable and upwardly mobile labor force (see Box 1.3 for an example).

BOX 1.3
Delta Cafés (Portugal and East Timor):
Programs for Disadvantaged Groups

The Delta Cafés Group, a multinational company based in Campo Maior, Alentejo, Portugal, is the Portuguese market leader for coffee, holding 38% of the market share and generating revenues of 160 million euros (World Business Council for Sustainable Development, 2003; World Business

Council for Sustainable Development, 2009). In 2000, the government of East Timor approached Delta about establishing operations in the newly independent country to revitalize its dilapidated coffee industry and to help alleviate the pervasive poverty there. Delta saw the opportunity to develop new markets and help rebuild East Timor's economy while generating revenues. Working with the government of East Timor, the UN, and local nongovernmental organizations (NGOs), Delta began holding capacity-building seminars with local farmers and contracted to purchase the coffee grown—at a fair market price. Delta has since launched a new brand of coffee, Delta Timor, which bears a logo designating its production in support of sustainable communities. Consumers have demonstrated their willingness to pay more for the socially responsible product, and the new brand is already profitable. For their partnership efforts, Delta and the government of East Timor received a 2003 Corporate Conscience Award for Positive Impact on the Community (Social Accountability International, 2003).

Finally, *collaborating with individuals, groups, and organizations across national and cultural boundaries* refers to the organization's positions with respect to international collaborations. The exclusionary workplace operates from a framework of one culture is competition-based, and is focused on narrowly defined national interests. The inclusive workplace sees value in collaborating across national borders, in being pluralistic, and in identifying global mutual interests (see Box 1.4 for an example).

BOX 1.4
La Siembra (Canada): International Inclusion Programs

La Siembra Co-op was incorporated in 1999 in Ottawa, Canada, as the first North American importer, manufacturer, and distributor of fair trade cocoa products (La Siembra Co-op, 2003; "25 years, 25 success stories," 2009). The company's products—hot chocolate, cocoa powder, sugar, and chocolate bars—are marketed under the name Cocoa Camino in natural health food and grocery stores in Canada and the United States. It was founded on the principles of equal and respectful trade relations, fair wages and working conditions, environmentally sound farming practices, and education. La Siembra sources its products from cooperatives of traditional family farms in

(Continued)

> **(Continued)**
>
> the Dominican Republic and Paraguay. La Siembra notes that each of its suppliers is formally registered with the Fair Trade Labeling Organization (FLO) as a fair trade producer. Further, La Siembra has received fair trade certification by TransFair Canada, the independent Canadian fair trade certification organization (TransFair Canada, 2003). The certification assures consumers that farmers receive higher than world market prices for their goods, often including organic and social premiums used for development programs (La Siembra Co-op, 2003). Consumers and corporate peers alike have recognized the company's efforts. La Siembra received the 2002 Socially Responsible Business Award at the 18th Annual Natural Products Expo held in Washington, DC (Ontario Co-operative Association, 2003).

There is accumulating research evidence that such corporate practices constitute good business. The benefits include (a) cost savings due to lower turnover of employees, less absenteeism, and improved productivity; (b) winning the competition for talent by being more attractive to women and members of minority groups; (c) driving business growth by leveraging the many facets of diversity, such as marketing more effectively to minority communities or to senior citizens; (d) improved corporate image with a positive impact on the company's stock standing; and (e) reaping the benefits of an increasingly global marketplace by employing workers from different nationalities in, or outside, their native countries.

Conceptual Framework and Organization of the Book

For too long the question posed by management in organizations has been "Is diversity good for business?" The conceptual model presented in this book suggests reframing the question to "How can diversity work for organizations?" Successful and seamless inclusion is the desired outcome of good diversity management. This, however, is not an undertaking for companies and employers alone. It needs to be reinforced and permeated through national and international laws and policies as well as via cultural tolerance in educational content and messages that the media convey concerning intergroup behavior. This broad perspective guides the conceptual framework for the book (see Figure 1.1).

The book is divided into three parts. Part I presents the macro, or large-systems, perspective on diversity: global demographic trends, legislation, and public policies in different countries. Part II presents the micro/mezzo—or smaller-systems—perspective on diversity: how diversity is defined in different countries, theories explaining diversity, interpersonal and cultural aspects, and communication in the workplace. Finally, Part III presents solutions or practical intervention approaches: diversity paradigms, the inclusive workplace model, and case studies demonstrating how corporations in different parts of the world can apply the model.

This book utilizes an interdisciplinary approach, drawing from different bodies of knowledge to provide the demographic, legislative, and theoretical background for understanding diversity from an international perspective. Applying the above principles, the book also offers practical guidelines that can help managers create an organizational culture that welcomes and utilizes the diversity of their workforce and ultimately creates the inclusive workplace.

Figure 1.1   Conceptual Framework and Organization of the Book

Macro Dimensions	Micro/Mezzo Dimensions	Practice Applications
Demographics trends	Individual and group aspects of diversity	Diversity management paradigms
Legislation	Theoretical explanations of intergroup relations	The inclusive workplace model
Public policy	Culture and communication	Practice applications for the model
Global economy	Interpersonal cross-cultural relations in the workplace	Cases for discussion

Summary and Conclusion

The focus on diversity in global business today is quite different from civil rights legislation and from affirmative action programs. It is no longer only a matter of righting past wrongs or of trying to achieve equality of opportunity by addressing underrepresentation of specific groups. Diversity efforts are focused on managing and engaging the company's heterogeneous workforce in ways that give it a competitive advantage. The progressive expansion of diversity compliance may be viewed as a continuum: equal employment opportunity

(EEO) legislation means that it is against the law to discriminate; affirmative action programs mean that companies need to take positive steps to ensure equal employment and promotion opportunities; and diversity programs are proactive and aim to achieve a diverse and heterogeneous workforce that values employee differences—and contributes to the local as well as global community.

It is important to state that diversity programs without the foundation of strong legislation and sound proactive public policy may be fleeting. Left to the business world's interpretation of "what is good for business," this trend may disappear—as others have in the past—when businesses decide that diversity management no longer benefits their financial goals. Reflective of this trend are often-used slogans such as "diversity makes business sense" and "diversity is good business." Although these phrases may suggest a useful and practical direction, their use often precludes consideration of ethical practices and major long-term organizational changes that may not be immediately linked to the bottom line. Understanding the full range of practical benefits of diversity management is an important motivator for corporations to invest additional resources in employee development concurrent with their business development; but in addition, the scholarly and public examination of this multifaceted issue has to include the important dimensions of morality, ethics, fairness, and human dignity.

Given the growing acceptance (though not necessarily adherence) of human rights as a value around the globe, promoting fairness and economic advancement for disenfranchised members of society is perceived as the right and ethical thing to do. It does also constitute good business by giving corporations a competitive advantage in recruitment, in customer relations, in marketing to the growing minority communities with purchasing power, and in developing a positive corporate image that translates into corporate profits. To alleviate both social and economic tensions in society as a whole, and as reflected within the workforce, work organizations must learn to not only remove barriers but to actively encourage full participation of members of diverse groups in society.

The premise of this book is that work organizations must create and sustain a culture that is accepting of individual differences—and one that encourages greater involvement in community, national, and international affairs. In other words, they need to become inclusive organizations, inside and out.

Note

1. Harex is a Korean-based, high-tech company that developed, among other things, an innovative gadget called ZOOP, which replaces credit cards, tollbooth operators, and bank debit cards.

PART I

The Global Context for Diversity Management

CHAPTER 2

Diversity Legislation in a Global Perspective

Equality and Fairness in Employment

All human beings are born free and equal in dignity and rights. They are endowed with reason and conscience and should act towards one another in a spirit of brotherhood.

—Universal Declaration of Human Rights
(article 1), adopted by the United Nations General
Assembly resolution 217 A (III) of 10 December 1948.

The second half of the 20th century witnessed an unprecedented global trend in antidiscrimination and equal opportunity legislation. A growing number of countries around the world have instituted legislation providing their citizens with wider protections against discrimination and workplace harassment. This trend began with the United Nations' (UN) 1948 Universal Declaration of Human Rights, continued with the equal opportunity movement in the United States and Western Europe in the 1960s, and blossomed in the 1980s and 1990s with constitutional revisions and a multitude of laws protecting the rights of individuals of diverse backgrounds.

In order to assure adherence to employment laws and regulations, to avoid penalties, and to reap the rewards of compliance with local rules in these different national and cultural contexts, managers must understand the legislative and business-related, social policy practices of countries in which they are doing business. Moreover, to practice in today's global economy, managers need a framework for understanding human rights that transcends individual national contexts. This chapter begins with a discussion of an international and overarching framework for managing workforce diversity that has its roots in the UN Universal Declaration of Human Rights. Next, it presents different antidiscrimination legislation in several regions of the world and some discrepancies between laws and common practices. Finally, we present some practical implications for international business practices.

The International Bill of Human Rights and Employment Rights

In democratic countries, legislation and social policy stem from a value system that is shared by a people and thus represent their collective wish to enforce these values. In order to examine diversity legislation from a global perspective, one has to look for an authoritative representative body that can speak to the value system of the majority of people on the face of the earth. The UN, with all its shortcomings, is the organization that comes closest to representing all people around the world. In an ideal world, this body would be composed of democratically elected governments of all world countries and thus be truly representative of all people. In reality, the majority of the governments that participate and vote in the UN General Assembly and its numerous committees are not democratically elected. This being so, a good place to start examining global values with respect to workforce diversity is still the UN International Bill of Human Rights[1] and its statements with respect to employment rights and equality in the workplace. Given the diversity of geopolitical interests represented at the UN, one could argue that where there is consensus on issues of human rights, these pronouncements represent minimum standards to which civilized countries should adhere.

The International Bill of Human Rights consists of the Universal Declaration of Human Rights; the International Covenant on Economic, Social, and Cultural Rights; the International Covenant on Civil and Political Rights; and the two optional protocols. The chart depicted in Figure 2.1 provides a graphic representation of the International Bill of Human Rights and indicates the articles that are relevant to employment.

The Universal Declaration of Human Rights, the first component of the International Bill of Human Rights, was adopted by the UN General Assembly in its resolution 217 A (III) of December 10, 1948. The Declaration consists of a preamble and 30 articles, setting forth the human rights and fundamental freedoms without any form of discrimination to which all men and women, everywhere in the world, are entitled. (For the complete Declaration, see Appendix 2.1.)

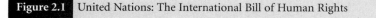

| Figure 2.1 | United Nations: The International Bill of Human Rights |

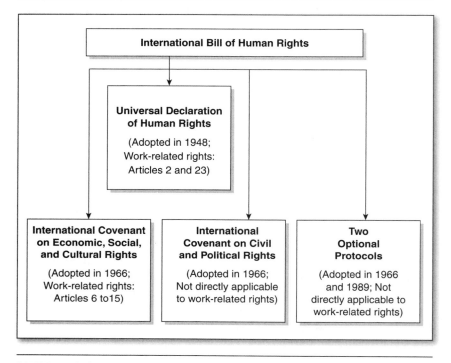

SOURCE: United Nations

Article 1 of the Declaration (cited at the very top of this chapter) lays down the philosophy on which the Declaration is based: first, the right to liberty and equality is the birthright of every human being, and it cannot be alienated; and second, human beings, as distinguished from other creatures, are rational and moral. For this reason, human beings are entitled to certain rights and freedoms that other creatures do not enjoy. Article 2, which sets out the basic principle of equality and nondiscrimination with respect to human rights and fundamental freedoms, forbids "distinction of any kind, such as race, colour, sex, language, religion, political or other opinion, national or social origin, property, birth or other status."

The Declaration assures every person, as a member of the human society, specific economic, social, and cultural rights (stated in Articles 22–27).[2] These rights are characterized as indispensable for human dignity, and the Declaration indicates that they are to be realized "through national effort and international cooperation." The rights most relevant to employment include the following:

- The right to social security
- The right to work

- The right to equal pay for equal work
- The right to rest and leisure
- The right to a standard of living adequate for health and well-being

It is important to note that although the different articles under the Declaration were designed to fit together harmoniously, there is potential tension between the articles that assure freedom of cultural and religious expression and those that assure equality, particularly as they apply to the workplace. For example, it is not uncommon in many cultures and religions around the world to have defined gender roles that specify behavioral expectations for women and men, not only within the family environment but also with respect to appropriate occupations and behaviors in the public arena. When these gender expectations create limitations on behaviors and communication patterns between men and women, they may challenge the principles of equality and fairness in the workplace. The debate over the ban on wearing religious attire in schools and in the workplace (the so called "headscarf ban") demonstrates the potential tension between multiculturalism and human rights (McGoldrick, 2006; Vakulenko, 2007) (see Box 2.1).

BOX 2.1
The Debate Over the Ban on the Wearing of Religious Attire and Religious Symbols in the Workplace

Aysegul Yilmaz wants to become a teacher after she finishes college, but the 21-year-old student will not be able to do so and still practice all elements of her religion. In Turkey, where Aysegul lives, it is illegal for Muslims to wear *hijabs*, the head scarves that cover a woman's head and neck but leaves the face clear (Nelson, 2003; BBC News, Muslim Veils, 2009). Predominantly Muslim, Turkey has banned *hijabs* in schools, workplaces, and other public locations because of the principle of state secularism promoted by the founder of modern Turkey, Mustafa Kemal Atatürk, in the beginning of the 20th century (McGoldrick, 2006). For example, a female defendant was ordered to leave a Turkish court, while her case proceeded, because she refused to remove her hijab (Nelson, 2003). At Turkey's Ankara University, theology faculty failed 150 students who were not permitted to attend class because of their *hijabs* ("Theological Students," 2002). In a landmark case (*Leyla Şahin v. Turkey*, 2005) the top European court of human rights set a precedent, determining that the ban on head scarves did not violate human rights. Leyla Şahin was a

(Continued)

(Continued)

student at Istanbul University when she was refused access to written examinations and was not allowed to enroll in courses because she was wearing the *hijab*. The Strasbourg-based Grand Chamber European Court of Human Rights has upheld the ruling of the lower court that the head scarf ban in Turkey did not violate the rights to freedom of thought, conscience, or religion guaranteed by an international human rights treaty. On February 9, 2008, the Turkish Parliament passed an amendment to the constitution allowing women to wear the *hijabs* in universities, only to have this amendment annulled by Turkey's Constitutional Court ruling on June 5, 2008, that removing the ban would run counter to official secularism (U.N. Refugee Agency, 2008; Birch, 2008).

Turkey is not the only country where *hijabs* and other religious attire are prohibited. Similar bans are found in Tunisia (which is also predominantly Muslim) and in Germany, where *hijabs* are banned in schools in half of its 16 states (German Courts uphold Muslim headscarf ban in schools, 2008; Browne, 2004; McGoldrick, 2006). In 2004, the French Senate and Parliament both overwhelmingly approved a law banning *hijabs*, yarmulkes (the Jewish skullcap), large crosses, the Sikh head cover, and similar religious apparel (Richburg, 2004). There are also different restrictions and various court rulings related to the ban on wearing the *hijabs* in other countries such as Italy, the Netherlands, Belgium, and Great Britain (Vakulenko, 2007).

Although opponents of these laws criticize them as limiting freedom of religion and of religious expression, proponents claim that they promote a secular society and assure freedom *from* religion in schools and in the workplace and therefore guaranty equality in the public arena. Opponents of these laws point to the restrictions on access to education and employment created by such bans, and the International Helsinki Federation for Human Rights, based in Austria, said it was against the French bill because it believed it violated human rights ("Chirac on Secular Society," 2003). If people's religious beliefs require them to wear, for example, the Muslim head scarf or the Sikh head cover, then their rights to work and to free choice of employment (Article 22 of the Universal Declaration of Human Rights) are, de facto, limited. Defending the law, French president Jacques Chirac declared in his December 17, 2003, address to the nation, "Secularism guarantees freedom of conscience. It protects the freedom to believe or not to believe." He further stated,

It is the neutrality of the public sphere which enables the harmonious existence side by side of different religions. Like all freedoms, the freedom to express one's faith can only have limits in the freedom of others, and in the compliance with rules of life in society. Religious freedom, which our country respects and protects, must not be abused, it must not call general rules into question, it must not infringe the freedom of belief of others. ("Chirac on Secular Society," 2003)

Since the French instituted the 2004 ban on religious attire, there has been a great deal of debate on the issues surrounding freedom of religious expression. In his highly publicized address to the Muslim world at the University of Cairo on June 4, 2009, U.S. president Barack Obama alluded to this controversy by stating that:

Moreover, freedom in America is indivisible from the freedom to practice one's religion. That is why there is a mosque in every state of our union, and over 1,200 mosques within our borders. That is why the U.S. government has gone to court to protect the right of women and girls to wear the *hijab*, and to punish those who would deny it. (*The Washington Post*, 2009. Transcript: President Obama's Cairo Address to the Muslim World)

These declarations demonstrate different approaches to resolving the inherent conflict between Article 2—the basic principle of equality that forbids distinction of any kind such as race, color, sex, etc.—and Article 18—that basic principle of freedom of thought, conscience, and religion that assures individuals' rights to manifest their religion and beliefs. The principles of *secularism* in the public arena (as in Turkey) and of freedom *from* religion (as in France) are used to justify a ban on prominent religious attire in schools and in the workplace while the principle of freedom *of* religion (as in the U.S.) is used to justify the support for allowing prominent religious attire in schools and in the workplace. Different countries find their own balance between religion, education, and the workplace, and, clearly, political considerations often influence these approaches (Smith, 2007).

Importance and Influence of the Declaration of Human Rights

The Universal Declaration is particularly relevant to the study of employment rights from a global perspective because no one country can serve as a model for other countries. The Declaration is truly universal in scope, as it preserves its validity for every member of the human family, everywhere, regardless of whether or not governments have formally accepted its principles or ratified the covenants.

The International Covenant on Economic, Social, and Cultural Rights, which includes the employment-related nondiscrimination articles, entered into force on January 3, 1976. As of July 2009 the Covenant had been ratified or acceded to by 169 states (United Nations, Treaty Collections, International Covenant on Economic, Social, and Cultural Rights, 2009; United Nations Fact Sheet No. 2 [Rev. 1], 2009):

Afghanistan, Albania, Algeria, Angola, Argentina, Armenia, Australia, Austria, Azerbaijan, Bahamas, Bahrain, Bangladesh, Barbados, Belarus, Belgium, Belize, Benin, Bolivia, Bosnia and Herzegovina, Brazil, Bulgaria, Burkina Faso, Burundi, Cambodia, Cameroon, Canada, Cape Verde, Central African Republic, Chad, Chile, China, Colombia, Congo, Costa Rica, Cote d'Ivoire, Croatia, Cuba, Cyprus, Czech Republic, Democratic People's Republic of Korea, Democratic Republic of the Congo, Denmark, Djibouti, Dominica, Dominican Republic, Ecuador, Egypt, El Salvador, Equatorial Guinea, Eritrea, Estonia, Ethiopia, Finland, France, Gabon, Gambia, Georgia, Germany, Ghana, Greece, Grenada, Guatemala, Guinea, Guinea-Bissau, Guyana, Honduras, Hungary, Iceland, India, Iran (Islamic Republic of), Iraq, Ireland, Israel, Italy, Jamaica, Japan, Jordan, Kazakhstan, Kenya, Kuwait, Kyrgyzstan, Lao People's Latvia, Lebanon, Lesotho, Liberia, Libyan Arab Jamahiriya, Liechtenstein, Lithuania, Luxembourg, Madagascar, Malawi, Maldives, Mali, Malta, Mauritania, Mauritius, Mexico, Monaco, Mongolia, Montenegro, Morocco, Namibia, Nepal, the Netherlands, New Zealand, Nicaragua, Niger, Nigeria, Norway, Pakistan, Panama, Papua New Guinea, Paraguay, Peru, Philippines Poland, Portugal, Republic of Korea, Republic of Moldova, Romania, Russian Federation, Rwanda, Saint Vincent and the Grenadines, San Marino, Sao Tome and Principe, Senegal, Serbia, Seychelles, Sierra Leone, Slovakia, Slovenia, Solomon Islands, Somalia, South Africa, Spain, Sri Lanka, Sudan, Suriname, Swaziland, Sweden, Switzerland, Syrian Arab Republic, Tajikistan, Thailand, The former Yugoslav Republic of Macedonia, Timor-Leste, Togo, Trinidad and Tobago, Tunisia, Turkey, Turkmenistan, Uganda, Ukraine, United Kingdom of Great Britain and Northern Ireland, United Republic of Tanzania, United States of America, Uruguay, Uzbekistan, Venezuela, Vietnam, Yemen, Zaire, Zambia, and Zimbabwe.

Despite this impressive number of states endorsing the Covenant, quite a few states either did not sign it or do not reinforce these principles in their national constitutions. For example, Saudi Arabia's constitution, adopted by royal decree of King Fahd in March 1992, includes no statement of equality related to gender, race, or ethnicity. Article 26 of Saudi Arabia's constitution declares, "The state protects human rights in accordance with the Islamic Shari'ah" (whose principles are different from those of the UN Declaration of Human Rights) (Constitution of the Kingdom Saudi Arabia, n.d.). It is important to note that the Covenants were originally conceived as multilateral conventions, which means that they are legally binding on only those states that have accepted them by ratification or accession. However, the precedent set by *Filartiga v. Pena-Irala* (1980)[3] indicates that they are currently recognized as "law of nations," a term that indicates an acceptance of international standards for judging human rights abuses, even in those states that have not accepted the covenants by ratification or accession.

Additional conventions relevant to workforce diversity include the International Convention on the Elimination of All Forms of Racial Discrimination, adopted in 1965; the Convention on the Elimination of All Forms of Discrimination Against Women, adopted in 1979; and the International Convention on the Protection of the Rights of All Migrant Workers and Members of Their Families, adopted in 1990.

Implementation

Having antidiscrimination legislation is an important first step, but to make a real difference in people's lives, the laws must be implemented and enforced. Many countries around the world do not have adequate legislation; others have appropriate legislation but with limited enforcement. In Australia, for example, current legislation has, to some degree, changed employers' views regarding discrimination in the workplace, but the legislation's impact on their actual practices is not very significant. Australian employers either do not fully understand the scope of the legislation or find ways to avoid its implementation (Bennington & Wein, 2000).

Often the obstacles for implementation are traditions and long-existing cultural practices that are discriminatory (for an example, see Box 2.2). One has only to examine the numerous reports of the UN Committee on Elimination of Racial Discrimination or those of the Committee on Elimination of Discrimination Against Women to realize that inadequate legislation and noncompliance are widespread. The following are a few informative examples:[4]

• The Committee on Elimination of Racial Discrimination in its March 2002 meeting expressed concern over the difficulties experienced by Roma (an ethnic minority group popularly referred to as "Gypsies") in Lithuania in "enjoying their fundamental rights in the field of housing, health, employment and education."

• The Committee on Elimination of Discrimination Against Women expressed concern over women's rights in Nigeria (July 1998). The committee noted, "Although education and training promoted equality between men and women, certain cultural and traditional practices and beliefs remained obstacles to women's full enjoyment of rights . . . including in the areas of . . . women's labour."

• The Committee on Elimination of Racial Discrimination reviewed the situation in Nepal (October 1999), noting that although the caste system in Nepal has been abolished by law, nevertheless this system still functions and appears embedded in parts of the Nepalese culture.

BOX 2.2
Equal Employment Legislation and De Facto Discrimination
Case Example: Belgium

Foreign nationals make up about 9% of Belgium's total population. Many of these were immigrants who came to Belgium immediately after World War II when workers were needed to fill labor shortages in the coal mining, iron, and steel industries. Workers were recruited from Italy, Spain, Greece, Morocco, and Turkey. The current population groups are the original workers, their descendants, and family members who were reunited with them (Smeesters, Arrijn, Feld, & Nayer, 2000). Although Belgium has adequate legislation with respect to racial and ethnic discrimination, the UN Committee on the Elimination of Racial Discrimination in its March 2002 meeting expressed concern about the increasing influence of racist and xenophobic political parties and "the difficult access of ethnic minorities to housing and employment."[5]

An elaborate study undertaken by the International Labour Organization (ILO) in the 1990s[6] provides some case examples that document discrimination in employment in Belgium. The researchers carefully selected testers who posed as job applicants. The testers were university students who were matched on major job-related characteristics with one difference: one of the testers was of Belgian origin and the other of Moroccan origin. It is important to note that Moroccan nationals make up 15% of all foreigners in Belgium, the largest group of non–European Union immigrants. The researchers report that the number of discriminatory cases amounted to 212 of 637 tests, constituting a discrimination rate of 33%. That is, in one third of the tests, the applicant of Belgian origin had a better chance of getting the job. The example below demonstrates the types of covert discrimination experienced by the testers.

Vacancy for a sales assistant in a fried-food outlet

Applicant of Belgian origin (Telephone)

The prospective employer inquired about the applicant's work experience and motivation, and then came the question of languages:

Employer: Do you speak German?

Applicant: Well, just a little—numbers . . .

Employer: But you really don't speak it? I'm sure you'll learn quickly. Come and see me tomorrow.

Applicant of Moroccan origin (Telephone)

The employer started off by asking the applicant if he spoke German.

Applicant: I can count.

Employer: That's not enough, you know. You are not suitable.[7]

A similar field experiment was conducted in the United States to examine the effects of perceived race on the decision of employers to call job applicants for interviews (Bertrand & Mullainathan, 2004). The researchers of the study, entitled "Are Emily and Greg more employable than Lakisha and Jamal?" sent fictitious résumés to help-wanted ads in Boston and Chicago newspapers. To manipulate the applicant's perceived race, résumés were randomly assigned African American or White-sounding names. The résumés with the White-sounding names received 50% more callbacks for interviews and the racial gap was uniform across occupation, industry, and employer size.

Diversity-Related Employment Legislation

Most democratic and many nondemocratic countries today ban job discrimination that is related to gender, race, and ethnicity. Some go further to forbid discrimination based on other characteristics like age, caste, social class, sexual orientation, and disability. In fact, this trend is so widespread that a growing number of insurance carriers are now offering employment practices liability insurance specific to foreign countries' labor laws (Maatman, 2000).[8]

A number of countries were assessed primarily using the ILO's database[9] to determine the extent to which countries worldwide offered antidiscrimination or equal rights legislation that is applicable to employment and work (see Appendix 2.2, Global Antidiscrimination and Equal Rights Legislation). The most popular forms[10] of antidiscrimination and equal rights legislation included protections based on gender or sex, equal remuneration, race, ethnicity or country of origin, religious beliefs, physical disability, and sexual orientation, respectively. More than 88% of the countries reviewed provided at least one of these protections. Other categories of protections offered in some countries include the following:

- HIV status (Philippines, South Africa, Zimbabwe) or health status (Cyprus)
- Marital status (Australia, Canada, Guyana, Ireland, Malawi, Netherlands, Trinidad and Tobago, United Kingdom, and Zambia)
- Pregnancy (Australia, Iceland, Israel, South Africa, United States)
- Aboriginal status (Canada)
- Political affiliation (Australia, Denmark, Malawi, Netherlands, Northern Ireland, Zambia, Zimbabwe)
- Family status (Canada, Malawi, South Africa)

The following are some examples of legislation on specific issues around the world.

Broad-Based Antidiscrimination Legislation

In the United States, civil rights legislation, from the 1960s and later, outlawed job discrimination on the basis of sex, race, color, religion, pregnancy, national origin, age, and disability (Equal Pay Act of 1963, the Civil Rights Act of 1964, the Rehabilitation Act of 1973, Vietnam Era Veterans Readjustment Assistance Act of 1974, Pregnancy Discrimination Act of 1978, Age Discrimination in Employment Act of 1967 and its amendments of 1978, Americans With Disabilities Act of 1990, and the Civil Rights Act of 1991). Canada's labor legislation is similar to that of the United States in the areas of employment discrimination and employment equity (Block & Roberts, 2000). Although the United States and Canada provide similar antidiscrimination protections, several differences exist. For example, Canadian laws extend to protect employees based on political beliefs and membership in organizations. The United States does not provide such protections for its employees except for membership in a union. Another difference is that the United States offers more extensive provisions to accommodate people with disabilities in employment, which is not as pervasive throughout Canadian jurisdictions (Block & Roberts, 2000).

Legislation banning discrimination against women, immigrants, and minorities in the labor force exist in most European countries, though often in weaker forms when compared with the U.S. laws. All European Union (EU) member states, except one, have constitutional provisions outlawing various forms of discrimination. The United Kingdom does not have a written constitution, but its general body of laws prohibits discrimination. As far as ordinary legislation is concerned, all EU member states' legal systems have regulations governing equal treatment and nondiscrimination in many facets of the employment relationship. Examples include access to employment, remuneration, and working conditions during employment (Commission of the European Communities, 1999). Yet the EU has often been criticized for not going far enough, in particular for the lack of a specific legal base for action going beyond equal treatment for men and women in the area of employment (O'Rourke, 1997). In 2000, the EU Council of Ministers' adoption of the directives on equal treatment of people regardless of their race and ethnic background in the labor force has signaled a trend of strengthening national legislation against racial and ethnic discrimination in employment. Some of the most advanced employment discrimination legislation in the European Union is that of the United Kingdom. It prohibits race, gender, and disability discrimination (the Race Discrimination Act of 1976, Sex Discrimination Act of 1975, and the Disability Discrimination Act of 1995). It is important to note that there are no statutory limits on compensation awards for employment discrimination in the United Kingdom.[11]

A similarly long list of diversity characteristics is included in Fiji's legislation. Fiji in its 1997 Amendment Act denies unfair discrimination on the basis of "actual or supposed personal characteristics or circumstances, including race, ethnic origin, colour, place of origin, gender, sexual orientation, birth, primary language, economic status, age or disability, or opinions or beliefs" (Fiji Islands Constitution Amendment Act of 1997, n.d.).

RACE—SOUTH AFRICA

South Africa's antidiscrimination legislation is relatively new and broad (Twyman, 2002). After a long rule by a tiny minority (White Afrikaners constitute only 13% of the population), the repressive apartheid regime was abolished in 1994, and the majority of the population (76% Blacks, 8.5% Coloureds, and 2.6% Asians) were finally able to share the power in a democratic process. The new constitution, adopted in 1996, declares that the country belongs to all who live in it "united in our diversity." Chapter 2, section 9, reads, "(3) The State may not unfairly discriminate directly or indirectly against anyone on one or more grounds, including race, gender, sex, pregnancy, marital status, ethnic or social origin, colour, sexual orientation, age, disability, religion, conscience, belief, culture, language and birth." There are two interesting elements of note about this declaration. First, the diversity list is far more inclusive than those of many other nations. Second, only "unfair discrimination" is banned, implying that it is possible to "fairly discriminate" and paving the way for affirmative action (discussed in the next chapter) (Constitution of the Republic of South Africa, 1996).

GENDER—JAPAN

In Japan's traditional society, discrimination against women was widespread and, until 1999, its laws were not as restrictive as those of other developed countries. The first law in the country's history introduced July 1, 1972, to address gender discrimination in the workplace was the "Law respecting the improvement of the welfare of women workers, including the guarantee of equal opportunity and treatment between men and women in employment" (Law No. 113). Other ordinances regarding the implementation of the law were enacted in 1986, and the law was amended through Law No. 107 of June 1995.

Though it was hailed as breakthrough legislation, it was so vague that employers were able to continue their discriminatory practices. Without legal repercussions, the law required only that employers "do their best" to rectify and curtail any gender-based discrimination. Job advertisements in newspapers continued to post "male only" jobs, and women college graduates continued to encounter difficulties in obtaining jobs with salary and benefits commensurate with or equal to those of their male counterparts. Additionally, the law included "protective" articles, such as restricting women labor at night. The following case illustrates the issue:

> In 1995, a student from India received a scholarship to study dental technology in Tokyo. Upon graduating from the program 3 years later, she looked for jobs in her field. Although she encountered no discrimination from employers because of her foreign origin, she was barred, as a woman, from applying for positions that required nighttime work.[12]

A 1996 landmark ruling on gender discrimination was a part of the impetus to change Japan's gender-related legislation. The case involved a group of women employees of Shiba Shinyo Kinko Bank who sued over unequal wages and denials of promotions. The courts awarded the 13 plaintiffs 340 million yen (approximately $3 million). On April 1, 1999, a new piece of legislation was introduced that rectifies the limitations of the previous law. Whereas the previous law required employers only to "do their best," the new law gave specific guidelines, such as (a) prohibiting discriminatory advertisements in the hiring process; (b) asking certain types of interview questions only to members of one gender is forbidden (such as asking a woman if she plans to leave her job once she marries or has children); and (c) making it easier to start a mediation process (it can be initiated unilaterally, rather than bilaterally). The law also repealed some of the "protective" provisions that were included in the previous law, such as restricting nighttime labor for women.[13]

EQUAL REMUNERATION—UNITED STATES

Equal remuneration legislation requiring work organizations to pay women (and men in some countries like Norway) equally for their work was by far the most common form of antidiscrimination or equal rights legislation throughout the world. Taking equal remuneration legislation into account, in addition to anti–sexual harassment and equal rights legislation, more than 75% of the countries reviewed offer some form of protection based on gender. It is interesting to note that the first major legislation signed by President Barack Obama, the Lilly Ledbetter Wage Bill, was aimed at closing a loophole in the U.S. legislation related to equal pay for equal work, making it easier to sue for wage discrimination. Lilly Ledbetter worked for 19 years at a Goodyear plant in Alabama and sued after she found that she was paid less than her male counterparts. The battle reached the Supreme Court, which ruled against her in a 5-4 decision. The high court's decision was based on the principle that a person must file a claim of discrimination within 180 days of a company's initial decision to pay a worker less than it pays another worker doing the same job. Ledbetter, who discovered this discrimination only after 19 years of working for the company, could not have possibly sued within this time frame. Under the new bill every new discriminatory paycheck would extend the statute of limitations. President Obama said that the bill "is by no means a women's issue, it is a family issue" (Davis, 2009; S.181: Lilly Ledbetter Fair Pay Act of 2009).

In most counties, a woman cannot claim that she has been discriminated against if she cannot fulfill reasonable physical requirements associated with performing a job and this can often affect her level of compensation. For example, in the United States, a woman applied for a job as a prison guard and was turned down because she did not meet the minimum height and weight requirements. She brought a class-action lawsuit under Title VII of the Civil Rights Act of 1964 alleging that she had been denied employment because of her sex, in violation of federal law. The U.S. Supreme Court affirmed a lower court's decision that the minimum weight and height requirement was reasonable and therefore not discriminatory (*Dothard v. Rawlinson*, 1977).[14] However, the 1991 Civil Rights Act now provides that a practice that is seemingly neutral (such as setting height and weight limits) but has discriminatory impact (in this case, excluding women) violates the law. For example, setting a high school education as the employment requirement for custodial work is neutral on its face, but can have discriminatory impact on individuals who had limited access to education, and therefore would be unlawful under the 1991 Civil Rights Act.[15]

It is important to note that although in the majority of cases of gender discrimination, women constitute the group that needs protection, the laws in most countries can be applied for men as well because they prohibit discrimination regardless of gender. For example, a 1982 U.S. ruling determined that a state university for women (Mississippi University for Women) could not constitutionally prohibit male students from enrolling for credit in its nursing school (*Mississippi University for Women v. Hogan,* 1982).

SEXUAL ORIENTATION LEGISLATION—INTERNATIONAL

Much less common in international legislation is protection based on sexual orientation. A cross-referenced search of the UN ILO's database, NATLEX, and research conducted by the International Gay and Lesbian Human Rights Commission (IGLHRC)[16] shows that over 20 countries, such as Australia, Canada, Denmark, Germany, Ireland, Israel, the Netherlands, South Africa, Sweden, and the United States, offer such protections. The map illustrates the countries worldwide that provide antidiscrimination legislation based on sexual orientation (see Figure 2.2 for the map and Table 2.1 for a listing of sexual orientation legislation by country).

ANTI–SEXUAL HARASSMENT LEGISLATION—INTERNATIONAL

Sexual harassment is a widespread and underreported form of gender-based discrimination and deserves special attention. It is aimed primarily at women, although men suffer from it too. Sexual harassment often goes unreported for two reasons: first, many women are afraid of losing their jobs and hence their livelihood. This is particularly true when they are in an economically or immigration-related vulnerable situation; for example, they are single mothers, sole breadwinners, and immigrants who are not familiar with the host country's language and legislation, or illegal immigrants who are afraid of being deported. Second, in many cultures, reporting sexual harassment victimizes the woman a second time. She is seen as having brought shame on herself and her family, as she is blamed for being promiscuous and sexually provocative. As a result of high-profile lawsuits and pressure from grassroots women's organizations, there is a growing awareness of women's rights, and additional efforts toward creating a work environment that is free of sexual pressure are being made. Around the world, more and more countries are banning sexual harassment in the workplace.

The legal definitions of sexual harassment and the protections provided under the law vary greatly from one country to the next. Those definitions are

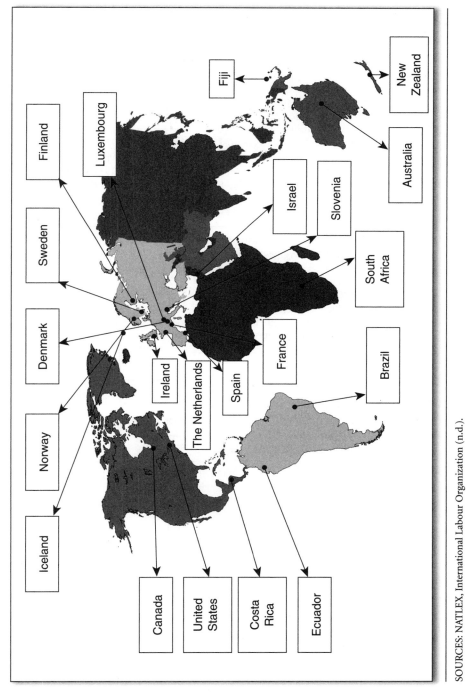

SOURCES: NATLEX, International Labour Organization (n.d.).

International Gay and Lesbian Human Rights Commission [IGLHRC] (1999).

Table 2.1	Worldwide Legislation Against Sexual Orientation Discrimination: Listing by Country

Country	Name of Legislation
Australia	• Capital Territory–Discrimination Act (1991) • Equal Opportunity Act (Gender Identity and Sexual Orientation) (2000), No. 52 • New South Wales—Anti-Discrimination Act (1977, 1998) • Northern Territory–Anti-Discrimination Act (1996) • State of Queensland–Anti-Discrimination Act (1991) • State of South Australia–Equal Opportunity Act (1984) • State of Tasmania–Anti-Discrimination Act (1998) • State of Victoria–Equal Opportunity Act (1995)
Brazil	• State of Mato–Constitution Article 10.3 (1989) • State of Sergipe–Constitution Article 3.2 (1989)
Canada	• The Canada Human Rights Act (1996) • Canadian Charter of Rights and Freedoms Section 15(1) (1982) • New Brunswick Human Rights Code [Human Rights Code. 1971, c.8, s.1; 1985, c.30, s.3]ª 3(1)
Costa Rica	• Law No 7771, Article 48
Denmark	• Act No. 459 on prohibition against discrimination in respect of employment (1996) • The Penal Code (1987), Act 626, Article 266
Ecuador	• Constitution (1998), Article 23
Fiji	• Constitution, Section 38(2) of the Bill of Rights (1998)
Finland	• Constitution (1998), Section 5 • The Penal Code (1995), Section 9 • Penal Code (1995), Chapter 47, Section 3
France	• The French Penal Code (1985) • The Code of Labor law (1986, 1990)
Iceland	• The Icelandic Penal Code (1996)
Ireland	• Prohibition of Incitement to Hatred Act (1989) • The Health Insurance Act (1994) • The Unfair Dismissals (Amendment) Act (1993) • Employment Equality Act (1998)

Country	Name of Legislation
Israel	• Equal Opportunities in Employment (1992)
Luxembourg	• Penal Code, Articles 454–457 (1997)
Netherlands	• The General Equal Treatment Act (1994) • Penal Code (1992), Articles 137c, d, e, and f; Article 429quater • In 1992 Constitution, Article 1 DC (1983)
New Zealand	• Human Rights Act, Section 21 (1993) • Human Rights Amendment Act (2001)
Norway	• Act No. 15 of (2001) (to amend Act No. 4 of 1977) • Work Environment Law (Clause added in 1998) • Penal Code, Paragraph 135a (1981)
South Africa	• Employment Equity Act 5 (1998) • Constitution of the Republic of South Africa (Act No. 108 of 1996) • Constitution (1996), Bill of Rights and Equality Clause (Section 9)
Slovenia	• Act 27 on Equality of Educational Opportunities (2007) • Penal Code (1996), Article 141 • Law About Work Relations, Article 6 (1998)
Spain	• Penal Code (1995), Article 22
Sweden	• The Prohibition of Discrimination Act (No. 307 of 2003) • Act No. 453 of 2005 (to amend Act No. 307 of 2003 to prohibit discrimination) • Act No. 480 of 2005 (to amend Act No. 307 of 2003 to prohibit discrimination) • Act No. 1089 of 2004 (to amend Act No. 307 of 2003 to prohibit discrimination) • Act No. 479 of 2005 (to amend the Prohibition of Discrimination in Working Life because of Sexual Orientation Act No. 133 of 1999) • Ordinance No. 146 (2006) (to amend Ordinance No. 170 of 1999) • Ordinance No. 1408 (2006) (to amend Ordinance No. 170 of 1999) • Ordinance No. 319 (2003) (to amend Ordinance No. 170 of 1999)

(Continued)

| **Table 2.1** (Continued) | |

Country	Name of Legislation
Sweden	• Act No. 310 of 2003 (to amend the Prohibition of Discrimination in Working Life because of Sexual Orientation Act No. 133 of 1999) • Prohibition of Discrimination in Working Life because of Sexual Orientation Act No. 133 of 1999 • Penal Code (1987), Chapter 16, Paragraph 9
Taiwan	• Gender Equality in Employment Act (2002), Chapter 2
United States of America	• Equal Employment Opportunity in the Federal Government (1998) (Executive Order 11478) • Executive Order 13087 (1998) (to amend Executive Order 1147) • States' civil rights laws (Twenty states and the District of Columbia offer such protections. The states include California, Colorado, Connecticut, Hawaii, Illinois, Iowa, Maine, Maryland, Massachusetts, Minnesota, Nevada, New Hampshire, New Jersey, New Mexico, New York, Oregon, Rhode Island, Vermont, Washington DC, and Wisconsin)

NOTES:

a. The New Brunswick Human Rights Code can be found on the New Brunswick Department of Justice Web site (www.gnb.ca/acts/acts/h-11.htm). This legislation was retrieved August 11, 2002.

SOURCES:

NATLEX, International Labour Organization (n.d.).

International Gay and Lesbian Human Rights Commission [IGLHRC] (1999).

Council of Labor Affairs. Executive Yuan Taiwan R.O.C. (2009).

important because when they are broad and vague, they leave more room for interpretation by the courts, and as a result, it is often more difficult to prosecute perpetrators under such laws. Examples of broad definitions include Nepal's civil code on sexual harassment, which applies to women only and states that sexual harassment is "any male touching the body parts of a woman (other than his wife) with a sexual intention." Under Malaysia's Code of Practice on the Prevention and Eradication of Sexual Harassment in the Workplace, sexual harassment means any unwanted conduct of sexual nature having the effect of verbal, nonverbal, visual, psychological, or physical harassment that (a) might, on reasonable grounds, be perceived by the recipient as placing a condition of a sexual nature on her or his employment; or (b) might, on reasonable grounds, be perceived by the recipient as an offense or humiliation, or a threat to her or his well-being, even with no direct link to her or his employment. Hong Kong's Sexual Discrimination Ordinance defines sexual harassment as any unwanted or uninvited sexual behavior that a reasonable person regards as offensive, humiliating, or intimidating, including unwelcome sexual advances or unwelcome requests for sexual favors.

South Korea's laws provide a more detailed definition. According to the Sexual Equality Employment Act and the Gender Discrimination Prevention and Relief Act, sexual harassment at work includes actions taken by a business owner, supervisor, or coworker that cause sexual humiliation to another worker through words or actions or creates an uncomfortable work environment. These actions may be in conjunction with job requirement or using the perpetrator's position in a way that creates the impression that if the victim will not yield to the sexual demands, the behavior will result in loss of a job or a disadvantage at work. These definitions related only to direct actions by a supervisor or a coworker. They do not include situations in which the work environment itself constitutes sexual harassment, such as the use of profane language by supervisors and coworkers and posting sexually explicit posters in the workplace. Other definitions are more specific and include both direct sexual harassment and indirect. The latter refers to an oppressive work environment. The Equal Employment Opportunity Commission in the United States defines sexual harassment as unwanted sexual advances in the workplace that include requests for sexual favors and other verbal or physical contact of a sexual nature when these advances are made either explicitly or implicitly a condition for getting a job, keeping a job, or getting a promotion. An important evolution of the law now requires that the judge or jury see harassment not through the eyes of a reasonable person but through the eyes of a reasonable *victim*. For example, what a man may not consider harassment may be considered so by a woman. Further, a work environment that is offensive, intimidating, or hostile also constitutes sexual harassment.[17] India's Supreme Court guidelines are more specific and include such unwelcome sexually determined behavior (whether directly or by implication) as (a) physical contact and advances; (b) a demand or request for sexual favors; (c) sexually colored remarks; (d) showing pornography; and (e) any other unwelcome physical, verbal, or nonverbal conduct of sexual nature.

Similarly, the scope of protections against sexual harassment varies greatly among countries. Some countries, such as the United States, the United Kingdom, and Hong Kong, provide a relatively wide scope of protections against sexual harassment in the workplace, whereas others provide limited (e.g., Malaysia) or no protections at all (e.g., Pakistan). The European community has moved toward providing a strong protection against sexual harassment in recent years. The directive on the equal treatment of persons in the labor market, adopted by the EU Council of Ministers on June 7, 2000, amended October 5, 2002, calls for all EU members to adopt antiharassment programs, to set up national bodies and civil remedies to ensure their enforcement, and to encourage employers to take measures to combat all forms of sexual discrimination and sexual harassment in the workplace.

A similar trend has taken place in Japan and Venezuela. In 1997, the Japanese Ministry of Labor issued recommendations that are modeled after the guidelines prohibiting sexual harassment of the U.S. Equal Employment Opportunity Commission. At about the same time, Japan's Equal Employment Opportunity Act was amended, requiring Japanese employers to establish company policies and internal complaint procedures on sexual harassment. Venezuela has enacted its sexual harassment law (January 1, 1999) as part of the Law on Violence Against Women and Family. The law establishes sexual harassment as a crime that is punishable by a prison term of from 3 to 12 months, and the offender must pay the victim double the amount of economic damages caused by the harassment, such as lack of access to jobs or promotions (Maatman, 2000).[18]

A survey conducted by CAW (Committee on Asian Women) examined the legal provision for protection and prevention of sexual harassment at the workplace among a select number of Asian countries.[19] The findings indicate that the legislative situation in Southeast Asia is mixed. Although there are clear legal provisions laid down for the protection and prevention of sexual harassment in places like Hong Kong and South Korea, such provisions are nonexistent in countries like Pakistan. Somewhere between are countries like Malaysia, which has a code of practice rather than legal provisions for employers to establish in-house mechanisms to combat sexual harassment. For a comparison of sexual harassment laws among eleven Asian countries, see Table 2.2.

Practical Implications

The moral principles of just treatment of members of diverse groups—outlined in the UN Universal Declaration of Human Rights and in the various state constitutions and legislation—have some practical implications for individual workers, for groups of workers, for work organizations, and for societies. Employees who are treated unfairly are less productive, less satisfied, and less loyal to their organizations. These issues will be dealt with in the next several chapters. Relevant to this chapter is the fact that these workers are more likely to initiate lawsuits against the offending work organization. The lawsuits can carry hefty financial repercussions for the organizations. As the noted sociologist Émile Durkheim predicted almost a century ago, a society that loses

(Text continued on p. 42.)

Table 2.2 Comparison of the Legal Provision for Protection Against Sexual Harassment at the Workplace Among Selected Asian Countries

COUNTRY— NAME OF LEGISLATION	QUESTIONS ADDRESSED REGARDING SEXUAL HARASSMENT IN THE WORKPLACE						
	1. Do legal protections against sexual harassment in the workplace exist?						
	2. Is there separate legislation or some section/clause of other labor laws?						
	3. How are victims protected? Are there specific rights defined in the law?						
	4. Are there any sections in the law on prevention of sexual harassment at the workplace?						
	5. Do administrative structures exist to facilitate the implementation of the law?						
	6. Is sexual harassment considered a criminal offense?						
	7. What is the minimum and maximum punishment permissible by law?						
	1	2	3	4	5	6	7
MALAYSIA— Code of Practice on the prevention and eradication of sexual harassment at the workplace	No	No legislation but a separate Code	The Code only refers to the responsibility of the employers to prevent sexual harassment.	The Code gives some guidelines for employers regarding prevention of sexual harassment.	No	No	The nature and type of penalty would depend on the nature of offense.
NEPAL— The Civil Code	Yes	Some clause or section of other laws	Under general law provision, they can lodge complaint with the court or appropriate authority.	No	No	Yes***	Minimum: 1 Rupee fine and 1 day in jail. Maximum: 500 Rupees fine and 1 year in jail.

(Continued)

Table 2.2 (Continued)

	1	2	3	4	5	6	7
SOUTH KOREA— Equal Employment & Work and Family Reconciliation Act	Yes	Some clause or section of other laws	When the sexual harassment occurs within the workplace, the employer should punish the sexual harasser right away or address the issue accordingly. And the employer cannot fire or give disadvantages to the person who is sexually harassed or who says that he/she is sexually harassed.	Yes	Yes*	No	The fine imposed as follows: (1) Maximum 10 million Won when the employer committed sexual harassment. (2) Maximum 5 million Won when the employer neglected the sexual harassment case or didn't address it appropriately. (3) Maximum 3 million Won when the employer did not conduct preventive trainings for sexual harassment.
SRI LANKA— Article 12(1) and (2) of the Constitution and criminal law	Yes	Some clause or section of other laws	No response	No	No	Yes	Minimum: 3 years Maximum: 10 years
THAILAND— The Labour Protection Law	Yes	Some clause or section of other laws	No response	No	No	No	Not stipulated

	1	2	3	4	5	6	7
TAIWAN – Gender Equality in Employment Act & Enforcement Rules for the Sexual Harassment Prevention Act	Yes	Some clause or section of other laws	The laws specify responsibility of the employers to prevent sexual harassment and to handle a complaint concerning sexual harassment.	Yes	Yes	Yes	(1) The fine imposed on the employer for negligence, failing to take preventive measures, or didn't address it appropriately is from minimum NTD 100,000 to maximum NTD 500,000. (2) The maximum punishment for the harasser is 2 years in jail or a fine of NTD 100,000.
HONG KONG— Sex Discrimination Ordinance	Yes	Separate legislation	They may lodge complaint in writing to the Commission. The Commission will then investigate the complaint and encourage conciliation between the parties in the dispute. If the complaint cannot be resolved, the Commission may also provide assistance in court proceedings should the victim decide to take his/her case to court.	Yes	Yes**	Yes****	To be determined by the court.

(Continued)

Table 2.2 (Continued)

	1	2	3	4	5	6	7
INDONESIA— Act 281 of the Criminal Law that regulates ethics	Yes	Some clause or section of other laws	No	No	No	No	The maximum punishment is 2 years and 8 months in jail or a fine of Rp. 4500.
ISRAEL— Prevention of Sexual Harassment Law, 5758 - 1998	Yes	A section of the Sexual Harassme nt Law refers to sexual harassme nt in the workplace	Victim's protection specified (e.g., concealing the victim's identity, no disclosure of past sexual experiences. etc.).	Yes, the law specifies steps employers must take to prevent sexual harassment and address complaints efficiently.	Yes	Yes	Up to 4 years in jail, monetary compensation of 50,000 INS (Israeli New Shekels), but the courts can award higher sums with proof of damages.
INDIA—Indecent Representation of Women Act Vishaka Guidelines and Indian Penal Code (Sections 294, 354, and 509),	Yes	Some clause or section of other laws	Superior guidelines refers only to the responsibility of the employers.	No	No	No	Minimum sentence of 2 years.

40

	1	2	3	4	5	6	7
JAPAN— Equal Employment Opportunity Law	Yes	Some clause or section of other laws	The law refers only to the responsibility of the employers.	No	No	No	Not stipulated.

NOTES:

* The Presidential Commission on Women Affairs, Employment Equality Committee in Labour Ministry.

** The Equal Opportunities Commission (EOC).

*** Depending on the nature of the offense committed.

**** Depending on the nature of the offense committed.

SOURCES:

Based on Committee on Asian Women (2000) cross-referenced with ILO's NATLEX database.

Council of Labor Affairs. Executive Yuan Taiwan R.O.C. (2009).

Hong Kong Legal Information Institute (2009).

Ministry of Labor in Korea (2009).

Ministry of Interior in Taiwan (2009).

Regev, D. (2007).

The Sunday Times (2007).

Vibhuti Patel (2005).

Vishaka Guidelines Against Sexual Harassment in the Workplace. (2009).

its organic solidarity—an internal compass for what is right and wrong—must turn to the courts for relief. The following two examples illustrate the financial implications of discriminatory behavior in the workplace.

> In one of Japan's largest sexual harassment lawsuits, the governor of Osaka region was ordered to pay the equivalent of $107,000 to a 21-year-old university student who worked on his election campaign. The governor, Knock Yokoyama, was found guilty by Osaka's District Court Judge Keisuke Hayashi, who determined that, in addition to sexually harassing the campaign worker (he was accused of groping her for one half hour aboard a campaign bus), the governor also tried to silence and intimidate her by offering her a gift, making false statements about her to prosecutors, and defaming her publicly. (Tolbert, 1999)

A similar example from the U.S. context pertains to racial discrimination.

> A federal appeals court in San Francisco upheld a $1 million punitive damage verdict awarded to a Black man subjected to repeated harassment on the job, including numerous racial slurs by coworkers. Although management tried to characterize the racial slurs as "jokes," the court did not accept their contention. Judge Margaret McKeown wrote for a unanimous panel of three judges of the U.S. 9th Circuit Court of Appeals, "This case should serve as a reminder to employers of their obligation to keep their workplaces free of discriminatory harassment." This award is one of the largest ever in a racial harassment case based solely on offensive language. ("Award Over Racism Upheld," 2001)

These examples demonstrate the costly consequences of noncompliance with legislation pertaining to diversity discrimination in the workplace. There is an additional dimension to international legislation that pertains to multinational corporations. These corporations often operate in host countries whose cultural framework and legislation are very different from those of the country where the company is headquartered. When a company sends its employees overseas, the question is often asked, Do the laws of the country of origin apply or those of the host country? This question is relevant to occupational safety laws, environmental pollution laws, as well as to discrimination and equal opportunities. In the past, the courts have stated that the relevant law was that of the host country.[20] The following case illustrates the implications for employment discrimination.

> In 1979, Arabian American Oil Company (Aramco), a Delaware corporation, hired Mr. Boureslan, a naturalized U.S. citizen born in Lebanon, as a cost engineer in Houston. A year later he was transferred, at his request, to work for Aramco in Saudi Arabia. Boureslan remained with Aramco in Saudi Arabia until he was discharged in 1984. After filing a charge of discrimination with the Equal Employment Opportunity Commission (EEOC), he instituted a suit in the

United States District Court for the Southern District of Texas against Aramco and Arabian American Oil Company. He sought relief under Title VII of the Civil Rights Act of 1964 on the ground that he was harassed and ultimately discharged by the respondents on account of his race, religion, and national origin. In dismissing this claim, the court ruled that it lacked jurisdiction because Title VII's protections do not extend to United States citizens employed abroad by American employers. The Court of Appeals affirmed this decision. (*Equal Employment Opportunity Commission v. Arabian American Oil Co.,* 1991)

Since then, however, new developments included in the U.S. Equal Employment Opportunity Commission's (EEOC) manual prohibit discrimination by an American employer even when the employer is operating abroad. Further, the EEOC manual also prohibits discrimination by a foreign employer that is controlled by an American employer (i.e., financial control, common ownership, common management, etc.).

Summary and Conclusion

This chapter examines global legislation related to equity and fairness in employment. In democratic countries, the laws represent a value system shared by the people. To identify such a shared value system globally, one has to search for a global representative body that can specify a similarly shared value system for all human beings. The United Nations, with all its faults (most governments represented are not democratic), is the closest to such a representative body. The Universal Declaration of Human Rights, adopted in 1948 by the UN General Assembly, stands on two philosophical principles: (a) the right to liberty and equality is the birthright of every human being and cannot be alienated; (b) human beings, as distinguished from other creatures, are rational and moral and therefore entitled to certain rights and freedoms. The International Bill of Human Rights provides the universal moral basis for nondiscrimination in employment because it forbids "distinction of any kind, such as race, colour, sex, language, religion, political or other opinion, national or social origin, property, birth or other status."

Some countries, such as the United States, Canada, and many members of the European Union, have broad-based antidiscrimination legislation that outlaws discrimination based on a wide array of characteristics such as gender, race, ethnicity or country of origin, religious beliefs, physical disability, and sexual orientation. South Africa's relatively recent legislation (the apartheid regime was abolished in 1994) provides a very broad protection from discrimination, listing a wide array of characteristics including "race, gender, sex, pregnancy, marital status, ethnic or social origin, colour, sexual orientation, age, disability, religion, conscience, belief, culture, language and birth."

Noncompliance with these laws may have severe consequences. Employees who are treated unfairly are more likely to be less productive and less loyal. Antidiscrimination diversity legislation has the potential to deter discriminatory employment practices because of its potential costly consequences. It is important to note that, depending on each country's cultural climate and court system, the success of such lawsuits, or even the likelihood that a victim of such action will press charges, greatly varies. Therefore, to avoid penalties and lawsuits and to reap the rewards of compliance, managers today must understand the legislative- and business-related social policies of the countries where they are doing business.

Appendix 2.1 Universal Declaration of Human Rights

UNIVERSAL DECLARATION OF HUMAN RIGHTS

Adopted and Proclaimed by General Assembly Resolution 217 A (III) of 10 December 1948

On December 10, 1948, the General Assembly of the United Nations adopted and proclaimed the Universal Declaration of Human Rights, the full text of which appears in the following pages. Following this historic act, the Assembly called on all member countries to publicize the text of the Declaration and "to cause it to be disseminated, displayed, read and expounded principally in schools and other educational institutions, without distinction based on the political status of countries or territories."

Preamble

Whereas recognition of the inherent dignity and of the equal and inalienable rights of all members of the human family is the foundation of freedom, justice and peace in the world,

Whereas disregard and contempt for human rights have resulted in barbarous acts which have outraged the conscience of mankind, and the advent of a world in which human beings shall enjoy freedom of speech and belief and freedom from fear and want has been proclaimed as the highest aspiration of the common people,

Whereas it is essential, if man is not to be compelled to have recourse, as a last resort, to rebellion against tyranny and oppression, that human rights should be protected by the rule of law,

Whereas it is essential to promote the development of friendly relations between nations,

Whereas the peoples of the United Nations have in the Charter reaffirmed their faith in fundamental human rights, in the dignity and worth of the human person and in the equal rights of men and women and have determined to promote social progress and better standards of life in larger freedom,

Whereas Member States have pledged themselves to achieve, in co-operation with the United Nations, the promotion of universal respect for and observance of human rights and fundamental freedoms,

Whereas a common understanding of these rights and freedoms is of the greatest importance for the full realization of this pledge,

Now, Therefore THE GENERAL ASSEMBLY proclaims THIS UNIVERSAL DECLARATION OF HUMAN RIGHTS as a common standard of achievement for all peoples and all nations, to the end that every individual and every organ of society, keeping this Declaration constantly in mind, shall strive by teaching and education to promote respect for these rights and freedoms and by progressive measures, national and international, to secure their universal and effective recognition and observance, both among the peoples of Member States themselves and among the peoples of territories under their jurisdiction.

Article 1

All human beings are born free and equal in dignity and rights. They are endowed with reason and conscience and should act towards one another in a spirit of brotherhood.

Article 2

Everyone is entitled to all the rights and freedoms set forth in this Declaration, without distinction of any kind, such as race, colour, sex, language, religion, political or other opinion, national or social origin, property, birth or other status. Furthermore, no distinction shall be made on the basis of the political, jurisdictional or international status of the country or territory to which a person belongs, whether it be independent, trust, non-self-governing or under any other limitation of sovereignty.

Article 3

Everyone has the right to life, liberty and security of person.

Article 4

No one shall be held in slavery or servitude; slavery and the slave trade shall be prohibited in all their forms.

Article 5

No one shall be subjected to torture or to cruel, inhuman or degrading treatment or punishment.

Article 6

Everyone has the right to recognition everywhere as a person before the law.

Article 7

All are equal before the law and are entitled without any discrimination to equal protection of the law. All are entitled to equal protection against any discrimination in violation of this Declaration and against any incitement to such discrimination.

Article 8

Everyone has the right to an effective remedy by the competent national tribunals for acts violating the fundamental rights granted him by the constitution or by law.

Article 9

No one shall be subjected to arbitrary arrest, detention or exile.

Article 10

Everyone is entitled in full equality to a fair and public hearing by an independent and impartial tribunal, in the determination of his rights and obligations and of any criminal charge against him.

Article 11

(1) Everyone charged with a penal offence has the right to be presumed innocent until proved guilty according to law in a public trial at which he has had all the guarantees necessary for his defence.

(2) No one shall be held guilty of any penal offence on account of any act or omission which did not constitute a penal offence, under national or international law, at the time when it was committed. Nor shall a heavier penalty be imposed than the one that was applicable at the time the penal offence was committed.

Article 12

No one shall be subjected to arbitrary interference with his privacy, family, home or correspondence, nor to attacks upon his honour and reputation. Everyone has the right to the protection of the law against such interference or attacks.

Article 13

(1) Everyone has the right to freedom of movement and residence within the borders of each state.

(2) Everyone has the right to leave any country, including his own, and to return to his country.

Article 14

(1) Everyone has the right to seek and to enjoy in other countries asylum from persecution.

(2) This right may not be invoked in the case of prosecutions genuinely arising from non-political crimes or from acts contrary to the purposes and principles of the United Nations.

Article 15

(1) Everyone has the right to a nationality.

(2) No one shall be arbitrarily deprived of his nationality nor denied the right to change his nationality.

Article 16

(1) Men and women of full age, without any limitation due to race, nationality or religion, have the right to marry and to found a family. They are entitled to equal rights as to marriage, during marriage and at its dissolution.

(2) Marriage shall be entered into only with the free and full consent of the intending spouses.

(3) The family is the natural and fundamental group unit of society and is entitled to protection by society and the State.

Article 17

(1) Everyone has the right to own property alone as well as in association with others.

(2) No one shall be arbitrarily deprived of his property.

Article 18

Everyone has the right to freedom of thought, conscience and religion; this right includes freedom to change his religion or belief, and freedom, either alone or in community with others and in public or private, to manifest his religion or belief in teaching, practice, worship and observance.

Article 19

Everyone has the right to freedom of opinion and expression; this right includes freedom to hold opinions without interference and to seek, receive and impart information and ideas through any media and regardless of frontiers.

Article 20

(1) Everyone has the right to freedom of peaceful assembly and association.
(2) No one may be compelled to belong to an association.

Article 21

(1) Everyone has the right to take part in the government of his country, directly or through freely chosen representatives.
(2) Everyone has the right of equal access to public service in his country.
(3) The will of the people shall be the basis of the authority of government; this will shall be expressed in periodic and genuine elections which shall be by universal and equal suffrage and shall be held by secret vote or by equivalent free voting procedures.

Article 22

Everyone, as a member of society, has the right to social security and is entitled to realization, through national effort and international co-operation and in accordance with the organization and resources of each State, of the economic, social and cultural rights indispensable for his dignity and the free development of his personality.

Article 23

(1) Everyone has the right to work, to free choice of employment, to just and favourable conditions of work and to protection against unemployment.

(2) Everyone, without any discrimination, has the right to equal pay for equal work.

(3) Everyone who works has the right to just and favourable remuneration ensuring for himself and his family an existence worthy of human dignity, and supplemented, if necessary, by other means of social protection.

(4) Everyone has the right to form and to join trade unions for the protection of his interests.

Article 24

Everyone has the right to rest and leisure, including reasonable limitation of working hours and periodic holidays with pay.

Article 25

(1) Everyone has the right to a standard of living adequate for the health and well-being of himself and of his family, including food, clothing, housing and medical care and necessary social services, and the right to security in the event of unemployment, sickness, disability, widowhood, old age or other lack of livelihood in circumstances beyond his control.

(2) Motherhood and childhood are entitled to special care and assistance. All children, whether born in or out of wedlock, shall enjoy the same social protection.

Article 26

(1) Everyone has the right to education. Education shall be free, at least in the elementary and fundamental stages. Elementary education shall be compulsory. Technical and professional education shall be made generally available and higher education shall be equally accessible to all on the basis of merit.

(2) Education shall be directed to the full development of the human personality and to the strengthening of respect for human rights and fundamental freedoms. It shall promote understanding, tolerance and friendship among all nations, racial or religious groups, and shall further the activities of the United Nations for the maintenance of peace.

(3) Parents have a prior right to choose the kind of education that shall be given to their children.

Article 27

(1) Everyone has the right freely to participate in the cultural life of the community, to enjoy the arts and to share in scientific advancement and its benefits.

(2) Everyone has the right to the protection of the moral and material interests resulting from any scientific, literary or artistic production of which he is the author.

Article 28

Everyone is entitled to a social and international order in which the rights and freedoms set forth in this Declaration can be fully realized.

Article 29

(1) Everyone has duties to the community in which alone the free and full development of his personality is possible.

(2) In the exercise of his rights and freedoms, everyone shall be subject only to such limitations as are determined by law solely for the purpose of securing due recognition and respect for the rights and freedoms of others and of meeting the just requirements of morality, public order and the general welfare in a democratic society.

(3) These rights and freedoms may in no case be exercised contrary to the purposes and principles of the United Nations.

Article 30

Nothing in this Declaration may be interpreted as implying for any State, group or person any right to engage in any activity or to perform any act aimed at the destruction of any of the rights and freedoms set forth herein.

SOURCE: © The Office of the United Nations High Commissioner for Human Rights. www .unhchr.ch/udhr/ index.htm.

Appendix 2.2 Global Antidiscrimination and Equal Rights Legislation Checklist of Protections Offered by Select Number of Countries

UNIVERSAL DECLARATION OF HUMAN RIGHTS (10 DECEMBER 1948)

	Race/ Ethnic Origin/ Country of Origin	Religion/ Religious Beliefs	Gender/ Sex	Equal Remuneration (pay)	Sexual Harassment	Physical Disability	Mental Disability	Age	Sexual Orientation[a]	Other	Total Number of Protections Offered per Country
AUSTRALIA	✓	✓	✓	✓	✓	✓	✓	✓	✓	A,B,C, D,F	14
AUSTRIA	✓	✓	✓	✓	✓	✓	✓	✓	✓	B,C,J,	12
BELARUS – RUSSIAN FEDERATION										J,G,L	3
BELIZE	✓				✓	✓	✓				4
CANADA	✓	✓	✓	✓	✓	✓	✓	✓	✓	B,E,G, H,I,J	15
CHINA			✓			✓	✓			A,B, C,J	7
HONG KONG	✓		✓	✓	✓	✓	✓			B,C, G,J,	10
CONGO				✓						K	2
CYPRUS	✓	✓	✓	✓				✓	✓	E,J, L,N	10
CZECH REPUBLIC	✓	✓	✓	✓						C,G, J,N	8

(Continued)

(Continued)

	Race/Ethnic Origin/Country of Origin	Religion/Religious Beliefs	Gender/Sex	Equal Remuneration (pay)	Sexual Harassment	Physical Disability	Mental Disability	Age	Sexual Orientation[a]	Other	Total Number of Protections Offered per Country
DENMARK	✓	✓	✓	✓	✓	✓	✓	✓	✓	C,F,J,L,M	14
EGYPT	✓	✓	✓						✓	L	5
FIJI	✓	✓	✓		✓				✓	A	6
FINLAND	✓	✓	✓	✓	✓	✓	✓	✓	✓	D,G,J, L,M,N	15
GERMANY	✓	✓	✓			✓	✓	✓	✓	C,J,L	10
GUYANA	✓	✓	✓	✓	✓	✓	✓	✓		B,C,F,J,	12
HUNGARY	✓	✓	✓			✓		✓		D,F,J,	8
ICELAND			✓	✓	✓	✓	✓		✓	C,J	8
INDIA			✓	✓						G	3
INDONESIA	✓			✓						A,K	4
IRAQ				✓							1
IRELAND	✓	✓	✓	✓	✓	✓	✓	✓	✓	B,J	11
ISRAEL	✓	✓	✓	✓	✓	✓	✓	✓	✓	B,C,J	11
JAMAICA			✓	✓						A	3
JAPAN		✓	✓		✓	✓	✓	✓		C,G,J	9

Country	Race/ Ethnic Origin/ Country of Origin	Religion/ Religious Beliefs	Gender/ Sex	Equal Remuneration (pay)	Sexual Harassment	Physical Disability	Mental Disability	Age	Sexual Orientation[a]	Other	Total Number of Protections Offered per Country
KOREA			✓	✓	✓	✓	✓			D,J	7
LITHUANIA	✓	✓	✓	✓	✓	✓	✓	✓	✓		9
MALAWI	✓	✓	✓		✓	✓		✓	✓	J	8
MALTA	✓	✓	✓	✓		✓				B,E,J,N	9
NAMIBIA	✓		✓		✓	✓				B,D,G	7
NETHERLANDS	✓	✓	✓	✓	✓	✓	✓	✓	✓	B,C, D,E,J	14
NEW ZEALAND	✓		✓	✓	✓			✓	✓	A,J,K,L	10
NIGERIA	✓	✓								K	3
NORWAY	✓		✓	✓	✓	✓	✓		✓	C,J	9
PHILIPPINES			✓		✓	✓	✓			A	5
POLAND			✓		✓	✓	✓			J	5
REPUBLIC OF SOUTH AFRICA	✓	✓	✓		✓	✓	✓	✓	✓	A,B,C, D,E,J	14
RUSSIAN FEDERATION	✓	✓				✓	✓			A,C,J,K	8

(Continued)

(Continued)

	Race/ Ethnic Origin/ Country of Origin	Religion/ Religious Beliefs	Gender/ Sex	Equal Remuneration (pay)	Sexual Harassment	Physical Disability	Mental Disability	Age	Sexual Orientation[a]	Other	Total Number of Protections Offered per Country
SAINT LUCIA			✓	✓							2
SAINT VINCENT AND GRENADINES	✓		✓	✓		✓	✓				5
SAUDI ARABIA	✓			✓							2
SWEDEN	✓	✓	✓	✓	✓	✓	✓		✓	C,J	10
THAILAND			✓		✓	✓	✓				4
TRINIDAD AND TOBAGO	✓	✓	✓			✓				B	5
TUNISIA	✓		✓		✓						3
UKRAINE	✓	✓	✓			✓				A,J	6
UNITED KINGDOM	✓	✓	✓	✓	✓	✓	✓	✓	✓	B,C,J	12

	Race/ Ethnic Origin/ Country of Origin	Religion/ Religious Beliefs	Gender/ Sex	Equal Remuneration (pay)	Sexual Harassment	Physical Disability	Mental Disability	Age	Sexual Orientation[a]	Other	Total Number of Protections Offered per Country
FALKLAND ISLANDS (MALVINAS) (U.K.)			✓								1
ANGUILLA (U.K.)	✓		✓								2
GIBRALTAR (U.K.)			✓	✓							2
ST. HELENA (U.K.)			✓								1
BERMUDA (U.K.)											0
NORTHERN IRELAND (U.K.)	✓	✓	✓							F	4
UNITED STATES OF AMERICA	✓	✓	✓	✓	✓	✓	✓	✓	✓[b]	C,D	11
VANUATU			✓								1

(Continued)

(Continued)

	Race/ Ethnic Origin/ Country of Origin	Religion/ Religious Beliefs	Gender/ Sex	Equal Remuneration (pay)	Sexual Harassment	Physical Disability	Mental Disability	Age	Sexual Orientation[a]	Other	Total Number of Protections Offered per Country
ZAMBIA	✓	✓	✓							B,F	5
ZIMBABWE	✓	✓	✓		✓	✓				A,F	6
TOTALS	39 (68%)	29 (51%)	48 (84%)	30 (53%)	29 (51%)	34 (60%)	26 (46%)	19 (33%)	20 (35%)		

(yes) protection offered

Other Categories Defined:

A = HIV status
B = marital status
C = pregnancy
D = affirmative action legislation
E = aboriginal
F = political affiliation
G = visible minorities
H = ancestry
I = source of income
J = family status
K = nondiscrimination—not elsewhere specified
L = general equal rights statement—not elsewhere specified
M = health status
N = language

NOTES:

a. The specific legislation offering protections based on sexual orientation is from the ILO's database NATLEX and the IGLHRC.

b. Twenty states and the District of Columbia offer such protections. The states include California, Colorado, Connecticut, Hawaii, Illinois, Iowa, Maine, Maryland, Massachusetts, Minnesota, Nevada, New Hampshire, New Jersey, New Mexico, New York, Oregon, Rhode Island, Vermont, Washington DC, and Wisconsin.

SOURCES:

NATLEX, International Labour Organization (n.d.).

Bureau of Democracy, Human Right and Labor (2009), retrieved Aug 10, 2009, from http://www.state.gov/g/drl/rls/hrrpt/2007/index.htm.

Notes

1. The International Bill of Human Rights can be obtained directly from the UN and can also be accessed from the UN's official Web site (www.un.org/Overview/rights.html). This section is based, in part, on UN Fact Sheet No. 2 (Rev 1): The International Bill of Human Rights. It can also be found on the World Wide Web at the UN's official Web site (http://unhchr.ch/html).

2. Although the UN Universal Declaration of Human Rights was initially drafted as a "secondary authority" (a legal term indicating that it is an ideal notion rather than enforceable law), it has become customary international law as a result of its long existence and acquiescence by a majority of countries. A case in point is a lawsuit brought in a U.S. court by a Mexican family against a Mexican official for acts of torture committed in Mexico against their son. The judge accepted their claims based on the UN Declaration of Human Rights. See *Filartiga v. Pena-Irala,* 630F.2d 876 (U.S. Court of Appeals, Second Circuit, 1980).

3. Please refer to the previous note.

4. These examples are taken from the committee's protocols. They can also be found on the official Web site of the Office of United Nations High Commissioner for Human Rights (http://www.unhchr.ch/tbs/doc.nsf/).

5. See the complete protocol of the UN Committee on the Elimination of Racial Discrimination, March 2002 (an electronic copy available on the World Wide Web at www.unhchr.ch/tbs/doc.nsf/).

6. For the complete study, conducted in several EU countries, see Zegers de Beijl (Ed.) (1999).

7. Smeesters, Arrijn, Feld, & Nayer (2000), p. 46.

8. For a discussion of implications of antidiscrimination laws to insurance claims, see Maatman (2000), pp. 34–35.

9. The United Nation's International Labour Organization has created a database, called NATLEX, that references over 55,000 national laws related to employment, social security, and related human rights. NATLEX is available to researchers and to the public (in English, French, or Spanish) through their publications and through their Web site (www.ilo.org/dyn/natlex/natlex_browse.home).

10. Over 20% of the countries reviewed had to have legislation in the appropriate category to be considered a most popular form of antidiscrimination legislation.

11. The United States is the only country that allows punitive damages awards. Punitive damages entail a sum of money designed to punish the defendants and to deter others from repeating the offense. Typically, punitive damages against large corporations range in millions of dollars.

12. Based on personal interview, July 2002. Per the interviewee's request, her name is kept confidential.

13. In the United States, the laws allow for "fair discrimination" in gender-related employment, when the discrimination is based on gender differences in physical abilities (e.g., *Dothard v. Rawlinson,* 433 U.S. 321 [1977]).

14. It is interesting to note that while the suit was pending, the Alabama Board of Corrections adopted a regulation that created male-only and female-only positions in the prison system. The effect was to exclude women from 75% of the jobs in the system. The plaintiff amended her suit to include a claim that the regulation violated federal

law. The three-judge panel held that both the statute and regulation violated Title VII. The court held that the applicant had shown the statute had a discriminatory effect, and the director had failed to show the challenged requirements were job-related. The court held, however, that the regulation fell within the narrow exception for bona fide occupational qualifications because most of the jobs in Alabama's atypical, unclassified system were just too dangerous for women. The Supreme Court affirmed the district court's decision with respect to the statute setting minimum height and weight requirements but reversed the district court's decision with respect to the regulation, which created male- and female-only positions.

15. The *Griggs v. Duke Power Company,* 1971 (which preceded the *Dothard v. Rawlinson,* 1977), determined that the Duke Power Company's intradepartmental transfer policy requiring a high school education and the achievement of minimum scores on two separate aptitude tests violated Title VII of the 1964 Civil Rights Act. Specifically, the U.S. Supreme Court concluded that neither the high school graduation requirement nor the two aptitude tests were directed or intended to measure an employee's ability to learn or perform a particular job or category of jobs within the company. The Court concluded that the subtle, illegal purpose of these requirements was to safeguard Duke's long-standing policy of giving job preferences to its White employees and was discriminatory against its African American employees. In fact, the Court determined that not only overt discrimination is illegal, but also practices that are fair in form but discriminatory in practice are against the law. This theory of the law, the "disparate-impact" theory, was chipped away in the *Dothard v. Rawlinson,* 1977, decision and almost eliminated in *Wards Cove v. Antonio,* 1989. The latter decision was so extreme that it motivated Congress to amend Title VII of the Civil Rights Act of 1964. In essence, the theory of discriminatory impact is now the law of the land.

16. The International Gay and Lesbian Human Rights Commission (IGLHRC) is a nonprofit, nongovernmental organization (NGO) based in the United States. IGLHRC's commitment is to individual and community human rights as well as eliminating discrimination or abuse based on sexual orientation, gender identity, or HIV status. For more information on IGLHRC, visit their Web site (www.iglhrc.org/).

17. *Mississippi University for Women v. Hogan,* 458 U.S. 718 (1982).

18. Interestingly, this seems to be based on a logic that is similar to the punitive damages awards granted in the United States (see note 11).

19. Established in 1992, CAW is a grassroots organization with 28 chapters in 13 Asian countries working actively to raise awareness of women workers rights in Asian countries. A more detailed description of the survey was published in the Asian Women Workers Newsletter. An electronic copy is available on the World Wide Web at http://cawinfo.net/.

20. The U.S. Congress, in some cases, has specifically indicated that particular legislation is extraterritorial. That is, Congress has the authority to enforce its laws beyond the territorial boundaries of the United States. Cf. *Foley Bros., Inc. v. Filardo,* 336 U.S. 281, 284–285 (1949); *Benz v. Compania Naviera Hidalgo, S. A.,* 353 U.S. 138, 147 (1957).

CHAPTER 3

Discrimination, Equality, and Fairness in Employment

Social Policies and Affirmative/Positive Action Programs

> *The inequality of rights has no other source than the law of the strongest. Was there ever any domination that did not appear natural to those who professed it? We ought not to ordain that to be born a girl instead of a boy, any more than to be born black instead of white, shall dictate a person's position through life.*
>
> —John Stuart Mill (1806–1873), English philosopher
> and influential liberal thinker of the 19th century.

The International Bill of Human Rights, as well as the various national laws described in the previous chapter, is aimed at banning discrimination and assuring equal opportunities to people regardless of their gender, race, ethnicity, age, disability, or other characteristics that are not relevant to their job-related skills. These laws are *negative* in that they prohibit discrimination in employment. In the past several decades, a new category of protections has emerged—social policies that are *positive* in that they aim to change the rules and provide advantages to groups that have traditionally been discriminated against. These social policies go beyond assuring equal rights to correct past wrongs. They are grouped under titles such as "positive action" in Europe (e.g., Caruso, 2003; Kennedy-Dubourdieu, 2007) or "affirmative action" in the United States (e.g., Libertella, Sora, & Natale, 2007). Other countries that have later adopted similar policies have used one or the other of these terms (see, for example, White, 2001; Sunstein, 1999; Sowell, 2004). This chapter begins with a discussion of different types of discrimination to provide the context for these policies and then turns to the specific policies in various countries whose aim is to actively promote equality and fairness in employment. It concludes with the public and political debate over these policies and the challenges they pose for business practices.

Discrimination and Equality in Employment

Originally morally neutral in its meaning, the word *discrimination* has acquired a negative value, particularly in the context of employment. *Webster's New World Dictionary* (2003), for example, reflects this duality by providing both meanings. The first definition is morally neutral, and the second is morally negative: "Discrimination: (1) to distinguish; (2) to make distinction in treatment; show partiality or prejudice" (*Webster's New World Dictionary,* 2003). The United Nations International Labour Organization (ILO) defines discrimination as "any distinction, exclusion or preference made on the basis of race, colour, sex, religion, political opinion, national extraction or social origin, which has the effect of nullifying or impairing equality of opportunity or treatment in employment or occupation" (United Nations Discrimination [Employment and Occupation] Convention, 1958). For the purpose of the current discussion on discrimination in employment we define the following:

> Discrimination in employment occurs when (a) individuals, institutions, or governments treat people differently because of personal characteristics like race, gender, or sexual orientation rather than their ability to perform their jobs and (b) these actions have a negative impact on access to jobs, promotions, or compensation.

There are several classifications of discriminatory acts that can help us in understanding the way discrimination is manifested in the workplace (Velasquez, 2006). First, discrimination can be overt or covert. *Overt* discrimination occurs as a result of an explicit policy or law that generates unequal treatment; *covert* discrimination is the result of an implicit side effect of another policy or decision. Second, discrimination can be individual or institutional. It is *individual* when a single manager or a coworker in conjunction with his or her individual prejudice performs the action or actions; it is *institutional* when it is performed as part of the organization's common practices or policies. Finally, discrimination can be characterized by the motivation behind it and can be either *intentional* or *unintentional.*[1] The following examples may help demonstrate these distinctions.

The first example comes from the July 1943 issue of *Mass Transportation* (see Box 3.1). Male supervisors of women in the workforce wrote these "Eleven Tips on Getting More Efficiency Out of Women Employees" during World War II. It is clearly prejudicial: "Numerous properties say that women make excellent workers when they have their jobs cut out for them, but that they lack initiative in finding work themselves," and derogatory, "You have to make some allowances for feminine psychology. A girl has more confidence and is more efficient if she can keep her hair tidied, apply fresh lipstick and wash her hands several times a day." Though it seems laughable today, the "advice" given to managers in this piece was considered serious and meant to be helpful.

The discrimination in this example is overt—clearly the authors were not aware there was anything wrong with their attitude and didn't make any attempt to hide their prejudice; it is institutionalized—this is not an act of a single manager but instructions given to all managers; and it is intentional— the intent of the authors was to treat women differently because women were perceived to possess inferior characteristics.

BOX 3.1
Discrimination Categorization:
Management Advice in 1943

The following is an excerpt from the July 1943 issue of *Mass Transportation*. This was written for male supervisors of women in the workforce during World War II ("Eleven Tips," 1943).

Eleven Tips on Getting More Efficiency Out of Women Employees:
There's no longer any question whether transit companies should hire women for jobs formerly held by men. The draft and manpower shortage has settled that point. The important things now are to select the most efficient women available and how to use them to the best advantage.

Here are eleven helpful tips on the subject from Western Properties:

1. Pick young married women. They usually have more of a sense of responsibility than their unmarried sisters, they're less likely to be flirtatious, they need the work or they wouldn't be doing it, they still have the pep and interest to work hard and to deal with the public efficiently.

(Continued)

(Continued)

2. When you have to use older women, try to get ones who have worked outside the home at some time in their lives. Older women who have never contacted the public have a hard time adapting themselves and are inclined to be cantankerous and fussy. It's always well to impress upon older women the importance of friendliness and courtesy.

3. General experience indicates that "husky" girls—those who are just a little on the heavy side—are more even-tempered and efficient than their underweight sisters.

4. Retain a physician to give each woman you hire a special physical examination—one covering female conditions. This step not only protects the property against the possibilities of lawsuit, but reveals whether the employee-to-be has any female weaknesses which would make her mentally or physically unfit for the job.

5. Stress at the outset the importance of time—the fact that a minute or two lost here and there makes serious inroads on schedules. Until this point is gotten across, service is likely to be slowed up.

6. Give the female employee a definite day-long schedule of duties so that they'll keep busy without bothering the management for instructions every few minutes. Numerous properties say that women make excellent workers when they have their jobs cut out for them, but that they lack initiative in finding work themselves.

7. Whenever possible, let the inside employee change from one job to another at some time during the day. Women are inclined to be less nervous and happier with change.

8. Give every girl an adequate number of rest periods during the day. You have to make some allowances for feminine psychology. A girl has more confidence and is more efficient if she can keep her hair tidied, apply fresh lipstick and wash her hands several times a day.

9. Be tactful when issuing instructions or in making criticisms. Women are often sensitive; they can't shrug off harsh words the way men do. Never ridicule woman—it breaks her spirit and cuts off her efficiency.

10. Be reasonably considerate about using strong language around women. Even though a girl's husband or father may swear vociferously, she'll grow to dislike a place of business where she hears too much of this.

11. Get enough size variety in operator's uniforms so that each girl can have a proper fit. This point can't be stressed too much in keeping women happy.

The second example (see Box 3.2) is more recent and comes from the experiences of African American employees in the U.S.-based Xerox Company (Comer, 2002).

> ## BOX 3.2
> ## Discrimination Categorization: Black Employees
> ## File a Discrimination Lawsuit Against Xerox
>
> The Equal Employment Opportunity Commission (EEOC) found that Black employees suffered from discrimination and a racially hostile environment at Xerox Corporation's Cincinnati facilities. Racist symbols such as swastikas and black dolls with nooses around their necks were displayed in the Xerox work areas, and racial slurs were directed at Black workers.
>
> In response, Bill McKee, spokesman for the company, said, "Diversity is one of our core values. It is part of the fabric of Xerox, rooted in our commitment to treat all people with dignity and respect." The EEOC report, however, indicated that "evidence shows that blacks, as a class, were subjected to racially hostile environment," and were disciplined more frequently as a class.
>
> SOURCE: Comer (2002).

The findings about the Xerox work environment actions can be characterized as discrimination that is (a) covert—this was not a stated policy of the organization (in fact, based on the company's statement, these actions seem to go against its stated policy); (b) institutionalized—these actions were not done by a single individual, nor as an isolated incident, but were widespread enough throughout the organization to constitute an unofficial subculture; and (c) intentional—the use of the racial slurs and the posting of offensive symbols were carried out with the intention of intimidating Black people and making them uncomfortable in the work environment.

Theoretical Perspectives of Discrimination and Affirmative Action

Affirmative or positive action policies originated from the notion that discrimination against whole groups that has been persistent, institutionalized, and long term cannot be remedied simply by banning such actions. Although antidiscrimination legislation is essential, these policies emerged out of the recognition that such legislation may not be enough to create a work environment that provides equality of opportunities for all, and may actually cement past inequalities.

Affirmative or positive action policies have two goals: (a) righting past wrongs—compensating groups that have been disadvantaged in the past with better opportunities in the present; and (b) achieving social goals of increasing the representation of traditionally disadvantaged groups in more lucrative jobs as well as management and leadership positions. The rationale behind these policies is that they redress past discrimination by giving preference in hiring and promotion to members of groups that have been discriminated against in the past. Considering that for a long time these groups have had limited access to education, high-paying and prestigious jobs, networks of influence, and promotion opportunities, they may continue to be deprived of these opportunities if not given such advantages until a more balanced representation can be achieved.

There are several theoretical paths explaining discrimination in employment and the need, or lack thereof, for affirmative action policies. "Neoclassical" economists assume that, in a competitive market, the "taste" for discrimination cannot be indulged because it would be too costly for employers (Becker, 1971; Figart, 2005). Employers would lose their competitive advantage if they do not utilize the wide range of skills and talents offered by women, members of minority groups, older adults, sexual minorities, and people with disabilities. If employers continue to discriminate against these groups, their productivity will be reduced, ultimately resulting in reduced income for employers. Strictly following this logic, there is no need for any policies that encourage employers to give equal opportunities to all because it is in their own economic best interest. The problem with this logic is that it assumes that discrimination is simply a "taste," disregarding the fact that this behavior is embedded in deeply engrained prejudicial perceptions that color people's evaluation of other people's skills, abilities, and talents. In other words, if one is prejudiced, say, against older people, he or she will make a series of inaccurate and often prejudicial assumptions (they are slow, inaccurate in their work, lacking in technical skills, etc.). Operating from a mind-set that affects perception of reality, an employer is not likely to objectively determine the prospective employee's real qualifications—for example, a woman's ability to manage an engineering team—and is less likely to hire her for a management job (Arrow, 1973, 1998). Decisions that are propelled by prejudices tend also to perpetuate them: the employer may never realize the potential economic loss for his or her business enterprise by not hiring that woman (e.g., her unique talents and her ability to better understand women customers). It has been suggested, therefore, that the economic process cannot be insulated from stereotypes held by employers and affecting their judgment (Bennington & Wein, 2000). Nevertheless, neoclassical economists generally argue for deregulating the labor market and removing legal and policy restrictions to allow employers to use pure economic principles in their employment decisions.

At the other end of the theoretical spectrum is the "equal opportunities" school that considers institutional and cultural factors as the cause of discrimination (McDonald & Potton, 1997; Roemer, 2002). Groups that have traditionally been discriminated against suffer from three types of interconnected barriers that may perpetuate the discrimination against them. The first is stereotyping, which excludes them from lucrative and desirable jobs; the second is exclusion from positions of authority, which perpetuates their image of being incapable of doing certain jobs; and the third is lack of role models and mentors within their groups who are in positions of power and influence and who can assist them in obtaining and retaining desirable jobs.

Unlike the neoclassical economists who believe that distributive justice will resolve on its own due to the forces of the market economy, equal opportunities theorists believe that the forces that have originally led to discrimination will also work to preserve it. For example, in the past—and to a somewhat lesser degree today—the dominant stereotype of women was that they could not handle the pressure of top management and such positions were entirely outside their reach (the infamous "glass ceiling"). As a result, for a long time there was no evidence to disprove this stereotype, and discrimination was perpetuated. Furthermore, because many positions are obtained through networking and many promotions are attained through mentorship and role modeling, there were no women available to support and mentor other women in their quest for management jobs.

The main argument of the equal opportunities school of thought is that ending discrimination does not create equal opportunities because women, Blacks, people with disabilities, and other groups that have been discriminated against do not have the same resources available to them as members of the dominant groups. The main argument against this school of thought is that preferential hiring is another form of discriminating.

Social Policies and Affirmative/Positive Action Programs

In contrast to the passive nondiscrimination dictated by the equal employment legislation described in the previous chapter, affirmative or positive action means that employers must act directly and aggressively to remove all barriers that prevent women and members of minority groups from having equal access to education, employment, and political processes. Although these policies do not equal quotas, some affirmative action plans may include quotas if courts find purposeful systemic discrimination in specific areas (Tomei, 2003).

LEGAL ARRANGEMENTS FOR AFFIRMATIVE AND POSITIVE ACTION POLICIES

Despite the public debate about these programs and the challenges presented in several judicial systems, governments around the world continue to legislate for affirmative or positive action in employment in favor of designated groups (International Labour Office, 2007). These programs operate under different legal arrangements. A review of select countries using the ILO's NATLEX database revealed information about 17 countries that currently have affirmative action policies. (Please note that the list is illustrative, not exhaustive; see Table 3.1.)

Table 3.1	Affirmative Action Legislation Worldwide (Select Countries)

COUNTRY/LEGISLATION (TARGETED GROUPS)

AUSTRALIA—Affirmative Action (Equal Employment Opportunity for Women in the Workplace) Act (1986, No. 91)

Private employers with 100 or more employees and higher-education institutions are required to create affirmative action programs. (*women*)

CANADA—Employment Equity Act (1995)

Employers are required to identify and eliminate employment barriers against persons in designated groups. As a part of that, employers are required to institute policies that ensure that designated groups are represented in the workforce. (*not specified*)

COLOMBIA—Law of Quotas No. 581 (2000)

The law promotes the participation of women in the public sector within positions that carry decision-making power in the Colombian government. It requires that at a minimum, 30% of all public sector positions at the National Department District, and Municipal level be filled by women. (*women*)

COSTA RICA—Electoral Code Law No. 7653 (1996)

The law guarantees the representation and participation of women in politics within Costa Rica as a method to eliminate discrimination in the public and political life of women. The law requires that women be allowed to be participants in any organization that is subject to public elections and to partake in the formulation and implementation of governmental policies. Furthermore, the law requires that all political parties ensure that at least 40% of all political positions subject to the popular vote be filled by women. (*women*).

ETHIOPIA—The Constitution of the Federal Democratic Republic of Ethiopia (1994)

Employers are required to promote the rights of women through remedial and affirmative measures that promote their well-being, including maternity leave with full pay. (*women*)

COUNTRY/LEGISLATION (TARGETED GROUPS)

FINLAND—Act respecting equality between women and men (1986)

Public authorities are required to actively promote gender equality by removing obstacles through training and education, as well as by placing men and women in work positions and creating equality in working conditions. (*gender*)

FRANCE—Law in Favour of Disabled Workers 1987 (Act 87- 517) (1987)

Public and private establishments or enterprises with 20 or more employees are obliged to employ workers with disabilities at a level of 6.0% of the total number of staff employed. (*persons with disabilities*)

HUNGARY—Provisions respecting gender participation in governmental councils, administrations, delegations, etc.—implementation and reporting methods (No. 110 of 1996)

Requires a minimum of 40% representation of men and women in all public committees that are made up of at least four members. In committees with two or three members both genders must be represented. (*gender*)

INDIA—The Persons With Disabilities (Equal Opportunities, Protection of Rights and Full Participation) Act (1995)

Requires that every appropriate government appoint a percentage of vacancies of not less than 3% for persons or class of persons with disability. (*persons with disabilities*)

IRELAND—Northern Ireland's Fair Employment Act (1989)

Requires that employers have workforce representation of the two religious communities, Protestants and Roman Catholics, equal to their proportions in the population at large through the establishment of Fair Employment Commission (FEC). (*religion*)

KENYA—The Employment Act (2007)

Allows employers to make use of affirmative action measure in order to eliminate discrimination and promote equality in the workplace. (*not specified*)

NAMIBIA—Affirmative Action (Employment) Act (1998)

Requires that employers create affirmative action programs to promote employment and give preferential treatment (providing employment and removing employment barriers) to individuals in designated groups. Establishes an Employment Equity Commission. (*women, disabled persons, and ethnic groups*)

(*Continued*)

Table 3.1 (Continued)

COUNTRY/LEGISLATION (TARGETED GROUPS)

NORWAY—Public Limited Companies Act 2003

Requires the boards of public limited companies to have each sex make up at least 40% of the representatives on the board. (*gender*)

SOUTH AFRICA—Employment Equity Act (1998) (Chapter III)

Employers (> 50 employees), employers with more than a specified annual turnover, and the state are required to take affirmative action measures for designated groups as well as develop an employment equity plan. Establishes a Commission for Employment Equity. (*Black people, women, and disabled persons*)

SWEDEN—Equal Opportunities Act (1991)

Employers are mandated to promote equal representation of both sexes in the workplace. This is to be accomplished through training and recruitment policies and by giving preference to applicants of the underrepresented sex. Employers with more than 10 employees are required to create an annual plan of action outlining positive measures to promote equal opportunity. (*gender*)

UNITED STATES—Executive Order 11246 (1965) and Affirmative Action Programs Rule (41 CFR Part 60) (1970)

Employers who conduct business with the federal government are required to develop affirmative action plans.

VIETNAM—Circular providing guidelines for implementation of Decree 72-CP of the government with respect to recruitment of labour (No. 16-LDTBXH)

Employers are required to give consideration to designated groups in the recruitment process as well as to give group members priority in employment (when more than one qualified applicant): war veterans, sick war veterans, or members of their families. (*disabled persons, women, and persons who have been unemployed for more than 1 year*)

Specifically, countries such as South Africa, Namibia, India, the United States, and the European Union all have differing ways of operating and implementing affirmative action programs:

- South Africa and Namibia have both adopted legislation requiring employment equity through means that include affirmative action—the Employment Equity Act Bi, 55 of 1998 in South Africa and the Affirmative Action (Employment) Act No. 29 of 1998 in Namibia.[2]

- In India, the 1998 Employment Equity Act specifies a commitment to implement affirmative action measures in order to ensure equitable representation by "designated groups" in all occupational categories and levels of the public workforce.

- The European Community passed the Equal Treatment Directive in 1976[3] but it was limited to equal pay and equal treatment and applied only to gender and not to race or any other groups. In 1984, a Council positive action recommendation was issued that suggested parallel action to be taken by governments to include industry and other bodies concerned in order to counteract prejudicial effects on employment.[4] Following the 1984 Council recommendation, several European Community members initiated positive action legislation and policies (specific examples are included in the next section). Article 13 of the Amsterdam Treaty declared the principle of equal treatment for the EU's increasingly multiethnic community and the need to fight against racism and xenophobia. Adopted in June 2000, the European Council Directive (2000/43/EC)[5] "implementing the principle of equal treatment between persons irrespective of racial or ethnic origin" placed far-reaching and specific demands on member states. It included the requirement to inform the Commission of measures taken by member states to implement the directive. It also stressed the need to promote "conditions for a socially inclusive labour market" in order to achieve the objectives of the EC Treaty.

- The United States has a relatively long experience with affirmative action programs. The term "affirmative action" first appeared in President John Kennedy's Executive Order 10925 of 1961. It reappeared 4 years later in 1965 when President Lyndon B. Johnson signed Executive Order 11246 requiring "employers doing business with the federal government to develop affirmative action plans to assure equal employment opportunities in their employment practices."

PRINCIPLES OF AFFIRMATIVE ACTION AND POSITIVE ACTION PROGRAMS

Programs to actively encourage a more representative workforce, as well as the incentives governments give to complying with such requirements, vary greatly from one country to the next. There are, however, several principles that are common to all such programs (Yang, D'Souza, Bapat, & Colarelli, 2006; Velasquez, 2006). Typically, affirmative/positive action programs:

- Are intervention measures
- Cut across, and attempt to influence, the operation of free-market mechanisms
- Aim to actively reverse past discrimination against specific groups
- Are intended as temporary actions, which will be withdrawn once the situation is rectified

The following discussion covers the three elements of these essential programs: (a) their specific goals and target population, (b) policies and activities covered by those programs, and (c) enforcement, incentives, and sanctions.

Specific goals and target population. In general, the goals of these programs are to provide better opportunities to population groups that have been discriminated against in the past and to increase their representation in public service jobs and in management and leadership positions. In the United States, for example, the goal of affirmative action programs is to compensate for past discrimination and to correct current discrimination by ensuring equal employment to members of minority groups and women. Similarly, the goal of positive action programs in Europe is to compensate population groups that have been discriminated against in the past by providing them with a competitive advantage at present (Caruso, 2003).

The South African affirmative action measures were implemented in order to ensure equitable representation by "designated groups" in all occupational categories and levels of the workforce. "Designated groups" are defined as Black people (Africans, Coloureds, and Indians), women, and people with disabilities (Employment Equity Act, No. 5 of 1998). It is important to note that although preferential treatment is meant only for "suitably qualified people," the definition of such suitability is very broad and may be a product of formal qualifications, prior learning, relevant experience, or "capacity to acquire, within reasonable time, the ability to do the job."

India, the largest democracy, has long been struggling with hierarchical social structures in the form of its traditional caste system (Deshpande, 2007; Sowell, 2004). The 1998 Employment Equity Act specifies a commitment to implement affirmative action measures in order to ensure equitable representation by "designated groups" in all occupational categories and levels of the workforce. In an effort to make its society more equitable, India employs "reservations"—a system of quotas in the public service system, set aside for minorities. The target populations for preferential treatment include three groups: the Scheduled Castes (about 16% of the population), the Scheduled Tribes (about 8% of the population), and the Socially and Educationally Backward Classes (also called "Other Backward Classes" and constituting about 52% of the population).

When examining affirmative or positive action policies from an international perspective, it is clear that each country's specific historical and cultural background dictates the nature of its policies. Two interesting examples illustrate this issue: The first example comes from India and South Africa. What distinguishes the affirmative action programs in both India and South Africa from most other national programs is that the target populations are not minorities but practically constitute a majority of the population. The second example comes from Norway. Although in most countries women are the focus of any gender-related affirmative action, in July 1998, Norway enacted Ordinance (No. 622 of 1998) Respecting Special Treatment of Men. This legislation creates special provisions for men in certain occupations, like childcare and education, in which they are not well represented (Hodges-Aeberhard, 1999).

Policies and programs. Affirmative or positive action policies and programs are designed to increase the number of qualified applicants from designated groups (depending on each country's definition of these groups) in the workforce. They usually employ two main strategies:

The first strategy involves *placing requirements on the composition of the public workforce.* This is done through specifying recruitment and promotion strategies for actual increase in representation of the designated groups (popularly referred to as quotas). India's "reservations" policy, which applies to public positions only, not to private employers, is a prime example of this approach. Under India's reservations policy, the federal government has set aside a quota of federal and state government positions to improve the representation of designated groups that were discriminated against in the past (Boston & Nair-Reichert, 2003; Sunstein, 1999). The quotas are designed to reflect these groups' representation in the population (indicated earlier) and include 15% for the Scheduled Castes and 7.5% for the Scheduled Tribes. No specific quota was set aside for the Other Backward Classes, though a 1963 Supreme Court ruling indicated that all reservations together should not exceed 50% of the positions. The responsibility for implementing affirmative action in India belongs to "designated employers," a term that includes all municipalities and most government organizations and larger organizations (defined either by the financial scope of their business or as having more than 50 employees). Each employer is required to conduct analyses of the employment barriers standing in the way of inclusion and promotion of the designated groups, prepare an employment equity plan, and report annually to the director general of the Department of Labour on the progress made in the implementation of such a plan. The employment equity plan has to state the objectives to be achieved each year, the affirmative action measures with timetables and strategies to be implemented to accomplish them, as well as procedures to accomplish the plan.

The second strategy involves *encouraging private businesses to actively recruit and promote* employees from the designated groups. Governments achieve this goal by providing businesses with incentives, like better access to government contracts. In the United States, for example, employers who initiate plans to ensure equal employment by actively recruiting minorities and women are given preferential access to government contracts. Similar public policies in some European countries, such as the United Kingdom's positive action, originate from the same ideology—compensating population groups that have been discriminated against in the past by providing them with a competitive advantage at present (other things being equal). In Belgium, for example, following the EC recommendation, a royal decree was passed that made provisions for the signing of an accord between the government and individual employers. The positive action programs were piloted with RTT—the national television company—and since then there have been more than 50 conventions signed with private sector employers. In each case, assistance has been given from a team of state-funded experts operating to a common set of positive action guidelines. In Italy, trade unions have introduced positive action into collective bargaining, and today many employment contracts contain positive action clauses (Chater & Chater, 1992).

An interesting case of positive action through legislation aimed at reducing religious discrimination is that of Northern Ireland's Fair Employment Act of 1989 (see Box 3.3). The goal of that legislation was to make the workforce representation of the two religious communities, Protestants and Roman Catholics, equal to their proportions in the population at large. This was attempted by granting far-reaching enforcement powers to the Fair Employment Commission (FEC). Despite this forward-thinking legislation, it is clear that inequalities in employment are rooted in the complexities of the histories, identities, and cultures of the two communities and are not easily eradicated via legislation (Rea & Eastwood, 1992).

BOX 3.3
Equal Employment Legislation and Religious Discrimination: The Case of Northern Ireland

Roman Catholics in Northern Ireland have suffered severe disadvantages in the labor market for a long time. Until 1989, Section 5 of the Government of Ireland Act 1920 was the only legal protection against religious discrimination for the citizens of Northern Ireland. It stated that the Northern Ireland Parliament was prohibited from making any law that would "give preference, privilege or advantage or impose any disability or disadvantage on account of religious belief or ecclesiastical status." Following Northern Ireland's civil rights movement of the 1960s and the surge in civil disorder, the governor of Northern Ireland appointed a commission headed by Lord Cameron to investigate the allegations of religious and political discrimination. The commission's 1969 report confirmed that injustices in the areas of housing and public employment led to the surge of civil unrest. Several declarations followed with the eventual result of the 1976 Fair Employment (North Ireland) Act that outlawed job discrimination on grounds of religion and political opinion in both public and private employment. A decade later, however, it became clear to the government that the 1976 Act was having a minimal impact on Catholic disadvantages in employment.

Interestingly, strong pressure to change this situation came from a group of Irish American lobbyists who urged U.S companies with investments in Northern Ireland to increase the numbers of Roman Catholics in their workforces. Articulating their position, the group drew the "MacBride Principles," named after one of the original signatories and modeled after the Sullivan Principles that were developed earlier to guide companies operating in South Africa.

These actions, in addition to reports on the status of employment discrimination, convinced the government of the need to introduce new legislation. The eventual outcome was the Fair Employment (Northern Ireland) Act 1989. The aim of the new legislation was to assure that the proportions of the two religious communities in employment would be equal to their proportions in the population at large.

The 1989 law provides for close auditing of employers' practices in achieving employment equality. It arms the Fair Employment Commission (FEC) with additional powers and resources. Specifically, it requires all employers of more than 10 people to monitor the religious composition of their workforce and to provide an annual report to the commission. Employers are also required to provide 3-year reviews of their recruitment, training, and promotion practices and policies. The penalties include not only fines for discrimination and failure to register and monitor but also exclusion from competing for government contracts and denial of any government grants.

The strong fair employment legislation in Ireland over the past few decades has played its part and there has been a substantial improvement in the employment representation, most markedly in the public sector but not confined to it. Catholics are now well represented in managerial, professional, and senior administrative posts. There are some areas of underrepresentation such as local government and security but the overall picture is a positive one. Catholics are still more likely than Protestants to be unemployed. There are emerging areas of Protestant underrepresentation in the public sector, most notably in health and education. This is evident at many levels including professional and managerial.

There has been a considerable increase in the numbers of people who work in integrated workplaces. At a time when public housing, for example, is virtually completely segregated, this represents another positive trend in the assessment of the implementation of the legislation. Evidence now suggests that unlike a generation ago when a person's religious affiliation determined

(Continued)

(Continued)

social mobility, now it is mainly education that is the determinant factor. Evidence also suggests that affirmative action agreements between the Equality Commission and employers have helped redress both Catholic and Protestant underrepresentation as a vital part of the process of change.

Despite this far-reaching legislation, it is clear that the animosity between the religious still exists and that, despite the remarkable progress, segregation by religion in employment situations remains a challenge in Northern Ireland.

SOURCES: Rea & Eastwood (1992); Osborne (2005).

Enforcement—incentives and sanctions. Some countries institute an official body that is responsible for evaluating compliance and enforcing the policies through sanctions or incentives. Sanctions include primarily monetary fines for organizations that do not comply with the policy. In South Africa, for example, the director general of the Department of Labour, who receives the employers' progress reports, has the powers to make compliance demands on the designated employers. A Commission for Employment Equity with a chair and eight members is appointed by the minister of labour to render advice on these matters. Penalties can range from 500,000 to 900,000 rand (roughly US$60,960–US$109,728).[6]

As a further example, Australia's Affirmative Action (Equal Opportunity for Women in the Workplace) Act, of 1999, requires that organizations with more than 100 employees have an affirmative action program in place. Even though the legislation was enacted in 1986, some employers did not respond to the legislation until the 1990s. Additionally, many organizations are not covered within the Act (less than 44% of those in the private sector are covered), and many women are excluded if they work part-time, have temporary jobs, or are in the category of low-paid employees. As a part of Australia's Affirmative Action Act, organizations are required to evaluate their employment statistics and human resources practices and to consult with women employee groups and with trade unions to develop an individualized affirmative action program. Organizations are also required to submit their reports and subsequent plans to the Affirmative Action Agency. Despite these aspects of the Act, the penalties for not complying with the requirement are limited and rarely enforced (Strachan & Jamieson, 1999; Konrad & Hartmann, 2001).

The Public Debate Over Affirmative and Positive Action Policies

The public debate over positive/affirmative action policies has focused on social justice and economic principles. Proponents of these policies claim three main arguments: the first is compensatory justice—past injustices need to be undone and compensation should be given to those who were disadvantaged as a result of discriminatory traditions or intentional policies; the second is distributive justice—the social goods and wealth of a country should be distributed equally; and the third is social utility—everyone in a society has something important to contribute, and the common good is best served by everyone's participation in the economic and social system. Opponents of these policies present arguments that can also be classified into three groups: first, reverse discrimination is another form of unfair practices that perpetuate discrimination, although it is now practiced on a different group; second, preferential policies go against the principles of individualism and interfere with the forces of a free-market economy; and, third, preferential practices may result in poor services and products because incompetent or unsuitable people may be appointed to jobs.[7] Some claim that affirmative action policies ultimately hurt the minorities they were designed to assist in the first place. Opponents of affirmative action posit that preferential treatment of minority groups engenders resentment among other groups, and perpetuates stereotypes about the groups that undermine the minority group as a whole (Cohen & Sterba, 2003). Further, even among proponents of strong social policies, there is uneasiness with policies that may amount to "quotas" and outright reverse discrimination because they undermine the real achievements of members of underrepresented groups and perpetuate the notion that members of these groups intrinsically lack the characteristics for success in employment and will always need special assistance.[8] The controversy around affirmative and positive action is reflected in the numerous challenges it faced in courtrooms throughout the world. It is interesting to note that despite the diversity of countries and jurisdictions, courts have generally supported the concept as an acceptable tool in the struggle to eliminate discrimination in employment.[9]

Affirmative or positive action programs have been challenged in the courts, mostly on grounds that they contradict a specific country's equal rights assurances under its constitution or legislation. South Africa's constitution presents a very interesting way of solving this dilemma. In banning unfair discrimination (see a comment earlier in the chapter), South Africa's constitution implies that fair discrimination is permissible. Chapter 10 of the constitution states that public administration must be broadly representative of the South African people. It further notes that although objectivity and fairness must be applied, an important goal is redressing the imbalances of the past and achieving broad representation. The South African constitution, unlike that of the United States, for example, sanctions affirmative action.[10]

Affirmative action policies were challenged in the U.S. courts repeatedly over the years when the courts were asked to reconcile these preferential policies with the equality principle stated in the Fifth and Fourteenth Amendments to the U.S. Constitution. Early Supreme Court decisions affirm these policies, but from the 1980s on, as the Supreme Court's composition became more conservative, the Court's decisions were less and less supportive. For example, in 1989 the United States Supreme Court ruled in favor of J. A. Croson Company, a nonminority-owned construction company that sued the city of Richmond claiming that its policy of setting aside at least 30% of the dollar amount of contracts to minority business enterprises was discriminatory. The Court found that because the city had failed to demonstrate the need for remedial action in the awarding of its public construction contracts, its treatment of its citizens on a racial basis violated the Constitution's equal protection clause (*Richmond v. J. A. Croson Co.,* 1989). Questions about the constitutionality of race-based set-aside policies emerged again in the *Adarand Constructors v. Pena* case, which came before the U.S. Supreme Court in 1995. The United States Department of Transportation awarded a highway construction contract in the state of Colorado to the Mountain Gravel and Construction Company. The contractor then sought bids for subcontracting. Although the lowest bid was posted by Adarand constructors, the contract was given to Gonzales Construction because of the latter company's composition of a large proportion of workers considered from disadvantaged backgrounds. The Supreme Court found that awarding the contract to Gonzales Construction based purely on the racial composition of the company was in violation of the Fifth Amendment's Due Process Clause (*Adarand Constructors v. Pena,* 1995). (See Box 3.4 for the Supreme Court's ruling in favor of White firefighters.)

BOX 3.4
Making the Case Against and for
Affirmative Action: The U.S. Supreme Court's
Ruling in Favor of White Firefighters and
the First Latina Supreme Court Justice

Eighteen White firefighters, including one Hispanic, sued the City of New Haven claiming racial discrimination. The case stemmed from a lieutenants' promotion examination administered to New Haven, Conn., firefighters in 2003. After no African American firefighters ranked high enough to be promoted to the rank of lieutenant, the city's Civil Service Board threw out the results and decided not to make any immediate promotions. The city claimed that it was simply trying to avoid being sued by the Black firefighters who argued that the test was unfairly skewed. A district judge sided with the city and tossed the suit out before trial. A year later, a three-judge Second Circuit panel backed that decision.

The U.S. Supreme Court agreed to hear the case in 2009 and in a dramatic ruling declared that the White firefighters were unfairly denied promotion because of their race, making this a reverse discrimination case. The Supreme Court's decision was closely split in a 5–4 ruling along conservative-liberal lines.

Writing for the majority opinion, Justice Anthony Kennedy noted: "Whatever the City's ultimate aim—however well intentioned or benevolent it might have seemed—the City made its employment decision because of race. The City rejected the test results solely because the higher scoring candidates were white."

For the dissenting justices, Justice Ruth Bader Ginsburg wrote that the majority's opinion "ignores substantial evidence of multiple flaws in the tests New Haven used. The Court similarly fails to acknowledge the better tests used in other cities, which have yielded less racially skewed outcomes." She expressed the justices' concern that the city of New Haven with almost 60% minority would be "served by a fire department in which members of racial and ethnic minority are rarely seen in command decisions" (Barnes, 2009; *Ricci v. DeStefano*, 2009).

There is an interesting caveat to this Supreme Court ruling—on the three-judge Second Circuit panel that ruled in favor of the city of New Haven was Judge Sonia Sotomayor, the first woman of Latin descent to be nominated and confirmed to the U.S. Supreme Court. The Supreme Court's decision came only weeks before the congressional confirmation hearings for Judge Sotomayor and it was used by Sotomayor's opponents to support their criticism of her as an "activist judge" who endorses reverse discrimination. On several occasions during her judicial career Sotomayor declared that she was "a perfect affirmative action baby." Recounting her modest upbringing (the daughter of parents who moved from Puerto Rico to the Bronx, her father died when she was only nine years old and her mother raised Sonia and her brother as a single mother, barely making ends meet), Sotomayor has credited Affirmative Action Programs with her admission to both Princeton and Yale.

(Continued)

(Continued)

She once said "affirmative action got me into Princeton" noting that her scores on standardized entrance examinations were lower than those of her classmates and that those test scores were overlooked by the admissions committees at Princeton and Yale because she was Hispanic and grew up in poor circumstances. "With my academic achievement in high school, I was accepted rather readily at Princeton and equally as fast at Yale, but my test scores were not comparable to that of my classmates," she said. "And that's been shown by statistics, there are reasons for that. There are cultural biases built into testing, and that was one of the motivations for the concept of affirmative action to try to balance out those effects." However, she did graduate summa cum laude from Princeton and was the editor of the Yale's law journal. Her comments came in the context of explaining why she thought it was "critical that we promote diversity" by appointing more women and members of minorities as judges.

SOURCES: Barnes, 2009; *Ricci v. DeStefano*, 2009; Savage, 2009.

The fate of affirmative action policies in the United States took a very interesting turn in the mid 1990s. In November 1996, the California voters approved Proposition 209, which amended the state's constitution and stated

Neither the State of California nor any of its political subdivisions shall use race, sex, color, ethnicity or national origin as a criterion for either discriminating against, or granting preferential treatment to, any individual or group in the operation of the state's system of public employment, public education, or public contracting.[11]

Proposition 209 was unsuccessfully challenged in the courts (it was upheld in the Ninth Circuit Court of Appeals, and the Supreme Court turned down a request to hear the case in November 1997, practically voiding all affirmative action initiatives). The state of Washington followed suit by passing a similar resolution in 1998, and other states have contemplated similar measures. President Clinton was known to have phrased the slogan "Don't end, amend!" about affirmative action programs, but under his presidency no new initiatives were generated to institute such amendments. Therefore, unlike the state of affairs in South Africa, the tension between affirmative action and the equality principles in the U.S. Constitution has remained a contentious issue.

The heated debate over affirmative action was centered at the University of Michigan's Ann Arbor campus in the early 2000s when two lawsuits were brought against the university due to its use of affirmative action policies in their admissions process (Perry, 2007). The first suit was brought by Jennifer Gratz, a high school student who claimed to have been rejected for undergraduate admissions due to reverse discrimination (*Gratz v. Bollinger,* 2003). The second suit was brought by Barbara Grutter, a Caucasian female who was rejected from the University of Michigan's law school. Grutter claimed that her application was rejected due to reverse discrimination (*Grutter v. Bollinger,* 2003). Both cases were brought before the U.S. Supreme Court and a decision was rendered on both in 2003. The Supreme Court ruled that the use of affirmative action in the undergraduate admissions process at the University of Michigan was unconstitutional as the process that was being utilized for admission was thought to resemble quotas too closely and was thus considered unconstitutional. The Court, however, ruled that the use of affirmative action in the process of admission at the University of Michigan's law school was in fact constitutional as it did not make use of any quotas but rather used an individualized and holistic view of applicants to make admissions decisions.

The debate over affirmative/positive action programs has reverberated throughout the world, with some countries implementing new affirmative action policies, while others roll them back. In Malaysia, for example, the affirmative action policies enacted after the 1969 race riots between the majority Malays and the minority ethnic Chinese Malays have come under attack in recent years for retarding the economic development of the country. The original goal was to help Malays catch up economically with ethnic-Chinese Malaysians, who make up around a fourth of the country's 27 million people but who control a disproportionately large share of businesses and trade. The hope was that private Malay entrepreneurs would eventually emerge to take control. Thus far, however, relatively few Malay entrepreneurs have capitalized on the race-based initiatives. In the meantime, some economists in Malaysia say that those same programs now threaten to undermine Malaysia's fortunes by making it tough for some non-Malay entrepreneurs to go up against competitors in countries such as China, Vietnam, and Singapore. Since taking office in April 2009, Prime Minister Najib Razak, a Malay, has moved to attract more foreign investors. He recently issued new rules allowing foreign investors to enter selected service, financial, and legal businesses without having to give up equity to local ethnic-Malay partners. "The world is changing quickly and we must be ready to change with it or risk being left behind," Mr. Najib told an investment conference on June 30, 2009. But he stressed in an interview that "we mustn't lose sight of the overall objective of a more equitable and just society" (Hookway, 2009). Some countries have even considered eliminating affirmative action policies altogether. On October 18, 2005, the Constitutional Court of the Slovak Republic determined that the provision of the *antidiskriminaèný zákon* (Anti-discrimination Act) regarding the positive (affirmative) action principle was unconstitutional. Two years earlier, in 2003, the Slovak government adopted specific measures containing programs of positive actions toward, and in favor of, the Roma population (a minority group, also known as "gypsies") that has suffered widespread discrimination. The Court has argued that "the Constitution prohibits both positive and negative discrimination for the reasons stated in this provision, i.e., having regard to sex, race, colour, language, belief and religion, political affiliation or other conviction, national or social origin, nationality or ethnic origin, property, descent or any other status." Therefore, the Court declared that adoption of specific compensatory measures, although generally recognized as legislative techniques for the prevention of disadvantages pertinent to racial or ethnic origin, was incompatible with the country's constitution and had to be dismantled (International Labour Office, 2007; Buzinger, 2007).

Summary and Conclusion

And while the law [of competition] may be sometimes hard for the individual, it is best for the race, because it ensures the survival of the fittest in every department.

—Andrew Carnegie, *The Gospel of Wealth,* 1889

Global affirmative or positive action programs aim to change rules and provide advantages to groups that have traditionally been discriminated against. They stand in contrast to the laws reviewed in the previous chapter because they encourage positive action (equal and even favorable treatment of certain groups) rather than prohibit negative treatment (discrimination) in employment. These types of policies go beyond assuring equal rights to correct past wrongs. Several principles of affirmative or positive action programs are common to all countries, although the program can greatly vary from one country to the next. Typically, affirmative or positive action programs provide measures for interventions; cut across, and attempt to influence, the operation of free-market mechanisms; aim to actively reverse past discrimination against specific groups; and offer temporary actions.

There are those who argue that business enterprises should not be burdened with concerns for people and society but be able to pursue single-mindedly their financial interests. It is argued that in a perfectly competitive free market, the pursuit of profit will by itself ensure that the members of society are served in the most socially beneficial way.[12] On the other hand, businesses operate in a social context, and they need to be ethical and abide by the rules of the host country. Understanding the legislation and social policies of the host country is important because it provides businesses with important knowledge of the value context in a specific country. From a practical perspective, businesses need to understand the legal context in order to practice legally and avoid lawsuits.

Although the legislation and public policies described in this chapter have been conceived with the good intentions of providing diverse groups with better opportunities, they have generated some unintended consequences that are not always positive for individuals and for the well-being of the nations. For example, affirmative action practices in South Africa have caused many Afrikaners (Whites) to leave the country. With not enough well-trained Black people to replace them, this "White flight" has had a negative impact on the South African economy. Another unintended side effect of these programs is the rush for people to classify themselves as members of a disadvantaged group in order to reap the benefits of preferential treatment (e.g., groups in India who want to be classified as "Backwards"). The backlash against these policies includes a call to dismantle the programs, a call that has been successful in some instances (e.g., California, see above).

Proponents of affirmative action programs are concerned that the recent trend to eliminate these programs may cause a sweeping reversal of the policies that will result in erosion of their achievements. They fear that without the sanctions and incentives of these programs, companies may no longer be proactive in recruiting and retaining women and minority workers, and the representation of these groups in the workforce will decrease. On the other hand, opponents believe that the combined effect of the legislation and public policies has already made enough of a difference, and that there is no need to continue with those programs. Their main concern is that if the programs drag on long enough, they will become an entitlement rather than a measure to remedy past inequalities. Both sides agree, however, that some form of time limit needs to be set on these programs. In the long run, the hope is that the impact of these programs—along with the existence of strong antidiscrimination—will result in a more egalitarian workplace that accurately represents the general population of each nation.

Notes

1. For a detailed discussion of discrimination categorizations, see Velasquez (2006), pp. 319–341.

2. The full text of these Acts is available in the ILO's national labor law database (NATLEX) on the Internet at http://natlex.ilo.org.

3. Equal Treatment Directive 76/207/EEC, 1976. Articles 1(2) and (3) state that "This Directive shall be without prejudice to provisions concerning the protection of women particularly as regards to pregnancy and maternity and this directive shall be without prejudice to measures that promote equal opportunity for men and women. In

particular by removing existing inequalities which affect women's opportunities in areas referred to in article 1(1) i.e., access to employment including promotion and to vocational training and as regards working conditions and social security."

4. The Council Positive Action Recommendation 84/635/EEC, December 1984.

5. Council Directive 2000/43/EC of June 29, 2000, Race Relations (Amendment) Act 2000 and the EC Article 13 Race Directive.

6. Exchange rate as of July 2009 as quoted at www.oanda.com/convert/classic.

7. For a discussion of the pros and cons of affirmative actions, see Tummala (1999), pp. 495–508, and Hodges-Aeberhard (1999), pp. 247–272.

8. See, for example, a discussion of quotas for religious groups in Ireland in Rea and Eastwood (1992), pp. 31–39.

9. For a thorough review of court cases in the United States, South Africa, and the European Court of Justice, see Hodges-Aeberhard (1999), pp. 247–272.

10. For a detailed discussion of South Africa's legislation and examples of court cases, see Hodges-Aeberhard (1999), pp. 247–272, and Tummala (1999), pp. 495–508.

11. State of California Constitution, article I, section 31.

12. For a discussion of the objections for enforcing corporate ethical standards, see Velasquez (2006), pp. 23–26.

CHAPTER 4

Global Demographic Trends

Impact on Workforce Diversity

Martha Farnsworth Riche[a] *and*
Michàlle E. Mor Barak

> *No more shall there be an infant that lives but a few days, or an old person who does not live out a lifetime; for one who dies at a hundred years will be considered a youth, and one who falls short of a hundred will be considered accursed.*
>
> —Isaiah 65:17–25

Global demographic trends echo this ancient prophesy. The working-age population in the developing world is exploding because more children than ever before are living to adulthood and to have children of their own. Concurrently, the workforce in the developed world is aging, also as never before, as more adults are living a full work life and surviving into retirement. Some demographers estimate that the average baby girl born today in the United States, France, or many of the developed countries has a life expectancy of as much as 100. (See, for example, Vaupel et al., 1998; Vaupel, 2001.)

Economic integration and societal globalization are diversifying the world's workforce in new ways, and demographic trends are amplifying this development. First, the working-age population is surging in less-developed countries. Their rapidly growing numbers of young people will continue to

---

a. Martha Farnsworth Riche, PhD, Center for the Study of Economy and Society, Cornell University.

increase the supply of new workers in the developing world as their children, born and yet to be born, eventually reach working age. Second, the world's more-developed countries are experiencing slowing rates of population growth, even population declines. Their static or declining numbers of young people, combined with improved health in mid and later life, is tilting their working-age populations toward mature age groups.

Meanwhile, global economic integration, based in part on differences in labor costs, is amplifying the role of migration in balancing labor demand and supply. Under such circumstances, people have traditionally migrated to find work; with global integration, employers also migrate to find workers. As a result, people from diverse backgrounds, with diverse human capital and diverse expectations, are increasingly encountering one another in the workplace. This diversity is accentuated by changes within national populations that are increasing the proportion of the workforce that is made up of nontraditional workers—particularly women but also older people, people with disabilities, and people with nontraditional sexual orientations.

This chapter provides an overview of global demographic trends that contribute to increasing workforce diversity throughout the world. We begin with international population trends—trends in the working-age population in different regions and migration trends across borders. We then describe some national population trends specifically related to gender, age, disability, and sexual orientation that contribute to increased diversity in the workplace.

International Population Trends

The world's population, virtually static throughout most of history, has grown to unprecedented size over the past 2 centuries, largely due to advances in health care that developed in the industrialized world, then spread to the developing world (see Figure 4.1). At the beginning of the 20th century, the world had 1.7 billion people. By 1960, after health advances had become widespread in the industrialized countries but before they became common in the developing countries, the world had 3 billion people. Then foreign aid programs took the new advances around the world, and its population surged past 6 billion by the century's end (Haub & Riche, 1994), and is slated to reach 8 billion by 2025 (United Nations, 2009a). Thanks to advances in curing infectious childhood diseases, sanitation, and public health, in most countries children live to adulthood and have healthy children of their own.

At the beginning of the 21st century, the world had about 1 billion adolescents and 1 billion more young children. If fertility rates continue to decline at their current pace, these young people will grow the world population to 9 billion as they have their own children during the next 50 years

(United Nations, 2009a). If rates do not decline, the United Nations sees the world's population growing an additional 2 billion, reaching nearly 11 billion in total. Thus, the childbearing decisions of today's young people will determine how large the world's population becomes.

The developing world already has unprecedented numbers of young people, many of whom would have died at young ages before the public health advances of the last half century. From an employment perspective, the primary challenge is absorbing the 3 billion people who doubled the world's population during the last 40 years of the 20th century. Age 39 or under in 2002, they are either working, looking for work, or looking for the education that will help them when they reach working age.

More than 60% of the world's population age 39 or under was Asian in 2000, compared with only 4% that was North American.[1] Africa had 15% of the

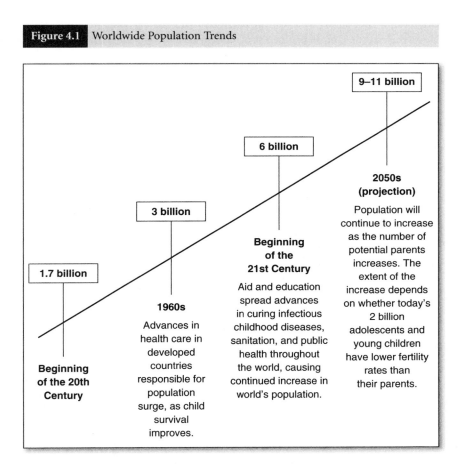

Figure 4.1   Worldwide Population Trends

world's under age 40 population, whereas Latin America (including the Caribbean) and the newly unified Europe each had nearly 10% (United Nations, 2001). Looking at just the population under age 15 in 2000, the source of today's young workforce entrants, Asia had more than 60%, Africa more than 18%, and all other regions accounted for a declining share. Asia clearly represents the center of gravity of the world's labor force now and in the future, whereas Africa increasingly accounts for net growth in the world's labor supply.[2]

Meanwhile, a second health-related trend is taking place in the developed countries and beginning to show up in the developing countries. Once more, science/medicine, public health, and public education have combined, this time to lengthen life expectancy. For the world as a whole, life expectancy at birth has grown by more than 20 years—to 69—just since 1950 (Population Reference Bureau, 2009b). Of course, there is still a wide gap in life expectancy between developed and developing countries. Currently, Japanese life expectancy is 83, compared with an average of 55 in all of Africa, where life expectancy at birth is also improving (from 38 as recently as 1950). Nevertheless, the United Nations projects a gradual slowing in this gap over the first half of the 21st century.

The great improvements in life expectancy during the 20th century largely resulted from successfully combating infectious childhood diseases—this is the source of the explosive growth in the world's actual and next-generation labor force. The current trends, however, are growing the labor force in a different way, by lengthening the number of working-age years for most individuals. This trend is measured by the years of life expected at age 45 (United Nations, 1999a). Although the data are sparse for developing countries, the trend toward more years after age 45 seems quite similar around the world. For instance, life expectancy at age 45 is about the same in the United States, China, and Brazil.

Some people jump to the conclusion that longer life expectancy in midlife or later adds unhealthy years to the end of life and thus grows the numbers of sick, old people. New research in several industrialized countries suggests that these new years are being inserted into the middle of adult life and pushing old age and disability back.[3] That is, active life expectancy (sometimes called healthy life expectancy) is growing at the same pace as life expectancy. People at a given age, say, 75 or 80, are healthier than people of that age were a few decades ago in terms of their activity levels (Manton, Corder, & Stallard, 1997; Manton & Gu, 2001). Moreover, researchers say that the current midlife population has generally better health than today's elderly did at their age. They also have higher educational attainment, which is directly correlated to better health in old age. These population characteristics suggest that this trend to healthier, more active older people will continue. The result is that "old age" is occurring at older ages, and the ability to work, if necessary, is commensurately extended.

This is good news for individuals, though it contains new challenges for societies. Perhaps the most important challenge is that for the first time in history, a country whose fertility rate is around replacement level (2.1 children, to replace both parents in the population) is beginning to experience roughly equal numbers of people in each living generation, except the oldest. The age composition of the U.S. population is a good example of this change (see Figure 4.2).

As recently as 1970, the U.S. age picture represented the classic "population pyramid," in which each younger generation outnumbered the next older generation.[4] In a revolutionary change, the U.S. population pyramid is turning into a "population pillar," with roughly equal-sized generations throughout the working ages.

Meanwhile, the contrast between less-developed countries, which manifest the classic youth-dominated population picture, and the developed countries as a whole is stark. This is because developed countries whose fertility rates have been below replacement level for a considerable time are looking at a population that contains more older people than younger ones. This is particularly so in Europe, whose population is currently projected to decline by nearly 5% between 2000 and 2050 (United Nations, 2009a). Already its population under age 15 is considerably smaller than its population age 60 and older. Of course, the situation varies from country to country, depending on both fertility rates and net migration. But in the industrialized world overall, increases in the workforce will depend more than ever on employing a higher proportion of people whose good health makes them capable of working. This essentially means employing a higher proportion of older people, thus contributing to increasing workforce age diversity.

TRENDS IN THE WORKING-AGE POPULATION

The United Nations regularly assesses the outlook for world population according to changing patterns in births and deaths (United Nations, 2009a). Between 2000 and 2025, the UN expects the working-age population, defined internationally as ages 15 to 64, to increase by more than one third.

However, the UN expects that the working-age population of the more developed countries (as currently defined) will barely grow—and to slightly decline as a share of the population (Table 4.1). In countries such as Germany, Italy, Japan, or the Russian Federation, the UN expects there to be fewer people ages 15 to 64 (Table 4.2). Even if fertility rates increase in these countries, the current deficit in young people cannot be replaced, except by immigration. Other countries, such as the United States, will have more people in those ages, but not enough to keep up with the pace of rapid population growth throughout the developing world as today's "youth explosion" reaches its working ages.

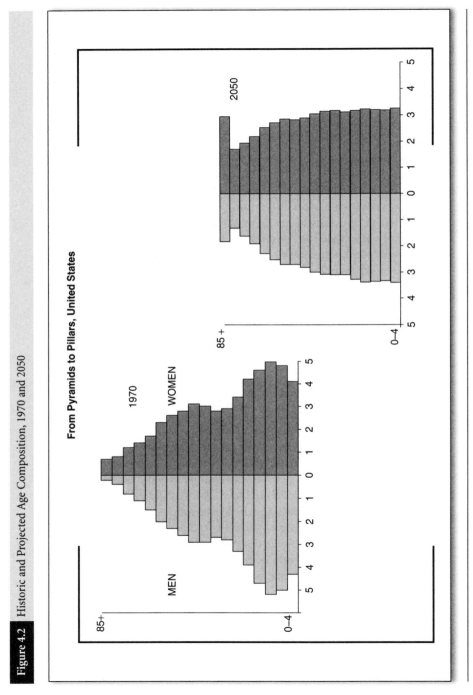

Figure 4.2 Historic and Projected Age Composition, 1970 and 2050

From Pyramids to Pillars, United States

SOURCE: U.S. Census Bureau (2000).

Given these contrasting growth rates, today's more developed countries can expect their share of the world's working-age population to drop from over 20% to 15% (Table 4.1). Africa will take up most of the slack: its working-age population will nearly double if current trends persist. The effect of AIDS on deaths is the major source of uncertainty in Africa, as the births that will feed this growth have already largely taken place.

In contrast, countries that typically have high fertility rates are experiencing substantial youth bulges, defined as a very high proportion of the population consisting of children under age 15.

In most countries, people have become accustomed to having children survive, and fertility rates are now declining. So over the next two decades, this bulge should be absorbed virtually everywhere except in Africa, which may contain more than one in four of the world's children in 2025 (Table 4.3). In that sense, Africa may be the last frontier of "excess" labor available for low-wage competition in their home countries or to fill jobs in developed countries with fewer working-age people.

The potential impact of HIV/AIDS on population growth injects some uncertainty into this overall picture. This impact is difficult to estimate, given the lack of reliable statistics about its prevalence in most countries. Estimates from the U.S. Census Bureau have suggested that although deaths from AIDS have dampened population growth rates in Africa, fertility is so high there that populations will continue to grow in most countries (Stanecki, 2002). However, in South Africa and Botswana, as well as Lesotho, Mozambique, and

Table 4.1   World Population, Ages 15–64 (in 1,000s)

	2000	% distribution	2025	% distribution
Africa	445,501	11.3	837,631	15.6
Latin America/Caribbean	325,450	8.2	452,420	8.5
Asia/Oceania	2,369,611	60.1	3,253,522	60.8
More developed regions	804,685	20.4	808,760	15.1
Total	3,945,247	100.0	5,352,333	100.0

SOURCE: United Nations (2009a).

Table 4.2 Population Ages 15–64, Selected Countries (in 1,000s)

	2000	% of world	2025	% of world
World	3,843,548	100.0	5,262,050	100.0
Europe	491,749	12.8	466,715	8.9
France	38,448	1.0	39,864	0.8
Germany	55,835	1.4	49,542	0.9
Italy	38,419	1.0	37,757	0.7
Japan	86,354	2.2	71,652	1.4
Republic of Korea	33,344	0.9	33,527	0.6
Russian Federation	101,846	2.6	87,394	1.7
United Kingdom	38,379	1.0	42,141	0.8
United States	190,190	4.9	227,147	4.3

SOURCE: United Nations (2009a).

Table 4.3 Trends in the Population Under Age 15 (in 1,000s)

	2000	%	2025	%
World	1,854,577	100.0	1,917,158	100.0
More developed regions	218,772	11.8	202,500	10.6
Africa	347,298	18.7	503,911	26.3
Latin America and Caribbean	165,739	8.9	146,471	7.6
Asia	1,138,059	61.4	1,073,511	56.0
Oceania	8,052	0.4	9,397	0.5

SOURCE: United Nations (2009a); percentages do not sum to 100% due to rounding.

Swaziland, AIDS is expected to decrease population over the next few decades. Population growth will also be dampened slightly in Asian countries such as Burma, Cambodia, and Thailand (Stanecki, 2002). Probably the most significant effect of HIV/AIDS on workforce demographics will not be on the numbers of workers but on the age structure of the workforce, particularly in countries where the pandemic has been severe. As people tend to contract AIDS relatively young, an estimated median survival rate of around 10 years means that the effect is felt among men in their 40s and women in their 30s. This dynamic works against the worldwide trend toward longer life expectancy, and to increasing shares of older workers.

MIGRATION TRENDS

Migration is the other element in population change, in addition to births and deaths. UN demographers have calculated how many migrants it could take to keep the working-age population the same size in various industrial countries over the first half of this century (United Nations, 2000a). Given the relatively lower numbers of children being born there, they calculated that Europe as a whole would need to receive a net 3.2 million migrants a year to keep its working-age population from declining. In contrast, the United States has enough births to keep its working-age population constant; thus immigration continues to grow that population.

Economic and demographic imbalances have increased the numbers, though not necessarily the proportion, of international migrants in recent decades, as well as their relative impact in specific countries (Massey, Arango, Hugo, et al., 2005; OECD, 2009; Sassen, 1988, 1999; World Bank, 1995; Zlotnick, 1994). This impact has been particularly pronounced in Western Europe (Table 4.4). Although annual migratory flows may be small relative to the size of world population, social and cultural differences tend to make migrants particularly visible.

Migration data are generally imperfect for workforce analysis because they are typically derived from records kept by countries as they "control" their borders (i.e., monitor and record entries) (Zlotnick, 1994). Tourists often become workers, as do students who stay beyond their schooling. Others enter by avoiding border controls altogether, while some countries, notably members of the European Union, have modified and even abolished such controls for member nations. At the same time, countries are much less likely to monitor and record exits.[5] Thus, the extent of return migration, particularly circular migration, is widely ignored, even though migration experts consider it of prime importance. The migration of workers from Eastern to Western Europe during the early part of the 21st century, and then their return home in the global economic crisis that began in 2007, is a notable example. This and other evidence suggests that globalization allows many international migrants to reinvent long-standing patterns of seasonal and temporary movement for work rather than choosing permanent settlement in a new country. However, this aspect of the global labor force is largely unmeasured.[6]

Overall, international agencies estimate that the level of transborder migration of people seeking work has not increased, relative to world population size. (Of course, world population has grown rapidly, doubling between 1960 and 1999.) Instead, economic integration has transformed the international division of labor. In the 1960s, developing countries exported primary commodities; now they are exporting labor-intensive manufactures, under either national or global ownership (Sassen, 1988; World Bank, 1995).

In addition, the direction of migration flows has changed. Since the 1960s, migration flows from less-developed countries—to both developed

Table 4.4   Percentage of the Labor Force That Is Foreign-Born in Selected Countries

	1997 (%)	2006 (%)
Austria	9.9	11.9
Belgium	8.6	9.2
Czech Republic	2.5	3.6
Germany	8.9	8.5
Italy	2.9	5.9
Japan	0.2	0.3
Korea	0.5	1.3
Norway	2.8	7.4
Spain	1.1	8.5
Sweden	5.2	4.3
Switzerland	20.5	21.0
United Kingdom	3.6	6.3

SOURCE: Organization for Economic Co-operation and Development (OECD), 2009 (Table A.2.3.).

and developing countries alike—have replaced the flows of Europeans in the opposite direction. Essentially, population stabilization or decline in Europe has replaced several centuries of European population explosion, which fueled European colonization of most of the rest of the world (Chesnais, 2000). In the meantime, population has exploded in the developing world. In search of work and livelihood, many leave their home countries for the developed countries (see, for example, Box 4.1). Certain migrants' need to find work sometimes meets demands in the host countries for their specific skills. For example, women from the Philippines have found a large international demand for their services as caregivers to children and to the elderly (see, for example, Box 4.2). Thus, slow population growth in most developed countries and rapid growth in developing countries are causing the foreign-born share of the population in developed countries as a whole to rise (World Bank, 1995) (see Figure 4.3). And it is becoming more diverse (Organization for Economic Co-operation and Development [OECD], 2009).

| Figure 4.3 | International Demographic Trends |

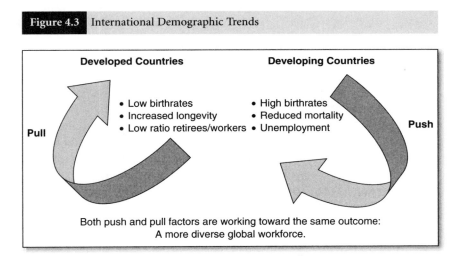

Developed Countries   **Developing Countries**

- Low birthrates   - High birthrates
- Increased longevity   - Reduced mortality
- Low ratio retirees/workers - Unemployment

Pull   **Push**

Both push and pull factors are working toward the same outcome:
A more diverse global workforce.

BOX 4.1
The Women Who Leave, the Children
Who Follow: Enrique's Story

In search of work and escape from poverty and hunger, many mothers from Central America and Mexico enter the United States illegally and leave their

(Continued)

(Continued)

young children behind in the care of relatives. Every year an estimated 48,000 youngsters from Central America and Mexico enter the United States illegally in an effort to reunite with their mothers. They travel any way they can, and thousands ride the tops and sides of freight trains. They leap on and off rolling train cars. They forage for food and water. Bandits prey on them. So do street gangsters, who have made the train tops their new turf. These trains have gained the nickname *los trenes del muerte*—the trains of death. None of the youngsters have proper papers. Many are caught by the Mexican police or by *la migra*, the Mexican immigration authorities, who send them back to their home countries. Enrique's story is a typical one:

Enrique was 5 years old when his mother, Lourdes, left him in his home-town Tegucigalpa, in Honduras, to immigrate illegally to the United States. Left by her husband, Enrique's father, and without any means to support her son, her older daughter, Belky, and herself, Lourdes decided to go to the United States, make money, and send it home until she could afford to bring her children to be with her. When she left, she promised to come back for them soon. She never returned. Throughout his childhood, moving from one family member to the other, Enrique dreamed of reuniting with his mother. At age 17, after six failed attempts to travel to the United States illegally, he was finally reunited with his mother in North Carolina. A few months later he learned that Maria Isabel, the girlfriend he left back in Honduras, had given birth to their daughter. Enrique sent money to bring Maria Isabel to the United States. In an ironic twist of fate, both Enrique and Maria Isabel decided to leave the baby behind with Maria Isabel's mother until they have enough money to send for her (Nazario, 2002, 2007).[7]

Mexicans, for instance, now account for the greatest share of foreign-born in the current U.S. population; but as recently as 1970, people born in Italy, Germany, and the United Kingdom, as well as in Canada, each out-numbered the Mexican-born (OECD, 2000). Today's fast-growing immigrant groups in the United States include people from the Philippines, Korea, and India, leading Chesnais to remark that the United States "is no longer primarily a European country" (2000). Or take Sweden, a major contributor to the U.S. population in the 19th century. Migration into Sweden turned positive (i.e., more people entered than left) during the 1960s (Council of Europe, 2000). Now there are more Swedes who were born in Iran than in Norway, more born in Iraq than in Germany, and more born in Turkey or Chile than in the United States or the United Kingdom (OECD, 2000).

BOX 4.2
The Price of Migration for Women
From the Philippines

Since she migrated from the Philippines 10 years ago, Marie has worked in the United States illegally as a caregiver to elderly people. When she works in a private home, room and board are provided, enabling Marie to send over 75% of her earnings to her family in the Philippines. She is expected to be on call 24 hours a day without overtime pay. From her meager wages, Marie cannot afford the trip back home to see her family. When she left the Philippines, her youngest child was 6 years old. That same child will be 18 by the time Marie sees her again (Tung, 2000).

Filipina women have found a large international demand for their services as caregivers to children and to the elderly. However, their experiences vary widely depending on the destination country. Filipinas work as caregivers most commonly in Saudi Arabia, Hong Kong, Japan, the United Arab Emirates, and Taiwan (Kang & Tran, 2003). Other countries such as the United States also employ a large number of Filipinas. However, most of the women live and work illegally in these countries, making it difficult to accurately estimate their numbers. Canada has been a popular destination since the introduction of Canada's Live-in Caregiver Program under which foreign workers live comfortably and have a chance to bring their families to Canada after 2 years (Baga-Reyes, 2003).

However, most countries' policies are not as generous as Canada's. For example, Taiwan, which is now the fifth most popular destination for Filipina women, has significantly less desirable economic conditions. Taiwan has set a minimum monthly wage of $TND 15,840 (Taiwanese new dollars; US$480), for a 40-hour workweek. However, after factoring in the cost of mandatory payments for food, accommodations, and monthly broker fees, the women are left with $TND 10,040 to $TND 11,840 (US$304 to US$359). Further, in order to obtain a job in Taiwan, most of the women had to pay a broker's placement fee. That fee can be as high as $TND 100,000, which is usually borrowed from the broker and paid later from the woman's wages (Kang & Tran, 2003). With all of the fees associated with the legal work opportunities in Taiwan, it is little wonder that many of the women head to countries such as the United States to work illegally for wages as little as $3 per hour, with no pay for overtime.

National Trends

Diversity in the workplace is a growing concern in many countries, and this concern extends well beyond the ramifications of international population trends. Simply put, shifts in the nature and location of economic activity are combining with social and demographic trends to increase the role of nontraditional workers, particularly women, in the paid workforce in all but the least developed countries. At the same time, international support for human rights—reinforced by messages delivered through global communications and entertainment networks—is blurring traditional patterns of workplace discrimination on the basis of religion; social class; caste; race, or ethnic origin; disability; or sexual orientation, as well as age and gender.

GENDER DIVERSITY

Increasing numbers and shares of women in the workplace may be the most important component of diversity at the national level in most of the world, not only because of their strengthened presence but also because their changing roles have a simultaneous effect at home and work. The largest increase in women's labor force participation in recent decades took place during the 1980s and 1990s. This trend is well illustrated by its evolution in Latin America. In 1980, little more than one quarter of the workforce was female in Central and South America; by 1997, women made up one third of the workforce in Central America and nearly two fifths in South America (Table 4.5) (United Nations, 2000b). Women's share of the workforce also grew significantly in Western Europe and the other developed regions during those two decades. Even in countries where women have traditionally been discouraged from working outside the home, they came to make up an increasing share of the measured labor force.[8] In Northern Africa, for example, women's share of the labor force rose from 20% in 1980 to 26% in 1997. In Western Asia, it went from 23% to 27%.

Whether women's participation rates are high or low, the gap between women's and men's rates is narrowing in most regions (Table 4.6) (International Labour Office, 2009). This results from two intersecting trends: increased rates of participation for women, and decreased rates for men, especially where pension schemes have encouraged early retirement. Changes in the age composition of the working-age population also may change women's share of the labor force. For instance, the share of women in the labor force may increase even more in countries where populations are growing older, as women tend to live longer than men. Many women need to support themselves in the absence of a husband; others seek activity outside a home that no longer contains children. In either circumstance, where women's educational attainment equals men's (or exceeds it), employers in most countries can expect challenges to practices that favor men at all levels of the workforce, including supervisory or executive positions.

In sum, women have been increasingly active economically in most regions, especially in regions where they had been relatively less active a quarter century ago. As a result, women's economic activity rates are increasingly similar around the world, except in regions where society constrains women's roles outside the home.

Table 4.5 Female Proportion of the Labor Force

	1980 (%)	1990 (%)	1997 (%)
Africa			
North Africa	19.8	25.3	26.2
Sub-Saharan Africa	42.2	42.5	42.8
Latin America and Caribbean			
Caribbean	38.2	41.2	42.8
Central America	26.9	30.2	33.1
South America	26.9	33.2	38.0
Asia			
East Asia	40.2	42.2	43.2
Southeast Asia	40.5	42.4	42.8
Southern Asia	30.8	33.7	32.9
Central Asia	47.4	45.0	45.6
Western Asia	22.9	25.0	26.6
Developed regions			
Eastern Europe	45.0	45.6	45.3
Western Europe	36.2	40.1	42.1
Other developed regions	38.6	43.0	43.9

SOURCE: United Nations (2000b).

Women's increased participation in the labor force is the result of several social and economic changes. In most countries outside Africa, large numbers of women have achieved control over their fertility, thus expanding their opportunities for education and employment. As a result, both activists and policymakers are now addressing employment-related barriers such as negative attitudes toward employed women and unfavorable public policies regarding family and childcare, part-time employment, maternity benefits, and parental and maternal leave. Meanwhile, both economic growth and expansion of services and other sectors that tend to employ large numbers of women contribute to increased employment of women.

Indeed, global economic development policy now makes fostering women's employment opportunities a priority in developing countries. World Bank economists have concluded that countries that limit women's employment lose as much as a percentage point of potential annual growth through inefficient allocation of productive resources (World Bank, 2001). Low investment in female education is also costly to poor countries. One influential study estimated that decreasing the already low gender gap in school enrollment in East Asia boosted its annual economic growth rate by 0.5% to 0.9% over South Asia, the Middle East, and sub-Saharan Africa between 1960 and 1992 (Klasen, 1999).

In addition to the economic benefits of turning dependents into producers, researchers have shown that women's paid employment increases human capital investment in children and thus in the future labor force.[9] Women who have other choices for their lives also tend to limit their childbearing, bringing fertility rates down so that the future labor force is of a size that the national economy can more readily absorb. This important development ensures that diversity issues regarding gender in the workplace will be increasingly salient in most countries, not just industrialized ones.

Both demographic and social changes have altered the pattern of economic activity over women's lives, creating new challenges for diversity management. Until recent decades, women in industrialized countries typically entered the labor force as soon as they completed their formal education, leaving within a few years to bear and raise children. Now, with secondary and higher education more common, entry rates are high for women in their 20s, rising through their 30s and 40s. Higher education simply makes it more costly for women to leave the labor force, as more education qualifies them for better-paying jobs and for jobs that provide advancement. This change is most visible in Europe and North America where patterns of economic activity for women have come to resemble patterns for men (United Nations, 1999a).

In these countries as well, relatively low levels of fertility mean that women whose children are grown are an increasingly important part of the labor force. In the United States, for instance, participation rates rose for older women as the well-educated baby boomers aged, and in 2008, the female workforce was

| Table 4.6 | Women's and Men's Economic Activity Rates |

	1998		2008 (preliminary estimates)	
	women	men	women	men
North Africa	24.6	75.1	28.1	73.4
Sub-Saharan Africa	59.6	81.6	61.5	80.3
Latin America and Caribbean	45.6	80.2	52.4	78.8
East Asia	70.7	82.4	68.2	77.9
Southeast Asia and the Pacific	57.3	81.6	56.8	82.2
Southern Asia	35.1	83.2	35.8	81.9
Middle East	21.5	75.6	25.4	75.1
Developed economies and the European Union	49.2	69.2	49.8	66.3
Central and South-Eastern Europe (non-EU) and CIS	50.2	69.5	49.5	68.3
WORLD	51.4	78.6	51.6	76.7

SOURCE: International Labour Office (2009).

roughly evenly divided between women under age 45 (generally considered the boundary between women's fertile and nonfertile years) and over it (U.S. Bureau of Labor Statistics, 2009). With two children or fewer and an increasing life expectancy, women in the more industrialized countries are spending a much smaller share of their adult life in parenting.[10] Thus, once women reach their 40s, equality, not diversity, is the issue for most, as they have effectively completed their conventional, gender-based responsibilities in the home.[11] And, given the prospect of extended work lives after their children have grown, younger women seem less willing to accept inferior access to skill development during the early years of their careers in countries where such delay is not penalized by employers.

Trends in Latin America and the Caribbean parallel women's participation trends in the developed regions, but here, as in other regions, women's participation rates have increased even more in the past decade. This suggests that women in less-developed regions may be less likely to afford to withdraw from the labor force to raise children, compared to women in more-developed countries. In Africa, where agriculture remains the primary industry, women have generally been active (though not usually in the paid labor force) throughout their lives, including their childbearing years, and little has changed. Indeed, in a few African countries, notably Mozambique and Rwanda, women's participation rates exceeded men's in 2008, while in Burundi, Ghana, and Sierra Leone, female participation rates were nearly equal (International Labour Office, 2009). Asia is much more heterogeneous, and economic activity rates by age differ widely among countries (International Labour Office, 2009; United Nations, 1999a). However, outside of countries where women face educational, cultural, and institutional barriers, with women increasingly in the paid labor force during their childbearing and child-rearing years, employer work-family policies are now an important aspect of diversity management around the world.

AGE DIVERSITY

Demographic change is increasing diversity in national workforces in yet another way as longer life expectancies expand the population of older people. Few people realize the important contribution of mortality improvement to population growth. Yet, throughout the 20th century, for instance, mortality improvement added more people to the U.S. population than did the significant amount of immigration the country experienced.[12] Current U.S. population growth derives as much if not more from "postponed" deaths as from immigration. In developing countries, most women and men who survive into old age must remain in the labor force. In developed countries, economic activity at older ages decreased in recent decades, mainly due to effective pension schemes that tended to allow or even encourage early retirement. The shift of employment away from agriculture has also had an effect as older people traditionally found useful work on family farms. However, in many countries this downward trend is now slowing or even reversing as workers consider how to fund a lengthening postemployment life, and governments worry about the sustainability of pension systems.

Developed or developing, most countries can expect to see larger numbers of older people in the workforce simply because improvements in mortality continue to increase the proportion of the working-age population that lives to the end of the normal work life, however that is defined. (This is the meaning of the term *population aging*—that fewer individuals die before they reach old age.) At the same time, the workforce contains a smaller proportion of young people as more of them extend their education. These two shifts have the general effect of making the workforce more diverse in terms of workers' ages.

In the United Kingdom, for example, the working-age population in 2000 (using the broad, international definition—age 15 to 64) contained almost as many people age 40 and older as under age 40. It was the same in Hungary. Even in South Korea, nearly 40% of the working-age population was estimated to be age 40 or older. In contrast, less than 30% were 40 or older in Pakistan where high fertility rates continue to grow the youth population (International Labour Office, 2002).

In countries that are experiencing workforce aging, some age-related diversity issues are obvious, such as those related to pay and benefits. For instance, rewarding workers for years they've spent on the job can produce disruptive inequities in the absence of visible skill acquisitions. Or skewing benefits to people who are raising children can cause trouble with those whose later life needs are quite different.

Other issues are less obvious. In cultures where older people are accustomed to higher status at work, larger numbers of older people mean that not all can be included among the relatively smaller numbers in the upper ranks of the workforce, even if employers are willing to delay promoting younger people and younger employees are willing to go along.[13] Family issues are also changing for workers in all parts of the life cycle. For instance, smaller families often mean that working men or women at any age may need to care for family members as there are fewer people available at home. As longer life expectancy does not ensure longer marital life expectancy, workers may acquire and lose family members through marriage and divorce as well as births and deaths, further diversifying the set of work-family issues.

RACIAL AND ETHNIC DIVERSITY

Similar issues surround the inclusion of racial and ethnic groups who have historically been allotted a subservient status in the national workplace. In many countries, such populations are growing even without significant migration because their fertility rates are high relative to the historically favored population.[14] (Higher fertility is generally associated with lower socioeconomic status.) Growth in numbers is combining with attitude change to promote attention to issues of inclusion, particularly in the workplace.

Around the world, the latter part of the 20th century saw a widespread change of attitude toward historically excluded populations—from discrimination and exploitation to tolerance and even inclusion. Granted, neither this change nor concomitant changes in policies and behavior have occurred rapidly or uniformly. Still, civil and human rights movements continue to work toward equalizing educational and employment opportunities across racial and ethnic lines. In the context of an integrated world economy, this advocacy increases the demand on employers to introduce and manage harmonious human relations policies in the workplace.

In the past few decades, immigration and fertility trends have made racial and ethnic diversity in the workforce an important issue in many industrialized countries. U.S. economist William Darity Jr. has asserted that "Germany's Turkish and other immigrant workers, France and the UK's African, Middle Eastern and South Asian workers, Japan's Korean workers, and Canada's non-White workers are in the same position as minority workers in the United States" ("Experts Speak," 1999, p. 81). However, many national workforces have long featured one or more varieties of excluded groups: castes and tribal groups in India, Blacks and "Coloureds" in South Africa, and Catholics in Northern Ireland are examples.

BOX 4.3
Ethnic Diversity in Malaysia

With a political majority of native-born Malays, or bumiputra, Malaysia made a commitment to use economic development to narrow the income gap with the ethnic-Chinese Malays via a set of affirmative action policies. These policies have had some success in reducing the income gap, partly because of programs to increase company ownership among native Malays. Thanks to substantial economic growth, even the Chinese-origin Malaysians have done well, with only foreign owners losing from this diversity program (Darity & Deshpande, 2000).

However, programs to close the income gap among workers have been constrained by lower levels of education, especially English language education, among Malays of rural origin. Meanwhile, the government has acknowledged that the policies, although successful in creating a Malay middle class, have also created a culture of entitlement (Arnold, 2002). Reporting the fallout from a corporate scandal, the *New York Times* quoted local executives as saying that "too often . . . managers win promotions because of their ethnic background and connections rather than their ability" (Arnold, 2002, p. W1). And those who prove competent are reportedly rewarded with more responsibility until it eventually overwhelms or even corrupts them.

The growing importance of the market in many countries is making private workplaces a particular focus of diversity concern because governments have tended to focus inclusion efforts on public education, government jobs, and political representation. For instance, India made a commitment in its constitution to address the sustained social and economic backwardness of its tribal groups and the groups at the bottom of its caste system. However, these groups are still vastly underrepresented among middle- and higher-income groups. In large part, this is due to the recent liberalization and privatization of much of the economy, which has both created funding problems for public education and constrained the growth of government employment (Darity & Deshpande, 2000). These trends limit the impact of government efforts, turning reformers' attention toward the private sector.

In some countries, the excluded group may actually be more numerous, as in Malaysia where native Malays outnumber people of Chinese origin and thus dominate the government (see Box 4.3). Or they may be equally numerous, as in Ghana, where citizens of East Indian and African origin each have their own political party and the electoral cycle determines which one can influence the workplace (Darity & Deshpande, 2000). So diversity issues in the workplace are not necessarily a question of numbers; nor are they a question of degree of economic development. According to Darity and Deshpande, "The universal persistence of racial and ethnic discrimination in labor markets in countries at all levels of development is a striking stylized fact of the modern world in the presence or absence of programs of redress for groups with inferior status" (p. 81).

Even when outright discrimination on the basis of group membership does not exist, educational differences tend to build a concrete barrier between workers of different racial and ethnic origins. Though individuals from minority populations may not have been deliberately excluded from the educational system, their relative poverty has generally hindered them from taking full advantage of it. Consequently, a country's efforts to overcome educational disparities generally herald efforts to improve representation in the workforce, particularly at higher levels. However, employers may need to undertake leadership if educational efforts are lagging workplace needs and workplace inequalities are hampering their ability to maximize workforce productivity.

ABILITY AND DISABILITY DIVERSITY

Global data are truly sparse in relation to people with disabilities. Some countries gather data through the census, but it tends to be unreliable (census methods are designed to count people, not collect information about their characteristics). Disability data reported as part of a program, rather than self-reported, tend to be more reliable—but that presupposes the existence of programs. Most existing programs produce data on work-related disabilities and compensation for them, not on people who can't get work because they have disabilities. Still, modern medicine is doing a better job of saving people's lives and may thus be indirectly growing the numbers of those with physical disabilities who not only survive longer but are also employable.

Developed countries generally provide benefits to people who have had disabilities from childhood. In some countries, these benefits are constructed in such a way as to discourage people with disabilities from finding paid employment because they would lose allowances that help them cope with costs they incur as a result of their disability. In other countries, this disincentive does not exist (International Labour Office, 2000). However, it is probably safe to say that in no case are these benefits sufficiently lavish to substitute for paid employment. In developing countries, according to the International Labour Organization, people who "have disabilities which prevent them from supporting themselves are usually unable to receive any benefit, except, possibly, social security where it exists"—and where it exists, it usually excludes most low-income earners, whether self-employed or wage earners (International Labour Office, 2000).

Thus, people with disabilities have a strong interest in removing barriers to potential employment. In countries with little or no population growth, people with disabilities can swell the labor supply. And, if for no other reason, longer life expectancies are likely to make governments less willing to provide lifetime support, however parsimonious, to people who incurred their disabilities as adults. These and other factors suggest that people with disabilities are likely to be a factor in increasing workforce diversity.

SEXUAL ORIENTATION DIVERSITY

The civil rights movement has fostered a continued striving for fairness toward all population groups in the workplace, including people with nontraditional sexual orientations. Similar to disability, global data on sexual orientation is hard to come by, and any information on sexual orientation that is collected through census data is most likely unreliable. (If people aren't willing to tell census takers their income, generally the least reported item, they are hardly likely to tell them their sexual orientation.)

Absent data, sheer population growth probably means that the number of people with nontraditional sexual orientations is growing. Moreover, other trends suggest that these groups may be growing relative to populations as a whole. Public opinion polls seem to suggest that younger people in developed countries are becoming more accepting of an array of sexual orientations; thus, more people may be willing to acknowledge their membership in these population groups.

Countries where labor is in short supply are likely to address barriers to full employment of all working-age adults, including those with nontraditional sexual orientations. This is all the more likely in that today's smaller families provide less economic shelter for people unwilling to confront hostility in the workplace.

Summary and Conclusion

Broad demographic trends spell more diversity in the global workplace as the world adapts to a new age in which most children survive to adulthood and most adults survive to old age. In industrialized countries, the biggest impetus for workforce diversity will come from population stabilization and population aging. Countries will choose between growing the labor force through immigrants or through employing more nontraditional workers. Either choice will increase diversity in the workplace. In developing countries, diversity will come from population growth, as foreign employers arrive to tap an underemployed and presumably less demanding workforce or as governments seek new forms of employment to provide jobs for their growing numbers.

Aside from these demographic dynamics, widespread improvement in education over the last century has created a more highly educated and thus more aspiring workforce around the world. In the developed world, working-age people are knowledgeable about their rights and about how to make sure they are observed. In the developing world, awareness of individual and group rights is one more lesson being learned from more advanced economies. This trend alone is probably sufficient to ensure that issues related to diversity will touch more and more workplaces in the years to come.

Notes

1. The quantitative comparisons made in this chapter use varying time periods and age groups. This is unavoidable given the paucity of comparable international data. Indeed, only recent initiatives on the part of international agencies and research institutions make such comparisons possible at all.

2. How well African governments tame the AIDS epidemic will, of course, affect the future size of the region's workforce.

3. James Vaupel, the leading demographer in this line of research, has a number of instructive publications.

4. The factors that slightly distort the lower half of this "pyramid"—the small Depression and the large baby boom generations—are not unique to the United States.

5. Zlotnick (1996) offers a concise summary of the problems in accounting for migration flows, including problems of classification and problems of comparability. As she points out, migration is politically sensitive along a variety of dimensions, and countries often prefer not to know the realities.

6. Sociologist Saskia Sassen has written extensively of the ways in which globalization calls for new ways of thinking about migration, especially in a workforce

context. For instance, circular migration is common, in which people prefer to work in one country to earn higher wages but to maintain their personal, cultural, and political interests by returning home on a regular basis. This migration can be temporary, just to earn a certain amount of money or acquire a certain amount of experience, knowledge, or credentials. It can be also be recurring, whether seasonally or simple commuting. See Sassen (1999) for an introduction to these and related issues.

7. Enrique's story was compiled by Sonia Nazario (2002), a writer for the *Los Angeles Times,* from interviews with Enrique, his mother, and several of his family members in Honduras. The writer and the photographer also documented his ordeal by retracing his journey riding trains and joining groups of immigrants crossing the borders illegally. The resulting story, documenting a typical journey of a child yearning to be reunited with his mother, appeared in six installments in the *Los Angeles Times.* It can also be located on the Internet (www.latimes.com/news/specials/enrique).

8. Women's work for household consumption is not included in labor force statistics, and their unpaid labor for family enterprises, including farms, also tends to be overlooked, although their products are sold or traded. Underreporting is particularly common in countries where the culture frowns on women's economic participation (Bloom & Brender, 1993). Moreover, in developing countries, the bulk of women working for pay are in the informal sector (where street vending is a typical activity). This sector also tends to be unmeasured, although the international statistical system has been considering initiatives to address this omission.

9. World Bank and other researchers have traced how poor people in developing countries spend additional income and found that women are more likely than men to spend it on food, clothing, medical care, and education for their children (World Bank, 2001).

10. In the United States, men and women each currently spend, on average, an estimated 35% of the years between ages 20 and 69 raising children (King, 1999).

11. People who are uncomfortable with the idea of women without gender role constraints like to assume that women's responsibility for children is followed directly by a responsibility to care for aging parents. However, to the extent that such care is needed (it is often shared with other siblings and is generally short term where it is needed at all), increases in life and healthy expectancy in industrialized societies are delaying it until later in the life of both parent and adult child. Consequently, women whose children are grown are more likely to have a significant number of work years with few or no caregiving responsibilities.

12. Demographers estimate that about half of the 2000 U.S. population would not have been alive had mortality rates remained at 1900 levels throughout the century (White & Preston, 1996).

13. At an international meeting of experts on aging populations in the late 1990s, one author heard representatives from Japan and China reject the possibility of extending the work life to ease pressure on old-age benefit systems because, they said, "How can we promote young men if older ones don't leave?"

14. Data are not readily available to make comparisons across national boundaries, in large part because the definition of excluded populations varies so much. Generally, population groups are excluded on the basis of caste, religion, language, race, or national origin.

CHAPTER 5

Socioeconomic Transitions

The New Realities of the Global Workforce

Martha Farnsworth Riche[a] *and Michàlle E. Mor Barak*

> *There is no difference among classes of people. All the world is of divine origin.*
>
> —*The Mahabharata,* ancient Sanskrit epic

> *National states currently face a new set of economic conditions that push toward the neutralization of borders and diminish, or at least alter, state sovereignty and unilateral state action. Further, ... the emerging human rights regime makes the individual regardless of nationality, a possessor of rights.*
>
> —Saskia Sassen, *Guests and Aliens,* 1999

Changes in the global division of labor are blurring traditional geographic and corporate boundaries. At the same time, a growing concern for human rights in countries around the world calls for the inclusion of previously excluded people in mainstream economic activities. Whether national or international, the confrontation of people with different cultures and characteristics in the workplace is an increasingly salient management concern. This chapter examines the economic and social forces that create a more diverse

---

a. Martha Farnsworth Riche, PhD, Center for the Study of Economy and Society, Cornell University.

workforce worldwide. We examine trends of worker migration, occupational diversity among migrants, and educational attainment and their implications for creating increased diversity in the global workforce.

Flows of employers as well as workers are an important feature of the integration of the global economy. This is due in large part to imbalances in labor demand and supply (as described earlier in Chapter 4, Global Demographic Trends). Migration of working-age people has traditionally contributed to resolving such imbalances (Sassen, 1999), and it is still a solution for many in developing countries, whether they are highly skilled or simply seeking a livelihood. However, the numbers now entering working age in the developing countries are far larger than those willing to leave their homeland, with the latter already exceeding the numbers that better-off nations seem willing to absorb. Instead, globalization is allowing these countries to export many of their employers, particularly those in labor-intensive, low-paying industries that make a product that is transportable.

In strictly economic terms, it makes sense to move such jobs to people who find them superior to their local alternatives. Even when these jobs stay put, they often fall to immigrants because native-born workers demand wages that could price the products out of the international market. Kabeer (2000) illustrates both situations in her study of Bangladeshi apparel workers in England and Bangladesh. In the English context, the immigrant workers see themselves as exploited, whereas in Bangladesh, the workers find the same jobs a significant improvement over alternatives. In short, the context matters: jobs that are low paying and low status in an industrialized country can be exported as higher paying and higher status to developing countries.

Either way, migration of workers or migration of employers, the resulting encounter of people from different places, with different cultures and capabilities, is an important source of workplace diversity. This is particularly so because societies tend to racialize immigrants, describing them as "aliens" when they arrive, "minorities" if they settle. Describing long-settled populations, including many born in the new country, Sassen (1999) remarks, "In France they are referred to as immigrés even when they have become French" (p. 143). Similarly, Zinn (1994) comments on the euphemism used in Italy to refer to immigrants from developing countries: "Consider that the Italian euphemism for the immigrants from developing countries is *immigrati extracomunitari*—that is, non-EEC immigrants. As a U.S. citizen, I am technically an *extracommunitare*, too, though in fact no one would really consider me as one" (p. 54). In the Netherlands, Sweden, and Belgium, most immigrants are described as "minorities," and in Britain as "ethnic minorities," although the United Kingdom has its own British ethnic minorities—Scottish, Welsh, and Irish (Sassen, 1999).

A significant foreign presence in industrial-country workforces is not new. Historical studies such as Sassen's document a large role for foreign workers in

Western European countries before modern times, and other large industrial economies had their birth in traditional immigrant-receiving countries such as the United States and Canada. More recently, some European countries made up for population losses during World War II by recruiting workers from abroad. The history of immigration in France, for example, indicates that the makeup of immigrants has drastically changed in recent years. Most of the workers who immigrated in search of work post–World War II were Poles, Belgians, or Swiss, who were in essence Europeans with physical characteristics not much different from those of the French. In recent decades many of the immigrants are Black Africans and Asians (Alba & Silberman, 2002; History of Immigration in France, n.d.). Germany, too, developed a "guestworker" recruitment strategy in pursuit of economic development. Thousands of workers were brought in from countries such as Turkey, Yugoslavia, and Italy to work on German assembly lines with the mutual expectation that the situation would be temporary (Martin, 1994). Zlotnick (1994) says that after World War II, "the scale of the population inflows experienced by the main labor-importing countries of Europe was large" (p. 366). Although outflows were also large, as migration to the United States and other immigrant-receiving countries continued, the general assumption in these countries that foreign workers would leave when no longer needed was flawed. Unlike recent "return" migrants from within the European Union (EU), large numbers of foreign workers came with their families and stayed, constituting an important source of today's workforce diversity.

Differences in national population growth rates are likely to make the issue of workforce diversity increasingly salient in Europe in particular. The shrinking share of young and new native workforce entrants described earlier should increase the proportion of foreign-born workers and their descendants, even if immigration flows do not rise.

Before the severe global economic contraction that began in 2007, other developed economies, including oil-producing countries in the Middle East, also attracted large numbers of foreign migrants, largely from developing countries. From about the mid-1970s, the rapid depletion of the supply of Arab workers made countries in the Gulf region cast their recruitment net eastward to South and East Asian countries. Almost concurrently, the major labor exporters in the Arab region (such as Jordan and the Yemen Arab Republic) also became labor importers because they had to fill vacancies created by the departure of their workers for employment in oil-exporting countries (Athukorala, 1986). In Kuwait, the population grew rapidly and changed in composition as a result of work-related migration. By 1985, non-Kuwaitis constituted a full 60% of the population and nearly 80% of the labor force in that country (Al-Tuhaih, 1986). It remains to be seen whether, and where, such flows resume when economic trends reverse again.

Although rapid population growth per se is not correlated with growth in emigration, simple population growth means that the same relative flows contain more people. Moreover, there is an association between development and emigration. Improving economic conditions in poor countries give more of their people the resources to take advantage of superior opportunities in countries with relative labor shortages (Commission for the Study of International Migration and Cooperative Economic Development, 1990). Even when these opportunities mean relatively menial jobs that natives often no longer wish to do, the relatively higher wage scale makes migration attractive. After all, a menial job today can provide the seed money for a small business tomorrow or serve as the first step on an attractive career ladder. In short, population trends are making culturally based workforce diversity a fact of life for virtually all industrial countries.

Worker Migration

Managing such diversity has certain predictable aspects, if only because worker migrations tend to be geographically and occupationally patterned. Most international migrants head for countries with which they share either an historic relationship or geographic propinquity. European Union countries that have traditionally been immigrant receivers have long-standing relations with countries in their former colonial empires. In these countries, the proportion of total employment that is foreign or foreign-born is currently steady, though the numbers are substantial.[1] For instance, this proportion was virtually the same in 1996 as it was in 1986 in France, the Netherlands, and the United Kingdom (Sassen, 1999). Meanwhile, the proportion of foreign or foreign-born workers grew in countries like Austria and Germany that are primary destinations for people from neighboring countries in Eastern Europe.

For example, in Germany the fastest growth in the stock of foreign workers between 1985 and 1997 was in people from "other countries" (OECD, 2000). More workers from the traditionally prime sources—Turkey, Yugoslavia, Italy, Greece, and Portugal—still came, but they were each outnumbered by arrivals from "other countries." Although the statistics don't identify those countries, based on neighboring Austria's experience, they were largely Eastern European. In Austria, the stock of foreign workers grew almost 60% between 1988 and 1999, nearly all from Eastern Europe.

Still, the relatively low level of current cross-border mobility within the EU is evidenced by the general reluctance of most people to migrate for work, given alternative, albeit less attractive opportunities at home. Even though movement within the Union became easier while earnings differences remained significant, Sassen (1999) reported that in the mid-1990s, only 5 million EU natives were working in an EU country that was not their country of citizenship. In large part, this development recognized the overall success of the EU, as member countries that until recently sent large numbers of worker emigrants—notably Ireland and the countries around the Mediterranean—began to receive immigrants from outside the Union instead, as well as welcoming return migrants home.

By and large, most intra-EU worker migration mitigates the diversity challenge because it replicates past flows that were geographically patterned by shared language, culture, or history. For instance, the Irish have historically chosen the United Kingdom over other European destinations; the Italians, Spanish, and Portuguese have tended to choose France; and the Finns choose Sweden. Many of these migrants took advantage of improved conditions to return home, but others settled permanently in the host country. To the extent that they did not fully assimilate with the native population, they and their descendants represented the first wave of diversity concerns.

EU resident workers from non-EU countries exhibit a similar geographic patterning and represent a second wave of diversity concerns—culturally distant, but with a partially shared past. According to Sassen (1999), foreign residents in the United Kingdom tend to be from former colonies in Asia or Africa. Similarly, the Netherlands absorbed large waves of immigrants from its former colony Suriname in response to political problems tied to Suriname's transition to independence (Dew, 1994). In contrast, the United Kingdom has almost no Turk or Yugoslav immigrants—they tend to be found in Germany (OECD, 2009). Similarly, the bulk of North African residents in the EU are in France. Spain demonstrates the importance of both colonial relationships and geographic propinquity. In 2006, more than 266,000 Ecuadorians were working in Spain; the next largest group was from Morocco (250,000) (OECD, 2009).

In consequence, workforce diversity in EU countries has tended to be relatively predictable. Countries with vibrant economies tend to attract immigrants from their former colonies and/or their relatively impoverished neighbors, augmented by workers recruited from such traditional labor-exporting regions as Turkey and North Africa. Although mature migration flows tend to diversify their destinations, new flows, such as those now coming from parts of Asia or Africa, tend to be concentrated along historically traditional lines.

Immigration is beginning to diversify workplaces in some of the former Communist economies of Eastern Europe, including countries that have joined an expanded EU. In the first years after the changeover, immigrants tended to be expatriates returning home, but law and policy changes regarding long-term residency have fostered an intensified immigrant inflow, notably in the Czech Republic and also in Poland and Hungary (OECD, 2009). By and large, inflows come from neighboring countries, but there has also been a significant inflow of highly qualified employees from EU countries to manage subsidiaries set up in Central and Eastern Europe (OECD, 2000). Overall, increasing variety in both the sources and the destinations of worker migrants is making workforce diversity salient in the industrializing world, too. The World Bank (1995) has estimated that about one half of the new migrants that leave developing countries each year go to other developing countries. Although data in these countries are sparse, they suggest that these migrants tend to stay within their regions—African migrants tend to go to other countries in Africa, Asian migrants to other countries in Asia. For example, many Ghanaians left Ghana in the 1980s with the great majority of them going to Nigeria (Frempomaa, 1986), and Chinese migration to Thailand has been commonplace for decades (Sowell, 1996). Oil-rich, labor-poor countries in the Middle East have been the most notable recipients of worker migrants, especially from a wide range of Asian countries. However, the growing numbers of emigrants from East and Southeast Asia have been seeking a greater variety of destinations—including the Philippines, the Republic of Korea, Japan, the United States, and Thailand (Zlotnick, 1994). Hostile reactions by close neighbors, as when Malaysia expelled thousands of illegal Indonesian workers in 2002, if repeated, also make distant migration destinations more attractive.

The Gulf States are a potentially interesting laboratory for studying workplace diversity because they combine both aspects of international worker migration—very low and very high skill levels—with ethnic and cultural differences. Oil exploitation in these countries involves large numbers of low-wage, dirty, and dangerous jobs, as well as many highly skilled construction and management jobs. Meanwhile, the resulting oil riches until recently created enough pleasant, largely public sector jobs to employ the native-born workforce. It will be interesting to follow developments as states such as Saudi Arabia move into a stage at which ever larger numbers of native-born youth outstrip the ability of the public sector to absorb them, thus forcing diversity in the private sector workplace.

Central America (particularly Mexico) and the Caribbean have been a major source of worker migrants, particularly to the United States. Mexico is by far the largest source of foreign-born labor in the United States, followed by the Philippines (OECD, 2009). Joining with large new flows of migrants from Asia, particularly from Korea, China, India, and Vietnam, these immigrants have increased concerns about workforce diversity throughout North America. Overall, however, this region is considerably more favorable to immigrants than is Europe where the effect of immigration on the more homogeneous workforce and societies became an important political issue in several countries as the 21st century got under way.

Occupational Diversity

The occupational patterning of migrants is also predictable in broad categories, if both sides of the migration equation are considered. On the one hand, migrant workers move primarily in search of higher income. Less obviously, their opportunities and their place in the workforce are determined by the evolution of the receiving economy, as well as by the capabilities they possess relative to workers in the host country.

Analyses that focus on the global division of labor highlight the role of migration in filling low-pay, low-status jobs in the service sectors of developed countries. The resulting workplace diversity is one in which the workers are different from both the employers and the customers, each calling for specialized diversity management. However, in countries where immigrants make up a particularly large share of the labor force, they are dispersed more widely across the occupational and industry spectrum. One clear trend in the industrial countries that are members of the Organization for Economic Co-operation and Development is toward dispersion across industrial sectors; another is an increasing share of temporary and highly skilled workers in the total flows (OECD, 1998). Both trends contribute to broader-based workplace diversity.

A long and rich literature explores the diversity of contributions that immigrant workers have made, including fulfilling seasonal demands, making up for shortages of appropriate native workers, or supplying special skills.[2] Currently, two trends dominate the role of immigrant workers in national economies, with different effects on workplace diversity.

First, advanced economies that reward and subsidize high educational attainment are increasingly experiencing a need for workers to perform unskilled tasks, particularly the service tasks that national economies cannot export. These jobs attract people from countries where well-paying jobs are few and wages generally low. In addition to making more money than they could at home, migrants also gain access to a wider array of opportunities—for their children as well as themselves. For example, South Korea, a traditionally homogeneous society, has created a migrant worker program in order to fill jobs that can be described with the "three Ds"—Difficult, Dirty, and Dangerous—because of native South Koreans' aversion to these jobs as the country prospered, starting in the 1980s (Seol, 1999). Similarly, during Nigeria's period of relative economic buoyancy in the 1970s, many of its neighbors, particularly Ghana, but also Burkina Faso, Togo, Benin, and Niger, suffered their worst setbacks. Large numbers of workers from those countries flocked to Nigeria in search of jobs and a better standard of living. There were professionals like doctors, lawyers, engineers, architects, university lecturers, teachers, and nurses; there were middle-level skilled workers such as technicians and artisans for the building industry; and there were thousands of unskilled laborers to fill the gaps shunned by Nigerians, such as domestic workers, construction laborers, conservancy workers, casual dockworkers, and hawkers for the food and beverage industry. Many of these were undocumented or in an irregular situation as regards entry, stay, or employment (Frempomaa, 1986).

The World Bank (1995) estimated in 1995 that this type of migration may have accounted for 70% of contemporary migrant flows. As Sassen (1988) points out, the concentration of immigrant labor in service jobs in developed countries is essentially the counterpart of the export of low-wage manufacturing jobs to developing countries. In both cases, economic integration is making labor specialization into a global rather than national phenomenon. Such migration increases the overall diversity of the workforce in the receiving country but not necessarily the diversity of its workplaces.

Agriculture is a common example of substituting foreign workers for native-born workers. The OECD reports that during the late 1990s, overall employment in agriculture decreased in several European countries while the number of foreign farm workers increased. In contrast, both overall employment and the numbers of foreign workers increased in the services sector in most of these same countries (OECD, 2000). Thus, workplace diversity varies across economic sectors. Nevertheless, the economic cycle affects all such arrangements, as foreigners' employment fluctuates more markedly than total employment.

Second, highly skilled people from developing countries often migrate in search of better opportunities than their home economies can offer. India is a notable example of a country whose educational system has outstripped its economic development. Emigration is easier for the highly skilled because they are more likely to have information about employment opportunities, including personal connections or experiences, as well as the resources to invest in migration.

Meanwhile, receiving countries often have special programs to facilitate such migration, especially for temporary workers. For example, the United States saw a dramatic increase in H1B visas during the high-tech industry boom of the 1990s. These visas allowed high-tech employers to import electrical engineers and computer programmers from places such as India and China for up to 6 years. However, when the boom became a bust, the number of visas decreased (from 195,000 visas in 2000 to 65,000 in 2003). Rather than importing workers and paying them relatively higher U.S. salaries, some companies began exporting the jobs to countries such as China and India where they can pay much lower local salaries (Hiltzik, 2003).

The increasing internationalization of Japan's economy prompted a revision of national immigration policy permitting easier access to temporary work visas by foreign nationals. In response to Japan's 1990 Immigration Control and Refugee Recognition Act (ICRRA), highly skilled workers in specified areas (e.g., engineering, medicine, law, and investment banking) have migrated from countries such as Brazil, Peru, and the United States (Friman, 2001; Sassen, 1994).

Although there is no indication that the natural human reluctance to leave home and family is any less pronounced among the highly skilled, in some countries policy failures by governments have encouraged large numbers of skilled people to emigrate. Scientists, especially doctors, university professors, and other professionals, have trouble finding work if a country's educational system has produced more than the country can employ. This is particularly true in countries with policies that depress capital formation and thus the demand for skilled labor (World Bank, 1995). In any case, this migration spreads workforce diversity to a variety of workplaces in receiving countries. Yet migrant workers are often completely disenfranchised. Because they lack political rights enjoyed by citizens and are unable to vote, organize politically, and bring pressure to bear on government, they can be among the most down-trodden in society, working under terms unacceptable to nationals. They are also vulnerable to expulsion if they become too assertive (Cholewinski, 1997; Guerin-Gonzales & Strikwerda, 1993; Linder, 1992).

Whether high- or low-skilled, large numbers of migrants work abroad for a limited period and then return home. In some cases, they may have earned enough money to better their situation at home; in others, the sending economy may have created new opportunities. Ireland used to be an example of the former; then it became a good example of the latter. Widespread prosperity in the EU also turned Italy, Spain, Greece, and Portugal from net exporters of workers to net importers.

Meanwhile, there is growing evidence that workers from both high- and low-skill segments think of themselves as part of a cross-border and even global labor market. When travel was costly and difficult, migrants settled in the new country for good, or at least until retirement. Now low-cost transportation and communication technology makes it possible for workers to call two places "home."[3] Rather than settle permanently in a new country, many worker migrants prefer to maintain their residence in their country of origin if they are allowed to freely circulate.[4] Managing diversity that results from this circular migration may require different tools and policies than managing diversity that represents permanent settlement.

Migration of Employers

In contrast to the previous period of economic globalization (1850 to 1914) when massive emigration of working-age people helped to resolve national imbalances between labor supply and labor demand, the current period of globalization has also featured mass migration of employers.[5] Essentially, in a liberalized trade environment, transnational corporations (mostly based in developed countries) export capital to reduce their labor costs and, indirectly, create new markets for their products (see Box 5.1). The resulting workplace can feature a cross-cultural confrontation of foreign management and domestic labor, sometimes complicated by in-migration of skilled personnel from still other countries.

BOX 5.1
Outsourcing: The Experience for the Displaced Workers and for Those Who Receive the Jobs

Myra Bronstein lost her job when her employer, Watchmark-Comnitel, out-sourced the company's software-testing positions to India. Before she left the company, she had a choice to make. She could either train her Indian replacement or forfeit her severance package. When commenting on her situation, Ms. Bronstein said, "I can assure you that this is one of the most stressful, demeaning, dehumanizing experiences of my life. No one should have to deal with the issues of being a newly laid-off person . . . while at the same time being forced to train their replacements." Ms. Bronstein is not alone. Many technology workers are given the choice of losing their severance packages or training their replacements (Cook, 2004).

The outsourcing trend is expected to continue. Forrester Research predicts that 3.3 million service jobs in the United States will be outsourced overseas by 2015 (Cook, 2004). Most of those jobs have been going to India where large centers are being built to write software, manage technical support, and provide customer service and other activities for U.S. corporations. The practice came under scrutiny in the United States when the media reported that laid-off employees who encountered problems in receiving public assistance in the form of food stamps were calling a customer service center that was located in India. The irony was not lost on public officials who ordered the subcontractor to relocate the food stamp customer service center back to the United States (MacPherson, 2004).

The reason for the outsourcing is obvious: cost savings. For example, Indian computer programmers earn about $12,500 annually, which is one sixth the average of U.S. programmers (Drajem, 2004). Sherry Toly, spokesperson for Watchmark-Comnitel, summed up the company's decision to outsource positions to India. "The situation was to close our doors or look at ways to reduce our operations so we can stay in business during a very, very difficult time" (Cook, 2004).

What does outsourcing mean to the workers in India? Some think that at such relatively low wages, the workers in India are living close to poverty, or worse. In fact, for college-educated young people in India, a job at a call center is considered a plum position ("The Good Life," 2003). Though the work may involve long hours on the phone or at a computer terminal and working around the clock, the pay is good relative to other jobs in India, and the work environment is typically pleasant. These jobs are highly desired by young educated people because of the scarcity of jobs in India, and often thousands of job seek-ers show up for job interviews when a new center opens up. Not every employer who has outsourced work is happy with the results. Wesley Bertch of Life Time Fitness had an Indian company write software for his company. He was initially drawn by the rate of $6 per hour, compared with $60 per hour for U.S. programmers. However, after receiving software filled with bugs, and then being charged to fix the errors, Bertch regretted his decision. Bertch has joined a growing number of businesses, such as Lehman Brothers, Capital One, and Dell Computers, that have reversed their outsourcing decisions and returned positions to the United States (Stone, 2004).

Foreign direct investment (FDI)—the net amount of investment by non-residents in enterprises in which nonresidents exercise significant management control—is an imperfect but nonetheless useful measure of this change because it is directly tied to production.[6] Foreign direct investment has increased considerably as a proportion of the world's capital formation, according to the United Nations Conference on Trade and Development (UNCTAD)—reaching nearly $2 billion in 2007 (United Nations, 2009b). In turn, employment by foreign affiliates grew from 19.9 million in 1982 to 77.4 million in 2008.

UNCTAD counts some 82,000 transnational corporations with around 810,000 foreign affiliates, spanning virtually all countries and economic activi-ties. However, the bulk of this investment (over half in 2008, according to UNC-TAD) still flows to the industrial economies, creating various forms of workplace diversity.[7] Sometimes the diversity impact is restricted to cultural differences in the executive suite, as in the failed merger/acquisition of the U.S. car producer Chrysler and the German producer Daimler-Benz. The German chairman of DaimlerChrysler, Juergen Schrempp, fired several leading executives at the Chrysler division in 2000, including American unit president James Holden, who was replaced by longtime Mercedes-Benz executive Dieter Zetsche. Schrempp, who laid off more than 40,000 employees after taking over Daimler-Benz in 1995, picked Zetsche because of his reputation for slashing jobs to cut costs. Indeed, soon after he was hired, Zetsche directed the layoff of 20% of the U.S. workforce at DaimlerChrysler's truck division, Freightliner, eliminating 3,800 jobs after orders fell. When the merger took place in 1998, top Chrysler officials made tens of millions of dollars in buyouts and other bonuses before leaving the company, with little regard for the long-term health of the business or its employees. Because of "golden parachute" clauses, which provided especially generous stock options in the event of a takeover or merger, former Chrysler CEO Robert Eaton personally netted $62.9 million (Roberts & White, 2000).

At other times, FDI pits managers from one country against workers in another, as exemplified by trade union and gender-based challenges to Japanese car executives in their U.S. plants. The Mitsubishi plant in Normal, Illinois, was one of the most automated yet least productive plants in the industry. It was also known for the abusive, humiliating—and illegal—way female workers were treated. Remarkably, the plant now is held up as a model of workplace reform, thanks to training, a zero-tolerance policy on discrimination and sexual harassment, and a mission statement that puts respect for others ahead of even vehicle quality.

Japanese management had been thinking of closing the plant due to the negative attention it was receiving. In 1998, Mitsubishi agreed to pay $34 million to settle a sexual harassment lawsuit brought by the Equal Employment Opportunity Commission on behalf of 500 female workers at the plant. The high-profile case dragged on for 3 years, sapping worker morale already depleted by a distant relationship between American workers and Japanese managers. The lawsuit told a story of a bleak workplace: sexual graffiti written on fenders about to pass female line workers, pornographic pictures taped on walls, male workers taunting women with wrenches and air compressors, and women who complained of being fired or passed over for advancement. Then in 2001, while the American plant manager and his team were working on changing the plant's culture regarding attitudes toward women, Mitsubishi agreed to pay a multimillion-dollar settlement to African American and Hispanic workers who were claiming racial and job discrimination. To the extent that strengthening the capacity for innovation is behind many of these joint ventures, managing workplace diversity can involve managing differences among employees who are relative equals in terms of workplace status and are affected by unacceptable breaches in their human rights.

The smaller but growing share of direct foreign investment going to developing countries has received more attention, in part because the diversity implications can be encouraging on the one hand, but troubling on the other. Essentially, declining transportation and telecommunications costs have combined with trade liberalization, capital mobility, and globalizing markets to integrate economic activity around the world (Perraton, Goldblatt, Held, & McGrew, 2000). These cost declines have combined with trends in labor supply to shift much manufacturing for the world market to several developing countries (Bloom & Brender, 1993). Indeed, the global slowdown that followed the peaking of world GDP in 2000 intensified competitive pressure on transnational corporations, thus accentuating the value of lower-cost locations. There is no reason to suspect that the subsequent, more severe global downturn has changed this relationship.

Perhaps for this reason, foreign direct investment in developing countries has proved relatively resistant to broad economic downturns. The UN reported that on a net basis (inflows less outflows), FDI flows were the only positive component of private capital flows to developing countries and transition economies during 2000–2001 (United Nations, 2002). However, these flows are unevenly distributed. In 2001, the five largest recipients accounted for more than 60% of the total inflows into developing countries (led by Mexico, China, and South Africa) all with large and growing underemployed workforces.

In addition to employing underemployed workers, such investment can support the development of the host economy by increasing access to technology, workforce quality, or export potential. Concerns arise when the investment exploits and abuses the country, particularly its natural and human resources. For example, in 1984 in Bhopal, India, because of low safety standards, an explosion at the U.S.-based Union Carbide chemical plant released a deadly gas that formed a cloud over a large populated area resulting in an environmental disaster and the death of an estimated 2,500 people (see Box 5.2). In other instances, export-oriented manufacturers may "slice the value chain" to remove labor-intensive, low-skill processes to countries with large numbers of people willing to work for low wages. Although in some cases these workers may improve their income, or acquire new skills, in other cases, workers may be exploited and even abused, as documented by organizations advocating the institution and implementation of minimum labor standards.[8]

BOX 5.2
The Bhopal Disaster: Economic Exploitation and Human Tragedy

In the early morning hours of December 3, 1984, the U.S.-based Union Carbide Corporation's chemical plant in Bhopal, India, exploded, killing thousands and creating the worst industrial disaster the world has seen. The Bhopal gas-leak disaster has raised a number of complex legal, ethical, economic, technological, sociopolitical, and ecological questions and issues (Dias, 1997). More than 10,000 people were killed (several thousand immediately and many more later as a result of injuries and diseases) and estimates put the numbers of people injured or disabled as a result of the explosion at about 2 million. Whole communities were displaced and impoverished. Commenting on the settlement reached by the Supreme Court of India in 1989 (the original claim of US$3 billion was settled for only US$470 million—a settlement considered by many jurists and human rights activists as grossly unfair) Justice P. N. Bhagwati noted, "The Court order places the value of Indian life at a ridiculously low figure because, after all, we are browns and blacks and not favored whites!"

(Continued)

(Continued)

Union Carbide initially blamed the Bhopal accident on Sikh terrorists. Later, the company blamed it on disgruntled employees who tried to sabotage the plant. However, most experts agree that the accident resulted from Union Carbide's use of inferior safety standards at the Indian plant, compared with those found in the United States. One example of the differences in standards is the leak-detection system that was used. At Union Carbide's Virginia plant, a computerized system was installed that kept track of pressures, temperatures, and chemical levels, indicating where a leak was occurring. At the Bhopal plant, gas leaks were detected by human sight or smell (Bhargava, 1986).

Implications for Diversity of Gender, Disability, and Sexual Orientation

Whether positive or negative, workplace diversity is an issue. Migration of both people and employers not only puts people from different countries into the same workplace, it also imports their cultural dispositions regarding other forms of diversity. Racial, ethnic, and religious diversity are almost a given in most situations involving cross-national origins. Age diversity can also be an issue because migrants tend to be young; and so can disability, because migrants tend to come from countries where there are not sufficient jobs to go around and investing in the disabled can be considered a "luxury." Probably the most sensitive and least discussed form of diversity relates to sexual orientation. Cultural taboos can bring a strongly disruptive element into workplaces where law and custom join to protect a range of choices.

Gender diversity is a major issue in most immigrant-receiving countries, though in some areas such as the Gulf States, women typically work in separate occupational and physical environments. A notable concern is the widespread employment of young women in export-manufacturing zones, reportedly because their culture and traditions make them malleable and easy to exploit (Elson, 1999). Southeast Asian girls, exploited economically and physically by older men from wealthier Asian countries, are probably the most negative image of today's workplace diversity. On the other hand, migration of employers, employees, information, and technology between countries can increase workers' awareness of their rights in the workplace (see Box 5.3).

BOX 5.3
Sexual Harassment and the High-Tech Industry

The United States and India are closely bound in the global computer software industry, and several Indian software exporters have affiliates in the United States, including the largest: Infosys Technologies Limited. The U.S.-based company's highest-paid employee, the head of global sales and marketing, resigned in 2002 after his executive assistant sued him and the company for sexual harassment (Arnold, 2002). According to the newspaper account, "The lawsuit . . . sent Indian software companies scurrying to make sure their policies comply with United States law."

Although Indian laws defined sexual harassment in the workplace in 1997, human resource specialists there said the issue had been largely ignored, in part because in India, women feared the stigma attached to reporting. However, in this industry large numbers of Indians work in overseas offices and at customer sites, making multicultural interaction more frequent and more fraught. After the litigation at Infosys, one large firm undertook an audit, put its reworked policy on its intranet, and increased cross-cultural sensitivity training for employees. Another firm with multiple overseas offices undertook a worldwide review of its employee conduct policy, which had been culture- and country-specific. As one executive put it, "We are sensitizing our managers in issues like gender discrimination, noncompetitive behavior, and age discrimination." And the Infosys chief executive concluded, "Multicultural interaction is becoming a very important part of our work environment."

These examples point out the multiple aspects of diversity in the workplace. Managing all these forms of diversity in an increasingly cross-national workplace requires an understanding of cultural differences. Where migrant workers are involved, employers need to effectively communicate the host country's workplace norms. Where migrant employers are involved, managers may have to address multiple constituencies, at home as well as in the host country.

Educational Trends and Workforce Diversity

The other important demographic element that has broad implications for diversity in the global workforce is the rising level of educational attainment around the world (see Table 5.1). In the developed regions, secondary education has become virtually universal for both men and women, although enrollment rates declined in Eastern Europe in the transition from communism to a market economy (United Nations, 2000b). Meanwhile, enrollment rates are increasing in developing countries, though more slowly for women than for men. Even in sub-Saharan Africa and Southern Asia, where girls are routinely excluded from education, total enrollment ratios are improving.

At higher levels of education, such as upper secondary, women are nearly as well represented as men—indeed, in some regions, they are better represented (Table 5.1). Thus, even in countries where most women have much less education than men, the expectations of educated women workers may not be so different from women workers in other parts of the world, albeit quite different from other women in their country, particularly the rural poor.

Table 5.1 Trends in Primary and Secondary Education

| | Secondary school-age population | Upper secondary | | | |
| | | gross enrollment ratio | | gender parity ratio | |
	2008	1999	2007 (2006)	1999 (2000)	2007
Arab States	41,274,924	47	52	0.93	0.97
Central and Eastern Europe	34,914,377	80	85	0.99	0.94
Central Asia	11,372,719	83	89	0.93	0.96
East Asia and the Pacific	210,345,842	46	63	0.98	1.03
Latin America and the Caribbean	66,454,258	62	74	1.13	1.14
North America and Western Europe	62,098,799	98	98	1.03	1.01
South and West Asia	244,938,755	31	39	0.72	0.81
Sub-Saharan Africa	108,601,797	19	26	0.84	0.78

SOURCE: UNESCO, Key Statistical Tables on Education. Consulted on 9/29/09 at www.uis.unesco.org/.

In a few places around the world, such as the Barefoot College in Tilonia, India, innovative educational initiatives are helping the rural poor in developing countries to improve their lives through educational attainment (see Box 5.4).

BOX 5.4
Barefoot College: Educating the Rural Poor

Urban engineers in India said it was technically impossible to build hand water pumps in Ladakh, a remote Indian region in the Himalayas at an elevation of 15,000 feet. However, a group of mostly illiterate drillers proved the engineers wrong. Not only did they install the pumps, but they also managed to get them to work throughout the winter when temperatures drop to −50 deg C (−58 deg F). Now, over 50,000 people benefit from the use of these hand pumps ("2004 Tyler Laureates," 2004). These illiterate drillers are a small sampling of the people who have benefited from Bunker Roy's Barefoot College.

Founded in 1986, Barefoot College was designed to alleviate the suffering of the rural poor in India. The school is located in Tilonia, a village of 2,000 people in Rajasthan, one of India's largest and poorest states where over 45% of men and 80% of women are illiterate. Additionally, more than half of the children between the ages of 6 and 14 do not attend school ("Barefoot College," 2003).

"We believe that paper-qualified, urban-trained experts and professionals can easily be replaced by people from the village," says Mr. Roy. "People in Tilonia do not need knowledge; they need confidence and assurance that the skills they already have are enough to improve their quality of life" ("Barefoot College," 2003). Barefoot College has helped students learn to be effective teachers, doctors, health care workers, solar engineers, hand pump mechanics, designers, accountants, and communicators ("Barefoot College," 2003). The end result is that the school has helped create jobs for nearly 7,000 people, including women and youths (United Nations Environment Programme, 2004). The benefits of Barefoot College do not end with the creation of jobs. It is also educating the next generation with its night schools. Over 150 schools were created to meet the needs of children who cannot go to school during the day, typically because they are too busy grazing sheep and goats. Therefore, the classes are offered at night and taught by local residents who have been trained at Barefoot College.

Contrary to typical trends in developing countries, the night schools have attracted more girls than boys, thanks to the advanced lighting system they use. The lighting increases the school's safety, which increases the likelihood

(Continued)

> (Continued)
>
> that parents will send their girls to school (B. Roy, personal communication, April 28, 2004). Barefoot College has earned awards from such prestigious organizations as the United Nations. Its accomplishments span an array of areas, including the environment (for powering the schools with solar electricity), children's parliament (which manages the night schools), promoting volunteerism, social entrepreneurship, and education. If imitation is the best form of compliment, then Bunker Roy and Barefoot College have received that honor as well. India's Department of Education has adopted the night school idea and approved the creation of 275 additional night schools in eight states ("Barefoot College," 2003).

Enrollment in higher education is also increasing around the world, although developed countries still maintain a substantial advantage, especially in the English-speaking countries outside Europe and Japan. Enrollments in tertiary education (including technical education) have been growing particularly rapidly in Asia, and also in Central and Eastern Europe (Table 5.2).

Table 5.2   Trends in Postsecondary Education

	Enrollment in tertiary education	
	1999 (2000)	2007
Arab States	5,165,102	7,146,174
Central and Eastern Europe	12,420,822	20,749,657
Central Asia	1,212,131	1,994,408
East Asia and the Pacific	23,081,655	46,451,377
Latin America and the Caribbean	10,664,030	17,757,024
North America and Western Europe	28,240,250	34,008,815
South and West Asia	12,059,852	18,409,207
Sub-Saharan Africa	2,136,026	4,139,797

SOURCE: UNESCO, Key Statistical Tables on Education. Consulted on 9/29/09 at www.uis.unesco.org/.

Taken together with population growth, educational improvements in the developing world are changing the comparative advantage of different populations in the global workforce. Although the developed countries will continue to have the world's best-educated populations, they account for a decreasing share of the world's educated working-age people. China alone is projected to have more working-age people in all educational categories than Europe and North America combined by 2020 (Lutz & Gui, 2000). Even if the pace of educational improvement in the developing countries falters, simple population growth will give these countries a majority of people aged 20–65 with a higher education by 2030, according to estimates from the International Institute for Applied Systems Analysis (IIASA). Already, the majority of adults who possess a secondary education (generally equated with the skilled workforce) live in the developing world (Lutz & Goujon, 2001).

The same combination of population and educational trends is also growing the less educated or unskilled population in developing countries, particularly in South Asia and sub-Saharan Africa. The numbers of adults with no education at all will continue to grow in sub-Saharan Africa and the Middle East over the next three decades, according to the IIASA estimates (Lutz & Goujon, 2001). The numbers with a primary education will grow substantially in all developing regions (except China and Central Asia, where growth will be most intense among working-age people with a secondary education).

Thus, from a labor supply standpoint, the world's working-age population at all educational levels is shifting from the developed to the developing world. Other things equal, the extent to which these economies absorb these workers productively will influence how many of them migrate in search of employment or how many transnational employers move to the developing world to find employees. Either outcome will increase diversity in workplaces around the world.

This broad-based improvement in the educational level of the global workforce also suggests an improved context for managing and implementing inclusive workforce policies. Ignorance is generally related to intransigence regarding interpersonal differences; education, to greater acceptance of those differences. Already surveys suggest that contemporary young people are more tolerant than their elders regarding many kinds of diversity, if only because global information and entertainment networks have increased their shared knowledge.

Summary and Conclusion

Workforces are becoming increasingly diverse, due largely to the interaction of demographic trends and economic evolution and to the successes of the international human rights movement. These trends should continue to promote diversity in the global workplace although the social tensions they engender, along with broader economic or political failures, could set them back in the short term. By and large, though, managing workforce diversity effectively will be necessary in a globalizing world and also benefit national economies as well as national and international employers.

For instance, countries can enhance their economic success via their ability to welcome workers from other countries. This is especially true for countries that are experiencing tight labor markets, either because economic growth is outpacing labor force growth or a particular sector needs staffing up. Ireland offers a useful example, as the government helped create a comparative advantage for transnational firms' sales and support call centers. As a result, some companies concentrated their European operations under one Irish roof, bringing in natives from all over Europe to help their compatriots with their purchases—in their own language—when they dialed a toll-free number from home (Cowell, 2000). Where public policy deliberately creates diversity, managing it requires attention from both government and society, including help if economic conditions change and foreign workers need or want to return home.

The globalization of information and entertainment, hastened by the Internet, is reaching virtually everywhere and, in the process, promoting more encounters among diverse people. Young people are more inclined to use these communications channels and thus to take these encounters for granted, fostering a greater acceptance of diversity. As diversity becomes more widespread, they may become impatient with elders who display the old reticence, or old patterns of discrimination.

At the same time, traditionalists may find it difficult to change long-held attitudes and beliefs. This is more likely to the extent that these attitudes are rooted in religion, which so many cite to explain their reluctance to accept workers who have diverse sexual orientations. And both governments and employers can be daunted by the financial costs of accommodating worker diversity, such as retooling the workplace to meet the needs of persons with different physical abilities.

Thus, part of the challenge of managing workforce diversity is managing the diversity of people's preconceived notions about those outside their own mainstream culture, especially those notions acquired when social norms and economic needs were different. In that sense, the demographics of diversity include managing the demographics of past attitudes as well as future workforce trends.

Notes

1. Migration figures should be viewed with caution, as described in Chapter 4, Note 5.

2. Sassen (1999) provides a good historical overview from the European perspective.

3. This choice is facilitated by the growing acceptance of dual nationality.

4. Sassen (1999) offers the examples of Polish women working as cleaners in Germany and Africans working in Italy. Street peddlers, selling objects made at home, are a common example; so is the growing number of computer-related technicians.

5. Williamson (1998) offers an insightful comparison of the current and early period of globalization, along with an instructive account of the earlier antiglobalization backlash.

6. For instance, FDI measures understate the growth of transnational corporations, which finance much of their growth internally or from capital markets (Perraton et al., 2000).

7. The United States continued to be the largest recipient of total FDI inflows in 2008 (United Nations, 2009b).

8. Kabeer (2000) provides an example of the difficulty of making this distinction. She found that work in an apparel factory was socially as well as financially empowering for Bangladeshi women, who are normally tightly controlled by family members. A particularly interesting insight came from the women who told her that being locked into the factory was a form of maintaining their purdah (seclusion) and thus a necessary condition for them to be able to work. This stands in sharp contrast to the Western activists who use such conditions as "proof" of exploitation.

PART II

Social Psychological Perspectives of Workforce Diversity

CHAPTER 6

Defining Diversity in a Global Context

Prejudice and Discrimination

Bury me standing; I've been on my knees all my life.[1]

This saying from Romany, the language of the Rom (or Roma) people, refers to the centuries-long discrimination suffered by this persecuted minority in Europe. The Rom are descendants of a wandering people who appeared in Europe in the 13th or 14th century, most likely a lost caste from India that was expelled or voluntarily left. Europeans originally thought that they came from Egypt, and hence they came to be called "Gypsies."

In recent years, there has been a tendency to downplay the adverse implications of diversity. A few years ago, I observed a diversity seminar in the Southern Californian branch of an international high-tech company. The trainer, with elaborated enthusiasm, exclaimed, "Isn't it wonderful—we are *all* diverse! *Each one of us* is different from the other." She went on to lead an exercise in which participants were asked to identify the qualities that make them "diverse." Those qualities included salient individual characteristics such as race, gender, age, sexual orientation, and disability but also included less significant attributes such as the region where they grew up, the high school they attended, and even their hair color and taste in clothing and foods. The trainer was clearly trying to help the participants develop empathy for people who are different from the mainstream in American society through identifying the qualities that make all people different. Her approach, however, represents a common confusion between benign differences and differences that have practical or even detrimental consequences in people's lives.

It is important to note that there is a fundamental difference between attributes that make a person a unique human being and those that—based on group membership rather than individual characteristics—yield *negative or positive consequences*. For example, growing up in rural China would create barriers to employment, whereas growing up in urban China could give a job seeker a significant advantage in the job market; being a man in Japan would be associated with more and better job opportunities than being a woman; and belonging to the lower castes in India would be a disadvantage in the workplace as compared with belonging to the upper castes.

Keep in mind that workforce diversity *is not* about the anthropological differences between people that "make them special" (using the terminology of that diversity trainer); diversity *is* about belonging to groups that are visibly or invisibly different from whatever is considered "mainstream" in society. In short, it is about being susceptible to employment consequences as a result of one's association within or outside certain social groups.

The interpersonal characteristics that create those group identities may be different in various parts of the world. Regional differences, for example, may be benign in some areas but consequential in others. If you grew up in northern California, your high school experiences might have been different from those of someone who grew up 500 miles to the south in Southern California, though you would not be treated differently in the workplace. However, if you grew up in southern Italy and applied for a job in northern Italy, a distance of about 400 miles, you might suffer negative consequences because employers might consider you less educated and less hardworking than your northern counterparts. This is due to the prevailing notion among northern Italians of southern Italians' inferior status (Verdicchio, 1999).

China is another country where significant regional differences have major implications for employment. A few years ago I was invited to lecture in several universities in Beijing. During my presentation at People's University, a student complained about the difficulties that she and her female colleagues would encounter in finding suitable jobs upon graduation. She noted the interaction between regional affiliation and gender in creating unspoken employment-determinant diversity categories in China: "There are four groups of job seekers in China in descending order of advantage: urban men, urban women, rural men, and rural women."

Geographic region, gender, race, ethnicity, or other distinguishable characteristics may thus define a person as belonging to a more- or less-favored group and can have either beneficial or detrimental consequences for one's job prospects. What are the positive or negative consequences of belonging to a more- or less-favored group? This chapter examines several concepts that are often used to express psychological processes and actual behaviors involved in intergroup relations that lead to the dominance or advantage of one group over another in society. As a first step, we need to understand how *group distinction categories*—what we commonly call diversity—are being defined around the world.

Workforce Diversity Defined

In the summer of 2001, I was fortunate to receive a grant from the Rockefeller Foundation to organize an international colloquium on global perspectives of workforce diversity. With the magnificent backdrop of Lake Como and the Swiss Alps, the 18 distinguished scholars from 14 different countries met at the Foundation's Villa Serbelloni in Bellagio. As the meetings got under way, it quickly became clear that the concept of workforce diversity did not travel well across cultural and national boundaries. The representative from China and the representative from Mexico both noted that if the term *workforce diversity* were to be translated to their respective national languages, it would not make sense. They indicated that the term "diversity" itself is usually used to describe the varieties in fauna and flora[2] and does not yet have the human resource connotation it has acquired in other parts of the world. The discussions at the Bellagio conference illustrate the challenge of generating terms that will have common meanings across national boundaries and facilitate effective communication aimed at solving problems of intergroup relations in the workplace. Although the U.S. human resource connotation of the word *diversity* is gradually catching on in many parts of the world (the European Union, South Africa, and India are some examples), the specific definitions may be different. A discussion of these definitions is, therefore, warranted.

As noted in the earlier chapters, the globalizing economy with its trends of immigration and worker migration makes workforce diversity an increasingly common phenomenon in many countries around the world. Europe's societies are becoming heterogeneous, and even traditionally homogeneous societies such as Korea and Japan are seeing greater diversity, primarily in their major cities. In recent years, research and scholarly work on diversity has been generated in parts of the world other than the United States. Consequently, there is a growing need for a broader and inclusive definition of *diversity* that will allow both scientists and practitioners to communicate clearly across cultural and national boundaries. Philomena Essed (1996, 2002) notes the difficulties posed by the use of the concept of diversity in her home country, the Netherlands, as well as the broader European perspective. She and other authors note the different connotations the diversity concept has in Europe. Point and Singh (2003) identified how the definition of "diversity" and its dimensions vary across Europe through an examination of diversity statements on 241 top companies' Web sites in eight European countries (Finland, France, Germany, the Netherlands, Norway, Sweden, Switzerland, and the United Kingdom). With respect to identifying the dimensions of diversity, gender was the most cited dimension, appearing on 83 Web sites, followed by culture on 79 Web sites. The multiracial, multicultural, and multiethnic meanings of diversity are dominant in online statements, especially in German companies. Diversity statements on the Web sites of UK companies feature race and ethnicity rather than culture, while French and German companies have statements about the broader notion of culture. "Cultural diversity" for the French includes both cultural expression and cultural differences. The United Kingdom was the only country with online statements that reported almost all the identified dimensions, while French companies disclosed the least information about diversity dimensions. Swiss and Norwegian online statements often mentioned workforce diversity without providing any specific dimension, whereas Finnish companies tended to provide a precise definition of "diversity."

The literature presents a plethora of definitions and there is confusion about the nature of diversity: Is diversity about demographic categories, different identities, various life perspectives, life conditions, or all of the above (Essed & de Graaff, 2002)? Because of these varying definitions and country-specific cultural context, there are different connotations to the term *diversity*. In the Netherlands, for example, "when you say 'diversity,' the Dutch ear will hear 'ethnic difference'" (Essed & de Graaff, 2002), and the word *diversity* is often used interchangeably with the word *immigrants*, as well (Glastra, Meerman, Schedler, & deVries, 2000). The following excerpt from an article by Helen Bloom (2002) further illustrates this point.

> To U.S. corporations, *diversity* is mainly about race, ethnicity, gender, religion, physical disability, age, and sexual orientation. To Europeans, *diversity* is about national cultures and languages—and it is a reality with which they have always lived. So when Americans tell Europeans to establish a diversity policy, their reaction is, "We already have diversity! It is not something we must invent or control. It's there by definition."
>
> Many Europeans don't even understand what Americans mean by *diversity*. In many European languages, the closest word to it emphasizes differences and implies categorization, partition, and separation. To them, then, the term means the reverse of the inclusion principles underlying U.S. diversity policies. In addition, European managers now connect the term with U.S. social and legal issues, and react against it: "If this is American stuff, I don't want to know it. Americans have unique problems. We want to do our own thing." For Europeans, that means finding ways to overcome linguistic and national differences in order to forge pan-European business strategies. (p. 48) [italics added]

A review of the business, organization, and human resource literature produced three types of definitions of *diversity:* (a) narrow category–based definitions (e.g., gender, racial, or ethnic differences); (b) broad category–based definitions (e.g., a long list of categories including such variables as marital status and education); and (c) definitions based on a conceptual rule (e.g., variety of perspectives, differences in perceptions and actions). The following sections explain this typology, and Table 6.1 provides examples for each of the definition categories.

NARROW CATEGORY–BASED DIVERSITY DEFINITIONS

The concept of workforce diversity originated in the U.S.-based organizational literature because, having defined itself early as a country of immigrants, the United States had to contend with diversity from its inception (Kurowski, 2002). Therefore, some of the initial definitions of diversity were anchored in the U.S. experience and its mixed racial/ethnic, census-based categories of diversity, such as Caucasians (or Whites), African Americans (or Blacks), Hispanics (or Latinos), Asian Americans, and Native Americans. The narrow category–based diversity definitions are determined by discrimination legislation and include gender, racial and ethnic groups, national origin, disability, and age.[3] These U.S.-based definitions are not necessarily transferable to other cultures or applicable in other countries[4] (Ferner, Almond, & Colling, 2005). As an illustration, Sheila Walker (2002) discusses the complexity of economic differences in distinguishing racial or ethnic differences in Brazil as compared with the United States. She states,

> The idea that wealth or any other variable can somehow rescind one's most significant racial origin, i.e., those that determine into which of the only two available categories one falls, is a foreign concept in the United States. In contrast, a Brazilian anecdote tells of a poor Afro-Brazilian who laments to a very affluent Afro-Brazilian about how hard life is in Brazil if one is black. The rich man's response is "I know. I used to be black." . . . Consequently, in Brazil, being black, or for that matter being white for the economically unfortunate, just may be a transitory state. . . . Even with respect to appearance, the lines drawn at the limits of the shared categories of black and white are in different places in Brazil and the United States. Many "white" Brazilians would be considered black in the United States by both appearance and ancestry. (p. 19)

Researchers and practitioners in other parts of the world also encounter difficulties when applying the U.S.-based, narrowly defined diversity. With its increasingly multicultural population (Maoris are now 14.5%, Pacific Islanders are 4.8%, and Asians are 5.5% of the population), New Zealand is coping with workplace diversity issues that are similar to those of other developed countries. However, Jones, Pringle, and Shepherd (2000) note that the U.S.-based notion of diversity may not be applicable there because it is "ethnocentric and culturally limited" (p. 378). Even when attempting to use narrow categories that will be applicable to each country based on its antidiscrimination legislation, such as religion in Ireland or castes in India, the result may be too limiting, and the definition may need to be updated periodically as laws evolve and change.

BROAD CATEGORY–BASED DIVERSITY DEFINITIONS

Over the years, as more scholars and practitioners became interested in the study of diversity, the definition of the term has expanded to include differences in race, gender, ethnicity, age, cultural background, social class, disability, and sexual orientation. An expanded definition of diversity may also include such variables as marital status and education as well as skills and years in the organization (e.g., Carrell, Mann, & Sigler, 2006; Harrison & Sin, 2006; Jackson & Joshi, 2010; Jimenez-Cook & Kleiner, 2005; Joplin & Daus, 1997; Kearney, Gerbert, & Voelpel, 2009; Point & Singh, 2003; Thomas, 1991). A common typology for this expanded definition provides a useful distinction between two types—visible and invisible:

• Visible diversity refers to characteristics that are observable or readily detectable attributes such as race, gender, or physical disability. Simply put, these are the characteristics you would notice on people walking down the hall, even if you knew nothing else about them.

• Invisible diversity refers to underlying attributes such as religion, education, and tenure with the organization. To be aware of a person's invisible diversity, you would need additional information from other sources (Cummings, Zhou, & Oldham, 1993; Jackson, May, & Whitney, 1995; Jackson & Joshi, 2010; Jackson, Joshi, & Erhardt, 2003; Kreitz, 2008; Tsui, Egan, & O'Reilly, 1992; Tsui, Porter, & Egan, 2002; Van Knippenberg & Schippers, 2007).

This distinction is important and has practical relevance. It is easier to form or harbor prejudices, biases, and stereotypes and to discriminate against people whose diversity characteristics belong to the first category of visible and readily detectable attributes. Invisible differences should not, however, be omitted from discussions of diversity. Individuals who are different from the organizational mainstream on those invisible characteristics can also experience discrimination and, as a result, have their work potential compromised. A case in point is sexual orientation, which can be invisible if a person chooses to keep it confidential but

(Text continued on p. 145.)

Table 6.1 A Typology of Diversity Definitions

Source	Definition of Diversity	Narrow Category–Based	Broad Category–Based	Based on a Conceptual Rule
The Diversity Task Force (2001)	*Diversity* includes all characteristics and experiences that define each of us as individuals.			√
Cox, T. (2001)	*Diversity* is the variation of social and cultural identities among people existing together in a defined employment or market setting.			√
Cox, T. (1994)	*Cultural diversity* means the representation, in one social system, of people with distinctly different group affiliations of cultural significance.			√
DiTomaso, N., Post, C., & Parks-Yancy, R. (2007)	*Workforce diversity* refers to the composition of work units (work group, organization, occupation, establishment or firm) in terms of the cultural or demographic characteristics that are salient and symbolically meaningful in the relationships among group members.			√
Dobbs, M. (1996)	Broadly defined, *diversity* may refer to any perceived difference among people: age, functional specialty, profession, sexual preference, geographic origin, life style, tenure with the organization, or position.		√	

Source	Definition of Diversity	Narrow Category–Based	Broad Category–Based	Based on a Conceptual Rule
Fleury, M. T. (1999)	We define *diversity* as a mixture of people with different group identities within the same social system.			✓
Glastra, F., Meerman, M., Petra, S., & de Vries, S. (2000)	The notion of *diversity* is predominantly used to refer to the variety of individuals and groups with whom work organizations are confronted in their labor markets, among their consumers and their employees.			✓
Gorman, F. (2000)	*Diversity* should be understood as the varied perspectives and approaches members of different identity groups bring to the workplace.			✓
Grant, B., & Kleiner, B. (1997)	In the workplace today not only does *diversity* imply difference in people based on their identification with various groups, but it is also a process of acknowledging differences through actions.			✓
Harrison, D. A., & Klein, K. J. (2007)	We use the term *diversity* to describe *the distribution of differences among the members of a unit with respect to a common attribute*, X, such as tenure, ethnicity, conscientiousness, task attitude, or pay. Diversity is a unit-level, compositional construct. . . . . Diversity is also attribute-specific. A unit is not diverse per se. Rather, it is diverse with respect to one or more specific attributes of its members.			✓

(Continued)

Table 6.1 (Continued)

Source	Definition of Diversity	Narrow Category–Based	Broad Category–Based	Based on a Conceptual Rule
Jackson, S. E., & Joshi, A. (2010)	The term "*diversity*" is now widely used by scholars to refer to the composition of social units . . . It is useful to differentiating among various types of diversity, because different types of diversity may have different consequences. *Relations-oriented diversity* refers to the distribution of attributes that are instrumental in shaping interpersonal relationships. Age, gender, and personality characteristics are examples of relations-oriented diversity. *Task-oriented diversity* refers to the distribution of attributes that are potentially relevant to the team's work. Organizational tenure, formal credentials and titles, and cognitive abilities are examples of task-oriented diversity. . . . *Readily-detected diversity* refers to differences among team members on attributes such as gender, age, nationality—attributes that are easily discerned. *Underlying diversity* refers to differences among team members on attributes that generally become known only through interaction, such as personality, attitudes, and skills.		✓	

Source	Definition of Diversity	Narrow Category–Based	Broad Category–Based	Based on a Conceptual Rule
Jimenez-Cook, S., & Kleiner, B. H. (2005)	Since the inception of the concept *of diversity*, it has evolved to take into consideration not only ethnicity, race, and religion, but also age, socioeconomic class, spiritual belief, disability, marital status, gender, sexual orientation, and more. . . . Organizations need to be influenced by and consider the needs of individuals with different learning styles, cultures, and life experiences.		√	
Harrison, D.A., & Sin, H. (2006)	*Diversity* is the collective amount of differences among members within a social unit.			√
Hartenian, L. & Gudmundson, D. (2000)	*Work force diversity* was defined, therefore, as the percentage of Asians, Blacks, and Hispanics employed by the firm. *[Defined for the purposes of a research study. Authors note diversity is more inclusive.]*	√		
ILO (2005)	A workforce at enterprise level which includes workers from different national, ethnic, cultural or language backgrounds, workers with physical or mental handicaps, etc.		√	

(Continued)

Table 6.1 (Continued)

Source	Definition of Diversity	Narrow Category–Based	Broad Category–Based	Based on a Conceptual Rule
Joshi, A., & Roh, H. (2009)	We define *diversity* as an aggregate team-level construct that represents differences among members of an interdependent work group with respect to a specific personal attribute.			✓
Kreitz, P. A. (2008)	Both cognitive and demographic *diversity* can be indicative of variety—i.e., differences regarding task-relevant resources such as knowledge, experience, and perspectives that reflect a potential for improved team performance.			✓
Kossek, E. E., & Lobel, S. A. (1996)	*Diversity* includes differences derived not only from ethnicity and gender but also based on differences in function, nationality, language, ability, religion, lifestyle or tenure.		✓	
Lai, Y., & Kleiner, B. H. (2001)	*Diversity* is not only formed by sex, but also by race, color, religion, and national origin.	✓		
Lau, D., & Murnighan, J. (1998)	We limit our consideration of *diversity* to demographic differences, focusing particularly on age, sex, race, and job tenure or status.	✓		

Source	Definition of Diversity	Narrow Category–Based	Broad Category–Based	Based on a Conceptual Rule
Moore, S. (1999)	It *[Diversity]* is used as a criterion to segregate people into certain jobs and certain organisational levels and it has to do with invisible as well as visible characteristics. . . . Generally though, strong indicators of diversity tend to include such dimensions as gender, skin colour, age, cultural background, accent and levels of physical ability. Weaker dimensions include other physical characteristics such as height and eye colour.		√	
Muller, H. J., & Parham, P. (1998)	*Workforce diversity* is understood as the presence in organizations of men and women from different cultural and racioethnic backgrounds, sexual orientations, physical abilities, and age.	√		
Nixon, J., & West, J. (2000)	It *[multicultural diversity]* includes such differences as age, economic status, education, family type, gender, personality type, race, religion, geographic origin, and sexual orientation. In addition, by defining diversity broadly as being everything that makes us different from others, including communication styles and work styles, all employees can "buy into" the value of building a culture that supports diversity.		√	√

(Continued)

Table 6.1 (Continued)

Source	Definition of Diversity	Narrow Category–Based	Broad Category–Based	Based on a Conceptual Rule
Ocholla, D. (2002)	*Diversity* is based on recognition of harmony in differences and emphasis on similarities in differences. This approach provides the patience and tolerance for recognizing, knowing, experiencing, embracing, benefiting and fulfilling each other as well as accommodating the unique social differences and quite often transforming them into similarities for the benefit of the majority. Current social relations, created largely through urbanization and globalization, assume that people increasingly appreciate each other's culture, cuisine, attire, religion, language, sports, music, art, interests, tastes and values.			✓
Parham, P. A., & Muller, H. J. (2008)	The definition of *diversity* has shifted from a group level phenomenon in which disparate treatment occurs to an exploration of individual differences.			✓
Prasad, P., Pringle, J. K., & Konrad, A. M. (2006)	*Workplace diversity* is a more relevant concept if it focuses on those differences that have been systematically discriminated against, irrespective of whether or not they receive legal protection. . . . Diversity is also about respecting and valuing differences, whether they are gender-, race- or ethnic–based differences in lifestyles, appearance, linguistic proficiency, communication and decision-making styles, etc.		✓	✓

Source	Definition of Diversity	Narrow Category–Based	Broad Category–Based	Based on a Conceptual Rule
Shackelford, W. (2003)	The new definition of *diversity* includes the traditional categories of race and gender. In addition, it includes people with disabilities, gays and lesbians, and other non-traditional categories. One of the most interesting categories being used by some employers is "diversity of thought"—which they say can be obtained by hiring individuals with different degrees, college affiliations, education or social economic backgrounds from their current employees.		√	
Svehla, T. (1994)	*Workforce diversity* encompasses a mosaic of races, ethnic and religious backgrounds, sexual orientation, personality orientations, family situations, ages, and physical abilities. Workforce diversity can also refer to diverse functions within an organization.		√	
Thomas, Jr., R. R. (2005)	*Diversity* is the differences and similarities that exist among the elements of a specific mixture. It does not refer solely to differentiating characteristics, nor to characteristics that are easily observable. Diversity is both dynamic and interactive. It cannot be predicted by external appearances.			√

(Continued)

Table 6.1 (Continued)

Source	Definition of Diversity	Narrow Category–Based	Broad Category–Based	Based on a Conceptual Rule
Thomas, Jr., R. R. (1991)	*Diversity* includes everyone; it is not something that is defined by race or gender. It extends to age, personal and corporate background, education, function, and personality. It includes life style, sexual preference, geographic origin, tenure with the organization, exempt or nonexempt status, and management or nonmanagement.		√	
Van Knippenberg, D., & Schippers, M. C. (2007)	*Diversity* is a characteristic of social grouping that reflects the degree to which objective or subjective differences exist between group members.			√

NOTE: In all definitions above, italics have been added.

which can trigger prejudice and discrimination if the information gets out. Although the first category refers only to observable characteristics, one of the major reasons why diversity of any type creates difficulty for groups is attributable to complex and often implicit differences in perspective, assumptions, and causal beliefs with which the observable differences are assumed to be correlated (Milliken & Martins, 1996). These categories, therefore, are not necessarily mutually exclusive (Chatman & Flynn, 2001) because often a visible characteristic such as ethnicity may be associated with a less visible one such as socioeconomic status. Diversity, then, often becomes the interaction of visible and invisible dimensions, the former leading to unproven assumptions about internal qualities. For example, Black South Africans are more likely to belong to the lower socioeconomic group than White South Africans. Considering the limitations of the broad-based definitions of diversity, Cooke (1999) notes, "The list [of diversity characteristics] has now grown so long that we may wonder how we will ever be able to create a workplace that is sensitive to the needs of all, and is still productive" (p. 6).

DEFINITIONS BASED ON A CONCEPTUAL RULE

In contrast to actually listing the common categories of diversity (e.g., age, gender, or race), there are some definitions that provide a conceptual articulation of diversity (e.g., Cox, 2001; DiTomaso, Post, & Parks-Yancy, 2007; Harrison & Sin, 2006; Joshi & Roh, 2009; Kreitz, 2008; Van Knippenberg & Schippers, 2007). For example, Linda Larkey (1996), one of the first to use a conceptual rule, defined diversity as,

> (a) differences in worldviews or subjective culture, resulting in potential behavioral differences among cultural groups; and (b) differences in identity among group members in relation to other groups.

The basic assumption is that members of a given culture are likely to share a set of symbols, values, and norms that are at the root of their common worldviews and behaviors (Baugh, 1983; Collier & Thomas, 1988; Triandis, 2003). These shared views and behaviors, in turn, create a sense of belonging among group members with respect to other groups (Ashforth & Mael, 1989; Giles & Coupland, 1991; Giles & Johnson, 1986; Konrad, 2003; Triandis, 2003). This group identity, therefore, although providing a sense of belonging among the group members, also fosters a perception of not belonging or exclusion from other groups. This is relevant to understanding perceptions and behaviors, such as prejudice and discrimination, toward members of other groups, regardless of whether they represent majority or minority views.

Several theorists and researchers have advocated a move away from contrasting disadvantaged and privileged groups with regard to diversity, suggesting instead an individualized approach. Roosevelt Thomas articulated this conceptual framework in his book *Beyond Race and Gender* (1991):

> Diversity includes everyone; it is not something that is defined by race or gender. It extends to age, personal and corporate background, education, function and personality. It includes life-style, sexual preference, geographic origin, tenure with the organizations . . . and management or nonmanagement. (p. 10)

Diversity trainers such as the one cited at the beginning of this chapter have readily embraced this approach. Many diversity trainers, as well as human resource managers, find this broad definition appealing because it allows them to pull everyone in the organization under the "diversity umbrella," thus avoiding the controversial process of identifying groups with or without power, those who are discriminating and those who are discriminated against. This politically acceptable approach also allows them to avoid alienating the powerful members of the majority groups who, in most organizations, are at the top of the management pyramid and who make decisions about organizational processes, including what kind of diversity training employees will receive. The very characteristic of this definition—including all differences under the diversity concept—that some find so appealing is also the limitation of this definition. By including all types of individual differences as "diversity," this definition suggests that *all* differences are equal and, therefore, trivializes those differences. The main criticism is that such expanded definitions reduce diversity to benign differences among people, thereby diluting the serious consequences of prejudice, discrimination, and lack of power that were clearly associated with the original set of diversity characteristics (Linnehan & Konrad, 1999). For example, the oppression and discrimination suffered by Black people in the United States or in South Africa can hardly be equated with the different treatment employees receive due to their tenure in an organization or their management position within a company.

Toward a Global Definition of Diversity

As a backlash to the all-inclusive definitions of diversity, some scholars, as noted above, argue that such broad diversity categories dilute the real meaning of diversity. They advocate focusing only on the distinction categories that have been most persistent over the years, and that have the most serious impact on employment, as a barometer of other societal consequences (Essed, 2002; Linnehan & Konrad, 1999; Linnehan et al., 2003; Nkomo, 2001). They specifically identify race, gender, and social class as the fundamental diversity categories (Essed, 2002). For example, Nkomo (2001) asserts that the expanded definition of diversity "overlooks the role of conflict, power, dominance, and the history of how organizations are fundamentally structured by race, gender, and class." Nkomo continues, "Race, gender and class create and maintain the most fundamental divisions in organizations. Diversity work must be about ending the domination of these systems of oppression." As another example, Linnehan and Konrad (1999) declare that broad-based definitions of diversity diminish the emphasis on intergroup inequality and sensitive historical and institutional problems related to stereotyping, prejudice, discrimination, and disadvantage. Similarly, Essed (1996, 2002) focuses on experiences of non-dominant groups of gender, ethnicity, and culture in her work.

Against the backdrop of the broad definitions, on the one hand, and the narrow ones, on the other, generating a definition of workforce diversity that will be relevant in different countries and applicable in various cultural and national contexts proves to be a challenge. Trying to name specific diversity categories that can be relevant across cultures and nations is a futile effort. For example, the distinction between Catholics and Protestants that is central to diversity in Ireland is irrelevant in predominantly Muslim countries such as Pakistan; the distinction between various castes used in India is irrelevant in Belgium; and the racial distinction utilized in South Africa is irrelevant in China. Generating terminology that will be applicable across cultural and national boundaries is, therefore, essential.

There are some general distinction categories that do seem to cut across many (though not all) national and local cultures. These include gender, race, ethnicity, age, sexual orientation, and disability. However, there are two problems in utilizing some of these distinction categories to define diversity:

1. Some of the distinction categories may have either a positive or negative impact on employment and job prospects in different countries. For example, in Western nations, younger employees are considered more desirable because they are perceived to have new ideas, better technological skills, and a more dynamic and flexible attitude. In Eastern and more traditional societies like China, the old are revered and believed to possess desirable qualities of wisdom and experience. Therefore, although age discrimination may be relevant in both types of societies, its impact might be very different.

2. These distinction categories are not exhaustive of the domain. Many countries utilize diversity categories that are not included on this list. For example, religious affiliation in Ireland, regional location (rural vs. urban) in China, and castes in India are powerful diversity categories that are not included in the list. A more recent example is HIV status, which has been identified as a distinct diversity category in both South Africa and Zimbabwe based on the terms used in these countries' antidiscrimination legislation. (For a discussion of antidiscrimination legislation, refer to Chapter 2 of this book.) Similarly, involvement in a lesbian or gay male relationship is punishable by

death in some countries, although in others it is tolerated or even embraced (Amnesty International, 2003).[5] These laws have direct bearings on how gays and lesbians are treated in the workplace and the freedom or lack thereof that they have to express their sexual orientation in everyday life, including the workplace.

The logical solution to the problem of finding a global definition for diversity that can be relevant in different cultural and national contexts is to define diversity by (a) the *process* of generating distinction categories—groups with a perceived common denominator in a specific national or cultural context, and (b) the *consequences* of belonging to these groups—the potential harmful or beneficial impact on employment and job prospects.

Therefore, the definition of *workforce diversity—in the global context—* utilized in this book is as follows:

> *Workforce diversity* refers to the division of the workforce into distinction categories that (a) have a perceived commonality within a given cultural or national context, and that (b) impact potentially harmful or beneficial employment outcomes such as job opportunities, treatment in the workplace, and promotion prospects—irrespective of job-related skills and qualifications.

This definition addresses the limitations encountered in applying some of the previous definitions to the global context. First, it provides a broad umbrella that includes any distinction categories that may be relevant to specific cultural or national environments without prespecifying the categories and without limiting the content of the domain. This approach does not list the distinction categories and therefore does not limit them to specific categories (e.g., to only gender, race, and ethnicity), thus allowing the inclusion of categories that may be relevant in some cultural contexts and not in others (e.g., regional differences or HIV status). It therefore overcomes the limitations of the narrow definitions of diversity because it is sufficiently broad to be relevant in various cultural and national contexts. Second, this definition emphasizes the importance of the *consequences* of the distinction categories and thereby overcomes the limitation of the broad definitions that include benign and inconsequential characteristics in their diversity categories. This second advantage is also a limitation because the use of consequences of diversity as part of the definition makes it difficult to use them as outcome variables in diversity research.

What are the adverse consequences of the diversity distinction categories? *Stereotypes, prejudice, discrimination, oppression,* and *exclusion* are terms used to describe attitudes and behaviors that often affect the distribution of resources and privileges in society that are based on group membership rather than on employment-related characteristics such as level of education, commitment, and job-related skills. Donald M. Taylor and Fathali M. Moghaddam (1994) define stereotypes, attributes, and discrimination as "mechanisms by which advantaged and disadvantaged group members perceive and interpret interactions that appear to be based on their category membership rather than on their individual characteristics" (p. 159). At the basis of both intergroup attitudes and behaviors are the diversity or group-affiliation categories used to make the distinction between the advantaged and the disadvantaged in each society. Now that we have defined diversity in the global context, we are ready to examine the attitudes and behaviors that are associated with these distinction categories.

Stereotypes and Prejudice

Each one of us holds stereotypical views of groups other than our own, and sometimes about our own group as well. For example, "the French have gourmet tastes"; "Italians are great lovers"; "the Chinese are hardworking"; "women are emotional and men are rational." These stereotypes serve a very practical function. Rather than starting with no information when we encounter a person from another group, we begin with a framework that gives us a sense of confidence that we know something about the other person. These impressions have been formed by a combination of social, cultural, and political influences that include previous chance encounters with people of that group, popular media images, cultural norms of tolerance, partial truths that we have picked from various other sources, as well as contextual variables that are influenced by current events (Bar-Tal, 1997; Bar-Tal & Labin, 2001). These perceptions are often inaccurate when applied to an individual member of a group, as well as to the group as a whole. Yet these perceptions and categorizations often steer expectations of an individual or group and serve to justify actions that may turn out to be harmful or immoral (Tavris & Aronson, 2007). For example, the myth of the "model minority," as applied to Asian Americans in the United States, refers to an "overachieving, supersuccessful ethnic group without significant problems" ("What 'Model Minority,'" 1998). This notion misrepresents the complex and diverse experiences of Asian Americans by "glossing over huge differences within a group of people who come from more than two dozen countries and include Asian Indian professionals and Vietnamese peasants" (Kamen, 1992, p. A1). As a result, the social needs of Asian Americans may be overlooked, and those who do not fit this model may be subjected to racial hostility and stress in the workplace and in the community. The dilemmas associated with identity-based stereotypes are fiercely declared by Ziauddin Sardar (2001), a Muslim living in England (see Box 6.1).

BOX 6.1
Ziauddin Sardar Statement on His
Identity and Subsequent Stereotypes

When people ask me where I am from, my standard reply is "Hackney." I wasn't actually born in Hackney, but I grew up in the borough. Hackney shaped my formative years and provides me with my childhood memories. It is home; and that's where I am from.

   This is a difficult thing for most White people to grasp. They look at me and exclaim: "Surely, you're Asian." However, there is no such thing as an Asian. Asia is not a race or identity: it is a continent. Even in Asia, where more than half of the world's population lives, no one calls him or herself "Asian." If you are not Chinese or Malaysian, then you are an Afghan or a Punjabi. Moreover, the meaning of the term changes from place to place. In the U.S., the Asian label is attached to Koreans, Filipinos and Chinese. In Britain, we do not use the term Asian to describe our substantial communities of Turks, Iranians or Indonesians, even though these countries are in Asia.

   . . . There are others who look at me and say: "Oh, you're Indian." Sixty years ago, before the emergence of Pakistan and Bangladesh, this would have been a passable description. But today "Indian" has become almost as meaningless as "Asian," largely because the two terms have coalesced. They are lazy references to people of Indian subcontinental lineage. But for Pakistanis, Bangladeshis, Sri Lankans and Nepalese, the label is offensive. By lumping these diverse communities into a single category, we make them invisible.

   . . . When I really want to tell people who I am, I say I am a Muslim. Their reaction is an unbelieving stare—betraying complete incomprehension. This is because, first, at a time when no one actually believes in anything, people who express a religious identity—Muslims or Catholics or Orthodox Jews— appear to be totally out of sync. Second, although "Asian" and "Indian" suggest amorphous yet containable differences, "Muslim" describes a specific and volatile difference. Muslims are not simply a brand of believers: they are rampant, dangerous and impenetrably different believers.

   . . . In certain circles, saying you are a Muslim almost amounts to a declaration of war. Among feminists, for instance, I am automatically a chauvinist who forces his wife to walk several paces behind him. At secular intellectual gatherings, I am dogmatic and irrational even before I open my mouth. For some people, my name alone suggests that I must be a supporter of military dictators and terrorists.

Often confused, stereotyping and prejudice are distinct concepts and their definitions differ:

A stereotype is a standardized, oversimplified mental picture that is held in common by members of a group.[6]

A prejudice is derived from the verb *to prejudge* and refers to a preconceived judgment or opinion held by members of a group.[7] Most commonly, a prejudice is perceived as an irrational attitude of hostility directed against an individual, a group, a race, or their supposed characteristics.

Both concepts have long been important building blocks in most theories that deal with intergroup relations, as we shall see in the next chapter. Willard Enteman (1996) describes the original meaning of the word *stereotype* as follows:

While the origin of the word "stereotype" has been almost entirely lost in the dim recesses of linguistic history, it is most closely associated with journalism as a trade. The older print people among us will remember that the original stereotype was called a *flong*, which was a printing plate that facilitated reproduction of the same material. The typesetter could avoid recasting type by using the stereotype. Thus, a stereotype imposes a rigid mold on the subject and encourages repeated mechanical usage.
. . . The purposes of the stereotype are the same as in the print history. They are grounded in laziness. In standard economics, efficiency is another term for laziness. The person who substitutes a stereotype for careful analysis simply does not want to work harder than necessary to achieve a superficially acceptable result. (p. 9)

The *stereotype* concept was originally developed with respect to ethnic groups and has been perceived as morally wrong. Its early definitions reflect this focus. For example, Jack Brigham (1971) defined a *stereotype* as "a generalization made about an ethnic group, concerning a trait attribution, which is considered to be unjustified by an observer" (p. 29). Stereotypes were originally considered undesirable because they were thought to be either (a) the result of an inferior cognitive process—that is, a process that utilizes overgeneralization or oversimplification—or (b) were morally wrong because they categorized people who had no desire to be categorized (Taylor & Moghaddam, 1994; Corrigan,

2004). Early studies (e.g., Katz & Braly, 1935) presented research participants with an ethnic group label and asked them to check off or rate the extent to which each of a long list of trait adjectives best described the ethnic group.

Several studies demonstrate both positive and negative stereotyping of various groups in different societies. In one study conducted in South Africa, 265 students completed a questionnaire that attempted to measure ethnic group identification and particular interracial attitudes. Significant indications of racist stereotypes were found in all racial groups, with a strong positive bias toward participants' own racial groups and a negative bias toward other racial groups (Slabbert, 2001). Another study examined stereotypes of older workers in New Zealand. The participants—including 2,137 members of New Zealand's largest union and 1,012 employers who belong to New Zealand Employer Federation—were asked to indicate whether they agree or disagree with a series of statements under the term "views of the older worker." The results indicate that the negative stereotypes held by both groups were "adaptability factors," such as resistance to change and problems with technology, particularly computer technology. The positive stereotypes also related to "adaptability factors," but in this case they were reliability, loyalty, and job commitment (McGregor & Gray, 2002). Littrell and Nkomo (2005) noted that gender stereotypes are the psychological characteristics differentially associated with women and men across many cultural groups. Having conducting a eight-year study she found that having entered careers traditionally dominated by White males, Black women have been subjected to a particular form of sexism shaped by racism and racial stereotyping (Nkomo, 2003). Moreover, gender stereotypes affect perceptions of leaders and managers (Littrell & Nkomo, 2005). Being the first woman as editor of a major newspaper in New Zealand in the mid-1980s, Judy McGregor (2006) examined the status of women in the New Zealand media dominated by men's pervasive power and women's representation at governance level, and in newspaper editorships and broadcasting executive positions. She found the little progress of women to top editorships and the status of them is still low, given the so-called "feminisation" of the media in the past 30 years.

Another example of gender stereotyping and discrimination in the workplace is the U.S. case of *Price Waterhouse v. Hopkins*. The woman at the center of the case, Ann Branigar Hopkins, was denied promotion to partner in the accounting firm because her interpersonal skills were considered too abrasive, although the partners strongly praised her skills and abilities to secure major contracts. Her partnership was initially delayed for 1 year. In that period, she was told that she could improve her chances "by walking, talking, and dressing more femininely." In the following year, she was again denied partnership. Hopkins then quit and took action against the firm. She filed a lawsuit charging gender discrimination under Title VII of the Civil Rights Act of 1964. After bouts in the federal courts, in a landmark decision, Hopkins eventually won and was awarded partner (Hopkins, 2006; *Hopkins v. Price Waterhouse*, 1985; *Hopkins v. Price Waterhouse*, 1987; *Price Waterhouse v. Hopkins*, 1989).[8]

More recent studies put less emphasis on the negative aspects of stereotyping and view stereotyping as a basic cognitive process that is not necessarily bad and not necessarily informed by prejudice (Blair, 2002; Devine, 2001; Greenwald & Banaji, 1995; Judd, Blair, & Chapleau, 2004; Levy, 1999; Lowery, Hardin, & Sinclair, 2001; Yarhouse, 2000). The emphasis in those recent works is on associations between daily events that result in the creation of stereotypes. Thus, a group may become associated with a particular characteristic, not as a function of explicit prejudice but out of a basic cognitive process (Taylor & Moghaddam, 1994). For example, in the early 1990s, media reports included several incidents of Korean immigrants in Los Angeles who physically defended their shops against robbers.[9] A stereotype of Korean immigrants as storeowners was reinforced, and perhaps another stereotype of Korean immigrants as fierce fighters may have emerged. However, sometimes a stereotype of a group may be generated based on popular media images from one country and be inappropriately applied for the same group in another country (Van Dijk, 2007). For example, beliefs about Muslim women suggesting that they are veiled and often sheltered are based on images from the Middle East, which are globally applied. Actually, in a U.S.-based study by Jen'nan Ghazal Read, Muslim women were well-educated, held progressive gender views, and were represented in the labor force (2002).

The concept of prejudice refers to people's attitudes toward members of other groups—expecting certain behaviors from them that are mostly pejorative. Gordon W. Allport (1954, 1979) in his seminal book *The Nature of Prejudice* defined *prejudice* as "an antipathy based on faulty and inflexible generalizations. It may be felt or expressed. It may be directed toward a group as a whole or toward an individual because he is a member of that group" (p. 9). The word *prejudice,* derived from the Latin noun *praejudicium,* means to prejudge. Although it is possible to have positive prejudice as well—that is, to think well about others without sufficient justification (e.g., reverence for the wisdom of the elderly)—the word *prejudice* has acquired a negative connotation. The two important elements in understanding prejudice are that it involves passing judgment on the other without sufficient warrant and that it involves negative feelings (Allport, 1954, 1979; Ponterotto, Utsey, & Pedersen, 2006). Prejudice is a schema of negative evaluations and characteristics that are attributed to groups perceived as racially and culturally different (Van Dijk, 1987, 2006). Philomena Essed emphasizes the ideological basis of prejudice noting, "The negative evaluations are generalizations based on insufficient or biased representations that are constituent elements of an ideology rationalizing and reinforcing existing systems of racial and ethnic inequality" (1995, p. 45). For example, in a study of interethnic perceptions, Gilbert, Carr-Ruffino, Ivancevich, and Lownes-Jackson (2003) found that African American males were more likely viewed as incompetent and not as courtly and mannerly as African American women and Asian American women and men. This was despite having similar job-related qualifications and history.

Geert Hofstede makes a distinction between two kinds of stereotypes. The first are *heterostereotypes*—perceptions about members of the other group; and the second are *autostereotypes*—perceptions about one's own groups (Hofstede & Hofstede, 2004, p. 326). It stands to reason that people will incorporate generally positive and favorable characteristics into their autostereotypes and generally negative and unfavorable characteristics into the way they perceive groups other than their own, their heterostereotypes. For example, the 2003 Iraq conflict brought to the surface negative stereotypes of allied nations that took different positions on the war. The French saw the Americans as arrogant and as bullies, and the Americans saw the French as naïve and greedy.

A similar process occurs with respect to prejudice. Negative attributes are associated with members of other groups, or *out-groups,* and positive characteristics are associated with members of one's own group, or *in-group.* In a study by Howard and Rothbart (1980), subjects were randomly assigned to one of two different groups in which they did not know anyone. They were then presented with a mix of positive and negative information about their group (the in-group) and the other group (the out-group). Subjects had more favorable expectations about in-group members and more negative expectations about out-group members, even though they did not personally know the members of either group. In addition, people tend to perceive their in-group as heterogeneous, whereas the out-group is seen as mostly homogeneous. Taylor and Moghaddam (1994) note that popular statements such as "I can't tell one from the other" and "They all look the same to me" reflect this perception of the out-groups as more homogeneous than the in-group, which is part of the stereotyping process (p. 163). Regardless of which group is considered the majority and which is viewed as minority in a particular cultural or national context, people perceive more variability in the characteristics of their own group than in the characteristics of out-groups. For example, in the old Hollywood western movies of the 1940s and 1950s, Chinese men were typically cooks, whereas White men could be cowboys, sheriffs, town mayors, and even horse thieves and villains.

In an effort to understand diversity, research has been conducted in recent years that examined various characteristics of the workforce and the attributes of specific groups. Some generalizations that have come out of this literature have been used in diversity trainings designed to help employees become more sensitive to prejudice and discrimination. These applications, however, are not always helpful or productive. For example, a U.S.-based training program taught managers preparing for assignments in China that if a subordinate does not look at his or her supervisor's eyes during a conversation, it is a sign of respect. What the trainees did not realize was that this may not always be the case. One manager who was later posted in the company's branch in Beijing reported that it took him a while to realize that one of his direct subordinates was averting his eyes not because of respect but because of resentment; that employee had a good reason for resenting the new American manager—he was demoted from his job to make room for the U.S. manager's position.

Sometimes generalizations about certain ethnic groups used in diversity training can actually backfire, as in the case of diversity training conducted at the Lucky Stores chain in 1988. The diversity workshops were designed to help participants identify gender- and ethnic-based stereotypes. In an interesting twist, one of the company's representatives took notes that detailed comments such as "black females are aggressive" and "women cry more." An employee of the company found the notes and attributed the content to the lack of promotions for women and ethnic minorities in the company. Employees then sued the company for discrimination and the notes from the workshop were entered into evidence. The employer was found guilty (Caudron, 1993).

It is important to remember that although it is legitimate to categorize groups and to study their common traits, behaviors, and beliefs, applying that information to specific individuals may be misleading and may constitute stereotyping. Greet Hofstede (1997) refers to this very point stating, "Stereotyping occurs when assumptions about the collective properties of a group are applied to a particular individual from that group" (p. 253). Individual behavior, although to some degree a product of the cultural group, is also highly influenced by the family of origin and, of course, the unique individual's characteristics. In order to avoid the negative aspects of stereotyping, all of these elements should be taken into consideration when viewing an individual whose culture is different from one's own (see Figure 6.1 on p. 157).

When encountering a member from another group, rather than rely on the oversimplified mental picture provided by a stereotype, one should recognize that the person's attitudes and behaviors are the result of the interaction among the person's unique individual characteristics, the family environment, and the values and norms that are common to his or her cultural group. The use of stereotypes and prejudices is an unfortunate abbreviated way of sizing someone up. It is much easier than making the effort required to actually know the other person.

Dehumanization and Oppression

Stereotypes and prejudices also make it easier to relate to the other person as not only different but inferior, and as such not worthy of equal rights and treatment.

The most extreme psychological mechanism in viewing members of other groups as inferior is dehumanization, and its behavioral manifestation is oppression. Thus, at the root of oppression is a systematic process of *dehumanization* of the target people. Oppression is the unjust or cruel exercise of authority or power, most often used by one group to dominate another. A developed society governed by rules of law needs a rational justification for practicing any form of domination. The psychological process involved in this justification includes relating to out-group members as less human, inferior, or fundamentally different in ways that make them undeserving of equal treatment. This logic has often been used in the past to justify oppression as a method for bringing enlightenment to "primitive" nations. A prime example is "the White man's burden" logic that was used to justify colonialism as an "obligation" of the European nations to bring enlightenment to the rest of the world. A remnant of this colonialism ideology is the paternalistic approach toward minorities of color in Europe. Philomena Essed (1991, p. 16) describes the manifestation of this ideology in the Netherlands under the title "the Dutch burden," indicating that this paternalism was motivated by "good intentions" to "help" Blacks cope with "modern" Dutch society.

The oldest and most extreme form of cross-cultural oppression and exploitation of work was slavery. Many conquering nations in the ancient world practiced this cruel form of dominance. Slavery served several goals— the first was to break the spirit of a conquered people by humiliating their leaders through enslavement; the second was to break their social structure by taking away productive members of society and tearing apart families and communities; and the third was to economically benefit the homeland through free labor by importing the slaves to the dominating country or by outsourcing production to distant shores (e.g., Britain's exploitation of India or Germany's location of concentration camps outside the homeland).

The Roman Empire was infamous for its efficient use of slavery for the purpose of expanding its dominance over other nations and reaping major financial gains from the practice. During the colonial years, exploitation of indigenous people took other forms; the most blatant example was the apartheid regime in South Africa and Rhodesia (now Zimbabwe). These historical roots are important in understanding discrimination because the same derogatory attitudes toward oppressed people remained ingrained in the colonizing nations, even after the end of their colonial rule.

Two examples of extreme forms of dehumanization and oppression are the enslavement and genocide of the African people by the colonizing nations and the enslavement and genocide of the Jewish people by the Nazis. The colonial nations viewed the African people as not quite human, and therefore the oppressors felt "justified" in taking their freedom away. Advertisements for the sales of slaves in the United States in the 18th century, proclaiming the work qualities of African slaves while depicting them in stereotypical straw

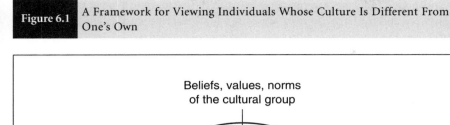

Figure 6.1   A Framework for Viewing Individuals Whose Culture Is Different From One's Own

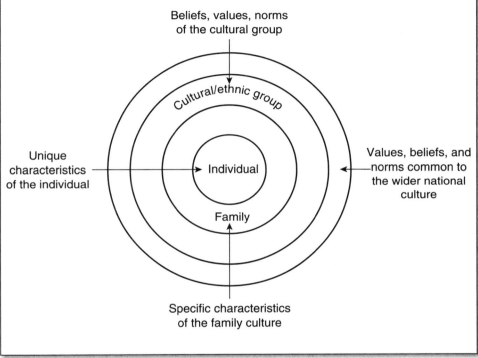

skirts, provide an example for the way this cruel and efficient industry created an image of the slaves as subhumans.

Similarly, the Nazis viewed the Jews as an inferior race and used their racist theory to justify the enslavement and genocide of the Jewish people. In 2000, the German foundation Remembrance, Responsibility, and Future was established by German law to provide $5 billion in funds to former slaves and forced laborers during World War II. Slavery and oppression were justified by cultural ideologies of racial superiority such as those of colonial Europe and of the Nazis. These cultural ideologies that are at the base of racism, sexism, ageism, ethnocentrism, and all the other "isms" characterize the dominant race, men, or specific ethnic group as being inherently superior to the other groups, simply because of their birthrights (e.g., race, gender, or ethnic origins) (Fernandez, 1991, p. 35).

Although there is no comparison between the harm done to a person who is enslaved and the harm done to someone who is discriminated against in the workplace, the psychological process at the root of these practices resides on a continuum. This discussion of oppression and dehumanization provides the basis for understanding the employment-related discrimination described in the next section.

Employment-Related Discrimination

Though originally morally neutral in its meaning, the word *discrimination* has acquired a negative value, particularly in the context of employment. Discrimination in employment occurs when (a) individuals, institutions, or governments treat people differently because of personal characteristics such as race, gender, or sexual orientation rather than their ability to perform their jobs; and (b) these actions have a negative impact on access to jobs, promotions, or compensation. The UN International Labour Organization (ILO) Discrimination Convention of 1958 (No. 111) defines discrimination as,

> Any distinction, exclusion or preference . . . which has the effect of nullifying or impairing equality of opportunity or treatment in employment or occupation as may be determined. In this convention the grounds for non-discrimination include race, colour, sex, religion, political opinion, national extraction or social origin. (Zegers de Beijl, 2000, p. 10)

Around the world, gender has been one of the most commonly used criteria for discrimination in the workplace. Although not as crude as robbing the others of their human qualities—as in the racist ideologies—the logic used to justify women's discrimination has relied on perceptions of a difference in their "destiny" in life, often citing religious justification. Consider the following statement:

> The paramount mission and destiny of women are to fulfill the noble and benign offices of wife and mother. This is the law of the creator. (Joseph P. Bradley, U.S. Supreme Court Justice, 1873)

Justice Bradley made this statement when, in 1873, the Supreme Court threw out a case by a woman who could not become a lawyer simply because of her gender.[10] A hundred years later, the prime minister of Japan made a similar statement:

First of all, I want women, as mothers, to become 100 percent wonderful mothers. Then I want them to become good wives. And I want them to become ladies capable of making contributions for society also. (Yasuhiro Nakasone, prime minister of Japan, 1984)[11]

Members of ethnic and national minorities have also been frequent victims of discrimination. A multinational study conducted by the UN's ILO found that discrimination against migrant and ethnic minority job applicants was widespread (Zegers de Beijl, 2000) (see Box 6.2). The average discrimination rates in the countries studied were around 35%. A particularly interesting facet of this study is that it was able to pinpoint the stage during which discrimination had occurred. Most of the direct discriminatory rejections occurred in all the countries in the first stage of the application process, resulting in these applicants being denied the opportunity to present their credentials. In other words, the discrimination occurred as soon as the applicants introduced themselves using foreign names that were not typical of their new country of residence.

BOX 6.2
Documenting Employment Discrimination Against Migrant Workers

In order to document the process of discrimination, the UN International Labour Organization (ILO) initiated a multinational study. The researchers utilized "situation testing," a research methodology that preserves the real-life quality of observations in a systematic and objective way. The process involved two testers, one belonging to the majority group in the country, the other to a minority group, who applied to the same position and interacted with the employer or manager who had the authority to make the hiring decision. The applicants were matched on criteria that concern an employer recruiting for a job, including age, educational background, and work experience. The main difference between the testers was their racial or ethnic background. Because the study used a highly controlled protocol, the results in actual hiring rates were attributable to the difference in race, ethnicity, or nationality backgrounds of the applicants. The study was applied in four European countries: Germany, the Netherlands, Belgium, and Spain. The results indicate that on average, migrants were discriminated against in one in three application procedures, with rates being highest in the Netherlands and lowest in Germany. Discrimination occurred in all three stages of employment— the initial inquiry, the job interview, and the actual offer of the job.

(Continued)

(Continued)

a. Discrimination during the inquiry stage. Discrimination was at its most flagrant during this stage. Migrants were often simply told that the vacancy had already been filled whereas the national applicant was invited for an interview. In some cases, the migrant applicant was told straight away that foreigners were not wanted.

b. Discrimination during the job interview. During this stage, there were a considerable number of cases in which the migrant candidate was asked for more qualifications than the native candidate or queried about residence status and work permit whereas the other candidate was not.

c. Discrimination in the job offer. During this stage, even when the migrant candidate was offered a job, the terms and conditions of employment tended to be inferior to those offered to the national applicant. In other words, migrant workers were treated as though they were undocumented foreigners (even though they were not) who could be easily exploited.

Vacancy for a Photographic Model

The following is an example of a discriminatory exchange that occurred in the inquiry stage in the German sample: The Turkish applicant called first and, after having introduced himself, was asked to give his height. When he stated that he was 1.82 meters, he was turned down for being too short; he was told that the minimum height requirement (not mentioned in the job advertisement) was 1.85 meters. Then, the German applicant telephoned. After giving his height (1.84 m), he was invited for an interview. When he then asked whether 1.84 meters would still be all right, he was given a reply in the affirmative.

SOURCE: Zegers de Beijl (1999).

Summary and Conclusion

Understandably, the concept of workforce diversity does not travel well across cultural and national boundaries. There is an underlying challenge in generating a term that will have common meanings across national boundaries and that will facilitate effective communications aimed at solving problems of intergroup relations in the workplace. Against the backdrop of the broad definitions on one hand and the narrow ones on the other, generating a definition of workforce diversity that will be relevant in different countries and applicable in various cultural and national contexts proved to be a challenge. The logical solution to the dilemma of finding a global definition for diversity that can be relevant in different cultural and national contexts is to define diversity by (a) the *process* of generating distinction categories—groups with a perceived common denominator in a specific national or cultural context, and (b) the *consequences* of belonging to these groups—the potential harmful or beneficial impact on employment and job prospects.

Often confused, stereotyping and prejudice are distinct concepts, and their definitions differ. A *stereotype* is a standardized, oversimplified mental picture that is held in common by members of a group. A *prejudice* is derived from the verb *to prejudge* and refers to a preconceived judgment or opinion held by members of a group. Most commonly, a prejudice is perceived as an irrational attitude of hostility directed against an individual, a group, a race, or their supposed characteristics. Stereotypes and prejudices also make it easier to relate to the other person as not only different but inferior and, as such, not worthy of equal rights and treatment. The most extreme psychological mechanism in viewing members of other groups as inferior is dehumanization, and its behavioral manifestation is oppression.

Discrimination in employment occurs when (a) individuals, institutions, or governments treat people differently because of personal characteristics such as race, gender, or sexual orientation rather than their ability to perform their jobs, and (b) when these actions have a negative impact on access to jobs, promotions, or compensation. Around the world, gender has been one of the most commonly used criteria for discrimination in the workplace. Other groups that have commonly been discriminated against are ethnic and national minorities.

This chapter presented several perspectives on diversity and suggested a definition that can be applicable to countries around the world. By-products of the adverse effects of diversity—stereotypes, prejudice, oppression, and discrimination—and their impact on the distribution of resources and privileges in society were discussed. Group membership or diversity characteristics, rather than employment-related qualifications such as level of education or job-related skills, were shown to have historically prevailed across the globe.

Extreme as well as not uncommon applications of these practices were pre-sented. The work environment is an important arena in which these mecha-nisms of intergroup relations are being played out. This is because of individual and group efforts to gain advantage in the competition for (real or perceived) limited resources or out of misguided, ill-informed, or blatantly malicious attitudes toward other groups. Most people derive their livelihood from their jobs, as well as personal identity and self-fulfillment. The conse-quences of mechanisms such as stereotypes and discrimination can be detri-mental to those affected, their families, and communities.

Notes

1. Quote from Fonseca (1996, p. 306).
2. Indeed, this was the common usage of the word *diversity* in the United States and in Europe before the term had acquired its human resource connotation. Darwin's use of the term demonstrates this: "When we reflect on the vast diversity of the plants and animals which have been cultivated, and which have varied during all ages under the most different climates and treatments . . . (Darwin, 1995, p. 71).
3. For example, U.S. federal laws prohibiting discrimination include Title VII of the Civil Rights Act of 1964, which prohibits employment discrimination based on race, color, religion, sex, or national origin; the Age Discrimination in Employment Act of 1967 (ADEA), which protects individuals who are 40 years of age or older; Title I and Title V of the Americans With Disabilities Act of 1990 (ADA), which prohibits employ-ment discrimination against qualified individuals with disabilities in the private sector and in state and local governments; and Sections 501 and 505 of the Rehabilitation Act of 1973, which prohibits discrimination against qualified individuals with disabilities who work in the federal government.
4. These narrow category–based diversity definitions are not entirely useless in a global context. Whether out of the United States or other countries, such definitions may provide an example or inspiration to other countries even if, in their respective contexts, they are not always or immediately applicable or transferable.
5. Different cultures have different perceptions and attitudes toward homosexu-ality, and these views are expressed in national legislation. An extreme view of homo-sexual relations was expressed by President Yoweri Museveni of Uganda who said: "Look for homosexuals, lock them up and charge them" ("Lock Up Gays," 1999). According to Amnesty International (2003), over 70 countries maintain laws that crim-inalize homosexuality. In 15 of these nations, homosexual acts can equal life in prison or death.
6. For an overview of definitions of the stereotype concept, see Taylor and Moghaddam (1994), pp. 159–166.
7. For the origins and societal perspective of prejudice, see Cox (1994), pp. 64–74.
8. Hopkins details her experiences in her book, *So Ordered: Making Partner the Hard Way* (1996).

9. One such example was a famous 1992 incident in Los Angeles, when a 15-year-old girl was shot in the back of the head in Los Angeles by a Korean storeowner who thought the girl was shoplifting. This incident was the result of long-standing tensions between Korean storeowners and African American residents (Ford & Lee, 1991).

10. A *Time* magazine article from June 4, 1984, "Getting a Piece of the Power: Women Barred From Partnerships Can Now Go to Court," described the 1984 Supreme Court unanimous ruling that it was illegal for law firms to discriminate against women in deciding on partnership simply because of their gender (p. 63).

11. *Japan Times,* May 15, 1984, p. 2.

CHAPTER 7

Vive la Différence? Theoretical Perspectives on Diversity and Exclusion in the Workplace

I refuse to join any club that would have me as a member.

—Groucho Marx, comedian and actor

Groucho Marx had a humoristic take on the sense of exclusion experienced by those who cannot belong to the inner circles of society. A similar sentiment of "us" and "them" is expressed in *The House on Mango Street*, Sandra Cisneros's (1984) depiction of a young girl growing up in a community of Mexican immigrants in Chicago:

> Those who don't know any better come into our neighborhood scared. They think we're dangerous. They think we will attack them with shiny knives. They are stupid people who are lost and go here by mistake.
>
> But we aren't afraid. We know the guy with the crooked eye is Davey the Baby's brother, and the tall one next to him in the straw brim, that's Rosa's Eddie V., and the big one that looks like a dumb grown man, he's Fat Boy, though he's not fat anymore nor a boy.
>
> All brown all around, we are safe. But watch us drive into a neighborhood of another color and our knees go shakity-shake and our car windows get rolled up tight and our eyes look straight. Yeah. That is how it goes and goes.

Why are people forming a strong sense of belonging to groups? What dynamics dictate intergroup relations? How can we explain conflicts and hostilities among ethnic groups? The previous chapter reviewed major concepts describing the social psychological mechanisms that contribute to attitudes and behaviors toward diversity in the workplace. This chapter examines theories that address the following questions: How are differences among groups created and why? Why are people that are different from the "mainstream" more likely to be excluded from positions of power and influence in work organizations?

Over the years of research and scholarly investigation, several theories have been generated that explain the nature of intergroup relations. This chapter begins with an examination of the concept of the inclusion-exclusion continuum and its relevance to today's diverse workforce. It explores research on organizational demography that points to the connection between diversity and exclusion and explores several social psychological theories on diversity and intergroup relations. The chapter elaborates on social identity theory, concluding with its implications for explaining diversity and exclusion in a global context.

Diversity and Exclusion: A Critical Workforce Problem

"Diversity makes business sense."

"People are our most precious commodity."

"We are gender and color blind."

"We do not discriminate, we incorporate."

These were some of the poster slogans that greeted me as I walked into the lobby of a large international high-tech company headquartered in Southern California. I was there at the invitation of the CEO to evaluate the company's diversity policies. As a first step, I interviewed employees, both men and women, from different levels in the organization and of various backgrounds. Personal disclosures by interviewees underscored the company's challenge of moving beyond its uplifting slogans to create a culture that is truly inclusive. Most White men expressed the belief that the company was "blind to ethnic and gender differences," and therefore fair in its practices. Women and members of racial/ethnic minority groups, however, reported different experiences: they primarily talked about lost job opportunities and missed promotions. The word most often used by interviewees was *exclusion*. They felt left out of social and informational networks and barred from the organization's decision-making process. One middle-aged minority manager, recalling the difficulty in rising to her current position, told me that her promotion was initially blocked because her supervisor expressed the belief that she "did not possess the communication skills needed for a managerial job" because she came from a different culture. "That was nonsense," she said. "I am very good at what I do, but I am a woman in a man's job. I am short, my skin is dark, and I have a funny accent. The fact was that I just didn't fit in—and management's solution was to exclude me."

One of the most significant problems facing today's diverse workforce is that of exclusion, both the reality experienced by many and the perception of even greater numbers of employees that they are *not* viewed by top management as an integral part of the organization (Hitlan, Cliffton, & DeSoto, 2006; Insch et al., 2008; Kalev, 2009; Kanter, 1992; Mor Barak, 2000b; Wood, 2008). The inclusion-exclusion continuum[1] is central to the discussion in this chapter and is defined below:

> The concept of inclusion-exclusion in the workplace refers to the individual's sense of being a part of the organizational system in both the formal processes, such as access to information and decision-making channels, and the informal processes, such as "water cooler" and lunch meetings where information and decisions informally take place (Mor Barak, 2000b, 2005).

The distinction between inclusion-exclusion and organizational involvement is that the latter's focus is on organizational activities that foster the development of policies and procedures aimed at creating an environment where individuals have better access to company knowledge and information channels (Lawler, 1992, 2008). The high-involvement approach to management focuses on moving power to lower levels in the organization so that workers could participate in important decisions about how work is done and take responsibility for their performance. Interestingly, the high-involvement approach seems to be easier to install in countries that have a democratic political tradition, perhaps because it places a great emphasis on allowing workers to make decisions, giving them feedback about the effectiveness of their performance, and challenging them to develp and use their skills and abilities (Lawler, 2008). The concept of inclusion-exclusion, by contrast, is an indicator of the way employees experience and perceive their position in the organization relative to its "mainstream." Sometimes the experience of exclusion is blatant, such as when a Suriname-born Dutch project manager was not invited to a meeting of other project managers and was later told by his boss simply, "I didn't think you needed to be there." But more often, it is subtle and unintentional. A woman who served as a CFO of a large health care company (and the only woman among the company's top management) once told me that during breaks in the company's top-management team meetings, the guys would continue the discussions on the way to, and while in, the washroom. When she finally protested on being excluded from these discussions, her colleagues belittled her concerns saying there was no need to make a fuss over such a trivial matter.

Though diversity distinction categories vary from one culture or country to the next, the common factor that seems to transcend national boundaries is the experience of exclusion, particularly in the workplace. Individuals and groups are implicitly or explicitly excluded from job opportunities, information networks, team membership, human resource investments, and the decision-making process because of their actual or perceived membership in a minority or disfavored identity group. Yet inclusion in organizational information networks and in decision-making processes has been linked to better job opportunities and career advancement in work organizations (O'Leary & Ickovics, 1992; Cunningham, 2007), as well as to job satisfaction, well-being (Mor Barak & Levin, 2002), job performance, and organizational commitment (Cho & Mor Barak, 2008; Findler, Wind, & Mor Barak, 2007), all of which are related to employees' intention to leave and actual turnover (Mor Barak, Levin, Nissly, & Lane, 2006). Some scholarly work, though clearly not enough, examined the interaction between diversity distinction categories, such as race/ethnicity and gender, pointing to the compounding complexity of understanding racial prejudice when entangled with sexism (Bell, 1990, 1992, 2004). Research indicates that racial and ethnic minority women commonly believe they are excluded from the organizational power structure and have the least access to organizational resources from among disfavored groups (Kossek & Zonia, 1993; Mor Barak, Cherin, & Berkman, 1998; Shorter-Gooden, 2004). In addition, ethnic minority women are often required to fit into the existing culture with respect to their behavior and appearance if they want to penetrate networks of influence or be given opportunities for career development and advancement (Claringbould & Knoppers, 2007; Kamenou & Fearfull, 2006). Employees' experience and sense of exclusion, therefore, may play a critical role in explaining both their lack of job opportunities and dissatisfaction with their jobs, respectively.

Theoretical Underpinnings of the Inclusion-Exclusion Construct

The universal human need to be included in social systems has its roots in the way people have traditionally satisfied their basic needs. Because human beings have always depended on one another for their livelihood and needed to work together in order to get food, shelter, and clothing, social inclusion has had an important survival function through the ages and across cultures (Baumeister & Leary, 1995). Festinger's social comparison theory (Festinger, 1954; Mussweiler, Ruter, & Epstude, 2006; Greenberg, Ashton-James, & Ashkanasy,

2007; Guimond, 2006) and Mead's symbolic interaction theory (Appelrouth & Desfor Edles, 2007; Denzin, 2007; Mead, 1982) provide insights into the role of inclusion-exclusion experiences of individuals in social systems. The social comparison process, as delineated by Festinger, postulates that individuals have the need to evaluate themselves and to assess their relative standing within groups. For this process, individuals use their employee peer group as a referent (Goodman & Haisley, 2007; Greenberg, Ashton-James, & Ashkanazy, 2007). A study of immigrant youth in Denmark illustrates the sense of exclusion that can result from the social comparison process. Hjarnø-Knudsen's (2000) research documented a series of social processes that produced a sense of negative self-image among these youth. For example, the teenagers could not fit into the mainstream of Danish society because they were not able to afford clothes and accessories similar to those of their classmates, and their school achievements did not measure up to those of their peers due to their poor command of the Danish language. The youths' cognitive process of social comparison to their peers left them frustrated and led to conflicts with their parents as well as with Danish authorities and institutions (Hjarnø-Knudsen, 2000).

The symbolic interaction process highlights the fact that individual interpretation and synthesis of symbols and objects in their environments drive both situational analysis and individual behavior. Mead (1982) describes this process as seeing oneself from the viewpoint of others in determining how one stands in the world. Together these social psychological theories provide us with the concept of the interior monologue—the internal evaluation process that individuals continuously engage in with regard to their social environment. Perceptions of inclusion or exclusion, therefore, are a form of an ongoing personal evaluation. These evaluations are the chief methodology that individuals utilize to assess their position within groups and organizations and are assumed to be universal, not culture specific.

Both processes—assessing one's own standing relative to others (social comparison) and seeing oneself from the viewpoint of others in determining how one stands in the world (symbolic interaction)—are methods we all use to deal rationally with our work environments. These theories imply that the perception of group inclusion is an important continuous process in the individual's desire to secure positive group affiliations. Perceptions of inclusion or exclusion, therefore, are a form of an ongoing personal evaluation and serve as the chief methodology that individuals utilize to assess their position within groups and organizations. This process is important for individuals such as women, people with disability, and members of racial and ethnic minority groups who have traditionally been excluded from the mainstream's networks of influence in work organizations.

A theoretical connection between worker inclusion-exclusion experiences and performance and satisfaction *outcomes* in organizational social systems can be extrapolated from the "sociometer model" of self-esteem (Leary & Baumeister 2000; Leary & Downs, 1995). The authors posit that other people's reactions, particularly the degree to which they accept and include individuals or reject and exclude them, are vital to a person's physical and psychological well-being. Research demonstrates that social and physical pain share common physiological mechanisms and that social exclusion is painful because reactions to rejection are mediated by aspects of the physical pain system (Campbell et al., 2006; Zhong & Leonardellie, 2008; MacDonald & Leary, 2005).

Because humans have always depended on others for their basic needs, they are motivated to maintain connections with significant people and social systems in their lives (Baumeister & Leary, 1995). Leary and Baumeister (2000) note that "it is safe to conclude that the human organism is characterized by a basic need to belong—a fundamental motivation to form and maintain at least a handful of meaningful social attachments. The power and importance of this motivation are sufficient to think that people might well possess an internal meter to monitor such relationships" (p. 11). This psychological gauge, or "sociometer," is the individual's self-esteem that acts as a personal indicator that allows people to monitor inclusion or exclusion reactions toward them from their environment (Leary, Schreindorfer, & Haupt, 1995; Leary & Baumeister, 2000). Triggered by an environment that is exclusionary, threats to one's self-esteem produce behavioral outcomes that are aimed at rectifying the situation by, for example, compensatory efforts to assimilate or by disengaging from the exclusionary system and linking with a more inclusive environment.

Research thus indicates that individuals from diverse groups commonly find themselves excluded from networks of information and opportunity (Abrams, Hogg, & Marques, 2004; Gray, Kurihara, Hommen, & Feldman, 2007; Pettigrew & Martin, 1989; McGuire, 2000). The reasons are varied. First, overt or covert racism, sexism, ageism, as well as other forms of discrimination may be the motivation for exclusionary practices (Larkey, 1996). These behaviors may be in the form of unintentional racism, in which unconscious avoidance behavior is expressed toward an individual or a group, or in the form of blatant racism, in which certain people are consciously excluded from information networks and job opportunities (Bernstein & McRae, 1973; *Bertrand & Mullainathan, 2004*; Gaertner & Dovidio, 1986). Second, economic self-interest can be the motivation for preventing access to power and economic resources from certain individuals or groups (Larkey, 1996). Such behaviors result in the continued job segregation of women and minorities, as well as the exclusion of these groups from development and promotion opportunities (Becker, 1957; Feagin & Feagin, 1988; Gray, Kurihara, Hommen, & Feldman, 2007). And, third, prevalent stereotypical perceptions and general sense of discomfort with those that are perceived as different (e.g., women, members of minority group) can be the reason for their exclusion from important organizational processes and resources (Kalev, 2009). People tend to feel comfortable with others with whom they share important characteristics, fortifying in-group/out-group perceptions and creating exclusionary behaviors (Abrams, Marques, 2004; & Hogg, Blau, 1977). Perception patterns of in-group/out-group variability contribute to attitudes that close the door on opportunities for those who are different. People expect fewer variations from the stereotype in out-group members than they do in in-group members because they typically perceive out-groups as more homogeneous on negative stereotypical characteristics (Vonk & Van Knippenberg, 1995; Linville, Fischer, & Salovey, 1989; Rubin & Badea, 2007). An out-group is perceived as a single unit, not a collection of possibly different individuals, and the result is that those who are different are not given opportunities to demonstrate their unique and individual characteristics. They are treated according to preconceived notions and prejudices. Further, this perception of homogeneity among out-group members is increased under conditions of competition (Corneille, Yzerbyt, Rogier, & Buidin, 2001; Sassenberg, Moskowitz, Jacoby, & Hansen, 2007). The processes described above increase the likelihood of exclusion of those who are different (i.e., women, ethnic and racial minorities, and members of groups that may be stereotypically defined or labeled as different), especially in situations of competition that are common in the workplace, such as competition for jobs, salary increases, and promotions.

Research on Organizational Demography Documenting Exclusion

Organizational demography has been used as a conceptual framework for diversity research for more than two decades (Aparna, 2006; Choi, 2007; Ely, 1994; Tsui & Gutek, 1999; Wei, Lau, Young, & Wang, 2005; Gonzalez & Denisi, 2009). According to Tsui and Gutek (1999, p. 13), "Organizational demography focuses on the distribution of worker characteristics along dimensions studied by other demographers (i.e., sex, race, ethnicity, national origin, age, migration, and emigration)." However, whereas diversity research focuses primarily on minorities, women, and other disadvantaged groups in the workplace, research on organizational demography is broader, examining the effect of demographic distributions on everyone in the organization. More specifically, the research questions center on the impact of demographic differences between and among worker attitudes and behaviors and toward the organization as a whole. Its proponents claim that unlike diversity research, which often has a strong policy and practice implication and is action oriented, organizational demography is geared to explaining the impact of organizational demography on any group in the organization (Aparna, 2006; Choi, 2007;

Gonzalez & Denisi, 2009; Tsui, Porter, & Egan, 2002; Tsui & Gutek, 1999; Wei, Lau, Young, & Wang, 2005). The study of organizational demography is, therefore, useful for examining the relationship between diversity and exclusion in work organizations.

Research on organizational demography indicates that being in the minority has significant effects on individuals' affective experiences in the workplace, including feelings of isolation and lack of identification in one-on-one relationships (Ibarra, 1995; Mor Barak et al., 2006; Roscigno, Lopez, & Hodson, 2009). Milliken and Martins (1996) indicate a strong and consistent relationship between diversity in gender, ethnicity, and age and exclusion from important workplace interactions. One of the most frequently reported problems faced by women and minorities in organizational settings is their limited access to, or exclusion from, vital and yet informal interaction networks (Gray, Kurihara, Hommen, & Feldman, 2007; McDonald, Lin, & Ao, 2009; McPherson, Smith-Lovin, & Cook, 2001; Petersen, Saporta, & Seidel, 2000). Ella L. J. Edmondson Bell and Stella Nkomo discuss both African American women's and Caucasian women's experience of exclusion in their book, *Our Separate Ways: Black and White Women and the Struggle for Professional Identity* (2001).

> Another barrier experienced by Black women is limited access to informal and social networks in their organizations. The African American women we interviewed felt they had less access to these networks in their organizations than White men and White women. As a result, they felt cut off from important organizational information and less accepted as full members of the organization. Many of the women spoke of the critical importance of informal networks in career advancement. In most corporations, excellent performance is necessary for advancement but is not the sole criterion. Getting ahead also depends on access to informal networks and the relationships those networks can foster—mentorships, sponsorships, and help from colleagues. Building these relationships requires that the women be part of the social networks with the company. . . . Similarly, the White women managers also believed that exclusion from the "old-boy network" was one of the barriers to women's advancement. (pp. 152–153)

Due to the duality of race and gender, African American women in managerial and executive positions are more likely to be excluded from informal social networks (Combs, 2003). These networks allocate a variety of instrumental resources that are critical for job effectiveness and career advancement, as well as expressive benefits such as social support and friendship. Information gleaned from informal social networks provides access to valuable job-related information, and can affect job stability and better promotion prospects (Gray, Kurihara, Hommen, & Feldman, 2007; Ibarra, 1993). In the context of gender relations, men's network cohesion with other men can prevent women from access to information, knowledge, and job opportunities and therefore contributes to exclusion of women in the workplace. Men can, therefore, shape rules at work that would help them maintain their advantages over women and they can also change the rules if necessary to keep women in more subordinate positions, often by devaluing the work that women do (DiTomaso, Post, & Parks-Yancy, 2007). As a result, women can feel "out of the loop," or excluded, from important information flows. Often interactions that take place informally have meaning that can be more consequential to labor market outcomes than formal decision-making processes. Thus the informality of the promotion system can particularly disadvantage those without well-placed mentors with powerful social networks (Gray, Kurihara, Hommen, & Feldman, 2007, p. 153).

The Federal Glass Ceiling Commission in the United States has identified "information isolation," or the exclusion from information networks, as one of the main barriers that blocks the career advancement of women, as well as ethnic minorities, particularly in the private sector (Federal Glass Ceiling Commission, 1995). A number of studies have found that women who do make it to elite positions are often "outsiders on the inside"; that is, they are less integrated in informal discussion networks and outside the influential, central circle of high-level contacts (Davies-Netzley, 1998; Fisher, 2006; Ibarra, 1993). This isolation means that women are excluded from top networks and informal relationships that are necessary for further career advancement (Gray, Kurihara, Hommen, & Feldman, 2007).

Although women and members of minority groups have made some inroads into traditional nonminority male job domains, organizational jobs remain largely structured along race, gender, and class lines with the more meaningful and prestigious jobs being held by men of the dominant group and of higher social echelons (Beggs, 1995; Tomaskovic-Devey, 1993). For example, recent statistics indicate that women at the highest levels of business organizations are still rare. Only 13 women serve as CEOs running the United States' largest 500 publicly traded companies (USA Today, January 2, 2009), and only 15.7% of corporate officer positions at Fortune 500 companies are held by women. Some researchers have speculated that the extreme overrepresentation of White men in organizational positions of authority may have a negative impact on women and non-White subordinates (Ely, 1994; Pfeffer, 1989; Ridgeway, 1988). For example, women in male-dominated organizations may attempt to assimilate—that is, to alter their thoughts, feelings, behaviors, and expectations at work to mirror those typically associated with men (Ely 1995; Ely & Thomas, 2001). The disproportionate representation of men over women in senior organizational positions may highlight for women their limited mobility and reinforce their perceptions of themselves as lower status than men (Ely, 1994).

There is ample evidence of the differential treatment experienced by racial/ethnic minorities and women in the workplace. For example, men believe that gender is a cue to competence and that, in the absence of any definite information to the contrary, the performer's gender becomes relevant in making job-related decisions (Forschi, Lad, & Sigerson, 1994). Women, on the other hand, either do not hold that belief or do so to a lesser degree. Forschi et al. (1994) concluded that this double standard is a subtle mechanism through which the status quo of gender inequality in the workplace is maintained. The supervisor-subordinate relationship provides a key insight into the workings of intergroup relations in the organization. The more dissimilar the supervisor and subordinates are in terms of race and gender, the less effective the supervisor perceives the subordinate to be (Goldberg, Riordan, & Zhang, 2008; Tsui & O'Reilly, 1989; Tsui, Porter, & Egan, 2002).

Being in the minority has significant effects on individuals' affective experiences in the workplace, including isolation in work groups and lack of identification in one-on-one relationships (Ibarra, 1995). Alderfer, Alderfer, Tucker, and Tucker's (1980) findings indicate that African American employees believe they do not receive as much important career information as their White counterparts. Similarly, women tend to have less access to a variety of measures of status in the organization, such as income, position, and information, than do men (Alderfer, 1986; Kamenou & Fearfull, 2006; McDonald, Lin, & Ao, 2009). Potential advancement ladders are shorter for women and less frequently allow them to climb to executive or administrative levels (DiTomaso, Post, & Parks-Yancy, 2007; Gray, Kurihara, Hommen, & Feldman, 2007; Gutek, Larwood, & Stromberg, 1986; Insch, McIntyre, & Napier, 2008; Scriven, 1984; Taylor, 1986). Because leadership and management qualities are defined mostly in masculine terms, these barriers persist for women (Nkomo & Cox, 1996).

Social Psychological Theories on Diversity and Intergroup Relations

Social psychological theories regarding diversity, social identity, and intergroup relations have been developed primarily in two locations, North America and Western Europe. Beyond these two regions, little or no attention has been paid to issues of exclusion in the workplace, perhaps because jobs have been scarce for the dominant groups as well. On a global scale, the research and scholarly work on individual and intergroup differences in the workplace has been disjointed. Although there are similarities in areas of research (e.g., gender and intergroup relationships), they are often examined under different frameworks and using different terminology. Taylor and Moghaddam (1994) echo the concern expressed by several authors before them (e.g., Berlyne, 1968; Kennedy, Schrier, & Rogers, 1984; Sexton & Misiak, 1984) that theory development in Europe and in North America has occurred with little mutual influence. What these authors have called the "isolationism" or "monocultural science" (p. 10)—the parallel tracks taken by theorists in these two regions—may have been the result of lack of awareness of each other's work or a general sense that theories developed in one region are not relevant to the other.

Although North American scholars have often identified their work under the title of "workforce diversity," European scholars and the few scholars from other countries who have published in this area usually identify their work under titles such as gender studies, demography of the workforce, labor migration, and guest workers. The difference is much more than semantic preferences but seems to stem from different perspectives and worldviews. North American researchers focus on diversity of the workforce (e.g., gender, racial, and ethnic differences), which emanates from the region's historical role in absorbing immigrants and a value system rooted in equal employment opportunity, antidiscrimination, and fairness paradigms. European research centers on immigration, worker migration, and gender work roles and the inherent social and emotional difficulties in integrating immigrants and women into each country's relatively stable social fabric and gender roles. The global trends of immigration and worker migration, as well as legislation and social policies related to the workplace noted in the first part of this book, underscore the need to examine theories generated in different parts of the world and to generate an integrated approach to understanding workforce diversity and intergroup relations.

THEORIES OF INTERGROUP RELATIONS: REALISTIC CONFLICT THEORY, EQUITY THEORY, RELATIVE DEPRIVATION THEORY, AND INTEGROUP CONTACT THEORY

A close examination of workplace miscommunications, conflicts, disputes, and even violence often reveals that they are the product of intergroup relations. The concept of intergroup relations refers to "any aspect of human interaction that involves individuals perceiving themselves as members of a social category, or being perceived by others as belonging to a social category" (Taylor & Moghaddam, 1994, p. 6). Given the definition of diversity presented in Chapter 6, theories of intergroup relations should provide us with a deeper understanding of why people create these diversity categories, why they include or exclude members of other groups, and how they affect workplace relationships.

There are several major theories of intergroup relations that are relevant beyond specific national contexts (Taylor & Moghaddam, 1994). A few theories are worth mentioning here: *realistic conflict theory* (RCT) is an economic theory that assumes that people act in self-interest and that conflict is caused by people's drive to maximize their own or their group's rewards to the detriment of other groups' interests (Sassenberg, Moskowitz, Jacoby, & Hansen, 2007; Sherif, 1966; Sherif & Sherif, 1953); *equity theory* emphasizes people's striving for justice and views perceptions of injustice as the cause for personal distress and intergroup conflict (Adams, 1965; Bolino & Turnley, 2008; Walster, Walster, & Berscheid, 1978); *relative deprivation theory* focuses on perceptions of inequality between one's own access to resources and that of others in the society resulting in intergroup conflict and emphasizes the emotional aspects (e.g., anger, outrage, and grievance) of oppression (DeVinney, Star, & Williams, 1949; Feldman & Turnley, 2004; Stouffer, Suchman, Crosby, 1976); and *integroup contact theory,* which sees the root cause for conflict in lack of contact between groups, or contact under unfavorable conditions, and holds that contact optimal conditions (e.g., equal status between the groups, common goals, integroup coalition and support of authorities, law or custom) could reduce prejudice and integroup conflict (Allport, 1954; Brown & Hewstone, 2005; Crisp, Turner, & Rhiannon, 2009; Pettigrew, 1998; Pettigrew & Tropp, 2006). A fifth theory that explains intergroup relations, *social identity theory,* stands out as a megatheory with wide international appeal. The next section describes social identify theory and its usefulness as a tool for explaining exclusion in the workplace.

SOCIAL IDENTITY THEORY—EXPLAINING EXCLUSION

Social identity theory is a cognitive social psychological theory that originated in Europe and gained popularity in North America and other regions of the world. It provides the connection between social structures and individual identity through the meanings people attach to their membership in identity groups such as those formed by race, ethnicity, or gender (Tajfel, 1982a). The theory postulates that people tend to classify themselves into social categories that have meaning for them, and this shapes the way individuals interact with others from their own identity group and from other groups (Tajfel, 1978, 1982a; Tajfel & Turner, 1986; Turner, 1987). In essence, an important way of a person's definition of self is through belonging to and membership in groups. As a result, people categorize others into groups and configure internal representation of them to fit the prototype of the category (Hogg & Reid, 2006). Once others have been placed in those mental categories they are viewed as the embodiments of their identity groups and not as unique individuals (David, 2009).

The central proposition of the theory is that people desire to belong to groups that enjoy *distinct* and *positive* identities (Tajfel, 1978). Through *social comparisons* between the in-group and out-group, in-group members will make an effort to maintain or achieve superiority over an out-group in some dimensions (Tajfel & Turner, 1986). Therefore, those who belong to groups with higher perceived social status will accept and *include* people they consider to be like them, while *excluding* those they perceive to be different from them (Tajfel & Turner, 1986; also see Pettigrew, Allport, & Barnett, 1958). Social identity theory was originally conceptualized as a megatheory, in that it can explain the universal effects of social categorization and group membership regardless of the specific type of group. It is this all-embracing orientation of social identity theory that makes it relevant for the study of diversity from an international perspective.

Origin and Significance

Originally formulated by Henri Tajfel and John Turner (1979, 1986), social identity theory was developed in an attempt to explain relations between groups from a truly social psychological perspective. The context for developing the theory is, in itself, an interesting example of intergroup relations—the intellectual relationship between North American and European social psychologists in the second half of the 20th century. Henri Tajfel was a central figure in a movement that took shape in the late 1960s to develop a distinctive European social psychology. Unlike their North American counterparts at the time who adopted models that described people as rational and living in cohesion, European social psychologists increasingly focused on concepts that reflected the discord and conflict present in society. Moscovici (1972), for example, expressed discontent with the existing models of what he called the "social psychology of the nice person" (pp. 18–19) (e.g., "the leader is a person who understands the needs of members of his group," and "understanding the point of view of another person promotes cooperation") and called for the development of models that are realistic and reflective of change and conflict at the intergroup level. The movement's emphasis was on giving the *social* aspects of social psychology relatively greater importance by focusing on the individual within the context of broad social structures (Taylor & Moghaddam, 1994).

As a megatheory, social identity has a wide appeal because it examines the connections between group membership and contextual social processes regardless of the specific type of group. It can, therefore, be applied to intergroup relationships with regard to the salient attribute of, for example, skin color, as it is manifested in South Africa or the United States, or to the saliency of language in creating a separate identity in French Canada, Wales, or Belgium (Tajfel & Turner, 1986). Over the years, social identity theory gained influence and served as an important impetus for social psychological research on intergroup relations and has inspired additional theoretical developments in

Europe, North America, and, to a lesser degree, other regions of the world (Taylor & Moghaddam, 1994; Hogg & Terry, 2000; Haslam & Ellemers, 2005; Cornelissen, Haslam, & Balmer, 2007).

Central Concepts and Propositions

Several concepts serve as the building blocks of social identity theory and are central to its propositions. This section expands on two areas of the theory that are relevant to understanding intergroup relations: (1) social categorization and intergroup discrimination and (2) social identity and social comparison.

(1) Social categorization and intergroup discrimination. Social categorization is a cognitive tool that is used to "segment, classify and order the social environment, and thus enable the individual to undertake many forms of social actions" (Tajfel & Turner, 1986, pp. 15–16). Early studies on categorization focused on nonsocial stimuli (Tajfel, 1957, 1959; Tajfel & Wilkes, 1963) indicating that we categorize objects to help us function in the physical world. For example, if we want to drive a nail to the wall and do not have a hammer, we'll look for another object in the same category of hard and heavy objects that can serve the same purpose, such as a brick or a stone. Or, if we find ourselves without an umbrella on a rainy day, we would look for an object that could similarly protect us from the rain, such as a plastic bag or even a newspaper. The same principle is at work with social stimuli— categorizing people (including ourselves) into groups with a perceived common denominator helps us function in the social environment. Social categories include groups such as Europeans, women, teachers, Muslims, Blacks, gays, and managers. Although categorization of both objects and people may serve to simplify the world, people are more complex than objects, in that values and norms, as well as one's own group identification, may influence social categorization and attitudes toward other. People tend to give members of their own group the benefit of the doubt in ambiguous situations that they would not give to members of other groups. In a workplace recruitment situation, for example, being fired or laid off from a previous job because of excessive absenteeism would typically count against an applicant's chances of being hired, but in a college-based experiment, both Black and White individuals gave the benefit of the doubt to members of their own group and not to members of out-groups (Chatman & Von Hippel, 2001). Similarly, people's social identification as Whites in Pettigrew et al.'s (1958) research, and their positive perception of their own group, made them more likely to exclude others when group identification was ambiguous (see Box 7.1 for a description of the experiment).

BOX 7.1
The Binocular Resolution Classical Experiments of Racial Categorization in South Africa: Prestige of Groups, Identification, and Exclusion

In a series of experiments conducted in the middle of the 20th century, a team of researchers (Pettigrew et al., 1958) tested the link associated with in-group identification, perception of group prestige, and social categorization. Their most famous study was conducted in the highly charged racial climate of South Africa in the 1950s during apartheid.

Pettigrew and his colleagues used a stereoscope, a device that presents a picture of a different face to each eye and merges those images in order to test how individuals classify the race of facial images that combine persons from two different racial groups. The researchers utilized the perceptual phenomenon of binocular rivalry to introduce considerable uncertainty into the task of recognizing the race or ethnic group of each face. The sample included a non-random purposive sample of participants representing the full diversity of ethnic groups in South Africa, both men and women and a variety of occupations. The participants were Afrikaners, English-speaking Whites, Coloureds[1], Indians, and Black Africans. Participants were given two seconds to view the pictures and classify the race of the image in the picture. They were allowed, however, to indicate uncertainly in assigning a category.

In interpreting the results, it is important to remember the prestige and privileges that were associated with belonging to each group in South Africa during apartheid, with Whites, particularly Afrikaners, assuming they were racially superior and enjoying a privileged life, Coloureds and Indians the semi-"neutral" group in the middle, and Black Africans the most oppressed.

The Afrikaner participants were more likely to place ambiguous images in the "extreme" group, Black African, rather than the "neutral" group, Coloured or Indian, and less likely to place any ambiguous image in the "extreme" category of White. Their decisions seemed to be informed by a motivation to keep their group as "pure" as possible by adopting a strategy of overexclusion from the European group and overinclusion in the African group. This experiment demonstrates that when people classify others into social categories, (a) their self-identification with a specific category affects their classification of others, and (b) the social context and group prestige and hierarchy affect the classification process (Pettigrew et al., 1958).

---

[1]A term used in the context of South Africa's apartheid culture to denote a person of mixed race.

Later studies replicated the findings in the United States with similar results for racial/ethnic categories relevant to that culture (Lent, 1970) and demonstrated that prejudiced individuals were more cautious in assigning racial categories in a presumed effort to preserve in-group and out-group distinctions (Blasovich, Wyer, Swart, & Kibler, 1997). In a series of studies in the Netherlands, Dotsch, Wigboldus, Langner, and Van Knippenberg (2008) examined whether prejudiced people also have more negatively stereotyped mental representations of faces of people in the out-group. Their studies examined people's attitudes toward Moroccans, a highly stigmatized immigrant group in the Netherlands. Their findings indicate that the more prejudiced people are, the more criminal-looking their prototype of Moroccan faces is. Because more prototypical exemplars are processed more fluently (Winkielman, Halberstadt, Fazendeiro, & Catty, 2006), prejudiced individuals may find it easier to categorize criminal-looking Moroccan faces as Moroccan than to categorize innocent-looking Moroccan faces as Moroccan. The authors suggest that this process may also function as a stereotype-maintaining device (Dotsch, Wigboldus, Langner, and Van Knippenberg, 2008).

With the increased interracial and interethnic marriages in recent decades, there is a growing awareness that racial and ethnic identification often does not fall along the lines used by social institutions in the past. For example, a man born to a British immigrant from Liberia and a White British woman may see himself as both White and Black and both European and African. Others are more likely to categorize him as belonging to one race or nationality or the other, depending on his dominant features. A prominent example is the U.S. president Barack Obama, the son of a U.S. mother born in Kansas and an African father born in Kenya with roots in three continents—America, where he was born and raised, Africa, his father's ancestry, and Asia, where he spent part of his childhood with his mother and Indonesian stepfather. His multicultural heritage was touted as strength by his campaign to highlight his openness to different life experiences, and as a weakness by his opponents to paint him as detached from the common American experience. Many issues of categorization related to President Obama's identity have emerged during his presidential campaign in a way that has never been experienced in the United States (or in most other countries for that matter) before. In a famous incident in a town hall meeting with Obama's opponent Senator McCain, a woman said that she "could not trust Obama because he was an Arab" (McCain refuted the claim) (Blumiller, 2008). A controversial cartoon intended to mock the stereotypes, bigotry, and misconceptions surrounding Obama's background, on the cover of the *New Yorker* magazine, depicted Barack and Michelle Obama in Arab and terrorist attires bumping knuckles as a U.S. flag is burning in the fireplace of the White House Oval Office (*The New Yorker* cover, July 28, 2008). On the other hand, some were asking "Is Obama Black Enough?" debating his authenticity as a Black man in America (Coates, 2007).

A Web-based survey of a probability sample at the University of Michigan in the United States asked students to categorize a set of photographs as White, African American, Latino, Asian American, American Indian, Pacific Islander, or other (Harris, 2001). The researcher found a significant discrepancy between the responses of the people who were the subjects in the photographs and those by the survey participants. More specifically, individuals who self-identified with multiple races were more likely to be identified by survey participants with only one racial group. Further, the categories chosen by the survey participants were related to the survey participant's own racial or ethnic category, similar to Pettigrew and his colleagues' findings. An interesting caveat is that White students who were roommates of non-White students were more attuned to the complexity of the images they saw and used more racial groups to more accurately classify the photographs.

Tajfel and his colleagues were also interested in the impact of social categorization on discrimination, and their now classic "minimal group experiments" were designed to examine that aspect of intergroup relations (for a description of these studies, see Box 7.2). The groups used in their experiments were designed to be "minimal," in that individuals were randomly assigned to experimental conditions, membership was anonymous, and criteria for social categorization was not linked to rewards to be allocated among the groups, thus eliminating conditions that may be associated with realistic conflict rooted in competition for resources (Taylor & Moghaddam, 1994). Their studies showed that even in a minimal group situation, in which none of the conditions associated with realistic conflict should be operating, people tended to discriminate against members of out-groups simply because they belonged to a different social category. Therefore, the mere categorization of individuals, either voluntary or assigned, is all that is necessary to create in-group favoritism and out-group discrimination.

BOX 7.2
The Classic Minimal Group Experiments

Tajfel and his colleagues knew that people favor members of their own group (in-group) over members of other groups (out-group). However, these investigators (e.g., Billing & Tajfel, 1973; Tajfel, Flament, Billing, & Bundy, 1971) were interested in identifying the minimal conditions necessary to produce prejudice and discrimination. They conducted a series of studies using minimal manipulations of group membership, hence the name minimal group experiments. The aim of these experiments was to test whether discrimination will result from minimal conditions that generate categorization.

The participants in the minimal group experiments were 64 boys of 14 to 15 years of age from a comprehensive school in Bristol. All the boys came from the same house and knew each other well. An early experiment (Tajfel et al., 1971) demonstrates the principles of the minimal group experiments. The experiment had two distinct parts:

1. Establish an intergroup categorization. The boys were brought together in a lecture theater and asked to estimate the number of dots flashed onto a screen (they were told that the experimenters were interested in the study of visual judgements). The boys were told that they tended to either overestimate or underestimate the number of dots. The experimenters pretended to mark the boys' answers, when, in fact, the boys had been randomly allocated to their groups. Also, there was no value attached to either overestimating or underestimating—both were seen as equally inaccurate.

2. The second part was to assess the effects of this categorization on intergroup behavior. When the boys were asked to allocate monetary rewards (on a set of matrices), overestimators consistently allocated more points to other overestimators and underestimators to other underestimators, although the identity of the others was not revealed to them.

The results demonstrate that although the groups were based on a meaningless classification and members had no contact with each other, they still showed a preference for the in-group.

The criteria for minimal groups are as follows (Schiffman & Wicklund, 1992):

1. No face-to-face interaction.

2. Personal identity of group members should not be known.

3. There should be no particular advantage to belonging to a particular group or logical reason for holding a negative attitude against the group (e.g., overestimators vs. underestimators).

4. There should be no advantage or gain for the individual as a result of making a particular decision about reward allocation.

(Continued)

(Continued)

5. The strategy employed when differentiating between groups should conflict with a more "rational" strategy.

Many studies that provide still more convincing evidence of the prejudice and discrimination resulting from even an arbitrary group categorization (Bourhis, Sachdev, & Gagon, 1994) followed in the footsteps of Tajfel and his colleagues' research. In one such experiment, Locksley, Ortiz, and Hepburn (1980) told the participants that they were being assigned to groups at random and were actually shown the lottery ticket that determined whether they were members of the Phi group or the Gamma group. Even with this explicit random assignment, study participants still showed a preference for members of their own group.

The minimal group experiments, and this last study in particular, are powerful demonstrations of prejudice and discrimination that can be generated even by the very minimal conditions.

(2) Social identity and social comparison. Identity, according to social identity theory, has two components: a personal component derived from idiosyncratic characteristics—such as personality, physical, and intellectual traits—and a social component derived from salient commonalities of group memberships, such as race, sex, class, and nationality (Ashforth & Mael, 1989; Tajfel, 1982a). Social identity is a perception of oneness with a group of persons (Ashforth & Mael, 1989; Cornelissen, Haslam, & Balmer, 2007; Haslam & Ellemers, 2005; Hogg & Terry, 2000). Sometimes, however, this perception of oneness is the result of being categorized by the larger society as members of a particular group. For example, despite their distinct cultural heritage and complex historical relationships, individuals who emigrate from countries such as Korea, China, and Japan are "lumped" into one group known as "Asian" when they live in North America or Europe (Choi, 2001). The differences between these individuals who come from very different countries, backgrounds, and histories are forgotten, with any uniqueness misunderstood at best (Fowler, 1996). However, over the years, individuals from these countries, and particularly the second-generation immigrants, have developed a sense of identity that is tied to being Asian Americans or Asian Europeans.

Social identity involves a process of self-categorization, along with an attachment of value to the particular social category (Pettigrew, 1986). Together, these two elements, group categorization and value attachment, constitute social identity (Turner & Giles, 1981). *Social identity* is defined as the individual's knowledge that he or she belongs to certain social groups, together with some emotional and value significance to him or her of the group membership (Tajfel, 1978, p. 63).

Social identity stems from the categorization of individuals, the distinctiveness and prestige of the group, the salience of out-groups, and the factors that traditionally are associated with group formation. Most important, and most relevant to the present discussion, social identification leads to activities that are congruent with the group's collective identity, that support institutions that embody their identity, and that foster stereotypical perceptions of self and others (Ashforth & Mael, 1989). *Social comparison* is the process that people use to evaluate themselves by comparing their group's membership with other groups. The basic hypothesis is that pressures to positively evaluate one's own group through in-group/out-group comparisons lead social groups to attempt to differentiate themselves from each other (Tajfel, 1978; Tajfel & Turner, 1986). The aim of differentiation is to maintain or achieve superiority over an out-group on some relevant dimension.

LIMITATION OF SOCIAL IDENTITY THEORY
IN UNDERSTANDING DIVERSITY AND EXCLUSION

One criticism of social identity theory is that it has tautological elements in its conceptualization: The first is the link between self-esteem and discrimination (self-esteem is described as the motive for discriminating against out-group members, as well as the consequence of this discrimination). The second is in defining social identity (the theory claims that when social identity is salient, individuals act as group members; yet if they don't act as group members, the theory explains it by claiming that social identity is not salient) (Abrams, 1992; Abrams & Hogg, 1988; Taylor & Moghaddam, 1994). Another criticism lies in the theory's very broad and rather generic view of social categories. Because the theory places all types of categorization as equal, it cannot account for the heightened significance of race, gender, and class in many cultures and nations due to their deep historical roots in both the Western world and in previously colonized countries. Finally, social identity theory conceptualizes identity primarily as self-defined. It therefore downplays the consequences of other groups defining individuals and affecting their sense of inclusion or exclusion.

IMPLICATIONS OF SOCIAL IDENTITY
THEORY TO DIVERSITY AND EXCLUSION

Every society and every organization consists of a large number of groups, and every person represents a number of these groups when dealing with other people (Alderfer & Smith, 1982). Demographic characteristics of organizations, such as race and sex distributions, help to shape the meanings people attach to their identity group memberships at work (Ely, 1994). As social identity theory has demonstrated, the way we perceive our social reality is significantly determined by our group memberships, such as gender and racial/ethnic affiliation. It follows that individual experiences vis-à-vis work organizations and their perceptions of organizational actions and policies will be affected by their identity group memberships. This social psychological perspective is useful to the current discussion because it indicates how identity groups shape applicant and worker experiences, perceptions, and behaviors in different employment settings. It is particularly relevant when membership in an identity group is associated with exclusion from employment opportunity and job mobility.

Tajfel and Turner (1986) conceptualize *group* as "a collection of individuals who perceive themselves to be members of the same social category, share some emotional involvement in this common definition of themselves, and achieve some degree of social consensus about the evaluation of their group and of their membership in it." Following from that, their definition of intergroup behavior is identical to that of Sherif (1966, p. 62): "any behavior displayed by one or more actors towards one or more others that is based on the actors' identification of themselves and others as belonging to different social categories." When a social group's status position is perceived to be low, it affects the social identity of group members. A group's *status* is the outcome of the social comparison process described earlier; it reflects the group's position on some evaluative dimensions relative to relevant comparison groups (Tajfel & Turner, 1986).

Low subjective status does not promote intergroup competition directly but rather indirectly through its impact on members' social identity. When faced with negative or threatened social identity, individuals may utilize one of the following strategies:

- *Individual mobility.* Individuals will attempt to pass from a lower-status to a higher-status group by disassociating themselves psychologically and behaviorally from their low-status group. For example, immigrants who feel that their social identity is devalued by the host society because most of the members of their ethnic group hold low status or menial labor jobs could choose to distance themselves from their co-ethnic peers though individual mobility (Shinnar, 2008). When the opportunities for upward mobility exist, low-status group members are often willing to choose individual upward mobility over a collective action. It is based on the assumption that the society is flexible and permeable and that through talent, hard work, or luck one can move from an undesirable group to a more desirable one (Turner & Tajfel, 1986). When successful, such a strategy will lead to a personal solution but will not make a difference in the group's status. An interesting example is women's social status in India. Although women have long had access to powerful professions such as in politics and medicine, they are still perceived as incompetent and not suitable for management and leadership. Despite having a woman as prime minister (Indira Gandhi was elected and served as prime minister of India from 1966 to 1977 and again from 1980 to 1984) and despite the number of women who have risen to top management positions in Indian organizations, women are typically stereotyped as being "less intelligent, less able to meet the demands of the job, less competent and in general have to work much harder than men to get the same results" (Nath, 2000).

- *Group mobility through "social creativity."* Group members may seek positive status for the group as a whole by redefining or altering the elements of the comparative situations (Shinnar, 2008). This coping mechanism is more psychological in nature compared to individual mobility and involves altering one's perceptions rather than taking direct action (Wright & Tropp, 2002). This could take place by, for example, changing the values assigned to the attributes of the group so that comparisons that were previously negative are now perceived as positive (such as the slogan used by African Americans, "Black is beautiful") (Tajfel & Taylor, 1986). Social creativity includes strategies such as: (a) seeking new elements for intergroup comparisons, such as comparing oneself to an outperforming in-group member, can be identity enhancing because it reflects positively on the group identity (Schmitt, Branscombe, Silvia, Garcia, & Spears, 2006); (b) redefining existing elements for such comparisons so that previously negative comparisons become positive; and (c) selecting an alternative referent group to which one's in-group is compared—instead of comparing one's group to the dominant majority, one may choose the referent group from other minorities. Group mobility through social creativity involves selecting new elements for intergroup comparisons leading to a more favorable evaluation. Individuals search for new, positive aspects of their group to justify the features not welcomed by other groups, or they seek features they deem as superior. As another example, a sample of non-English-speaking, non-European, international university students from 32 countries was studied to determine whether their sense of belonging to an international student identity group would counterbalance their sense of exclusion within the university. The researchers found not only that the students' group identification increased but also that it positively predicted improved self-esteem for the members. This research was insightful in two ways. First, it demonstrated that being perceived by *others* as a group was all that was needed to create a new group identity; and, second, it demonstrated that this new group identity gave them a more positive sense about themselves as foreign students (Schmitt, Spears, & Branscombe, 2003). This study provides support to the rejection-identification model (Branscombe, Schmitt, & Harvey, 1999) proposing that although perceived prejudice has psychological costs, those costs are suppressed by increased identification with one's minority group.

- *Social competition.* Members of a group may seek to improve their status by direct competition with the higher-status group. This coping mechanism refers to engagement in social action in order to promote change in the status quo and improve social comparisons that are unfavorable to one's own group. In the case of Mexican Americans, an example for social action to promote a more positive group identity is the Chicano movement of the 1960's. Deaux, Ried, Martin, and Bikmen (2006) found that immigrants of color who have been in the United States for more than eight years were more likely to reject social inequality and engage in collection action to improve the conditions of their group. The assumption underlying the social competition coping mechanism is that "the nature and structure of the relations between social groups in the society is characterized by marked stratification, making it impossible or very difficult for individuals, as individuals, to divest themselves of an unsatisfactory, underprivileged, or stigmatized group membership" (Tajfel & Turner, 1986, p. 9). In this system, individuals interact with one another based on their respective group memberships and not as individuals. To achieve positive distinctiveness, they may try to reverse their position relative to the other groups. This challenge, however, may generate conflict and antagonism between the subordinate and the dominant groups, in that it involves redistribution of scarce resources and a reassignment of power. A prime example of this conflict is the use of affirmative action policies to give disadvantaged groups better opportunities and the debate over reversing those policies, particularly when the economy is down and jobs are scarce. Although it is commonly believed that the antidote to categorizations that breed exclusion is more social contact between individuals from different groups, Geert Hofstede (1997) warns that contrary to popular belief, intercultural encounters among groups do not automatically breed mutual understanding. In fact, such contacts, unless they are prolonged and allow individuals from each group to really get to know individuals from another, usually confirm each group's previous perceptions of the other group. Isaac Olawale Albert[2] ("Nigeria—Watchdog Goes Back to School," 2002), commenting on the situation in Africa where tribal conflicts are a common occurrence, concurs:

> When "diverse peoples" meet, most especially as a result of social and geographical contacts, a culture shock is produced. It is within this framework that diversity becomes a development question that must be carefully managed. If well managed, diversity could be a major asset to society.

Summary and Conclusion

This chapter examines theories that address the following questions: How are differences among groups created and why? Why are people that are different from the "mainstream" more likely to be excluded from positions of power and influence in work organizations? Over the years of research and scholarly investigation, several theories have been generated that explain the nature of intergroup relations. The need to belong to social groups appears to be universal. The theories discussed in this chapter demonstrate that people are motivated to seek inclusion and avoid exclusion and that this basic human need transcends cultural and national boundaries. Further, individuals seek to belong to groups that are associated with higher status and prestige in society. Belonging to such groups is central to individuals' identity and their sense of worth.

A theoretical connection between worker inclusion-exclusion experiences and performance and satisfaction *outcomes* in organization social systems can be extrapolated from the "sociometer model" of self-esteem (Leary & Downs, 1995). Other people's reactions—particularly the degree to which they accept and include individuals or reject and exclude them—are vital to a person's physical and psychological well-being. Triggered by an environment that is exclusionary, threats to one's self-esteem produce behavioral outcomes that are aimed at rectifying the situation by, for example, compensatory efforts to assimilate or by disengaging from the exclusionary system and linking with a more inclusive environment.

Social identity theory provides the connection between social structures and individual identity through the meanings people attach to their membership in identity groups such as those formed by race, ethnicity, or gender. The theory postulates that people tend to classify themselves into social categories that have meaning for them, and this shapes the way individuals interact with others from their own identity group and from other groups. The central proposition of the theory is that people desire to belong to groups that enjoy *distinct* and *positive* identities. Therefore, those who belong to groups with higher perceived social status will accept and *include* people they consider to be like them, while *excluding* those they perceive to be different from them (Tajfel, 1982a).

The inclusion-exclusion continuum, introduced in this chapter, is linked to important psychological processes such as self-esteem, depression, anxiety, and a general perception that one's life has meaning. This is particularly relevant for members of disadvantaged or stigmatized groups who may suffer the psychological consequences of being excluded. Therefore, this need to be included in social groups is a strong motivator in human behavior. Though one needs to be aware of the inherent competitive nature of identity groups, what one gains in status the other may lose; taken together, these theories tell us that work organizations may gain a more loyal, satisfied, and committed workforce by becoming more inclusive.

Notes

1. For research scales that assess this construct in the context of diversity, see the Appendix.

2. Dr. Isaac Olawale Albert, of the Peace and Conflict Studies Programme in the Institute of African Studies, University of Ibadan, Nigeria.

CHAPTER 8

Culture and Communication in the Global Workplace

The Jack Welch of the future cannot be me. I spent my entire career in the United States. The next head of General Electric will be somebody who spent time in Bombay, in Hong Kong, in Buenos Aires. We have to send our best and brightest overseas and make sure they have the training that will allow them to be global leaders who will make GE flourish in the future.

—Jack Welch, CEO of U.S.-based General
Electric in a speech to GE employees[1]

To succeed in managing a workforce that is increasingly diverse and multinational, managers need knowledge about cultural differences and similarities among nations. They also need to be sensitive to these differences, which can contribute to their effectiveness in cross-cultural communication. Human behavior and interpersonal interactions are reflective of the values and norms of specific societies. These cultural values and behavioral norms differ between societies, but until recently, they have been considered quite stable within societies. In recent decades, however, this perception has been changing as scholars became more aware of the impact of the global trends of immigration and worker migration on national cultures (see Chapters 4 and 5). In today's global business world, a manager has to understand cultural differences among societies and their meaning in business relations. In addition, she or he needs to be sensitive to cultural nuances within societies that are associated with the diversity of that society. In this chapter, we examine the cultural context in the global workplace and analyze communication patterns that facilitate or block effective cross-cultural communication.

The Cultural Context for the Global Workplace

What is *culture?* The Latin origin of the word refers to the tilling of the soil, although the common everyday use of the word refers to refinement, particularly through education, literature, and the arts. In this book, we refer to the broader meaning of the word *culture* as used by social scientists. There are many definitions of culture in the social psychological and anthropological literature,[2] but the most widely accepted definition is the one proposed in the mid-20th century by Kroeber and Kluckhohn (1952) after analyzing 160 definitions of the concept of *culture* and synthesizing the following definition:

> Culture consists of patterns, explicit or implicit, of and for behavior acquired and transmitted by symbols, constituting the distinctive achievements of human groups, including their embodiments in artifacts; the essential core of culture consists of traditional (historically derived and selected) ideas and especially their attached values; culture systems may, on the one hand, be considered as products of action, on the other as conditioning elements of further action. (p. 181)

Using the analogy of computer programming, Hofstede & Hofstede (2005) call culture "software of the mind," noting that the patterns of thinking, feeling, and acting embedded in a culture are like "mental programs." They define *culture* as "the collective programming of the mind which distinguishes the members of one group or category of people from another" (p. 4). Although culture does not determine the exact behavior for human beings the way programs dictate how computers function, it does delineate the expectations, actual or anticipated, and behaviors within a specific social context. Others define *culture* as a "set of beliefs and values about what is desirable and undesirable in a community of people, and a set of formal or informal practices to support the values" (Javidan & House, 2001, p. 292). Understanding societal culture can be complex because it includes two sets of elements at once: the first are the ongoing cultural practices that inform us about the current perceptions of specific cultures, and the second are the strongly held values that inform us about aspirations and direction that cultures wish to develop (Javidan et al., 2005).

If culture is the sum of the learned and shared patterns of thought and behaviors that are characteristic of a given people, how are national cultures around the world different from one another? To answer this question, Hofstede (1980, 1997, 2001; Hofstede & Hofstede, 2004), a Dutch social scientist, embarked on a multinational study examining national cultures. In his initial book, *Culture's Consequences* (1980), Geert Hofstede presented a statistical analysis of about 117,000 questionnaires collected in 1967 and 1973 from employees working in IBM subsidiaries in 40 different countries. Studying individuals who worked for the same organization was assumed to provide the researchers with a good environment for studying national cultures because all the employees were thought to share the same organizational culture and environment. This allowed the researchers to focus on the differences in the participants' responses as indicative of national cultural differences. In other words, the researchers assumed that being employed by the same organization (IBM) has created a common organizational culture and, therefore, whatever differences in values and norms would be evident between employees who worked in different countries would be the result of national cultural differences. The most important result of this analysis was a theoretical formulation of four value dimensions for representing differences among national cultures: power distance, uncertainty avoidance, individualism-collectivism, and masculinity/femininity. A fifth dimension—long versus short-term orientation—was added a decade later (Hofstede, 1991).

It is important to note from the outset that Hofstede's research (e.g., 1980, 1990, 1991, 2001) was widely lauded for its breakthrough contribution to the study of culture (e.g., Kirkman, Lowe, & Gibson, 2006; Søndergaard, 1994), yet it was criticized for its lack of scientific rigor and even outright cultural bias (e.g., Ailon, 2008; McSweeney, 2002). Because of its enduring and widespread influence, we devote the following sections to discussing the strengths of the work as well as its limitations.

CULTURAL VALUE DIMENSIONS

Social anthropologists have long agreed that all societies face the same basic problems—they differ only in their answers to the problems.[3] Hofstede (1980), based on an earlier framework developed by Inkeles and Levinson (1969), examined culture in the different countries along four axes: *power distance*—the relationship with authority and social inequality; *individualism vs. collectivism*—the relationship between the individual and the group; *masculinity vs. femininity*—the tendency toward assertiveness in contrast to modesty; and *avoidance of uncertainty*—the control of aggression and expressions of emotions. Interestingly, Hofstede (1980) found that national culture, as measured along these axes, explained more of the differences in work-related values and attitudes than did position within the organization, profession, age, or gender. Following the discovery and write-up of the four original cultural dimensions stated above, Hofstede (2001) decided to add a fifth dimension to his model. This dimension was based on the answers of student samples from 23 countries to the Chinese Value Survey (CVS). The study's instrument was developed by Michael Harris Bond in Hong Kong based on values suggested by Chinese scholars and seemed was to reflect Confucian teachings in both of its poles. The fifth dimension was *long- versus short-term orientation*—the tendency for thrift and perseverance and respect for tradition and fulfilling social obligations. Table 8.1 provides the definitions for each dimension with some country-specific examples.

Table 8.1   Dimensions of Cultural Difference

Dimension	Definition[1]	Country-specific examples[2]
Power distance	*Power distance* refers to the extent to which the less powerful members of institutions and organizations within a country expect and accept that power is distributed unequally.	Large power distance: Malaysia, Guatemala, Panama, Philippines, Mexico Small power distance: Austria, Israel, Denmark, New Zealand, Ireland
Individualism vs. collectivism	*Individualism* pertains to societies in which the ties between individuals are loose. *Collectivism* pertains to societies in which people are integrated into strong cohesive in-groups, which throughout a lifetime continue to protect them in exchange for unquestioning loyalty.	High individualism: USA, Australia, Great Britain, Canada, the Netherlands High collectivism: Guatemala, Ecuador, Panama, Venezuela, Colombia
Masculinity vs. femininity	*Masculinity* pertains to societies in which gender roles are clearly distinct. *Femininity* pertains to societies in which social gender roles overlap (both men and women are supposed to be modest, tender, and concerned with quality of life).	High masculinity: Japan, Austria, Venezuela, Italy, Switzerland High femininity: Sweden, Norway, the Netherlands, Denmark, Costa Rica

Dimension	Definition[1]	Country-specific examples[2]
Avoidance of uncertainty	*Avoidance of uncertainty* refers to the extent to which the members of a culture feel threatened by uncertain or unknown situations—the extent to which they need predictability in the form of written and unwritten rules.	Weak uncertainty avoidance: Greece, Portugal, Guatemala, Uruguay, Belgium Strong uncertainty avoidance: Singapore, Jamaica, Denmark, Sweden, Hong Kong
Long-term vs. short-term orientation	Long-term orientation refers to the fostering of virtues oriented toward future rewards, in particular, perseverance and thrift. Short-term orientation refers to the fostering of virtues related to the past and present, in particular, respect for tradition, preservation of "face," and fulfilling social obligations.	Long-term orientation: China, Hong Kong, Taiwan, Japan, Korea Short-term orientation: Zimbabwe, Canada, Philippines, Nigeria, Pakistan

NOTES:

1. Definitions for the four cultural dimensions are drawn from Hofstede (1997), pages 28, 51, 82, and 113, respectively, and the fifth cultural dimension is drawn from Hofstede (2001), pages 356 and 359.

2. Country-specific identifications in this table and throughout the chapter are based on Hofstede's study among IBM employees worldwide and Michael Bond's CVS study among students. Scores and rankings for the more than 60 countries included in the original study on each of the four cultural dimensions can be found in Hofstede (1980, 1997) and those for 23 countries included in the CVS study on the fifth dimension can be found in Hofstede (2001).

SOURCE: Adapted from Hofstede, 1980, 1997, 2001.

These five dimensions have clear implications for individual and group expectations related to acceptable behaviors in the workplace. Whether employees expect their supervisor, for example, to be authoritative and give clear instructions that they will closely follow or whether they expect to operate independently and have egalitarian relationships with their supervisors depends to a large extent on the cultural perception of power distance in their society. Below is a description of the cultural differences in expected and acceptable behaviors in the workplace, according to Hofstede's five axes.

POWER DISTANCE

In large power distance societies, such as Latin countries (Latin American and Latin European, like France and Spain), as well as Asian and African countries, the hierarchical system in society is considered existential. Applying this principle to the workplace, supervisors and subordinates consider themselves as existentially unequal. There are many supervisors and many layers of management with large salary differentials between people at the top and at the bottom, as well as in between. Subordinates expect to be told what to do, and superiors are entitled to special privileges. Hofstede & Hofstede (2005) note that, in high power distance societies, "The ideal boss, in the subordinates' eyes, is a benevolent autocrat or 'good father'" (p. 55). In contrast, in small power distance societies, such as the United States, Canada, Great Britain, and Denmark, subordinates and supervisors consider themselves as existentially equal. The hierarchical strata in the organizations are considered permeable, providing the possibility for both subordinates and supervisors to move up or down the ladder, and supervisors are expected to be accessible to subordinates. The ideal boss is "a resourceful, and therefore respected, democrat" (Hofstede, & Hofstede, 2005, p. 56). There is evidence that congruence between managers' societal values of power distance and the culture of the organization in which the manager works can reduce job-related stress. For example, Joiner (2001) found that managers in Greece, a country characterized by a large power distance, were comfortable with the so-called Eiffel Tower organizational culture, characterized by centralization and formalizations, and that the congruence between this type of organizational culture and the Greek culture contributed to reduced levels of stress among the managers.

INDIVIDUALISM VS. COLLECTIVISM

The individualism/collectivism dimension refers to the extent to which people see themselves as an integral part of a social group with primary alliance to the group or as separate individuals with primary responsibility for themselves and their very immediate family only. In collectivist societies, such as many Latin American countries as well as Arab-speaking countries, people are born into extended families or other in-groups, which continue to protect them in exchange for loyalty. This reality is evident in the workplace where the relationship between the employer and the employees in the organization is seen as a family relationship. There are mutual obligations with strong loyalty on the part of the employee connected to an employer's commitment for protection and security in return. In a strong collectivist-oriented context, there is a clear preference for group-oriented human resource management practices (Aycan et al., 2007). Employee loyalty in this context refers to an unwritten contract that requires employees to be faithful to their duties, to their managers and cowork-ers, and to their organization. It means that they will follow orders, behave according to expectations, and do the best job they know how to do (Umiker, 1995). Hiring preference is given to relatives, first to relatives of high-ranking members of the organization and then to others. The assumption underlying this practice is that hiring relatives of employees reduces the company's business risk (due to familiarity with the new hires) and increases employee loyalty. Even when employees do not perform to expectation, they can still expect to hold onto their jobs because of the family loyalty value. A strong collectivist orientation, such as in many countries in the Middle East, often translates into commitment to the work organization (Robertson, Al-Khatib, & Al-Habib, 2002). A study of 365 employees from Saudi Arabia, Kuwait, and Oman provides support for the proposition that a collectivist orientation is associated with a strong group com-mitment and belief in participatory work ethics (Robertson et al., 2002).

A typical employee in the United States (individualist society) would most likely view his or her employer as rewarding individual initiative and effort, whereas a typical Korean employee (collectivist society) is more likely to say that his company rewards collaboration and working together rather than alone (Javidan & House, 2001). In individualist societies, such as the United States, Australia, Great Britain, and Canada, people are expected to act on their own interests. The relationship between employees and employers is based, therefore, not on group loyalty but on complementing self-interests. Employers' decisions related to hiring and promotions are expected to be based on skills, achievements, and merit; favoritism and nepotism are strongly dis-couraged. In approaching work assignments, employees in a collectivist society would emphasize working together and will view the relationships as more important than the task, whereas the reverse will be true in the individualist society where the task will prevail over the relationship. A study comparing social support of employees in a U.S.-based company with that of employees in its former subsidiary in Israel found significant differences that are rooted in the collectivist-individualist leanings, respectively, of these two societies (Mor Barak, Findler, & Wind, 2003). Using the statistical method of factor analysis, which allowed the researchers to identify clusters of relationships between variables, the researchers examined the sources of social support for employees in the two societies. They found that employees in the United States clearly delineated between three types of support providers: their supervisor, their coworkers, and support providers from outside the work environment—their spouses/partners, family members, and friends. The Israeli employees did not make such distinctions. For the Israeli employees, living in a collectivist society, the lines between supervisors, coworkers, and family/friends networks were blurred because a coworker, or supervisor for that matter, could also have been a friend or a family member.

MASCULINITY VS. FEMININITY

The masculinity/femininity dimension refers to the extent to which dominant values in the society emphasize assertiveness, competition, and material achievements, attributes associated with masculine qualities, as compared with feminine qualities such as relationships among people, care for others, and care for quality of life in general. Hofstede (1980, 1997, 2005) justifies anchoring these qualities in the gender-related terminology of the ancient, universal, gender-role differences between men as hunters, fighters, and providers and women as caretakers and nurturers of the family. In masculine societies, such as Japan, Italy, Mexico, and the United States, assertiveness, ambition, and competitiveness are expected and rewarded in the work context. In contrast, employees who show modesty, solidarity, and care for others are valued more in feminine societies such as Sweden, Norway, the Netherlands, and Denmark. In feminine societies, there is a preference for solving work-related conflicts by compromise and negotiation, whereas in masculine societies, power struggles and direct confrontation may be more common in conflict resolution. Managers in feminine societies take into consideration their employees' needs and strive for consensus, whereas managers in masculine societies are expected to be assertive and decisive. The balance between work and family is also very different in both types of societies. In the Scandinavian countries (identified as feminine societies), fathers often take time out from work to take care of a young or sick child. In a review of paternity leave statistics in the EU, Dermott (2001) reported that almost all fathers in Sweden take some leave, half of those in Denmark take leave, and 33% of fathers in Finland take paternity leave. In contrast, in masculine societies, the mother typically takes care of the children, and the father is expected to continue with his work as usual. In some countries, such as Japan and South Korea, the traditional cultural expectation was that women retire completely from the workforce once they had their first child and devote full time to raising their children. When Britain's prime minister Tony Blair limited his schedule but continued to work when his fourth child, Leo, was born May 2000, a public debate ensued about the justification of such an action with some criticizing his action as irresponsible and others hailing it as an example for paternal responsibility. Britain is, of course, near the masculine end of the scale.

AVOIDANCE OF UNCERTAINTY

Avoidance of uncertainty is a dimension that refers to the extent to which people in a society feel anxious about ambiguous situations and the steps that they are willing to take to create stability through formalization of rules and regulations. In high uncertainty avoidance societies, such as Belgium, Japan, and France, there are many rules that govern the behavior of employees as well as the work process. In contrast, in low uncertainly avoidance societies such as Great Britain, Jamaica, and South Africa, there are fewer regulations and a general belief that there should not be more rules than are strictly necessary. High job mobility is prevalent and expected in societies with low uncertainty avoidance, and job stability and lifetime employment are more common and cherished in societies with high uncertainty avoidance. Hofstede and Hofstede (2005) note the importance of the anxiety component of uncertainty avoidance and its impact on time orientation in the work context:

> In strong uncertainty avoidance societies people like to work hard, or at least to be always busy. Life is hurried, and time is money. In weak uncertainty avoidance societies people are quite able to work hard if there is a need for it, but they are not driven by an inner urge towards constant activity. They like to relax. Time is a framework to orient oneself in, but not something one is constantly watching. (p. 183)

LONG- VERSUS SHORT-TERM ORIENTATION

The long- versus short-term orientation is the fifth dimension that was added after the introduction of the original four dimensions to address differences in East-West cultural orientations. Designed by Chinese scholars and reflecting Confucian principles, the Chinese Value Survey (CVS) provided the initial evidence for this dimension among students in 23 different countries (Hofstede, 2007; Hofstede & Bond, 1988). Long-term orientation refers to the fostering of virtues oriented toward future rewards, in particular, perseverance and thrift. Short-term orientation refers to the fostering of virtues related to the past and present, in particular, respect for tradition, preservation of "face," and fulfilling social obligations.

In long-term-oriented cultures, a person's responsibility for family and for work are not separate and not viewed as in competition. In fact, the two seem to support each other and therefore family enterprises are very common. The long-term pole on the continuum is associated with persistence, perseverance, and tenacity in pursuit of goals and this value orientation is seen as supporting entrepreneurial initiatives. These values are paired with the values of thrift and a sense of comfort with hierarchy, all leading to the availability of capital and to a stable work relationship within a family or close-knit work enterprise. At the other end of the continuum, the short-term orientation places great emphasis on personal steadiness and stability, which could suppress risk-seeking behaviors that are required to support entrepreneurial activities.

On the continuum of long- versus short-term orientation, Asian countries scored toward the long-term pole while the rest of the countries scored at the medium- or short-term pole. The top long-term scorers were China, Hong Kong, Taiwan, Japan, and Korea (Hofstede, 2007). No Western countries scored more than medium term; the United States, Britain, and Canada scored in the short-term orientation range, as did countries of Africa. High scores on the long-term dimension were strongly correlated with the countries' economic success in the last quarter of the 20th century (Hofstede & Hofstede, 2005, p. 223). The authors note that long-term orientation is identified as a major explanation for the explosive growth of the East Asian economies during that period.

CRITIQUE OF HOFSTEDE'S FRAMEWORK

Hofstede's original work received wide acclaim for its pioneer nature and has since been cited and used in many research projects around the world, but it was also criticized for its less than rigorous theoretical framework and less than perfect research methods (e.g., McSweeney, 2002). The strengths of the work included an ambitious effort to measure and quantify the values that distinguish one culture from another along five unified dimensions, and a demonstration of the significance of national cultures to management theory and practice. As a result, the book promoted sensitivity to cultural diversity in the workplace at the very time that global businesses were expanding. It also undermined the assumption that management knowledge that originated in the United States could be universally applied and emphasized the need to learn different cultures and adapt management practices to local values and norms. The typology that Hofstede put forth in his work has been widely applied and has become exceptionally influential (e.g., Baskerville, 2003; Bhagat, 2002; Bing, 2004; Chandy & Williams, 1994; Hart, 1999; Søndergaard, 1994; see also Kirkman, Lowe, & Gibson, 2006; Triandis, 2004).

Hofstede's work has been criticized on several levels, including its limited conceptualization of culture, its less than rigorous methodology, and its inherent Western cultural bias (e.g., Ailon, 2008; Baskerville, 2003; Eckhardt, 2002; Harrison & McKinnon, 1999; Kitayama, 2002; McSweeney, 2002; Robinson, 1983; Singh, 1990). The work was criticized because it seemed to identify culture with nations and because it has operated under the assumption that within each nation there was a uniformed culture. This notion of a unified national culture is particularly problematic in light of the increased diversity within nations. One glaring example from Hofstede's (1980) initial study was the use of an all-White sample (because of the apartheid regime of the time) to represent the totality of the South African national culture. Another stream of criticism related to the validity and reliability of the study's measures as well as the limited research methodology. For example, even though the total number of questionnaires was very large—117,000—this number includes both waves of the questionnaire that were administered in 1968–69 and again in 1971–73. The large number in and of itself does not ensure representativeness. In fact, in some of the countries the samples were very small (e.g., 58 in Singapore and

37 in Pakistan). Hofstede's (1991) claim that the sample sizes were sufficient because to the homogeneity of values within national samples is highly questionable because the basic premise of homogeneous national cultures cannot be substantiated (McSweeney, 2002). Finally, an interesting analysis by Ailon (2008) uses a mirroring technique to deconstruct Hofstede's book *Culture's Consequences* (1980) using the book's own assumptions and logic. The author demonstrates that, despite his explicit efforts to remain "culturally neutral," the book's specific Western cultural lens is evident throughout the chapters. For example, with respect to the uncertainty avoidance (UA) dimension Ailon notes, "Hofstede strongly disagrees with the claim that company rules should not be broken, thus expressing low UA value" (1980, p. 423). The book itself, however, manifests what appears to be a very high intolerance for the unpredictable ambiguous, or uncertain. In other words, it manifests very high UA. (p. 893). Ailon finds several inconsistencies in both theory and methodology and cautions against an uncritical reading of Hofstede's cultural dimensions.

A central concern among all of Hofstede's critics is the author's central premise that *national cultures are uniform* and therefore could be represented by relatively small samples (1981, p. 65) and could be measured, quantified, compared, and graphed quite precisely on the continuum of each of the five dimensions. McSweeney (2002) notes that "If the aim is understanding then we need to know more about the richness and diversity of national practices and institutions—rather than merely assuming their 'uniformity' and that they have an already known national cultural cause" (p. 112). Ailon (2008) sums up her criticism with a positive note, highlighting Hofstede's pioneering work on the backdrop of the period of his initial research, "Hofstede, it should be remembered, worked within the discursive limits of the 1970's, and he did so impressively, at least in so far as the popularity of Culture's Consequences indicated" (p. 901).

It is important to remember that the cultural dimensions offered by Hofstede's work were in many respects the first attempt to scientifically characterize the very broad concept of culture in a multinational context. Judging by the numerous researchers who found this conceptual framework useful, the author's contribution has been enormous. Yet, as national cultures become more diverse with an influx of immigrants, migrant workers, and the migration of businesses (painstakingly demonstrated in the first part of this book), it is important to pay attention to diversity within national cultures. Any manager who attempts to shortcut her or his learning process by looking for broad brush characterizations of "uniform" national cultures may be doing a disservice to her- or himself. It has been the premise of this book all along that in today's increasingly diverse workforce, a more nuanced understanding of, sensitivity for, and proficiency in the cultural differences not only *between* but *within* national cultures is essential.

THE GLOBE STUDY

A different attempt to identify cultural dimensions in an international context is the Global Leadership and Organizational Behavior Effectiveness research program (GLOBE). GLOBE is a multiyear program of cross-cultural research designed to examine the relationship between societal culture, organizational culture, and organizational leadership effectiveness (House, Hangers, Javidan, et al., 2004; Javidan, House, Dorfman, Hangers, & De Luque, 2006). The project was conceived by Robert J. House from the Wharton School at the University of Pennsylvania in 1991 who assembled a team of approximately 170 social scientists and management scholars from 61 countries representing major geographic regions throughout the world to collaborate on the study. The researchers collected data from over 17,000 middle managers in three industries: financial services, food processing, and telecommunications, as well as archival measures of country economic prosperity and the physical and psychological well-being of the cultures studied.

GLOBE has several distinguishing features. First, it is truly a cross-cultural research program. The constructs were defined, conceptualized, and operationalized by the multicultural team of researchers. Second, the industries were selected through a polling of the country investigators, and the instruments were designed with the full participation of the researchers representing the different cultures. Finally, the data in each country were collected by investigators who were either natives of the cultures studied or had extensive knowledge and experience in that culture.

The authors derived nine cultural dimensions from the literature and measured them both as practices (the way things are) and values (the way things should be) (Javidan, Dorfman, De Luque, & House, 2006). The nine cultural attributes that were described in the study were:

- Performance Orientation: The degree to which a collective encourages and rewards group members for performance improvement and excellence
- Assertiveness: The degree to which individuals are assertive, confrontational, and aggressive in their relationships with others
- Future Orientation: The extent to which individuals engage in future-oriented behaviors such as delaying gratification, planning, and investing in the future
- Human Orientation: The degree to which a collective encourages and rewards individuals for being fair, altruistic, generous, caring, and kind to others
- Institutional Collectivism: The degree to which organizational and societal institutional practices encourage and reward collective distribution of resources and collective action
- In-Group Collectivism: The degree to which individuals express pride, loyalty, and cohesiveness in their organizations or families
- Gender Egalitarianism: The degree to which a collective minimizes gender inequality

- Power Distance: The degree to which members of a collective expect power to be distributed equally
- Uncertainty Avoidance: The extent to which a society, organization, or group relies on social norms, rules, and procedures to alleviate unpredictability of future events.

The study authors focused on leadership, which they defined through a process of cross-cultural discussions as "the ability of an individual to influence, motivate, and enable others to contribute toward the effectiveness and success of the organizations of which they are members" (House, Hangers, Javidan, et al., 2004, p. 15). The principal outcome of the study was the development of six universally shared dimensions of leadership: charismatic/value based, team oriented, self-protective, participative, humane oriented, and autonomous.

Cross-Cultural Communication

Effective interactions in today's global business world depend to a great extent on the ability to convey a clear message that people in different cultures can comprehend in the way the communicator intended them to understand it. Business communication can be interpreted very differently depending on the cultural orientation of a particular country. For example, in masculine societies an effective manager is one who communicates directly, assertively, and even aggressively. Those from feminine-leaning societies may interpret such behavior as unfriendly, arrogant, and even rude. A Swedish manager reading a help-wanted advertisement for a salesperson in the United States might be taken aback by the requirement that the qualified candidate be "aggressive." On the other hand, British managers may interpret a Chinese manager's modesty and humility in stating his qualifications as a weakness.

An incident in the city of Najaf during the 2003 war in Iraq (see Box 8.1), demonstrates one leader's bold and effective use of nonverbal, cross-cultural communication that probably saved many lives that day. Unable to speak Arabic and with no interpreter on site, the commander of the U.S. Army's 101st Airborne Division was unable to use language to communicate his nonaggressive intentions to the Arabic-speaking crowd. In a spur-of-the-moment decision, he instructed his soldiers to kneel on one knee, smile, and point their weapons to the ground. This vulnerable yet friendly posture was clearly understood by the crowd that responded likewise by smiling and sitting on the ground. Luckily, in the Najaf incident, the nonverbal body language was sufficiently universal to convey the peaceful intentions of the soldiers and to prevent what could have been a deadly incident.

BOX 8.1
Leadership Through Effective Cross-Cultural Communication Saves the Day in Najaf

Early in June 2003 during the U.S. war in Iraq, the U.S. Army's 101st Airborne Division on a mission to secure the area entered the city of Najaf. It was an uneventful patrol. The search turned up nothing. The Shia Muslim population, which traditionally has not supported Saddam's rule, seemed curious and friendly, but didn't get too close. The local population had cautiously welcomed the U.S. troops. Word came from the Grand Ayatollah Sistani that he was willing to meet with the American commander, but he asked first that the U.S. soldiers secure his compound.

As the troops started down the road toward the Ayatollah's compound, the crowd that assembled there to watch the American soldiers mistook their intentions to mean that they were progressing toward the Imam Ali shrine located in Najaf. The Imam Ali shrine is the burial site of the prophet Muhammad's son-in-law and considered one of the holiest sites in the world for Shia Muslims.

The once-friendly crowd became alarmed and chaos ensued. Earlier warm greetings were replaced with angry shouts and gestures as hundreds of people attempted to block the soldiers' way. Clerics appeared with a message from the Grand Ayatollah that the soldiers were progressing at his invitation, but their message was drowned out.

Realizing the explosive situation at hand and unable to verbally convey his peaceful intentions, the colonel told his men to stay calm. He instructed the soldiers to smile, get down on one knee, and point their weapons to the ground. The puzzled soldiers reluctantly complied. A hush fell on the crowd. Then slowly the crowd responded in kind—relaxing, smiling, and sitting on the ground. The tension was diffused, but the colonel realized that the situation was still potentially volatile. "Turn around," he ordered his men, "just turn around and go." The soldiers complied, and as they were leaving, the colonel turned around and bowed apologetically to the crowd as if saying, "Sorry for the misunderstanding." A potentially deadly confrontation was prevented.

SOURCE: Chilcote (2003).

Although in the business world the stakes do not often involve human lives, they do involve people's livelihood. Cross-cultural miscommunication can result in lost opportunities—such as losing a job or a business deal—that could be detrimental to the financial and economic well-being of individuals and organizations. Conversely, effective cross-cultural communication can open up employment and business opportunities that may not be otherwise available to the participants.

Effective Cross-Cultural Communication

Communication, in its most basic form, is the use of symbols to convey meaning. Symbols can include words, tone of voice, gestures, or use of objects (artifacts). Broadly defined, communication is multidimensional (Neuliep, 2008) and relates to three types of goals: instrumental goals (e.g., performing tasks), relational goals (e.g., negotiating conflicts), and identity management (e.g., conveying a desired self-image) (Bernstein, 1975; Clark & Delia, 1979; Halliday, 1978).

Cross-cultural communication is particularly challenging and involves several potential barriers to communication that are related to the use of verbal and nonverbal methods to convey meanings that may or may not be the same in the cultures of origin of the participants (see Figure 8.1 for illustration).

When people use symbols that elicit meaning in another person, whatever the original intent was, or even without conscious intent, they are still communicating. Often the message that is received may be different from the one that was intended because of cultural barriers on the part of receivers and transmitters. Take, for example, gender differences in perceptions of sexual meanings. A man may perceive a woman's behavior as flirtatious when her original intent was simply courteous and entirely nonsexual, leading to severe misunderstandings. Add to that the cultural layer when, for example, it is entirely acceptable and chivalrous for a French businessman to compliment a woman colleague on her dress in the French cultural context. An American businesswoman might perceive the exact same behavior as inappropriate and may even interpret it as sexual harassment. Miscommunication occurs when the original intent of the person transmitting the message is different from the meaning that is received by the other person, and it is more likely to occur between participants who belong to different cultures.

VERBAL COMMUNICATION

The use of different languages often creates a barrier to communication because one or both sides are not as articulate as they could be in their native tongues. For example, a Dutch person who speaks Flemish but is also fluent in French may not be as familiar with the vocabulary, grammar, and idioms of the language as would be a native French speaker. Articulating her

Figure 8.1 Barriers to Effective Cross-Cultural Communication

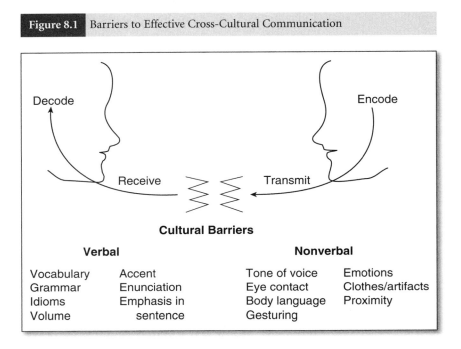

thoughts (encoding) would be more difficult for her, and the end message may not be exactly what she intended to convey. In addition, her accent, enunciation, and emphasis in sentence intonation (the "music" of the language) may make it difficult for the listener to clearly comprehend what she was saying and to be distracted from the message.

When conducting international business, the choice of which language to use (e.g., one's own or the host country's language) is more than a practical matter. It is a choice of whether to signify national pride on the one hand, or to demonstrate respect for the host country's culture on the other. Foreign leaders often speak their own language and communicate through an interpreter, even when they are fluent in the host country's language, to show a sense of national pride. For example, when the supersonic plane the *Concorde* was designed, there was a bitter argument between the French and the British who collaborated on the project, perhaps reflecting the age-old rivalry and animosity between the two countries.[4] At one point, work was halted after the French insisted that the plane should have a Gallic final letter "e" in its name, whereas the British stolidly referred to it as "Concord." Eventually the French spelling was adopted (Arnold, 2003). On the other hand, saying a few words, such as "hello" or "good evening," in the host country's language can go a long way. When J. F. Kennedy gave his famous speech in front of the Berlin town hall and said, "All free men, wherever they may live, are citizens of Berlin, and, therefore, as a free man, I take pride in the words, '*Ich bin ein Berliner*'" (I am a Berliner), more than a million West Berliners responded with a roar of approval.[5] Similarly, when Bill Clinton spoke at the funeral of Yitzhak Rabin, the prime minister of Israel who was assassinated because of his work toward peace in the Middle East, he began his English speech by saying two words in Hebrew, "*Shalom Chaver*"—"Goodbye (also doubles as Peace) My Friend." The people of Israel were so touched by this gesture that these words later appeared in poems, in everyday phrases, and on bumper stickers. Willy Brandt, the former German chancellor, once commented, "If I'm selling to you, I speak your language. If I am buying, *dann mussen Sie Deutch spechen*" (then you must speak German) (Nurden, 1997, p. 39).

Linguistic diversity is an important aspect of global diversity. Managing a workforce that does not share a common language can present a major challenge to both employees and management. Although most of the discussion related to the use of foreign languages in business refers to international organizations with business partners or subsidiaries in different countries, verbal communication may also present a challenge within countries. In Guinea, for example, a large segment of the population barely speak French, the official language of Guinea (Auclair, 1992); and in South Africa's metropolitan area of Alexandra, nine major Bantu languages are claimed as home language, and many residents also speak some English, Afrikaans, or Portuguese (McCall, Ngeva, & Mbebe, 1997).

Often, misunderstandings occur when one person is not familiar with all aspects of the other's language. A classic example of such mistaken translation resulted in a horned Moses holding the Ten Commandments in the famous Michelangelo statue (circa 1513). The original biblical Hebrew text describes Moses coming down Mount Sinai after meeting God "with his face radiating" or literally with rays of light coming out of his face (Exodus 34:29). However, the Hebrew word for *ray* is the same as the word for *horn—keren*. Michelangelo, relying on Jerome's vulgate translation of the Old Testament, which apparently confused the two meanings, sculpted the famous statue of Moses with two horns protruding from his head. On the other hand, sometimes the use of a foreign language can add a different dimension to the discussion because people who are not native speakers can pick up errors that native speakers will not see. Adler (1991) describes an example of a business using this perceptual characteristic to its advantage: the Canadian National Railway gives reports written in English to bilingual francophone employees to proofread and reports written in French to bilingual anglophones for proofreading.

LANGUAGE FLUENCY AND CULTURAL FLUENCY

When dealing with foreign languages and different cultures, language fluency and cultural fluency are not the same, although they are related. Language fluency refers to the possession of linguistic skills that allow one to function much like a native speaker of the language. Cultural fluency refers to the ability to identify, understand, and apply the communicative behaviors of members of the other group; it is the ability to go back and forth between two cultures, to send and receive messages in a way that assures that the meanings of the messages of both the sender and receiver regularly match (Glazier, 2003; Molinsky, 2005; Scott, 1999). Children of immigrants who grew up speaking the language of their parents at home, but without connection to their broader cultural heritage, are facing great difficulties when returning to their homeland, although they may speak the language fluently. For example, according to U.S. laws, legal aliens who committed a crime may be deported to their home country. After the 9/11 terrorist attack in 2001, the United States began enforcing its immigration laws more vigorously and more immigrants who committed crimes were deported. Among the deportees was a large group of Cambodian nationals who grew up in the United States and were highly acculturated to the American culture. Although their parents spoke Khmer at home, they did not teach them about their cultural heritage because they wanted to forget the horrors of the Khmer Rouge and the Pol Pot regime. As a result, although they were fluent in Khmer, these deportees experienced great difficulties adjusting to the Cambodian way of life and culture.[6]

NONVERBAL COMMUNICATION

Nonverbal barriers to cross-cultural communication include body language—movements, gestures, and postures—as well as the use of artifacts such as personal adornments and the physical setting. Trust and respect are often conveyed through nonverbal rather than verbal communication. A case in point is controversy in the U.S. media ignited by President Obama's bow to the Japanese emperor during his Asian tour in November of 2009. Some interpreted the bow as a culturally sensitive sign of respect, but others noted that this is an indication of subservience that is unbefitting a U.S. president (MSNBC News, 2009; National Public Radio News, 2009). Obama's defenders attributed the bow to his multicultural background and worldly awareness, while his critics thought it was a sign of his naiveté and a behavior unbefitting the presidency citing a tradition that the U.S. president bows to no one. The supporters also noted that the bow, a typical Asian form of greeting, was also accompanied by a very Western firm handshake, while the critics noted that the very low bow, practically a ninety-degree angel, was a gesture of extreme deference and subordination. Either way, it is clear that this one nonverbal gesture spoke volumes and was discussed more than any of the speeches the president and his hosts gave during the tour. In addition to body gestures, artifacts can also be used to transfer important information and those too need to be understood and interpreted in their specific cultural and national context (see Box 8.2 for an example of the use of the physical setting to convey respect in different cultures).

BOX 8.2

How Can the Important Guest Sit at the Head of a Round Table? The Use of the Physical Setting to Convey Respect in Business Communication

To convey respect to a high-ranking visitor, Europeans and North Americans have the person sit at the head of a rectangular table. A round table is typically reserved for occasions when the participants are presumed to be equals. A prime example is the famous legend of King Arthur of Camelot and his Knights of the Round Table. King Arthur conveyed the equality among his chosen knights through the use of a round table. Similarly, in modern times, the representatives to the UN Security Council all sit at a round table. The assumption of these Western cultures is that there is no way to identify a more- or less-respected seat at a round table and therefore no way to indicate the relative ranking of the participants

In the Chinese culture, on the other hand, the ranking of the participants can be clearly identified by the way they sit at a round table: the highest ranking participant in a meeting will be seated directly facing the main entrance to the room, and the rest of the participants, in descending order of rank, will be seated to his or her left and right sides until the lowest-ranking person will have his or her back to the entrance. This follows a similar logic of circular-ranked importance expressed in the Chinese perception of geography. The Chinese tradition indicates that the imperial palace is the most important place in the world, and from there, in circles of decreased importance, are the other areas of Beijing, the rest of China, and the rest of the world.

Clothing has long been used to communicate rank (e.g., the cardinal robes and the queen's crown), mood (e.g., mourning clothes), occasion (e.g., wedding outfits in different cultures), and even seasons (e.g., the geisha's seasonal kimono colors or light and dark business attire in the West, depending on the time of year). Clothes are an extension of the body and closely relate to the person's gender, age, socioeconomic status, and national origin. When doing business in a foreign country, one often faces the question of whether to wear the business attire that is common in one's own culture or in the host country.

Although in modern times the Western business suit goes a long way for men, it is not the same for women. Western clothes may be perceived as inappropriately revealing by many cultures, and wearing them might be interpreted as disrespectful to the host culture and be perceived as offensive. On the other hand, wearing a traditional outfit, such as the Muslim attire of *abaya, burqah,* or *hijab,*[7] may be seen as confining or even degrading by Western women. The U.S. Army's policy of "strongly encouraging" army servicewomen to conform to Saudi rules and wear *abayas* while serving in Saudi Arabia has long been controversial.[8] When Madeleine Albright, the U.S. secretary of state during the Clinton presidency, visited Egypt and Saudi Arabia in 1999, she found a middle-ground solution. Although she did not wear the traditional Muslim attire that is expected from women in that country, she wore dresses and skirts that were longer than the ones she wore in Washington. She also donned a wide-brimmed hat, thus walking the fine line between conveying respect for her hosts' culture and her own. In contrast, Mahatma Ghandi, the father of modern India and the leader of its liberation movement from Great Britain, wore just a loincloth during his visit to England in 1931, shocking the conservative British society. The British media interpreted his attire as "primitive" and disrespectful, but Ghandi was sending a clear message of independence and defiance as well as respect for Indian culture and traditions: "It was a rejection not only of the material products of Europe, but also of the European value system with its criteria of decency" (Tarlo, 1996, p. 75).

CROSS-CULTURAL COMMUNICATION STYLES

A question that is very relevant for any business transaction is whether and to what extent members of a particular cultural group will alter their preferred communication style when interacting with members from another cultural group. Utilizing the theoretical perspective presented earlier, will members of collectivist cultures become more direct and task oriented in their communication with members of individualist cultures? Will members of individualist cultures become more concerned with the needs of others and in preserving harmony in the transaction? Or will one or both groups become more entrenched in their own communication style?

It is plausible to assume that adapting to the other's communication style will generate a perception of similarity and familiarity that will contribute to creating a positive atmosphere in cross-cultural encounters (e.g., Byrne's 1971 similarity attraction paradigm; Foley et al., 2006; Lee & Gudykunst, 2001). On the other hand, because cross-cultural encounters create uncertainly and provoke anxiety, participants may resort to the familiarity of their own cultural norms and even more strongly exhibit their normative communication styles (Lau, Lam, & Deutsch Salamon, 2008; Laurent, 1984; Tse, Francis, & Walls, 1994). A study conducted in New Zealand supports the latter (see Box 8.3).

BOX 8.3
Are Members of a Cultural Group Interacting With a Member of Another Group More Likely to Change Their Original Communication Style or Reinforce It?

Pekerti and Thomas (2003) examined intercultural and intracultural communication styles between two groups in New Zealand: Anglo-Europeans, representing a low-context individualist culture, and East Asians, representing high-context collectivist culture. Participants in the experiment were 96 students at a large New Zealand university, one half of whom were Anglo-European New Zealanders (Pakeha) and one half of whom were students from Asia (primarily from China) who were first generation with less than 10 years in New Zealand (to control for acculturation). Students were randomly assigned to one of two conditions—interaction with members of their own cultural group or interaction with members of the other cultural group.[9] The assignment was ranking of 15 crimes by their severity, and participants were given no more than 15 minutes to rank the crimes by consensus. The interactions were videotaped and coded by independent observers for the occurrence and intensity of each cultural communication behavior. The results showed that interacting with members of a different culture increased the tendency to use the cultural communication style of their own culture. Specifically, in interactions with Anglo-Europeans, the Asian students were more likely than they were with members of their own culture to accommodate and change their opinions in order to preserve harmony. A similar trend was apparent with the Anglo-Europeans students who were more likely than they were with members of their own cultural group to be direct and task oriented in their interaction with Asian students. The authors attribute this behavior to the uncertainly involved in cross-cultural interactions, which increases people's tendency to rely on their own cultural norms. The authors conclude that in cross-cultural communication, the dominant tendency is exaggeration of one's own cultural behaviors rather than adaptation.

The tendency to resort to the familiarity of one's own cultural norms may be even stronger when facing a conflict. Sometimes due to misunderstanding, cultural ignorance, or fear of losing face, this behavior could have a toll both in human relationships and in financial outcomes. Mangaliso (2001) describes an incident in a South African mining company that mushroomed into a labor dispute and a prolonged strike that cost the company greatly—all because management was unable to appropriately communicate with its workers. In the beginning of the labor dispute, the workers invited top management to address them on the issue in a public forum. Management denied their request, however, and responded instead by sending messages through envoys and written statements posted on bulletin boards. In the high-context collectivist culture of the South African workers, management's impersonal and task-oriented communication was entirely inappropriate. It failed to take into consideration the South African concept of *ubuntu,* meaning humaneness, consideration for compassion and community—similar to the Chinese concept of *quanxi,* the Korean *chaeboel,* and the Spanish *simpatia* (mentioned in Chapter 9) all indicating a cultural emphasis on relationships (Sanchez-Burks & Lee, 2007; Triandis, Marin, Lisansky, & Betancourt, 1984). Frustrated and humiliated, the workers began a strike that lasted for more than 2 weeks and resulted in several hundreds of employees being fired and several million dollars of company losses. One of the employee representatives was reported to have said, "The only thing that employees wanted was for top management to come and address us. Just to speak to us" (Mangaliso, 2001, p. 23). In retrospect the strike and its costly consequences could have been avoided if management understood the cultural context of its workers and was able to communicate with them in an appropriate manner.

Summary and Conclusion

To succeed in managing a workforce that is increasingly diverse and multi-national, managers need to understand cultural differences and to become competent in cross-cultural communication. This chapter examines the cultural context of the global workplace and analyzes communication patterns that facilitate or block effective cross-cultural communication.

Research on cultural dimensions and the wealth of research inspired by Geert Hofstede's pioneering work provide an important context for understanding cross-cultural interactions in the workplace. His four axes of *power distance* (authority and social inequality), *individualism vs. collectivism* (cohesion and loyalty to the group), *masculinity vs. femininity* (competition in contrast to care for others) and *avoidance of uncertainty* (tolerance for ambiguity) have clear implications for individual and group expectations related to acceptable behaviors in the workplace. Whether employees expect to be rewarded, for example, for individual excellence or for a team effort depends to a large extent on the cultural perception of individualism versus collectivism in their society. The GLOBE project, led by Robert J. House, examined nine cultural dimensions of leadership worldwide through a longitudinal study in 62 world cultures. The principal outcome of the study was the development of six universally shared dimensions of leadership: charismatic/value based, team oriented, self-protective, participative, humane oriented, and autonomous.

Defined as *the use of symbols to convey meaning*, communication in today's global environment has become largely cross-cultural. Cross-cultural communication involves several potential barriers that are related to the use of verbal and nonverbal methods to convey meanings that may or may not be the same in the cultures of origin of the participants. Miscommunication occurs when the original intent of the person transmitting the message is different from the meaning that is received by the other person, and it is more likely to occur between participants who belong to different cultures. Often, misunderstandings occur when one person is not familiar with all aspects of the other's language, is not fluent or articulate in the language used for the business transaction, or miscommunicates or misreads nonverbal communication such as movement or gestures.

Effective communication with employees, customers, shareholders, regulators, and other business partners presents a serious challenge, even when conducted within the same cultural framework. The challenge is compounded when communication involves two or more diverse cultural contexts. When one partner to a business communication misreads the cultural clues encoded in the other person's message, the transaction can result in a misunderstanding, hurt emotions, conflicts, and lost business opportunities. On the other hand, making the effort to understand other cultures and to communicate effectively within them can go a long way in fostering trust, conveying respect, and eventually securing mutually beneficial business deals.

Notes

1. Javidan and House (2001), p. 289.
2. For a summary table of key definitions of culture, see Erez and Earley (1993).
3. See, for example, Margaret Mead (2001) and Ruth Benedict (1989).
4. The interesting historical/political context to the inception of the *Concorde* project: The project was designed in response to the space race between the United States and the Soviet Union in the 1960s. Its goal was to demonstrate the technological abilities of Western Europe as a center of world power, independent from the United States and the Soviet Union. This was the impetus for France and England to put aside their historical animosity and work collaboratively on this project. Sources: History of the supersonic airliner. (2001, July 5). CNN [television broadcast]; The World. (2003, October 23). National Public Radio [radio broadcast].
5. "Text: Kennedy's Berlin speech." BBC News, U.K. edition, June 26, 2003. http://news.bbc.co.uk/2/hi/europe/3022166.stm. Retrieved May 23, 2004.
6. The World. (2003, October 23). National Public Radio [radio broadcast].
7. *Abaya* is a head-to-toe, traditional Muslim dress made from black, lightweight fabric that has two layers; *burqah* similarly provides cover from head to toe and, in addition, covers the face so that only the eyes are exposed, sometimes behind a netlike fabric; *hijab* is a traditional Muslim head scarf.

8. Lieutenant Col. Martha McSally has led a long struggle to end this policy by the Pentagon. McSally, who was the first woman U.S. service member to fly in combat, was stationed in Saudi Arabia where she was forced to wear the *abaya* and travel in the rear seats of vehicles in accordance with local custom. Congressman Langevin joined McSally's fight and called the Army's requirement "gender discrimination," saying that "Women make first-class soldiers and should not be treated like second-class citizens." Langevin seeks to author legislation to ban forced wearing of the *abaya* by American servicewomen in Saudi Arabia. Source: Congressman Langevin (2002, May 8) [press release]. (www.house.gov/apps/list/press/ri02_langevin/050802abayaamend.htm)

9. The study used a 2 × 2 (culture × condition) design; and in assignment to the two experimental conditions, the researchers used blocks by gender, age, and culture to control for possible effects of these variables on the outcome variable of communication style.

CHAPTER 9

Interpersonal Relationships in a Global Work Context

Jeffrey Sanchez-Burks[a] and Michàlle E. Mor Barak

First day back from vacation, Diego, a Mexican engineering specialist working for a large multinational corporation based in Germany, received his next project assignment. The automotive plant's assignments typically lasted 6 to 8 months and involved highly interdependent multifunctional teams that worked under intense deadlines. Diego glanced at the names of the other people assigned to the team. It was not usual that the members would be unfamiliar with one another, but Diego recognized the names of three new team members. He had heard that they were all highly regarded for their skills in their areas of expertise. However, from what he had heard about their previous assignments, he worried that their exclusive and impersonal focus to tasks and time schedules and, frankly, their unfriendliness would not work well with the rest of the team. In previous assignments, Diego's teams had enjoyed a friendly atmosphere (they would go out for drinks together, sometimes inviting each other to their homes on the weekends). In Diego's opinion, that made the team productive and successful. He worried that the new team would experience little harmony and much interpersonal conflict.

With trepidation, Diego decided to ask for another assignment fearing the lack of interpersonal harmony, despite the high level of collective talent, would impede the team's ability to succeed on their core objectives. Upon hearing the request, Markus, the German project coordinator, was surprised about Diego's concern. For Markus, the issue was straightforward: the new people were excellent professionals who would help the team produce better outcomes with a shorter time schedule, and therefore Diego's concern for the team's productivity was unfounded.

---

a. Jeffrey Sanchez-Burks, PhD, is an Associate Professor of Management and Organizations at the Stephen M. Ross School of Business at the University of Michigan.

As demonstrated by this incident, people from different cultures often bring very different sets of assumptions about appropriate ways to coordinate and communicate in business relationships. Culture infuses meaning into the social situation. Whereas interpersonal harmony may be regarded as essential to task success in one society, such as in Mexico, it may be seen as less consequential in another, such as in Germany. As we will discuss in this chapter, one's perceptions, values, and behavior in such situations reflect deep-seated beliefs about the nature of interpersonal work relationships. To understand and manage these differences requires understanding the nature of cultural diversity and how it influences relational and communication styles.

There are different levels of cultural diversity, as described in Chapter 6. Some levels are more obvious to the observer than others. The most salient level of diversity to workers and scholars alike is demographic differences such as gender, ethnicity, or nationality. These categories are important to the extent that a person's identity and others' perceptions of them are influenced by these social categories. For example, ethnic preferences and prejudices can affect dynamics between a Japanese sales representative and a Peruvian distributor discussing logistics in Lima. The mere perception of differences in demographic category, such as "Japanese" and "Peruvian," can facilitate or sabotage business relations depending on one's beliefs (see Chapter 7 for a discussion of social categorization's impact on intergroup and interpersonal relationships).

The other, more implicit level of difference that people encounter in a global marketplace entails cultural variation in cognitive, communicative, and relational styles. Although the markers of diversity at this level can be difficult to observe directly, they nonetheless exert a powerful influence on people's preferences and team dynamics, as illustrated in the opening example (Sanchez-Burks, Nisbett, & Ybarra, 2000; Sanchez-Burks, Bartel, & Blount, 2009). Broadly, culture refers to shared understandings made manifest in act and artifact about what is true, good, and efficient (Redfield, 1941; Sanchez-Burks & Lee, 2007; also see Chapter 6 for an expanded discussion on culture). These shared understandings about proper relational styles found within cultures create particular challenges for intercultural business that have less to do with differences in ethnicity and much to do with deep-seated cultural variation between groups. This variation is revealed in how members of two cultures make sense of a situation, the appropriate way to convey bad news, and the extent to which one should or should not mix business and personal matters with colleagues and business partners. As a result, this level of cultural diversity can derail what might otherwise be a promising intercultural partnership.

This chapter begins by describing how culture shapes the mental models people use to coordinate and communicate thought and action. We then discuss an organizing framework for these diverse cultural mental models. We describe how cultural mental models influence people's emotional involvement or detachment with coworkers and business partners and beliefs about the importance of interpersonal harmony and conflict. Finally, we discuss how this diversity shapes communication styles and the challenges this cultural variation presents to creating a worldwide inclusive workplace.

Cultural Styles and Relational Mental Models

There is no such thing as an interpersonal style that is culture neutral. As a result of a cognitive bias social psychologists refer to as *naive realism* (Ross & Ward, 1996), we mistakenly assume that what is considered in our immediate environment to be appropriate and proper forms of behaving and communicating reflect the natural way things should be and are therefore universally correct. Even when we become aware of cultural differences, this bias often leads us to devalue others' relational work style as "incorrect" and "unprofessional." Indeed, the particular cultural contexts in which people are raised and begin their careers create culturally unique relational mental models.

Relational mental models influence our perceptions and the way we communicate and relate to others. Bartlett (1932, 1958) is credited with first proposing the concept of a relational mental model, which he referred to as a mental model. He arrived at the concept from studies of memory he conducted in which participants misremembered details of stories that were not actually in the original stories. He suggested that participants' use of preexisting mental models to understand the story shaped their interpretation and subsequent recall of the stories' details. Bartlett's work, replicated and elaborated in subsequent social cognition studies, provides insights into how mental models serve as a framework for encoding, understanding, and remembering information. Later studies (e.g., Knight & Nisbett, 2007; Nisbett & Miyamoto, 2005; Nisbett, Peng, Choi, & Norenzayan, 2001; Quinn & Holland, 1987) have demonstrated the importance of mental models in understanding culturally related variation in cognition. Relational mental models refer specifically to cognitions about interpersonal relationships in specific situations (Baldwin, 1992; Baldwin & Dandeneau, 2005). Cultural mental models allow people to coordinate thought and action by creating shared expectations about how a social interaction should unfold, what behaviors are appropriate, and which elements of an interaction are important to notice (Baldwin, 1992; Baldwin & Dandeneau, 2005; Fiske & Haslam, 1996). In many Latin American societies, for example, it is inappropriate to abruptly end one business meeting in order to avoid being late to another appointment. The relational mental model used in Latin cultures places priority on the relationship in the present moment. This can be contrasted with the relational mental models found in European American or Swiss cultures where proper social interactions involve strict adherence to punctuality and schedules. (For an illustration of attempts to alter relational mental models for punctuality norms, see Box 9.1.) Within each society, relational mental models facilitate interpersonal harmony by providing shared expectations about, for example, when to end one meeting and begin the next. Problems arise, however, during intercultural encounters when people are guided by different relational mental models. For example, the Mexican is likely to interpret his European American colleague's abrupt ending of the meeting according to the minute hand on the clock as "rude" and impersonal. Likewise, the European American will perceive his Mexican colleague's lack of respect for punctuality as "unprofessional." Both are interested in successful business relationships; however, the relational mental models they bring to the table influence their specific approach toward achieving this goal.

BOX 9.1
Relational Mental Models About Time in Ecuador

The Ecuadorian national government recently launched a campaign to eliminate the social practice of arriving 15 to 30 minutes late to business meetings and social events (jokingly referred to as running on "Ecuadorian time"). Citing the financial costs of tardiness, which is estimated at $724 million a year, the campaign began with a national "clock synchronization ceremony." Hundreds of officials gathered in the heart of Quito's downtown to mark a ceremonious start to the drive. The population was urged by President Lucio Gutierrez to be on time "for the sake of God, the country, our people, and our consciences" ("Ecuador Punctuality," 2003).

Researchers have documented relational mental models that are unique to a particular culture and mental models that reflect broad cultural dimensions. In China, there is a culture-specific mental model based on *quanxi* (Tsui & Farh, 1997) in which one is expected to attend carefully to the interconnections among business colleagues and partners. In Korea, a mental model reflecting *chaebol* (Kim, Y. Y., 1988), or company familism, structures business relationships to reflect both work and personal features. Mexican business relationships reflect a *simpatia* mental model (Diaz-Guerrero, 1967; Sanchez-Burks, 2002; Triandis et al., 1984), which places importance on proactively creating rapport and personal connections. In contrast, the influence of *Protestant relational ideology* in European American culture (Sanchez-Burks, 2002; Sanchez-Burks, 2005)) maintains a sharp distinction between the relational mental models used at work and outside work. (For an example of how differences in European American and Mexican relational mental models lead to different memories of "what just happened" in a team meeting, see Box 9.2.)

BOX 9.2
What Just Happened in That Meeting?

In a series of field studies on workgroups, Mexican, Mexican Americans, and European Americans were asked to view recordings of team meetings and later report what they could remember about what happened in the meeting. Although there were no cultural differences in their ability to recall task-related information such as progress on the agenda or questions raised, there was significant difference in their memory for interpersonal dynamics. European Americans were far less likely than either the Mexicans or Mexican Americans to recall interpersonal and social emotional dynamics, such as one person being rude or friendly to another or one person being interrupted by another (Sanchez-Burks et al., 2000).

Relational mental models characterized as broad cultural dimensions include independence-interdependence, high/low context, and individualism-collectivism (Hofstede & Hostede 2005; Triandis, 1996). The distinction between independent and interdependent self-construals, for example, focuses on a relational mental model in which perceptions, emotions, and behavior are focused on the individual in the situation, compared with a mental model in which the focus is the connection relationships within the group. Both culture-specific and these broader-level mental models serve as the foundation for how people from different cultures interpret, communicate, and approach interpersonal relationships.

The influence of relational mental models is revealed in numerous interpersonal dynamics of business relationships. At the micro level, for example, relational mental models influence the degree of nonverbal coordination between two people interacting. People attentive to relational concerns tend to unconsciously mirror the gestures and posture of their counterparts in a social interaction and as a consequence increase interpersonal rapport (Chartrand & Bargh, 1999; Sanchez-Burks et al., 2000; Van Swol, 2003). For example, if one of the parties to a conversation is speaking softly and not using hand gestures, after a while, the attentive observer is likely to do the same, which will increase the first person's sense of comfort and create more harmony in the relationship. When people are "out of sync" in their nonverbal gestures as a result of diversity in relational mental models, it can increase levels of anxiety and can actually reduce one's performance in the situation. This was demonstrated in a study conducted in a Fortune 500 company, in which a European American interviewed a pool of European Americans and Latinos under instructions to subtly mirror the nonverbal gestures of half of the applicants (e.g., lean forward when the applicant leaned forward) and not mirror the gestures of the other half. Videotaped recordings of the interviews were shown to experts who evaluated the performance of the applicants under these two conditions. The study found that interview performance was contingent on level of nonverbal coordination for the Latino applicants but significantly less so for the European American men and women (Sanchez-Burks, Bartel, & Blount, 2009). Thus subtle cultural differences in relational mental models between interviewer and applicant can sabotage the success of intercultural workplace interactions. Such findings illustrate how important understanding cultural diversity in relational mental models can be for individuals and the organization. For organizations to sustain effective recruiting and selection efforts, and thus an important competitive advantage in the marketplace, they must manage such implicit cultural diversity.

The influence of relational mental models on attention can also affect managers' perceptions of what motivates their subordinates. DeVoe and Iyengar (2004) report in a study on employees of a multinational retail bank that the intrinsic motivation of subordinates (e.g., a desire to work hard because of one's personal interest in the project rather than for financial rewards or threats of punishment) is more likely to be noticed by Japanese and Mexican managers than European American managers, presumably because the latter are guided by relational mental models that are less sensitive to such personal information.

In sum, experience and socialization within different cultural contexts create culturally unique relational mental models. In turn, these relational mental models provide specific templates that guide our perceptions, communication, and behavior in social situations. In organizations, these relational mental models shape a variety of dynamics, including what people notice and take away from business meetings and the degree to which they coordinate their nonverbal behaviors and are affected by the overall level of coordination. These mental models also influence managers' perceptions of what motivates their subordinates and their accuracy vis-à-vis subordinates' actual interests and motivations. Together, the notion of culturally grounded relational mental models provides a foundation for understanding what people from different societies "bring to the table" in diverse organizations and international business ventures. In the next section, we discuss specific organizing frameworks for understanding cultural diversity in relational mental models. These frameworks provide a way to understand how cultural mental models produce variation in beliefs about notions of professionalism, proper networking strategies, and beliefs about harmony and conflict.

Diversity in Interpersonal Relationships

EMOTIONAL DETACHMENT VERSUS EMOTIONAL INVOLVEMENT

Cultural divides that challenge intercultural relationships often stem from the way individuals integrate or differentiate two types of relational mental models: task-focused mental models and social-emotional mental models. When people are guided solely by a task-focused mental model, they focus exclusively on elements of the situation directly related to the task, such as whether progress on the agenda is being made, steps are being taken to meet upcoming deadlines, and other issues related more to the job than the people involved. In contrast, people guided solely by social-emotional mental models will focus their attention and effort on emotional and interpersonal concerns.

As shown in Figure 9.1, the level of integration of these two mental models varies along a continuum. In cultures where these concerns are combined, people maintain a dual focus on task and interpersonal concerns. Dual attention does not necessary mean equal attention at all times. That is, emphasis on relational concerns relative to task concerns and vice versa can vary from one culture to the next and between individuals in the same culture. It does mean, however, that there is no sharp distinction between the two areas and that they are intertwined. For example, a manager will coordinate her group's efforts to be productive while closely managing interpersonal harmony. Workers in these societies are more likely to mingle work and personal issues, go out with their coworkers on the weekend, and have a preference to work with their family and friends (Kacperczyk, Sanchez-Burks, & Baker, 2009; Morris, Podolny, & Sullivan, 2008). At the other end of the continuum are societies with more differentiated relational styles. Here, managers work hard to maintain a sharp divide between one's work and personal life. At work, people operate with an implicit understanding to put personal matters aside and to avoid emotions and other concerns believed to harm one's image of the polite but impersonal professional (Heaphy, Sanchez-Burks, & Ashford, 2009). Smooth team dynamics are managed by maintaining a strict focus on the task at hand. As one manager with a strong differentiated style reported in an interview on the meaning of professionalism, "It is a death wish to talk about personal matters or get emotional at work."

There is tremendous cultural variation in the form and content of social-emotional mental models. In East Asian societies, workers preserve harmony passively by not "rocking the boat," whereas in Latin societies, people proactively create harmony through open displays of warmth and graciousness, even to strangers. Despite disparate ways of fostering social-emotional ties, interdependent styles are common in much of the world, including East Asian, Latin, and Middle Eastern societies (Ayman & Chemers, 1983; Earley & Erez, 1997; Hampden-Turner & Trompenaars, 1993; Markus & Kitayama, 1991). These differences can be complex, blurring the lines between culture and nationality. For example, immigrants and members of ethnic groups whose culture of origin used the interdependent cultural mental model are highly likely to use it even when living in a differentiated cultural context (e.g., the United States). Research has provided evidence that Latinos (both Mexicans and Mexican Americans) are guided by a concern with socioemotional aspects of workforce

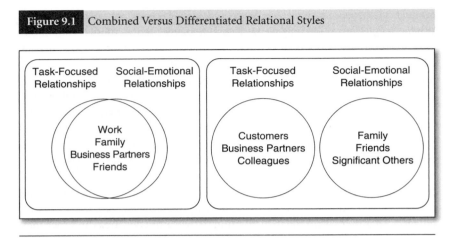

Figure 9.1　Combined Versus Differentiated Relational Styles

SOURCE: Adapted from Sanchez-Burks, 1999.

relations to a far greater degree than are Anglo-Americans, and the relationship holds true even when the Latinos reside in a differentiated culture such as the United States (Sanchez-Burks et al., 2000).

There can also be gender differences in interpersonal style. For example, women have been found to be more attentive than men to social-emotional aspects of work relationships and therefore more likely to use the interdependent relational style, even in cultural contexts in which the differentiated style is more prevalent, such as in North America (Reardon, 1995). However, in contrast to cultural differences, research suggests that gender differences can be quite inconsistent, emerging in some studies but not others (Holtgraves, 1997; Sanchez-Burks, Lee, Choi, Nisbett, Zhao, & Jasook, 2003; Tannen, 1990). At this point, it appears that differences in relational styles that may exist between men and women are exhibited within a particular culture, appearing to be smaller in magnitude relative to differences between cultures. For example, although American women may have more interdependent self-construals than American men, they are less interdependent than Japanese men and more independent than Japanese women (Kashima, Yamaguchi, Kim, Choi, Gelfand, & Yuki, 1995).

An exception in this general tendency toward interdependent relational styles is the United States, particularly European Americans. Here, acting "professional" means suppressing authentic displays of social emotionality, maintaining a divide between one's work and personal life, and not letting interpersonal issues stand in the way—the "emotional overcoat" theory (Mann, 1999). In fact, professional emotionality is prescribed in these cultures where employees are expected to be courteous in a friendly way and not display strong emotions, either positive or negative, in the workplace. Bringing authentic emotionality to the workplace (e.g., being sad, depressed, or overly happy) is frowned on and considered unprofessional behavior. Employees may be expected to display "scripted" emotions such as the "Have a nice day" script for many jobs in the service sector in which workers are required to be at all times cheerful and helpful to customers to encourage a positive experience and repeat service (e.g., training programs for telemarketers teach them how to speak on the phone with a smile in their voice so the smile will be obvious to the person on the other end of the phone line). Other organizational positions having less customer contact, as well as jobs such as lawyers, physicians, and nurses, are expected to be cool and emotionally detached in order to project professional competence (Mann, 1999). In either of these cases, the prescribed job-related emotional script typical in the differentiated cultural context requires workers to put effort into acting out emotions they do not feel or to suppress emotions they do feel in order to meet the emotional scripts of their jobs.

Variation in how social and task concerns are structured appears also at the social network level. Morris and his colleagues (2008) investigated the overlap between work and social ties among Citibank employees in Spain, China, Germany, and the United States. They asked bank branch employees how much they interact with coworkers during their time off, for example, on the weekend. Whereas the Spaniards and Japanese indicated it was quite common to interact with the same people inside and outside work (see combined style later in this chapter), Americans were significantly less likely to show such overlap (see differentiated style). Moreover, data from the U.S. General Social Survey (GSS) shows that this trend is becoming stronger for Americans over time (Kacperczyk et al., 2009). Mor Barak and her colleagues (2003) compared the support network structure between employees of high-tech companies in Israel and in the United States. They found a striking difference: in the United States, the support network structure was very distinct and segregated by type of provider (three clear factors emerged: supervisor, coworkers, and family/friends), whereas in Israel, the network structure was highly interconnected (no factors emerged in the confirmatory factor analysis). Israelis, like the Japanese and the Spaniards in the previous study, utilize a combined style and are more likely to interact with their coworkers after work. As a result, they made no distinction between support provided by their supervisor and coworkers and their family and friends. The Americans, by contrast, hold a differentiated style and make a clear distinction between support provided by people from their work context and those from outside the work context (Mor Barak et al., 2003).

Previous studies point to the fact that cultures of interdependence promote well-being in contrast to cultures of independence, which tend to foster psychological distress (Bellah, Madsen, Sullivan, Swidler, & Tipton, 1985).

Cultures of interdependence are composed of social structures that promote the good of the collective and the group's responsibility for taking care of its own. Social institutions in independent cultures, in contrast, support individual autonomy and personal fulfillment with the expectation that the individual will take care of his or her own needs. The result is a more fragmented support network with less communication between its various parts and gaps in support that reduce its positive impact on well-being.

In sum, understanding the degree to which an individual's relational mental models reflect a combined versus differentiated style provides a basis for anticipating the challenges that will arise when people from cultures using these two styles attempt to work together. These challenges include coordinating differences in the beliefs about the importance of social-emotional elements of work relations, their role in defining appropriate and professional behavior, and expectations about blending or differentiated work and nonwork social worlds.

CONFLICT AND HARMONY

Relational styles influence one's beliefs about conflict and its consequences (e.g., whether relationship conflict in a team is a threat to task success). The more that social-emotional elements are removed from one's workplace relational mental model (see differentiated style), the less vulnerable the team is perceived to be to social-emotional disruptions. According to Neuman, Sanchez-Burks, Goh, and Ybarra (2004), managers in combined-style cultures interpret conflict as an inherent barrier to success: a team, collaboration, or partnership without interpersonal harmony can rarely be productive (see Diego's alarm at the team's composition in the case vignette at the beginning of this chapter). On the other hand, managers in differentiated cultures, although not enjoying interpersonal discord, do not perceive it necessarily to be a limiting factor for a team's success (Markus's attitude to the team's composition in the case vignette demonstrates this approach). In a survey conducted in the United States, China, and Korea, Neuman and his colleagues (2004) asked managers and business students to what extent task and relationship conflict were a roadblock to success, if at all (see Figure 9.2). Virtually all of the managers believed that task-related conflict was a barrier to success, surprising only in that research demonstrates that under certain circumstances it may provide a source of synergy and remedy to groupthink (for reviews, see Jehn & Bendersky, 2004). However, only the European Americans, particularly men, had a different belief about the effects of relationship conflict—as one manager stated, "It [relationship conflict] is unfortunate but not devastating." Research also demonstrates that the negative effect of process conflict on the other types of conflict (e.g., task, relationship) over time may be limited when members are able to resolve their process conflicts at the start of their time together (Greer, Jehn, & Mannix, 2008).

The implication of these different beliefs about relationship conflict is that when conflict does arise in cross-cultural relationships (as it often does whenever people must work closely in interdependent tasks), people's reactions will differ likewise, and these different reactions may trigger a spiral downward in dynamics that extends far beyond the initial conflict. For example, a Korean manager may become anxious that the team's ability to succeed may be limited because of the interpersonal conflict and, hence, try to exit the team or work hard to restore interpersonal harmony. In contrast, the American is less likely to ruminate over the issue and prefers to "let bygones be bygones" rather than continue to focus on interpersonal difficulties over task-specific issues. Thus, beliefs about relationship conflict rather than actual effects of relationship conflict may pose the more serious threat to cross-cultural working relationships. Decisions about which teams to join, who to invite, and if and when to attempt an exit from the team will all reflect these beliefs about how much interpersonal harmony and relationship conflict affect a team's ability to succeed in their mission.

Interpersonal Relationships and Cross-Cultural Communication

Successful cross-cultural communication relies on many shared understandings about emotional displays, indirect cues, and face,[1] to name a few. In every culture, people's internalized cultural norms and values inform the way they communicate with other people and may explain some difficulties in cross-cultural communication that cannot be explained by the use of different languages alone. For example, consider the following conversation between an American plant manager (Patrick) and his Mexican supervisor (Francisco):

Patrick: It looks like we're going to have to keep the production line running on Saturday.

Francisco: I see.

Patrick: Can you make it on Saturday?

Francisco: Oh, yes . . . Patrick, did I tell you that my son's birthday is this Saturday. My family is going to have a big party for him.

Patrick: Oh, how nice. I hope that everyone has a wonderful time.

Francisco: Thank you, I knew that you would understand.

Patrick: OK, so see you on Saturday.

Figure 9.2   Beliefs About the Effects of Task and Relationship Conflict

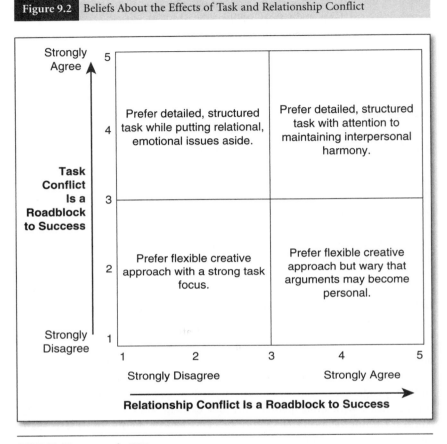

SOURCE: Neuman et al., 2004.

Will Francisco show up on Saturday? Would Patrick be justified in being upset if his supervisor does not show up? Culture and context rather than language per se are necessary to explain the likely miscommunication between Patrick and Francisco. In the following sections, we describe how culture shapes one's communication style and the implications of this diversity for cross-cultural communication in a global marketplace. We begin by discussing communication patterns that reflect different points along the cultural continuums of high/low context and individualism-collectivism. Next, we describe how these cultural continuums create communication contexts that differ in their orientation toward face and relational concerns versus instrumental concerns and preferences for direct versus indirect communication.

Theoretical Perspectives on Interpersonal Cross-Cultural Communication

All business transactions, whether within the same culture or across different cultures, involve communication. Business-related communication includes activities such as exchanging information and ideas, decision making, motivating, and negotiating (Adler & Gundersen, 2008). An important theoretical construct used to differentiate among cultural communication styles involves the continuum of *low-context to high-context* cultures (Hall, 1959). Members of high-context cultures, such as Japan, China, Mexico, and Chile, exchange information using a communication style in which the content and meaning of the information is derived from contextual cues in the setting, with only minimal information explicitly derived from a literal interpretation of the transmitted message itself. In such communications, the words convey only a small part of the message, and the receiver needs to fill in the gaps based on understanding of the context and of the speaker. In contrast, members of low-context cultures, such as the United States, Australia, and Germany, exchange information through transactions that are the opposite: most of the information is conveyed within the transmitted message itself. The actual words rather than the context contain the intended meaning (Hall, 1976). Thus, high- and low-context cultures differ in the degree to which one must attend to interpersonal and contextual cues in the situation in order to understand what is taking place and what is being communicated. These cues are essential for understanding in high-context cultures and substantially less important in low-context cultures.

A second theoretical distinction between cultures that is relevant to communication is the continuum of *collectivist to individualist* cultures. These terms are part of a broad theoretical formulation to differentiate cultures across the globe (Hofstede, 1980; Hofstede & Hofstede, 2005; Triandis, 1996, 2003) (see Chapter 8). At this point, suffice it to say that individualist cultures are those that value autonomy and independence whereas collectivist cultures are those that value reciprocal obligations and interdependence. In collectivist societies such as many Latin American countries, countries in Africa, and Arab-speaking countries, people are born into extended families or other groups that are structured to remain highly interdependent and loyal to one another in all spheres of life.

In Guinean culture, for example, as is the case in most of Africa, the deep sense of commitment to the extended family intertwines in subtle and complex ways with the working life. It is not uncommon, therefore, to see employees leaving work to settle family matters and to be absent for a couple of days to mourn relatives in remote villages (Auclair, 1992). In societies steeped in individualism such as the United States, Australia, Great Britain, and Canada, people are expected to act according to their self-interests rather than those of the collective and are not viewed as an inextricable part of a larger social group (Bellah et al., 1985; Javidan & House, 2001). In collectivist societies, the group is primary, and individuals are derived from their social relationships and group memberships. In individualist societies, it is the individual that is primary, and social affiliations are proprieties of the individual, each person having a unique collection of memberships and relationships (Wagner, 2002).

Cultures often cluster along the cultural continuums described thus far. Research reveals links between the cultural context continuum of low to high context and the cultural value continuum of individualism and collectivism. That is, cultures that have a collectivist value system (with an emphasis on "we" rather than "I") also tend to have a high-context orientation, whereas individualist cultures (with an emphasis on "I" rather than "we") are often more low context in nature (Gudykunst, Ting-Toomey, & Chua, 1988; Ting-Toomey, 1988, 2007). Moreover, the cultural patterns described earlier as having differentiated versus combined relational styles also tend to covary with these dimensions. High-context collectivists tend to exhibit a combined relational style (blending task and social-emotional ties), whereas low-context individualists more often show a differentiated relational style (Sanchez-Burks & Lee, 2007).

How does the cultural context affect communication styles? We examine this question according to three interrelated dimensions: (a) face and harmony orientation; (b) relationship versus task orientation; and (c) direct versus indirect communication (see Table 9.1).

FACE AND HARMONY ORIENTATION

The concept of "face" refers to "the public self-image that every member of a society wants to claim for him/herself" (Brown & Levinson, 1978, p. 199). Earley (1997) defines it more broadly: "Face refers to both internal and external

Table 9.1   Cultural Context and Communication Orientation

	Cultural Context	
Communication Orientation	**High-Context Collectivist**	**Low-Context Individualist**
Face Orientation	Other-face concern	Self-face concern
Relationship vs. Task	Relationship oriented	Task oriented
Direct vs. Indirect	Indirect communication	Direct communication

presentations of oneself, and it is based on both morality defined in a social structure as well as a socially constructed representation by others" (Earley, 1997, p. 14). Although the concept of face may manifest itself differently in various cultures and has been mistakenly attributed as primarily an Asian culture preoccupation, everyone has a concept of face that influences his or her behavior and action. In collectivist, high-context cultures such as in Indonesia, for example, it would be inappropriate for a manager to praise individuals too highly in front of their peers. Instead, the group as a whole should be praised when things go well (Foster, 1998). Harmony, which too has been mistakenly attributed to only Asian cultures, is the process through which face is regulated in a particular cultural context (Earley, 1997). As described earlier, the Mexican value placed on *simpatia* similarly emphasizes the importance of interpersonal and group harmony (Diaz-Guerrero, 1967; Triandis et al., 1984). In their communication with others, members of low-context individualist cultures are more likely to be concerned with self-face and have a preference for congruence between their private self-image ("authentic self") and their public self-image ("social self"). In contrast, members of high-context collectivist cultures are more likely to be concerned with other-face in their interpersonal communication and negotiations (Ting-Toomey, 1988, 2007). The roots of this focus on the other-face in the Asian cultures can be found in the Confucian principle that one needs to continually deepen and broaden one's awareness of the presence of the other in one's self-cultivation (Tu, 1985).

RELATIONSHIP VERSUS TASK ORIENTATION

As indicated earlier in the chapter, different cultures use relational mental models that emphasize by varying degree either instrumental goals or relational goals. Here we discuss the impact of these relational mental models on cross-cultural communication. Communication in the combined task/relationship mental model or the differentiated mental model focus on either achieving a task or the relationship as it relates to the task (see Box 9.3).

BOX 9.3
Communicating Through the Exchange of Business Cards: Task-Oriented Versus Relationship/Task-Oriented Cultures

Exchanging business cards is a decades-old tradition within the business community, a tradition that originated in the United States and Europe. The

(Continued)

(Continued)

reason for this custom was straightforward: to provide the very basic information about the bearer of the card so that the other person would remember the card owner's name, job title, company affiliation, and contact information for pursuing future business opportunities. Developed within the Western cultural context, it was clearly task oriented.

Businesspeople in Asian countries such as China and Korea have adopted this custom, but with a cultural twist. Whereas Western business people pay no attention to the way they hand out their cards, Chinese people take great care about the process of giving and receiving a business card: they hold the card with both hands and with a bow present the card with the print facing the recipient of the card. Coming from a relationship-oriented cultural mental model, the method of presenting the card is aimed to convey respect and establish trust. Presenting the card with both hands symbolically indicates that the presenter of the card is honest, has nothing to hide, and is not holding back.

An American businessman who was coached ahead of time about this custom found himself in an awkward situation in meeting a Chinese colleague. The two of them were handing their cards to one another at the very same time. Holding their cards in both hands, neither one had a free hand to take the other's card, let alone accept it with both hands as is customary. Finally, the Chinese man graciously put his card on the table and took the American's card and then picked up his card from the table and handed it to his American colleague, thus completing their "cultural dance."

An example that demonstrates the discrepancy between the Western differentiated task orientation and the Eastern combined relationship/task orientation is the following incident. An American professor was invited to give a series of lectures in several universities in China. Her hosts exhibited the very warm hospitality that the Chinese people are known for by lavishly wining and dining her. On the morning of the last day of the visit, with her flight scheduled for noon, her hosts insisted on showing her a traditional tea ceremony. Although she appreciated their gracious hospitality and the great effort they had made to find a teahouse that would agree to perform the tea ceremony in the morning rather than the typical afternoon/evening time, she was anxious about the risk of missing her flight. Unbeknownst to her, during the tea ceremony, arrangements were made by one of the hosts for a car that would take her to the airport on time for her flight. Relaxing on the plane (that she did not miss after all), she reflected that a typical American host would have been more concerned with getting her to her plane on time (differentiated task orientation) than spending additional time in developing the relationship in a social atmosphere (interdependent relationship/task orientation).

DIRECT VERSUS INDIRECT COMMUNICATION

The most universal communication strategy used to preserve face and harmony, particularly when conveying bad news, is the use of indirectness (Brown & Levinson, 1978). Indirect communication refers to the difference between the literal meaning of what one says (semantic meaning) and the intended meaning (see Figure 9.3 for an example of public displays of indirectness). For example, when a coworker proposes an alternative marketing approach that you do not think is particularly well thought out, you might say, "It sounds interesting" (indirect communication) in order to avoid saying what you really think: "It's a half-baked idea" (direct communication). Thus, you have not hurt your coworker's feelings and allowed her or him to save face.

Indirectness is an important communicative strategy that varies according to cultural context, individualism-collectivism, and relational styles. In cultures where face and harmony are important, people use face-saving communication strategies such as indirectness to avoid conflict and preserve status structures. Members of collectivist, low-context cultures exchange information primarily on the basis of direct, explicit communication that is focused on precise, straightforward words. In contrast, members of individualist, high-context cultures exchange information primarily on the basis of implicit, indirect communication that is focused on shared experiences developed over time (context) utilizing indirect and nonverbal meaning.

Summary and Conclusion

There is no such thing as an interpersonal style that is culture neutral. People hold assumptions and beliefs about the nature of interpersonal work relationships that are rooted in their cultural context. In this chapter, we focused on a continuum of relational mental models that help explain different types of relationships and communication patterns in different cultures. Relational mental models are the mental models that structure our perceptions and the way we communicate and relate to others. At one end of the spectrum is the *differentiated relational mental model* where there is a clear division between *task-focused* relationships in the business environment and the *social-emotional* relationships with family, friends, and significant others. At the other end of the spectrum is the *combined relational mental model* where both task-focused and social-emotional relationships are intertwined in both the work and the family arenas. In organizations, these relational mental models shape a variety

Figure 9.3   "Keep Off the Grass," Stated Directly (U.S.), and the Same Message, Stated Indirectly, "Since We Have Broad Road, Why Should We Open Small Paths" (China)

of dynamics, including what people notice and take away from business meetings and the degree to which they coordinate their nonverbal behaviors and are affected by the overall level of coordination.

We then examined cross-cultural communication in low-context versus high-context cultures (where information is received primarily in the message itself as compared with from sources such as the settings and the relationships) and in collectivist versus individualist cultures (where emphasis is placed on reciprocal obligations and interdependence within the extended family and community as compared with an emphasis on autonomy, independence, and self-interest). We presented an organizing theoretical model that utilizes the concepts of other-face versus self-face, relationship versus task, and indirect versus direct communication in conjunction with high/low and collectivist/individualist cultures.

Finally, we examined communication patterns and the impact of communication styles on cross-cultural interactions in the global workplace. Members of high-context cultures exchange information using a communication style in which the content and meaning of the information is derived from contextual cues in the setting, with only minimal information explicitly derived from a literal interpretation of the transmitted message itself. In contrast, members of low-context cultures exchange information through transactions that are the opposite: most of the information is conveyed within the transmitted message itself; the actual words rather than the context contain the intended meaning.

In conclusion, even when the parties communicating share a language and belong to the same culture, misunderstandings are not uncommon. Add to that the layers of cultural expectations and beliefs, gender relations, and national loyalties, and the possibilities for misunderstanding and conflict dramatically increase.

Note

1. The concept of "face" refers to "self-definition in the context of social observers," or "self-definition in one's social system" (Earley, 1997, pp. 3–4). Face includes all aspects concerning how we present ourselves and how others perceive us and, at the same time, serves as a basis for self-evaluation. We expand on this concept later in the chapter.

PART III

Managing a Diverse Workforce in the Global Context

The Inclusive Workplace

CHAPTER 10

Diversity Management

Paradigms, Rationale, and Key Elements

> Now the Star-Belly Sneetches
> Had bellies with stars.
> The Plain-Belly Sneetches
> Had none upon thars.
> Those stars weren't so big. They were really so small
> You might think such a thing wouldn't matter at all.
> But because they had stars, all the Star-Belly Sneetches
> Would brag, "We're the best kind of Sneetch on the beaches."
> With their snoots in the air, they would sniff and they'd snort,
> "We'll have nothing to do with the Plain-Belly sort!"
> And whenever they met some, when they were out walking,
> They'd hike right on past them without even talking.
>
> —Dr. Seuss, *The Sneetches and Other Stories*[1]

In his classic children's story about imaginary creatures named Sneetches, Dr. Seuss demonstrates how an irrelevant characteristic such as having or not having a small star on their bellies created two camps of Sneetches and affected their relationship with one another. The story goes on to introduce Mr. Sylvester McMonkey McBean with his "very peculiar machine" that could put stars on the Plain-Belly Sneetches. Once the Star-Belly Sneetches realized that they could no longer tell the difference, they asked Sylvester McMonkey

McBean to remove their stars! And so it went with one group going through the machine to put stars on their bellies while the other was going through it to remove their stars, "Until neither the Plain nor the Star Bellies knew whether this one was that one . . . or that one was this one" (p. 21). Like any good children's story, this tale has a happy ending with the Sneetches realizing that "Sneetches are Sneetches and no kind of Sneetch is the best on the beaches" (p. 24). Unfortunately, many cross-cultural conflicts do not have such an enlightened and happy ending. This story is often used in diversity-training programs because its moral teachings apply to adult situations as well as children's.

In this chapter, we examine diversity management programs and policies. We define the concept, examine its historical context, analyze two prominent paradigms for diversity management, and conclude by identifying its key characteristics and limitations.

Defining Diversity Management

In response to the growing diversity in the workforce around the world, many companies have instituted specific policies and programs to enhance recruitment, inclusion, promotion, and retention of employees who are different from the privileged echelons of society. Just as the privileged groups may vary from one country to the next (e.g., urban men of Han descent in China, White men in the United States, or Protestant men in Northern Ireland), so too do the disadvantaged groups (e.g., the lower castes in India, North African immigrants in France, or women in Korea). Although equal rights legislation and affirmative/positive action policies have helped disadvantaged groups obtain access to a variety of jobs not previously open to them, it is their exclusion from circles of influence in work organizations that has kept them from fully contributing to and benefiting from their involvement in the workplace. Diversity management policies and programs are designed to create a welcoming organizational environment to those groups that, in the past and through the present, have not had access to employment, in general, and to more lucrative jobs, in particular.

The term *diversity management* originated in North America but has slowly taken hold in other regions and countries of the world (e.g., Hays-Thomas, 2004; Kaiser & Prange, 2004; Nyambegera, 2002; Ozbilgin & Tatli, 2008; Palmer, 2003; Palmi, 2001). Below is a brief definition of the term:

> Diversity management refers to the voluntary organizational actions that are designed to create greater inclusion of employees from various backgrounds into the formal and informal organizational structures through deliberate policies and programs.

With the globalizing economy and the increase in multinational corporations, diversity management no longer refers solely to the heterogeneity of the
workforce within one nation but often refers also to the workforce composition
across nations. The first type, *intranational diversity management,* refers to
managing a diverse workforce of citizens or immigrants within a single national
organizational context. An example would be a German company instituting
policies and training programs for its employees to improve sensitivity and provide employment opportunities to members of minority groups and recent
immigrants in its workforce. The second type, *cross-national diversity management,* refers to managing a workforce composed of citizens and immigrants in
different countries (e.g., a Korean company with branches in Japan, China, and
Malaysia establishing diversity policies and trainings that will be applicable in
its headquarters and also in its subsidiaries in these countries). Each of these
types of diversity management presents different challenges and dilemmas, and
each requires a different set of policies and programs. In addition to practicing
within the laws and social norms of its home country, cross-national diversity
management requires employers to take into consideration the legislative and
cultural context in other countries, depending on where their workforce resides.
For example, a company based in South Africa has to abide by the South African
equal rights legislation, which compels it to treat men and women equally. If
the same company has a branch in Saudi Arabia, however, it will have to treat
its employees according to the laws of that country, which are inspired by the
shari'ah and follow the Islamic tradition of prescribed gender roles. In South
Korea, as another example, the cultural norms dictate that married women with
young children leave their careers and devote their time to their families.
Therefore, while a U.S. company is likely to provide training and promotion
opportunities to young women (in compliance with antidiscrimination legislation), its Korean subsidiary may view such policies as a waste of time, considering the Korean cultural norms (Lee, 1997; Park, 2008).

Cox (2001) notes, "The challenge of diversity is not simply to have it but
to create conditions in which its potential to be a performance barrier is minimized and its potential to enhance performance is maximized" (p. 16).
Diversity management refers not only to those groups that have been discriminated against or that are different from the dominant or privileged groups, but
to "the mixture of differences, similarities and tensions that can exist among
the elements of a pluralistic mixture" (Thomas, 2005, p. 93). Using a jar of jelly
beans (colorful candy) as a metaphor, Thomas (1996) emphasizes that diversity management is dealing with the collective mixture of all workers, not just
the recent additions to the organizational workforce:

> To highlight this notion of mixture, consider a jar of red jelly beans and
> assume that you will add some green and purple jelly beans. Many would
> believe that the green and purple jelly beans represent diversity. I suggest that

diversity, instead, is represented by the resultant mixture of red, green and purple jelly beans. When faced with a collection of diverse jelly beans, most managers have not been addressing diversity but, instead, have been addressing how to handle the last jelly beans added to the mixture. . . . The true meaning of diversity suggests that if you are concerned about racism, you include all races; if you're concerned about gender, you include both genders; or if you're concerned about age issues, you include all age groups. In other words, the mixture is all inclusive. (pp. 146–147)

Further, diversity management can create a competitive advantage in areas such as marketing, problem solving, and resource acquisition (Cox, 2001). Therefore, diversity management is not the sole domain of the human resource function in the organization (as has been the case with affirmative or positive action initiatives) primarily aimed at compliance with legal requirements. It is a systematic organization-wide effort based on the premise that for organizations to survive and thrive there is an inherent value in diversity (Cox, 2001; Kreitz, 2008; Orlando, 2000). However, it is important to note that careful research in a global context suggests that diversity management can have both positive and negative consequences as well as no change at all and that a more nuanced approach to the link between diversity management and organizational outcomes is in order (Kochan, Bezrukova, Ely, Jackson, & Joshi, 2003; Jackson, Joshi, & Erhardt, 2003; Thomas, 2005).

From Equal Rights Laws, to Affirmative/Positive Action, to Diversity Management

The current business focus on diversity is quite different from equal rights legislation and from affirmative/positive action programs. The latter are about trying to achieve equality of opportunities by focusing on specific groups and righting past wrongs. Diversity efforts focus on managing and handling the diverse workforce to give the company a competitive advantage. All these may be viewed as a continuum: equal employment opportunity (EEO) legislation means that it is against the law to discriminate; affirmative action programs mean that companies need to take positive steps to ensure equal opportunities; and diversity management is proactive and aimed at promoting a diverse and heterogeneous workforce. The emphasis of the latter is on the business advantage that it can provide to organizations. More and more companies are realizing that there could be a business benefit for having diversity management programs or, at the very least, to including language about it in their public relations materials. For example, IBM's chairman and CEO Sam Palmisano points to the link between diversity management and the core business at IBM. Highlighting IBM's long involvement with equal opportunity and diversity initiatives, Palmisano notes

that "diversity policies lie as close to IBM's core as they have throughout our heritage. Today, we're building a workforce in keeping with the global, diverse marketplace, to better serve our customers and capture a greater share of the on
demand opportunity" (IBM Web page, 2009). The importance of diversity management programs for global companies is a recurrent theme in the statements
of many executives (for a sample of statements in speeches by senior officers of
Nikkeiren, Japan's Business Federation, see Ozbilgin and Tatli, 2008, pp. 52–56).
Emphasizing the global angle of diversity management, Tiane Mitchell Gordon,
senior vice president for diversity and inclusion at American On Line (AOL),
notes that diversity management has a strategic role: "It really is about looking at
how we can influence and impact our business from a different lens to understand how, as a global company, we have to be more culturally aware" (Schoeff,
2009). Cox (2001) notes that "the globalization of business is a trend that makes
diversity competency crucial for many organizations" (p. 124) because both large
and small companies increasingly derive a significant portion of their revenues
from other countries in the world.

An interesting explanation for the difference between equal opportunity
legislation and diversity management comes from Australia and uses the analogy of wild animals in the zoo.[2]

> Imagine your organisation is a giraffe house. Equal opportunity has been very
> effective widening the door of the giraffe house to let the elephant in, but
> home won't be best for the elephant unless a number of major modifications
> are made to the inside of the house. Without these changes the house will
> remain designed for giraffes and the elephant will not "feel at home." (Krautil,
> 1995, p. 22)

In the United States, where the term *diversity management* originated, there
was a gradual progression over the years from Title VII of the 1964 Civil Rights
Act that mandated equal employment opportunity (EEO), to President Lyndon
Johnson's 1972 Executive Order 11246 that outlined affirmative action, and culminating in diversity management policies and programs developed in the
1990s and the 2000s. In Australia, the same progressive development took place
with antidiscrimination legislation and affirmative action policies requiring the
removal of barriers and the implementation of policies that encourage full
employment of groups defined by personal characteristics such as gender, race,
physical ability, ethnic heritage, and family responsibilities (Kramar, 1998).
There, too, diversity management has been seen as the natural next step for
effective management in the future competitive business environment (Burton,
1995; De Cieri, 2003),[3] and many of Australia's most profitable companies have
adopted productive diversity policies in different ways (Pyke, 2007).

The EU as a whole has developed a strong commitment to equality and
positive action policies. Across Europe, there is a trend to strengthen legislation

against discrimination as indicated by directives on equal treatment of people irrespective of their race and ethnic backgrounds and on the equal treatment of persons in the labor market, adopted by the EU Council of Ministers in 2004 (EU Directive 2000/43/EC Art 13).[4] Different countries within the union, however, have implemented varying levels of protections and initiatives, and some have adopted affirmative or positive action programs while others have not.[5] Accordingly, companies in different countries may or may not institute, or even aspire to implement, diversity management policies and programs, and those that have been developed will vary in scope and organizational commitment. In a series of comparative studies, the International Labour Organization (ILO) evaluated antidiscrimination and diversity-training initiatives in different countries in the EU (Wrench, 2007). The studies indicated that Spain, for example, was one of the few industrialized migrant-receiving countries that at the time of the study had not introduced antidiscrimination legislation to protect nonnational workers; and in general, there was very little or no awareness of the potential problem of ethnic or racial discrimination. Therefore, although there were some labor initiatives coming from local government organizations, trade unions, NGOs, and some multinational companies, the trainings were aimed at antidiscrimination, not at diversity management (Angel de Prada, Pereda, & Actis, 1997). Even in countries that have already instituted equal rights laws and public policies that promote diversity, the general organizational culture may not have been ready for the next step of diversity management. In the United Kingdom, for example, diversity management was perceived as premature during the 1990s in several cases unless it followed antiracism and equality trainings (Taylor, Powell, & Wrench, 1997). It is important to remember that the prerequisite for diversity management is having a diverse workforce. Although recruitment of diverse employees can be a goal of diversity management, if there is little diversity in the organization, the focus should be on recruitment strategies and not on diversity management per se. In the Netherlands, for example, a heterogeneous workforce is still more of an exception than a rule. Although the demographics have changed quite dramatically in the last two decades, the workforce is still quite segregated. Most business diversity efforts are focused on recruiting customers, not employees. Therefore, companies need to focus on applying positive action policies in workforce recruitment before they can exercise diversity management (Abell, Havelaar, & Dankoor, 1997; Tsogas & Subeliani, 2005).

In some countries such as South Africa where a nonracial, democratic constitution came into effect in 1996, equal rights legislation was implemented at just about the same time as its affirmative action policies, and many of its companies have been trying to almost simultaneously design and implement diversity management programs. The results of both equal rights laws and the affirmative action policies in South Africa are already evident in the increased proportion of Black managers, though these rates are still far from their representation in the wider society. As the racial and cultural profile of South African organizations continues to change, the process of managing diversity is becoming more important (Horwitz, 2002). The situation in Brazil is quite similar to that of South Africa, with both legislation and government measures to combat employment discrimination taking place relatively recently.[6] Brazil, however, is quite different because it has long been a heterogeneous society, the product of several migration flows relatively early in its development. As a result, Brazilians take pride in their tradition of nonprejudicial national ideology. Nevertheless, inequalities do exist, and the concern of Brazilian companies with the practice of managing cultural diversity is quite recent and relatively limited. Although the population in Brazil is rather diverse, those companies that have developed programs are primarily subsidiaries of U.S enterprises (Fleury, 1999; Perez-Floriano & Gonzalez, 2007).

As is evident from this brief review, equal rights legislation and affirmative/positive action policies are prerequisites for the development of diversity management because they create the social, legal, and organizational environment on which diversity management initiatives can be based. In some countries, the development was sequential and took decades, whereas in others, the development was rapid and almost co-occurring.

Diversity Management Paradigms

In recent years, several paradigms have been offered for diversity management that underscore its unique characteristics and purpose. This section highlights two of the prominent approaches—the human resource (HR) paradigm and the multicultural organization (MO) paradigm.

THE HUMAN RESOURCE PARADIGM IN DIVERSITY MANAGEMENT

Conventional HR practices tend to produce and perpetuate homogeneity in the workforce as a result of the A-S-A (attraction-selection-attrition) cycle (Schneider, 1987; Schneider, Smith, & Paul, 2001). Typically, individuals are *attracted* to organizations that appear to have members with values similar to their own. In turn, organizations *select* new members that are similar to their existing members because their hiring continues to make everyone feel comfortable (García, Posthuma, & Colella, 2008). Recruiting practices often emphasize hiring people from sources that have historically been reliable and selecting candidates whose characteristics are similar to those employees that have been successful in the past. As a result, employees who do not fit in well with the dominant organizational culture eventually leave or are fired, creating a selective *attrition* process that supports and maintains a workforce that is homogeneous (Schneider, Smith, & Paul, 2001). In the long run, this trend is unhealthy for organizations in that it limits their talent pool, their long-term growth and renewal, and their ability to adapt to environmental changes and tap into new markets.

In recent decades, human resource managers have recognized the need to adopt effective diversity management practices in order to overcome barriers for diversity and reap the rewards of a diverse workforce. Kossek and Lobel (1996) summarize the three prevailing HR approaches to diversity management and offer an original approach of their own. The authors later expanded on the model and made the connection between human resource management practices, workforce diversity, and individual, group, and organizational outcomes (Kossek, Lobel, & Brown, 2006). The four approaches are presented in Table 10.1 and elaborated below.

Diversity enlargement. This approach focuses on increasing the representation of individuals of different ethnic and cultural backgrounds in the organization. The goal is to change the organizational culture by changing the demographic composition of the workforce. For example, the Norwegian government backed a draft law that would oblige companies to appoint women to at least 40% of their directorships ("Oslo Push," 2003). The assumption is that the new employees will conform to existing practices and that no additional intervention will be needed. The mere presence of increasing numbers of employees from different backgrounds will result in a culture change that will bring the desired results. Often this approach is motivated by compliance to laws and public expectations of political correctness rather than a deep understanding of the business need for diversity (Kossek & Lobel, 1996).

Diversity sensitivity. This approach recognizes the potential difficulties introduced by bringing together individuals from diverse backgrounds and cultures in the workplace. It attempts to overcome these difficulties through diversity training that is aimed at sensitizing employees to stereotyping and discrimination while also promoting communication collaboration. The assumption embedded in this approach is that increased sensitivity to differences will improve performance. Although this is sometimes the case, in other instances, particularly when the training is not linked to corporate goals and initiatives and not supported by its long-term policies, it can create more harm than good. Emphasizing differences can backfire by reinforcing stereotypes and highlighting intergroup differences rather than improving communication through understanding and common interests (Kossek & Lobel, 1996). (See Box 10.1 for an example of a diversity training gone awry.)

Table 10.1 The HR Approach to Diversity Management

HR Approach	Goal	Strategy	Assumptions
Diversity Enlargement	Change organizational culture through changing the composition of the workforce	Recruit employees from diverse backgrounds	New hires will change the culture by their mere presence—no need for additional intervention
Diversity Sensitivity	Overcome adversity and promote productive communication and collaboration	Train to increase sensitivity and improve communication	Increased sensitivity to differences will affect performance
Cultural Audit	Identify obstacles faced by employees of diverse backgrounds and modify company practices accordingly	Audit current practices through surveys and focus groups and generate changes to address these deficiencies	Problems are caused by the dominant cultural group in the organization and need to be addressed by that group
Strategy for Achieving Organizational Outcomes	Achieve organizational goals through diversity management	Integrate diversity management with HR policy areas and other company strategic choices	Diversity management practices have to be linked to desired individual and organizational outcomes

SOURCE: Based on Kossek and Lobel, 1996.

BOX 10.1
A Diversity Training Gone Awry:
The Texaco "Jelly Bean Jar" Incident

Diversity training ought to be well planned and executed. Sometimes, the efforts to improve openness and understanding between groups may reinforce negative images and even prejudice. Rather than facilitating open communication and improved relationships, the end result might be divisive and offensive. An example of a diversity training gone awry is the infamous Texaco 1994 "jelly beans" incident that was featured in a lawsuit against the company (Eichenwald, 1996). The lawsuit, filed by the company's African American employees, alleged racist remarks as part of the company's culture. Among other incidents of prejudice and discrimination in the company, the lawsuit alleged that in a diversity training sponsored by the company, a comment was made by one of the managers that "All the black jelly beans seem to be glued to the bottom of the bag," a remark that was interpreted as derogatory toward African Americans. In its defense, the company commissioned an independent counsel who reported that there was nothing inherently derogatory in any of the references to jelly beans. Indicating that the jelly beans reference was a common image used in diversity training,[7] the independent counsel suggested that it may have been a reference to inequities imposed upon African Americans by society, rather than a criticism. The case ended with a $176 million settlement announced November 15, 1996 (De Meuse & Hostager, 2001; Olson, 1997; "Texaco Independent Investigator's Report," 1996).

Cultural audit. This approach aims at identifying the obstacles that limit the progress of employees from diverse backgrounds and that block collaboration among groups in the organization. The audit is usually performed by outside consultants who obtain data from surveys and focus groups and then identify areas in which employees who are different from the dominant group feel that they are blocked from performing to the best of their ability. Although this is a customized approach that is tailored to specific organizational cultures, the recommendations for change are typically based on the notion that the source of the problem is in the dominant cultural group (typically, in North America, White male) and that the change must come from within that group (Kossek & Lobel, 1996). An example of a cultural audit is Ford Motor Company's global employee satisfaction survey. The survey, called PULSE, is distributed annually among all of the company's salaried employees (in 2002, 71% of employees participated in the survey). Employee satisfaction with diversity is one of the 12 dimensions assessed by the survey, and the results are used to assess Ford's commitment and performance in achieving a diverse workforce (Ford Motor Company, 2002).

Strategy for achieving organizational outcomes. This approach, proposed by Kossek and Lobel (1996) as a comprehensive framework for HR diversity management, focuses on diversity management "as a means for achieving organizational ends, not as an end in itself" (p. 4). Using this strategy, managers have to identify the link between diversity management objectives and desired individual and organizational outcomes. Organizational strategic choices are viewed in the context of environmental drivers such as the changing labor market composition, the global economy, the shift to a service economy, and the legal and governmental pressures. Analyzing environmental drivers can help the organization determine the specific benefits it expects to gain from its diversity management and how those are linked to its overall business strategy. For example, if innovation is a business strategy for the company, it is in its best interest to cultivate multicultural diverse teams because creativity and responsiveness to new markets, primarily in today's global economy, are more likely to be found in diverse work teams.

THE MULTICULTURAL ORGANIZATION
PARADIGM IN DIVERSITY MANAGEMENT

Cox (1994, 2001) presents a diversity management paradigm that includes three types: the monolithic organization, the plural organization, and the multicultural organization. Diversity management, according to this paradigm, should strive to create multicultural organizations in which members of all sociocultural backgrounds can contribute and achieve their full potential.

The monolithic organization. This is an organization that is demographically and culturally homogeneous. For example, most Chinese companies are monolithic from a cultural and ethnic perspective, as the overwhelming majority of their employees are ethnically Han Chinese. They are not, however, monolithic from a gender perspective because there are many women in the companies. Women, though, are more commonly employed at the lower levels of the organization, whereas most of the managers, particularly at the top levels, are men (Powell & Graves, 2003). A monolithic organization in North America or Europe will have a majority of White men and relatively few women and members of ethnic and racial minorities. Typically, women and racial/ethnic members of minority groups, both men and women, will be segregated in low-status jobs such as receptionists and maintenance people that do not have a significant impact on organizational policies and practices (Cox, 1994, 2001). A monolithic organization will have a culture that will perpetuate the homogeneity of its workforce through its hiring and promotion practices. There will be an expectation that members of diverse groups will assimilate into the culture of the majority with minimal degrees of structural and formal integration. In other words, because one cultural group manages the organization almost exclusively, both the practices and policies of a monolithic organization are biased in favor of the majority group. Not surprisingly, intergroup conflict is expected to be minimal in such an organization because it is basically homogeneous and is composed of one dominant cultural group. Given the globalizing economy, a monolithic organization will be at a competitive disadvantage, and its homogeneity will become more difficult to maintain given the influx of women and members of minority groups into the workforce around the world.

The plural organization. This is an organization that has a heterogeneous workforce, relative to the monolithic organization, and typically makes efforts to conform to laws and public policies that demand and expect workplace equality. It will take active steps to prevent discrimination in the workplace such as audits that assure equality of compensation systems and manager trainings on equal opportunity issues and sexual harassment. Although women and members of minority groups are represented in larger numbers, they make up only a small percent of the management, particularly top management, and are still expected to assimilate into the majority culture. Examples of plural organizations include companies in which members of minority groups constitute a sizable proportion of the workforce but only a small percent of the managerial positions. Although there is greater structural and formal integration in the plural organization, institutional bias is rather prevalent and intergroup conflict is significant, primarily because the increased presence of women and members of ethnic and racial minority groups is not accompanied by serious efforts to make them a truly integral part of the organization. Cox (1994, 2001) attributes the increased intergroup conflict in plural organizations in the United States to the backlash against affirmative action programs and the resulting sense among majority group members that they are being discriminated against because of no fault of their own. Cox (1994) identifies the plural organization as the most prevalent type in the North American business environment, but this organizational type is also prevalent in other areas of the world such as Europe, Australia, India, and South Africa.

The multicultural organization. This is more an ideal than an actual type because very rarely do companies achieve this level of integration. However, Cox (1994, 2001) indicates that it is important to understand this type and use it to create a vision for effective diversity management. The multicultural organization (MO) is characterized by a culture that fosters and values cultural differences—truly and equally incorporates all members of the organization via pluralism as an acculturation *process,* rather than as an *end* resulting in assimilation. The MO has full integration, structurally and informally, is free of bias and favoritism toward one group as compared with others, and has only a minimal intergroup conflict, thanks to the above characteristics that result from effective management of diversity.

Cox's (1994) typology of the monolithic-multicultural organizational continuum presents "pure" types that are rarely found in reality but are useful from an analytic standpoint. Although it was generated primarily for the North American context, it is useful for other countries as well because diversity of the workforce is increasingly central, even in traditionally homogeneous societies. By outlining these types, particularly the extremes, Cox's typology is helpful in providing work organizations with a vision of the model they need to strive for in designing their diversity management strategies.

The Impetus for Implementing Diversity Management

Why do companies implement diversity management strategies? There are three types of arguments in favor of diversity management, each with its own slogan (Table 10.2):

1. "Diversity is a reality that is here to stay." Businesses have to adapt to the new realities of an increasingly diverse workforce. In the United States, it was the report by the Hudson Institute, Workforce 2000, and the one that followed it, Workforce 2020, that served as a wake-up call to businesses, describing in compelling statistical detail the future trends of the workforce (Johnston & Packer, 1987; Judy & D'Amico, 1997). One of their central predictions was that the workforce will grow slowly and the proportion of older adults, women, and members of minority groups will continue to increase. Earlier chapters in this book described diversity trends in other countries as well, demonstrating that the global economy contributes to increased diversity in practically every region of the world.

Table 10.2 Motivation for Implementing Diversity Management

Slogan	Argument
"Diversity is a reality here to stay."	The pool of current and future employees is becoming more diverse, and businesses have no choice but to adapt to this new reality.
"Diversity management is the right thing to do."	Companies have an obligation to promote social justice and implement principles of compensatory justice through their policies and programs.
"Diversity makes good business sense."	Diversity management can give companies a competitive advantage in the global economy.

2. "Diversity management is the right thing to do." This is the moral and ethical reasoning for diversity management. At the heart of this argument is the notion of equal opportunities regardless of individual characteristics such as gender, race, and sexual orientation. This includes providing all potential employees with equal access to jobs in the organization and providing current employees with comparable pay for jobs of comparable worth (Velasquez, 2005). Another ethical principle, compensatory justice, is the foundation of affirmative action programs (Kellough, 2006). This principle suggests that society has an obligation to overcome historical discrimination against specific groups of people to compensate those who have been intentionally and unjustly wronged (Kellough, 2006; Velasquez, 2005). Therefore, work organizations have a social obligation to participate in compensating groups that have been wronged in the past—Blacks in South Africa or Catholics in Northern Ireland.

3. "Diversity makes good business sense." Diversity management can provide businesses with a competitive advantage. Here the logic is that by managing diversity, companies have much to gain (Cox, 2001; Kochan et al., 2003), including (a) cost reductions due to lower absenteeism and turnover, (b) advantages in the competition for talent in the workforce (Thomas, et al., 2002),[8] (c) reduced risk of discrimination lawsuits due to a more just and nondiscriminating environment, (d) more effective marketing to diverse customer pools (Kossek, Lobel, & Brown, 2006; Pradhan, 1989), (e) increased creativity and innovation through diverse work teams (Weiss, 1992; Kossek, Lobel, & Brown, 2006), (f) government contracts for which minority- or gender-balanced businesses are given preference, and (g) improved corporate image, which generates public goodwill. More will be said about benefits to companies in the next chapter.

Elements of this three-pronged rationale for adopting diversity management are evident in the mission statement and corporate ethos of many companies. For example, Jay C. Rising, president of Automatic Data Processing (ADP), states, "Our goal is to have a workplace that is fully inclusive, one that enables us to leverage the talents of a multi-cultural organization" (Automatic Data Processing [ADP], n.d.); and the mission statement of Hanes and Boone (one of the largest law firms in the United States) indicates,

> Our greatest asset is our people. They make Haynes and Boone a special firm by embracing core values that foster a healthy work environment, a commitment to being the best and an attitude of service to others. While our people make a positive difference for our clients, they do the same for their local communities by dedicating substantial personal time and funds to pro bono work and community service. We are equally proud of the ethnic, gender and cultural diversity of our people and our success in hiring, retaining and promoting women and ethnic minorities. (About the Firm, 2002–2003)

These types of mission statements have been adopted by companies outside the United States as well. For example, the diversity statement of Woolworths Holdings, a South African–based retail group, pronounces,

> Woolworths believes in a diverse workforce and embraces the principles of employment equity to achieve an appropriate balance for the group. The group has demonstrated its commitment to employment equity by adopting a diversity statement forming the basis for implementation. (Woolworths Holdings Limited, 2004)

Similarly, the corporate statement about diversity from AstraZeneca, a leading U.K.-based pharmaceutical company, proclaims,

> Our definition of diversity includes all our different personal skills and qualities as well as race and gender, where advancement depends solely on ability, performance and good teamwork. We encourage our people to share their knowledge and ideas across boundaries—to build high performance teams that recognise and value our differences—teams that celebrate diversity but which also embrace common goals. Across the business, diversity is high on the agenda and continuous improvement is at the heart of our approach. And we have a clear focus on the future—an aspiration to become a true culture of diversity. (AstraZeneca United Kingdom, 2004)

Characteristics and Limitations of Diversity Management

The goal of diversity management is to transform the organizational culture from a majority-oriented to a heterogeneous-pluralistic culture in which different value systems are heard and thus equally affect the work environment. Diversity management has a dual focus: the first is enhancing social justice by creating an organizational environment in which no one is privileged or disadvantaged due to characteristics such as race or gender; the second is increasing productivity and profitability through organizational transformation (e.g., Cox, 2001; Ozbilgin & Tatli, 2008; Thomas, 2005). Accordingly, diversity management has three key components:

1. Diversity management is voluntary. Equal rights legislation is enforced through sanctions (monetary fines or incarceration), and affirmative/positive action policies are enforced through incentives (government contracts); but diversity management is self-initiated by the companies themselves. It is not enforced or coerced but is entirely voluntary.

2. Diversity management uses a broad definition of diversity. Whereas both equal rights legislation and affirmative or positive action policies specify the groups that are to benefit from the laws or public policies (e.g., specific castes in India or Blacks in South Africa), companies that implement diversity management often use broad and open definitions of diversity. One of the reasons for this broad and often vague definition is that they make diversity programs inclusive and reduce potential objections from members of the majority group.

3. Diversity management aims at providing tangible benefits to the company. Diversity management is seen as a business strategy aimed at tapping into the full potential of all employees in the company in order to give the company a competitive advantage, whereas in the past, employees of different backgrounds (e.g., race/ethnicity or gender) were labeled as unqualified by managers if they did not conform to values and norms of the majority. The logic of diversity management is that it allows every member of the organization to bring to the workplace his or her unique perspective, benefiting the organization as a whole. Expected benefits of diversity management include such outcomes as broad appeal to diverse clients—because diverse employees communicate better with diverse clients; better products—because diversity of opinions leads to creativity; and improved sales—because diverse employees better understand the needs of diverse clients (Cox, 2001; Ozbilgin & Tatli, 2008; Thomas et al., 2002). Ford Australia, for example, realizing that attracting women as customers is imperative for its future growth, sought to increase the proportion of women among its workforce. Since 2000, Ford Australia has funded the Ford of Australia Women in Engineering Scholarship Program, an undergraduate scholarship program aimed at encouraging more women to enter the field of automotive engineering. As a result of that program, in 2002, women had increased to a 43% share of the company's total university graduate intake. Similarly, in order to attract diverse clients, Telstra Corporation Limited recruited employees who could speak up to seven different languages to staff its multilingual customer service centers. These multilingual sales consultants take an average of about 2,700 calls each month with increasingly positive feedback from customers who prefer explaining their telecommunication problems in their native tongues.

Though these key components of diversity management—being voluntary, using a broad definition of diversity, and providing tangible benefits to the company—represent strength in the current business context, they can potentially bring the demise of the concept in the long run. First, the *voluntary nature* of diversity management means that it may not survive during difficult economic times. The concern here is that if forced to make a choice among competing expenditures, diversity programs may be cut back or eliminated altogether because their benefits often take a long time to materialize. Second, the *broad definitions of diversity* mean that the most vulnerable groups in society—racial minority groups, people with disabilities, and women—may not receive the protection they deserve because resources will be spread across many groups. The concern here is that the slogan "Everyone is diverse" dilutes the implications of historical injustices and discrimination that have denied certain groups access to opportunities and resources. And, finally, the emphasis on the *practical benefits* suggests that once diversity management is no longer perceived as beneficial to companies, it will disappear. It is, therefore, essential that diversity management will be based not only on the principle of providing tangible benefits to the companies but also on a strong moral and ethical commitment to diversity.

Summary and Conclusion

The globalizing economy and the increase in the number of multinational corporations make diversity management a necessity for companies that want not only to survive but thrive during this time of economic, social, and cultural changes. *Diversity management* refers to the voluntary organizational actions that are designed to create through deliberate policies and programs greater inclusion of employees from various backgrounds into the formal and informal organizational structures. Diversity management, compared with its predecessors (equal opportunity legislation and affirmative action programs), is proactive and aimed at creating an organization in which all members can contribute and achieve to their full potential.

The reasons for implementing diversity management include having to adapt to the new reality of a workforce that is increasingly diverse, doing the right and moral thing, and gaining a competitive advantage. Diversity management has three main characteristics: it is voluntary; it uses a broad definition of diversity; and it aims at providing tangible benefits to the company. Finally, implementing diversity management can give companies a competitive advantage in areas such as problem solving, corporate image, and marketing.

The challenge of diversity management is to break the harmful cycle that equates cultural difference with social/economic disadvantages. Therefore, although the emphasis on the business advantage of diversity management is probably a good motivator for companies to enact diversity programs, it does not mean that moral and ethical missions should be neglected or overlooked. To overcome these potential limitations, diversity management has to focus on both enhancing profitability and fostering social justice.

Notes

1. Geisel, T. S. [Dr. Seuss] (1961). *The sneetches and other stories* (pp. 3–4, 21–24). New York: Random House.

2. Roosvelt Thomas Jr. (1999) has used a similar metaphor as the theme for his book *Building a House for Diversity: How a Fable About a Giraffe and an Elephant Offers New Strategies for Today's Workforce.*

3. The Australian Commonwealth Government established the Industry Task Force on Leadership and Management Skills. The task force published a report in 1995 known as the Karpin Report, which included several recommendations associated with promoting equality and diversity. Burton's (1995) article demonstrates that diversity management is consistent with the Karpin Report's recommendations for effective management.

4. See Chapter 2 on international legislation.

5. One has to be careful about broad generalizations with respect to EU countries because legislation and public policies may vary greatly from one country to another. For example, France has long had a policy that implies (when translated) that "diversity statistics" are illegal to compile. Hence, it is difficult to know for certain whether the goals of diversity, equality, and nondiscrimination are being achieved—in both the private and the public sector.

6. The Brazilian National Program of Human Rights was created in 1996 to implement international human rights declarations, including the ILO 111 convention on employment discrimination, though the latter was ratified by the Brazilian government earlier in 1965 (Fleury, 1999).

7. See a quote from Thomas (1996), pp. 109–210, earlier in the chapter referring to the jelly bean image with respect to diversity management.

8. For example, during the high-tech boom of the 1990s, countries like Canada, Germany, and the United Kingdom revised their immigration policies to attract skilled workers from other countries like China and India in order to supply the much-needed workforce for their computer and high-tech industries.

CHAPTER 11

An Overview of the Inclusive Workplace Model

Managing the Globalized Workforce Diversity

Global managers have exceptionally open minds. They respect how different countries do things, and they have the imagination to appreciate why they do them that way. . . . Global managers are made, not born.

—Percy Barnevick, CEO of Swedish-Based Asea Brown Boveri[1]

The economic, social, and demographic trends described earlier in the book create an environment that is a fertile ground for intergroup conflicts. The legislative and social policy initiatives taken by individual countries and by international organizations mitigate potential harmful effects and define "the rules of the game" for work organizations. It is important to understand, though, that these trends are not only a backdrop or context for organizations to consider, they also define the *scope* of what companies need to consider as their domain when they design diversity policies and programs. In order to avoid the pitfalls and reap the benefits of a diverse workforce, employers need to adopt a *broader vision of inclusion*, a vision that includes not only the organization itself but also its surrounding community and its national and international context.

The conceptual model for the inclusive workplace introduced here and elaborated in the next chapters includes both the value base and the practice applications that foster inclusion, not only within the organization itself but also with the larger systems that constitute its environment. The process of applying such policies and programs presents several problems and obstacles (Mor Barak, 2000b; Mor Barak, 2005). Some of the barriers to the model's implementation include suspicions and mistrust of those who are different, generational misconceptions (Wong, 2008), cross-cultural misunderstandings, organizational uniformity of thoughts and ideas (Barbosa & Cabral-Cardoso, 2008), and short-term goals. At the same time, a broad vision for diversity management has a potential for generating important benefits, such as a better work environment for workers and their families (Bond, 2007; Winfeld, 2005) that in turn will contribute to a more productive and loyal workforce, advantages to the company in recruitment and in the competition for talent, positive corporate reputation (Thiederman, 2008), and improvement in the public's goodwill toward the company, including customers and stakeholders.

Diversity Management and the Inclusive Workplace

The concept of the inclusive workplace refers to a work organization that is not only accepting and utilizing the diversity of its own workforce but is also active in the community; participates in state and federal programs to include population groups such as immigrants, women, and the working poor; and collaborates across cultural and national boundaries with a focus on global mutual interests (see Box 11.1 for the definition of the inclusive workplace).

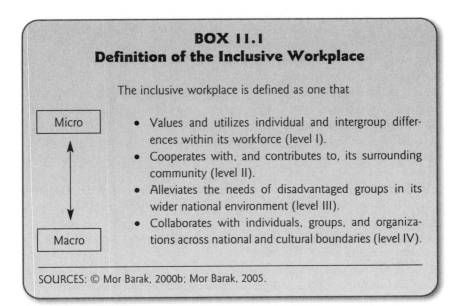

BOX 11.1
Definition of the Inclusive Workplace

The inclusive workplace is defined as one that

Micro

Macro

- Values and utilizes individual and intergroup differences within its workforce (level I).
- Cooperates with, and contributes to, its surrounding community (level II).
- Alleviates the needs of disadvantaged groups in its wider national environment (level III).
- Collaborates with individuals, groups, and organizations across national and cultural boundaries (level IV).

SOURCES: © Mor Barak, 2000b; Mor Barak, 2005.

The model has a strong value base that is manifested at each of the systems levels. It also has policy and practice applications that are unique to each of the levels from the micro to the macro. The more traditional diversity policies and programs have targeted the organization's own workforce, improving the employment opportunities of such groups as women (e.g., Bilimoria et al., 2008; Syed & Murray, 2008); members of racial, ethnic (Smith, 2008), sexual-orientation (Colgan et al., 2007), and religious-minority groups; and people with disabilities. The inclusive workplace emphasizes the same ideas but is targeting a wider scope of diversity. It synthesizes into a cohesive framework the accumulated body of knowledge on diversity within organizations with what we have learned in recent years about business responsibility and involvement with the community along with the projected developments on the global scene. Through programs with the community, such as job preparation workshops or employees volunteering to teach at a local high school, the organization is inclusive of diversity groups that may not be represented in its own workforce; it helps community residents acquire the education and job preparation that will give them access to better jobs, and it helps the community as a whole improve its living conditions. Through collaborations with state and national programs for disadvantaged groups, such as former welfare recipients, domestic violence victims, or recent immigrants, the organization is inclusive of a combination of diversity characteristics that typically bar individuals from even applying for certain classes of jobs or from having a job at all. Finally, through fair and culturally sensitive and respectful international collaborations, the organization is inclusive of cultural diversity that may go beyond national boundaries. These practices are beneficial not only to the recipients of the additional services and programs but also to the organization itself.

In recent decades, the public expectations for corporate "good citizenship" behaviors have not only increased but have also been redefined. The more the public hears of corporate greed, corruption, and faulty procedures that result in exploitation and disaster, the less patience it has for corporate indifference and unethical behavior. At the same time, it is no longer enough for companies to conduct their business with integrity and responsibility toward their shareholders. The globalized public now expects businesses to add another fundamental quality—integration with society (Schwartz & Gibb, 1999). The inclusive workplace offers a model for integration with society via expanding circles of inclusion: through inclusion of the organization's own workforce as well as programs with the community—at the state level or across national borders— the organization can be inclusive of diversity groups that may not be represented in its own workforce.

The following chapters introduce each level of the model, identify its value base, and examine policies and practices that make the workplace more inclusive. The barriers and benefits associated with implementing these programs are presented. Each chapter concludes with a case illustration that describes the organizational context and the circumstances that motivate companies to initiate inclusive policies. They illustrate some mistakes that were made and demonstrate interesting and creative programs and initiatives that promote a more inclusive organizational environment. Questions for further analysis and discussion follow each case.

Note

1. Javidan and House (2001), p. 292.

CHAPTER 12

The Inclusive Workplace: Level I

*Inclusion Through Diversity
Within the Work Organization*

> *By application of the theory of relativity to the taste of the reader,
> today in Germany I am called a German man of science and in
> England I am represented as a Swiss Jew. If I come to be regarded as
> a "Bête noire" the description will be reversed, and I shall become a
> Swiss Jew for the German and a German for the English.*

> —Albert Einstein in a letter to the
> *London Times,* November 28, 1919[1]

The first level of the inclusive workplace, *diversity within work organizations,* relates to the organization's internal relations with its own employees and reflects the "micro" system level, that of individuals and groups within the organization. Whereas an exclusionary workplace is based on the perception that all workers need to conform to preestablished organizational values and norms (determined by its "mainstream"), the inclusive workplace is based on a pluralistic value frame that relies on mutual respect and equal contributions of different cultural perspectives to the organization's values and norms (Cox, 2001; Stevens, Plaut, & Sanchez-Burks, 2008). For example, an exclusionary workplace will hold a 1-day orientation for new employees, during which they will be introduced to expectations regarding norms and behaviors in the company ("this is how we do things around here"). An inclusive workplace, on the other hand, will utilize continuous, multiway communication methods, such as open management-employee meetings and open e-mail communications,

256

to learn of its employees' concerns and expectations. It will constantly strive to modify its values and norms to reflect the diversity of its workforce. Figure 12.1 illustrates the value base for level I of the inclusive workplace model and identifies the values on either side of the inclusion-exclusion continuum. Note that most organizations will be somewhere along this continuum. Few would be at either extreme.

Inclusive Policies and Practices

A variety of policies and practices constitute inclusion at level I—from recruitment through mentorship and training, to cultural audit and linking diversity practices to strategic goals. What distinguishes an inclusive workplace from an organization that merely implements diversity initiatives is the comprehensive approach to diversity that is part of an overall organizational strategy. This approach includes an organization-wide diversity evaluation, or audit, that should lead to goals that are tailored to the organization's unique culture and will result in implementing appropriate diversity policies and practices. The *cultural audit* is usually performed by outside consultants who obtain data from surveys and focus groups to identify areas in which employees who are different from the dominant group feel that they are blocked from performing to the best of their ability. Based on this assessment, diversity goals are then set forth, with the general purpose of creating a more inclusive work environment and as *a strategy for achieving organizational outcomes* (see Chapter 10 for more

Figure 12.1	The Inclusive Workplace: The Value Base for Level I

Inclusion and Diversity Within Work Organizations		
	Value Frame	
System Level	**Exclusion**	**Inclusion**
	←	→
Individuals and Groups Within Organizations	Conformity to preestablished organizational values and norms that reflect the "majority" or "mainstream"	Pluralistic, coevolving organizational culture that keeps changing to reflect diversity of values and norms

details on both cultural audit and diversity management as a strategy for achieving organizational outcomes). In this section, we discuss a variety of diversity policies and practices that an organization can implement to create an inclusive work environment.

Surveys of diversity initiatives in selected multinational corporations indicate that these companies are planning, implementing, and evaluating a large number and variety of diversity initiatives, not only in the United States but also internationally (Ferner, Almond, & Colling, 2005; Wentling, 2004; Wentling & Palma-Rivas, 2000). Most of the companies surveyed had diversity statements in their mission as well as their annual reports and regularly communicated their diversity initiatives to their employees. These diversity initiatives typically cover five principal areas and included (a) *management leadership*—senior management taking the leadership in major diversity projects such as using consultants to conduct needs assessment and designing diversity trainings and programs; (b) *education and training*—conducting seminars and workshops to increase diversity awareness and skill building and to help employees understand the need for, and meaning of, valuing diversity; (c) *performance and accountability*—developing diversity action plans to meet the goals of specific business units and the organization as a whole and holding managers accountable to these goals by linking diversity performance to compensation; (d) *work-life balance*—offering flexible work arrangements such as telecommuting, job sharing, working at home, and part-time work assignments to accommodate diverse needs and lifestyles of employees; and (e) *career development and planning*—establishing career development and planning initiatives for women and members of underrepresented groups to ensure fair promotion opportunities for high-potential employees and to increase diversity representation in managerial-level jobs.

In addition to actively recruiting members of diverse groups, the most common approach to diversity within work organizations is providing sensitivity training and workshops to employees. Often triggered by lawsuits, diversity trainings vary from 1-hour lectures to a series of ongoing seminars. They typically use experiential, emotional, and sometimes confrontational techniques to raise awareness about personal harm caused by the "isms": sexism, racism, ageism, heterosexism, and others. When the training is long term and well conceptualized, the benefits include an increased familiarity and reduced bias against members of out-groups. However, often employees resent these diversity-training sessions because they are seen as forced, short-term affairs with no clear connection to the organization's strategic goals (Henderson, 1994; Kalev, Dobbin, & Kelly, 2006; Lynch, 2001). In the United States, for example, corporate diversity trainings are quite popular, with more than half (66%) of all U.S. companies providing diversity training to their employees (Paluck, 2006).

Other efforts to promote diversity and inclusion within organizations include initiatives aimed at (a) establishing organizational responsibility such as appointing a corporate officer to oversee the company's diversity efforts and appointing/electing diversity committees comprised of employees from various departments and levels within the organization; (b) encouraging managers' responsibility for diversity through such mechanisms as evaluating managers on their diversity performances; and (c) empowering employees of diverse backgrounds through networking and mentorship programs (Kalev, Dobbin, & Kelly, 2006).

Although most diversity efforts in work organizations focus on management initiatives and on developing managerial diversity skills, Thomas (2005) points out that it is just as important to develop the awareness and skills of individual employees at all organizational levels. He advocates that individual employees learn how to become *effective diversity respondents*—people who act with confidence, wisdom, and effectiveness when interacting with others who may be significantly different from them. He further notes that individuals need to develop *diversity maturity,* that is, a combination of knowledge about diversity and a comfort with the dynamics of diversity relationships. Investing in the development of advanced diversity skills is important, not only for organizations that will benefit from improved relations and better teamwork among their employees but also for individuals who will benefit from improved career trajectories. Thomas argues that "individuals also have a personal responsibility to manage diversity effectively. In fact, unless they do so, the organization as a whole cannot be effective with diversity" (2005, p. 90). It is clearly in the best interest of organizations to elevate their employees' diversity skills while at the same time creating an organizational environment that allows all qualified employees to perform at peak effectiveness (see Box 12.1).

BOX 12.1
A Company's Diversity Inclusion Programs (Level I): The Case of DCM Shriram Industries (India)

DCM Shriram Industries Ltd., headquartered in New Delhi, India, produces a variety of products including sugar, alcohol, fine chemicals, and rayon tire cord. The company's values, stated under its "corporate ethos," indicate a commitment to promoting respectful interactions among all employees and to improving workers' living standards and conditions. In the context of India's past traditions of gender-segregated and caste-oriented society, DCM Shriram's human resources philosophy includes two components: The first is similar to

(Continued)

(Continued)

what U.S.- and European-based companies entitle "diversity training"—a commitment to integration-oriented efforts that include educational and skill-development programs to all employees (regardless of gender and origin) to open up promotion and management opportunities. These efforts also include employee clubs geared toward promoting interaction among employees from different groups and between employees and management. The company's human resources philosophy indicates a belief in "achieving corporate goals through . . . human resource development, career planning and skill-upgrading" and in "building and supporting worker-management relationships."

The second element is more unique to developing countries that are poor in governmental and community services. The company's efforts to promote a positive and inclusive work environment for employees include not only educational, skill-upgrading, and social interaction programs for the company's employees but also family-welfare and community initiatives for the employees and their families. Again, in the context of a traditional class-segregated society such as India's, where a person's identity is largely determined by his or her family of origin, providing services to the family has a deeper meaning than the family-work balance associated with such programs in Western Europe and North America. Under this umbrella, DCM Shriram maintains facilities for housing, sports, and cultural events, as well as libraries and reading rooms for the benefit of employees and their families. Additionally, the company invests in its surrounding communities, where its employees and their families live. One of the company's efforts included the development of a low-cost water purifier especially for rural areas. Through supporting schools, hospitals, and vocational and community centers and through providing family medical services, including free immunization and dental/vision treatment programs, the company is investing in its workforce and its community.

SOURCES: Anand, 2003; Graham & Whiteside Ltd., 2003; DCM Shriram Industries Ltd., n.d.; *The Wall Street Journal,* 2009.

Barriers and Benefits of Implementing the Inclusive Approach at Level I

Organizations that implement inclusive policies and practices may need to overcome barriers on several fronts, but they will be able to reap the benefits, both for individual employees and for the organization as a whole.

BARRIERS

The main barriers have to do with managers' and employees' attitudes and behavior. Specifically, prejudice (biased views) and discrimination (biased behaviors), either overt or covert, are at the core of the barriers for implementing inclusive policies at the workplace. In today's "politically correct" environment, people may be embarrassed to show their ignorance about other cultures, may not want to invest time and energy in learning about those cultures, or may perceive diversity initiatives as a threat to their job security. The barriers traditionally suffered by women, older adults, and ethnic/racial minorities were typically the result of competitive relationships between identity groups in the workplace and often confounded by cross-cultural misunderstandings. These barriers include lack of support in career planning; marginalized status; failure to give nontraditional employees the breadth of experience required for job advancement; social isolation, particularly in management positions; and an unsupportive working environment (Fassinger, 2008; Hyun, 2006; Konrad, 2003). Executives interviewed about the challenges of implementing diversity initiatives reported encountering difficulties in changing attitudes about diversity throughout the workforce, making management more diverse, and changing attitudes or raising diversity competency among managers (Marquis et al., 2008). Figure 12.2 provides a summary illustration of the main barriers and benefits of implementing the inclusive workplace at level I.

An example of a company taking steps to identify and overcome barriers to inclusion is the experience of Sanlam, a financial services company headquartered in Bellville, South Africa. Sanlam developed an employment equity policy as required by the country's 1996 Employment Equity Act. In 1999, the

Figure 12.2   The Inclusive Workplace: The Practice Model for Level I

Barriers	Benefits	
	Individuals	**Organization**
• Discrimination • Prejudice • Perception of threat to job security	• Access to advancement and job promotions • Improved income and benefits • More decision-making power	• Business growth and productivity • Cost savings (e.g., lower turnover, less absenteeism) • Positive image with employees, customers, and financial institutions

company surveyed its employees and compiled an in-depth report of the barriers to equity within the company. When it was later decided that the company's diversity management initiatives were not progressing quickly enough, the decision was made to link managers' performance bonuses to their diversity management performance (United Nations Global Compact, 2001).

BENEFITS

By enacting policies that facilitate inclusion of all employees, the employment barriers traditionally suffered by women and minorities can be overcome. Such policies open the doors to job advancement and promotions that have clear monetary benefits to individual employees and their families. They also open up channels of communication and enhance employees' decision-making power. Research into the benefits of diversity for organizations was relatively scarce in the 1980s and early 1990s. Much of the "case for diversity" during that time was built on ideological and deductive reasoning. More research into the benefits of diversity practices has been generated since then, focusing on more clearly defining and measuring diversity and on examining the causal connection between diversity management and organizational outcomes.

There is now accumulating evidence that the benefits of inclusive diversity practices center around three areas: (a) *the opportunity to drive business growth and productivity* by leveraging the many facets of diversity, such as marketing more effectively to minority communities or to senior citizens (e.g., Erhardt, Werbel, & Shrader, 2003; Pitts, 2009; Richard, 2000); (b) *cost savings* due to lower turnover, less absenteeism, and improved productivity and *winning the competition for talent* by being more attractive to women and members of minority groups (Marquis et al., 2008); and (c) the positive effect that diversity management has on *the company's image and stock prices* (Robinson & Dechant, 1997; Wright, Ferris, Hiller, & Kroll, 1995).

An example for benefit (a) above, that of the connection between diversity and business growth and productivity, is a study conducted in the banking industry that documented an association between racial diversity and improved performance (Richard, 2000). The study's sample included 63 banks from three states in the United States—California, Kentucky, and North Carolina—and was based on a combination of financial information (obtained from quarterly reports to the Federal Reserve) and a questionnaire to solicit human resource information on racial composition (obtained from human resource managers in the companies). Although the study's first hypothesis, that racial diversity was positively associated with a company's performance, was not supported, its second hypothesis, that this relationship was moderated by the organization's business strategy, was. More specifically, higher racial diversity was positively related to a company's performance when a company pursued a growth strategy, and it was negatively related to performance when the company pursued a downsizing strategy. Another study investigated the relationship between demographic diversity of the executive board of directors and organizational performance. The results indicated that board of directors' diversity was positively associated with both return on investment and return on assets, thus apprearing to have an impact on the overall organizational performance (Erhardt, Werbel, & Shrader, 2003). A third study in this category is a survey of U.S. federal employees that investigated the relationship between diversity management, job satisfaction, and work group *performance*. The findings indicated that *diversity management* was strongly linked to both work group *performance* and job satisfaction, and that people of color saw benefits from *diversity management* above and beyond those experienced by White employees (Pitts, 2009).

An example for benefit (b) above, that of cost savings that may result from diversity management initiatives, is the experience of Nextel Communications. In 2001, Nextel focused its attention on ascertaining the impact of its diversity trainings. The initiative, called the "All-Inclusive Workplace," tracked changes in employee retention and corporate financial benefits that could be attributed to diversity training. The results showed that roughly 10% of the improvement in retention was due to the training; the overall decrease in turnover was 2.2% or 371 individuals. To put it simply, the training was responsible for 36 people continuing to work at Nextel. This is significant considering that turnover costs an average of $89,000 per employee, which makes the total savings for the company approximately $3.5 million. Accordingly, based on an impact assessment using the cost of diversity training, Nextel figured its saving as a $1.63 net benefit for every dollar spent on the diversity training (Kirkpatrick, Phillips, & Phillips, 2003). In general, the literature suggests that diversity initiatives can help companies increase the skill base and range of talent among employees, managers, and executives. In part, this may be because companies that recruit from a wider pool of candidates have access to and are able to hire a larger number of exceptional personnel, thus affecting the organization's bottom line (Marquis et al., 2008). IBM certainly benefited from its diversity initiatives, as indicated by Ted Childs, IBM's former vice president for workforce diversity. "A consistent heritage of diversity translates into a strong reputation that helps us attract and keep talented employees"(Alsop, 2004, pp. 158–159).

Finally, an example for benefit (c) above, improved company image and stock price, is provided by a study that examined the impact of exemplary versus faulty corporate diversity practices on companies' stock prices (Wright et al., 1995). The study employed event study methodology that is commonly used in financial economics research. This procedure was used to determine if there was a significant change in the price of a company's stock on the days immediately surrounding the announcement of an event of interest, indicating either exemplary or faulty diversity practices. In this study, the event chosen as an indicator of exemplary diversity practices was the announcement of the annual Exemplary Voluntary Efforts Award by the U.S. Department of Labor. Nominees for the award must be free of problems with compliance with the Equal Employment Opportunity Commission, must show a commitment to equal employment opportunity with demonstrated results, and must show a desire to go beyond "business as usual" practices. Data for this portion of the study included 34 award-winning companies over 7 years. The event chosen as an indicator of faulty diversity practices was the announcement of major settlements by companies found to be guilty of labor discrimination. Data for this portion of the study came from the *Wall Street Journal Index* and the Dow Jones News Retrieval and included 34 companies whose announcements came out during the same 7 years as the award-winning announcements (1986–1992). Companies included in both data sets represented a variety of industries and different sizes, all traded on the New York or American Stock Exchange during the period of the study. The results indicated that announcements of companies receiving awards for high-quality, voluntary diversity programs were associated with positive and significant stock price changes for those companies and that announcements that convey that companies were guilty of discriminatory practices were associated with negative and significant stock returns for those companies. Though the association was limited to the days immediately following those announcements, this study demonstrates that high-quality diversity efforts contribute to sustaining a competitive advantage and are valued in the marketplace (Wright et al., 1995). Creating a hospitable environment for all employees and building a reputation of a company with a diverse workforce can go a long way to improve a company's bottom line. Customers from diverse backgrounds expect the workforce to look like them and are more likely to do business with a company that has a positive image with respect to diversity. Similarly, diversity initiatives and a progressive corporate image can make the stock appealing to socially responsible investors (Alsop, 2004).

Case Illustration: Level I—Inclusion Through Diversity Within Work Organizations—Denny's, Inc.

All human beings have differences. . . . We need to recognize that.

—Rachelle Hood-Phillips,
Chief Diversity Officer, Denny's, Inc.

On December 11, 1991, the Thompsons, an African American family, went to Denny's to celebrate Rachel Thompson's thirteenth birthday. It wasn't the celebration they had anticipated. After waiting what seemed like an inordinate amount of time to be seated, they told their waitress that it was Rachel's birthday so she was entitled to a free meal under Denny's popular birthday promotion. The waitress ignored the request and the baptismal certificate that the Thompsons presented as proof of their daughter's age. Instead, she went to get her manager. Unfortunately, the manager did not offer a better remedy. The manager asked for proof of Rachel's age but rejected the baptismal certificate. Instead, he said he would accept a school ID card, which Rachel promptly presented. Again, the manager rejected the proof. He asked for the baptismal certificate again, which Mrs. Thompson slid over to the manager. At that point, the manager accused Mrs. Thompson of throwing things at him and started yelling at her. Finally, the Thompsons left Denny's without having eaten. The happy occasion was shattered for both Rachel and the entire Thompson family (story recounted from Adamson, 2000).

The Thompsons' experience is just one of many such accounts from African Americans who visited Denny's in the 1990s (Riesch & Kleiner, 2005). Denny's, once famous for its breakfast menu, became infamous for its discrimination, generating immense negative publicity for denying service to African Americans at several of its restaurants across the United States. In addition to discriminating against its minority customers, Denny's purchased no supplies from minorities and had few minorities in its management.

After paying $54 million to settle a pair of class-action lawsuits, Denny's has undergone a major transformation to change the level of diversity within the company as well as improve the way employees treat customers. Their efforts have been rewarded with widespread praise and numerous awards, including *Fortune* magazine's choice as the number one place for minorities to work. In the words of Denny's former CEO Jim Adamson, "Denny's has gone from worst to first" (Adamson, 2000). Despite all of these changes, Denny's still faces a negative public image and continual lawsuits for discrimination.

HOMOGENOUS HISTORY

Most famous for its "Original Grand Slam Breakfast," Denny's offers a variety of breakfast, lunch, and dinner menu options. Starting in 1953 as a donut shop named Danny's Donuts, Denny's has grown into the largest full-service, family-style restaurant chain in the United States with over 1,000 locations. Denny's became an international company in 1969 when it opened a restaurant in Acapulco, Mexico. It now operates in seven countries, including the United States.

A major stain appeared on Denny's history after two class-action lawsuits for discrimination were filed in 1993 (*Ridgeway v. Flagstar Corporation and Denny's, Inc.* Civ. No. 93–20202-JW and *United States of America v. Flagstar Corporation and Denny's, Inc.* Civ. No. 93–20208-JW). The cases accused Denny's (and Denny's parent company at the time, Flagstar) of repeated civil rights violations, primarily against African Americans. Some claimed that Denny's required African Americans to pay for meals prior to consumption. When challenged, employees told customers that other African Americans had left without paying, so prepayment was required. Some African American customers were charged a cover charge prior to being served.

"Blackout" periods were instituted at some restaurants, during which time the number of African American patrons was limited. In many cases, with or without a blackout period, service was refused to African Americans. Denny's employees would simply deny or delay seating, claiming that the restaurant was too full. Frequently during the delay, other later-arriving, non–African American customers were seated or served.

Denny's denied complimentary "birthday meals" for African Americans or in some cases required burdensome proof of a child's age. This was the case for the Thompson family who were denied a birthday meal for their daughter on her thirteenth birthday.

Denny's sometimes forced the removal of African Americans from its restaurants. This frequently occurred after a customer claimed that he or she was not being treated properly. Denny's employees would then claim the customer was being hostile and order his or her removal, either by the security guard or by the police (U.S. Department of Justice, 1993).

Although not every Denny's restaurant or employee was guilty of discrimination, the problem was systemic, as evidenced by other practices. Denny's had only one African American franchisee and had no minority suppliers in the early 1990s. Denny's board of directors consisted almost exclusively of White men.

Initially, Jerry Richardson, the CEO of Denny's parent company, Flagstar, denied and fought the charges filed in the lawsuits. Faced with growing negative publicity, Richardson signed a pact with the NAACP in 1993 to help solve the company's problems. He agreed to hire more minorities and increase the number of purchases from minority-owned businesses. Despite these efforts, the evidence continued to mount, eventually causing Denny's to settle the lawsuits.

Denny's losses from the lawsuits and widespread negative publicity were significant. In addition to having to pay $54 million to settle the class-action lawsuits from 1993, many customers refused to patronize Denny's. In a 1996 survey, Denny's found that 66% of African American customers refused to eat at the chain's restaurants (Henderson, 2001).

Additionally, Denny's had to absorb operational expenses associated with its class-action settlement. Under the consent decree from the settlement, Denny's was required to perform the following activities for 7 years, starting May 24, 1994 (U.S. Department of Justice, 1993):

- Retain a civil rights monitor, a person experienced with the monitoring and enforcement of civil rights. The monitor was responsible for investigating any new discrimination claims arising after the settlement.
- Develop and administer a nondiscrimination training program. Training was mandatory for every employee of Denny's and Denny's franchises. The training had to be approved by the monitor.
- Test franchise and company-owned restaurants to ensure compliance with the consent decree.
- Notify the public that Denny's will operate in a nondiscriminatory manner. The consent decree mandated the percentage of various ethnicities that were required in Denny's advertisements, with specific rules for counting the seconds of face time for various ethnicities in television commercials.

THE NEW FACE OF DENNY'S

Denny's was faced with the daunting task of changing its behavior and image. To accomplish this, Denny's parent company, Flagstar, hired a new CEO, Jim Adamson, in 1995. Adamson has a history of reversing bad company positions, including helping Revco emerge from bankruptcy and improving Burger King's financial woes (Talaski, 2002). Adamson also possessed a unique diversity perspective. When he was a child, Adamson lived in Japan and Europe because of his father's military travels. As a result of his experiences in those countries, Adamson has developed a deep appreciation for diversity and considers it important from a business perspective (Adamson, 2000).

One of Adamson's first steps was to create a chief diversity officer position. He recruited Rachelle Hood-Phillips, with whom he worked at Burger King, to fill the role. Hood-Phillips had spent her career successfully building and managing diversity at Fortune 500 companies.

In addition to creating this new position, Adamson denounced discrimination at employee meetings and other events. He publicly warned that he would fire any employee or franchise owner who discriminated or challenged the diversity changes he implemented.

DIVERSITY CHANGES

Together, Hood-Phillips and Adamson implemented many changes to improve Denny's diversity (Adamson, 2000). As Adamson concedes, the consent decree initiated some of the practices. Denny's, however, added many additional activities. Hood-Phillips developed methods to effectively measure and track diversity at the company. Her work enabled Adamson to tie diversity to managers' bonuses. For example, 25% of the senior management team's incentive bonus was tied to the advancement of women and minorities.

Denny's diversity training may represent some of the company's best efforts to correct its diversity issues. It teaches employees how to empathize with customers. More important, employees are taught how to reflect their empathy back to the customer and show their concern about a problem. Training teaches sensitivity for every culture, not just for African Americans. For example, employees are taught that it is inappropriate to ask a Hispanic customer to show a green card, regardless of the reason.

Security guards are taught to be more sensitive to customers. Many of the security guards are off-duty police officers who believe that early intervention in situations and monitoring of certain customers will prevent problems. However, Denny's teaches the guards that such actions may actually create more problems than they prevent. This point is demonstrated with videos that show various scenarios in which misinterpretations lead to disaster when mishandled. For example, in one scene, a security guard follows a patron who doesn't stop at the register to pay. The guard confronts the patron, which leads to a bad situation. In fact, the patron left his money on the table before leaving, as the video later shows. Security guards are trained to watch the restaurant generally, without making guests feel uncomfortable, and respond to situations only when instructed by the store manager.

Every employee must attend diversity training. The consent decree mandates that an employee attend a diversity session within 90 days of joining Denny's, with a second session within 270 days. Denny's tightened those requirements to 75 days and 225, respectively. Most employees, however, attend the sessions much sooner than the deadlines.

The diversity training that Denny's uses has a substantial price tag. According to Adamson, Denny's spends several million dollars each year on compliance and training (Adamson, 2000). However, the training has been so effective that Denny's was released from the oversight of its civil rights monitor at the end of 1999, a year earlier than mandated by the consent decree (Adamson, 2000).

Despite being released from oversight, Denny's continues to investigate every incident or claim of discrimination. A toll-free number is posted in every restaurant to help Denny's identify and investigate problems. Denny's policy is not to tolerate any discrimination. It has strict discipline standards for dealing with employees who discriminate or repeatedly perform questionable actions. Further, any customer that discriminates or uses racial slurs is asked to leave the restaurant immediately.

In addition to all of the training that Denny's is providing, the company has also made substantial improvements in the diversity composition of its workforce, from top management to servers and cooks. Denny's started with its board of directors. In the early 1990s, the board comprised primarily White men; now 50% of board members are women and/or minorities. Throughout all levels of the organization, the change in diversity is evident—54% of senior managers are women and/or minorities, 29% of nonsenior managers are minorities, and 47% of all Denny's employees are minorities.

Denny's has not only increased the number of minority employees, but it also has increased the number of minority franchise owners from 1 in the early 1990s to 120 in 2002. Because the franchisees, on average, own more than one restaurant, the minority franchisees own a total of 472 restaurants, which represents 46% of all Denny's restaurants. In many cases, Denny's has provided funding to help minority owners get started.

Denny's has increased its purchases from minority-owned suppliers from $0 in 1992 to $90 million in 2002, representing 15% of Denny's annual purchases, four times the national average. As with its minority franchisees, Denny's has helped fund some of the businesses. For example, one of Denny's suppliers was on the verge of bankruptcy. Adamson devised a creative financing arrangement that loaned money monthly to keep the business operating. The business sold items to Denny's and then repaid the loan monthly after receiving payment for the goods.

In addition to changing its business practices, Denny's has been active with philanthropic activities, supporting numerous human and civil rights organizations. Three campaigns in particular have been a large focus of Denny's efforts.

- In 2002, Denny's initiated a 3-year fund-raising campaign to promote human and civil rights. In the first year, Denny's raised $1.2 million for the National Civil Rights Museum. In 2003, Denny's targeted a $1 million donation to the King Center.
- In 2002, Denny's partnered with the Hispanic College Fund to initiate Denny's Scholastic Stars Sweepstakes. Denny's has pledged $250,000 to provide scholarships to Hispanic students over a 3-year period.
- In 2008, Denny's launched a new initiative in partnership with The Tom Joyner Foundation called The Denny's Single Parent Student Scholarship. The scholarship program is aimed at helping single-parent students attending Historically Black Colleges and Universities (HBCUs) meet the challenges of raising a family while earning a postsecondary education ("Denny's Promotes Diversity Leader," 2008).

To let the public know about all of the changes and recapture some of its lost customer base, Denny's spent several million dollars on an ad campaign targeting minority customers. The campaign illustrated the changes at Denny's, especially the increased number of minority franchise owners and suppliers. Although this new campaign was a fulfillment of the consent decree, Denny's delivered more than was required.

AWARDS AND IMPACT

The efforts at Denny's have been noticed by numerous organizations. Denny's has won awards for being a friendly place for women and minorities to eat and work. Awards have come from *Family Digest* magazine, the National Association for Female Executives, *Asian Enterprise* magazine, *Latina Style* magazine, and the Center for Responsible Business.

However, the most significant awards that recognize Denny's achievements are from *Fortune* magazine and the NAACP. In 1998, *Fortune* ranked Denny's as the second-best place for minorities to work. Denny's went on to rank number one for 2000 and 2001, remaining in the top 10 consistently since 1998. *Fortune* ranks companies based on a comprehensive list of diversity factors including (a) how well minorities are represented in the general workforce, (b) how many are among the most senior officials and highest-paid employees, (c) whether minorities are promoted into management at the same rates as nonminority employees, (d) whether managers are held financially accountable for meeting diversity goals, (e) how successfully people of color have been integrated into succession plans, (f) the strength of purchasing programs with minority-owned businesses, (g) the use of minority-owned underwriters or pension-management firms, and (h) the portion of charity going to minority-benefiting programs ("Best Companies for Minorities," 2003).

In 1997, the NAACP presented Denny's with the Fair Share Corporate Signatory Award for Minority Business Development. The Anne Arundel (Maryland) branch of the NAACP named Denny's "Corporation of the Year" for 1996. Additionally, in 1996, the NAACP named Jim Adamson "CEO of the Year."

Denny's has also been selected to the 2006 and 2007 Black Enterprise 40 Best Companies for Diversity, receiving high honors as Most Improved Company. In selecting the top 40, BE conducts a comprehensive outreach effort to the CEOs and diversity executives of the top-grossing 1,000 publicly traded companies and the 50 leading global companies with significant U.S. operations. BE's corporate diversity survey focuses primarily on activities related to the participation of African Americans and other ethnic minority groups in four key areas: supplier diversity, senior management, board involvement, and employee base ("Denny's Named Among Top Performers," 2009).

In addition to the awards, Denny's efforts have resulted in increased business. In 1998, Hood-Phillips conducted a follow-up survey and found that 39% of African Americans would not eat at Denny's. Although that number is still significant, it is substantially lower than the findings from 1996, when 66% of African Americans refused to eat at Denny's (Henderson, 2001). The 2-year change in attitude represents an additional 1 million African American customers for Denny's (Adamson, 2000).

CONTINUED LEGAL TROUBLE

Despite the changes made at Denny's, legal trouble persists. Numerous lawsuits have been filed against the company since the 1993 class-action cases (Riesch & Kleiner (2005); Texas Civil Rights Project, 1999; "Trooper Sues," 2003). The claims were familiar: denial of service, mistreatment, racial slurs, and other discrimination practices. The plaintiffs ranged from students, to a police officer, to a reverend. Denny's has also faced sexual harassment and discrimination charges from at least one employee (U.S. Equal Employment Opportunity Commission, 2002).

One case involved a group of Chinese and African American students from Syracuse University. They claimed that in 1997 they were refused service and then kicked out of the restaurant by one of the security guards. The students claimed that they were then beaten by the security guard and a mob of 10 White customers. Denny's civil rights monitor recommended the dismissal of one of the employees involved in the incident. The franchise owner protested, claiming no discrimination had occurred. However, he agreed to terminate the employee. For many, the story was not only disturbing but also believable, considering Denny's past. The district attorney, however, threw out the case. Upon reviewing the evidence, he determined that the students orchestrated the entire string of events from beginning to end. Customers reported that the students were obnoxious and intoxicated, using profanity directed toward employees. The scuffle outside involved only one other customer, who threw a punch at the students. The students refused to cooperate with police who arrived at the restaurant (Tuchman, 1997).

Another case in January of 1999 involved two Muslim men who went to a Denny's in Montana for lunch and requested that the cooks use a separate skillet so as not to contaminate their meals with pork. Halfway through their meals they discovered pork hidden in their food. They were offered new meals after complaining to the manager only to find bacon within the new meals as well. A Montana Human Rights Bureau investigator concluded that the Denny's employees deliberately placed the pork in the Muslim customers' meals. Another case of blatant discrimination occurred in September of 2003 when an African American Florida Highway Patrol Officer, Barbara Levy, went to Denny's with five other uniformed officers during her lunch break. When the meals arrived, Officer Levy discovered a small plastic pig on her plate. When the cook was asked about the incident, his response was, "Well, that's what you are, a black pig," The officer filed a discrimination lawsuit (Riesch & Kleiner, 2005).

In a 1999 lawsuit, an African American couple claimed they were ignored for nearly an hour while only White customers were seated and served. However, Denny's had a videotape of the incident that showed the couple was in the restaurant not for an hour but just 10 minutes. Additionally, the videotape showed several African American and Hispanic customers being seated during the 10 minutes ("Denny's Catches Phony Discrimination Claim," 2000).

Responding to one of the discrimination lawsuits, Rachelle Hood-Phillips said, "I wish we could have been faster and more efficient. But let's not confuse the delay of service with discrimination." She noted that the number of discrimination lawsuits against Denny's has declined steadily since 1993, with only four filed in the first half of 2001 ("Family Sues Denny's," 2001).

Questions for Discussion and Further Analysis

1. Could Denny's have managed their diversity issues better? Why or why not?

2. Why do you think Denny's is facing continuing discrimination lawsuits? Do the lawsuits indicate that Denny's policies and practices are not working? Are there other explanations? If you were a consultant, what would you advise the company to do at this point?

3. Jim Adamson stated that he would fire anyone who discriminated or challenged his new policies. What message did this statement send to the employees? What impact do you think it had on employee morale and customer relations?

4. Was Jim Adamson effective in improving Denny's diversity and public image? Why or why not?

Summary and Conclusion

This chapter presents level I of the inclusive workplace model: inclusion through diversity within the work organization. It relates to the organization's internal relations with individuals and groups of employees. A variety of policies and practices constitute inclusion at level I—from recruitment, through mentoring and training, to cultural audit and linking diversity practices to strategic goals. What distinguishes an inclusive workplace from an organization that merely implements diversity initiatives is the comprehensive approach to diversity that is part of an overall organizational strategy.

Diversity initiatives typically cover five principal areas and include (a) *management leadership,* (b) *education and training,* (c) *performance and accountability,* (d) *work-life balance,* and (e) *career development and planning.* In addition to actively recruiting members of diverse groups, the most common approach to diversity within the work organization is providing sensitivity training and workshops to employees. Although most diversity efforts in work organizations focus on management, it is just as important to develop the awareness and skills of individual employees at all organizational levels.

The main barriers to implementing inclusive policies at this level are attitudes and behaviors of prejudice and discrimination within the company. These barriers include lack of support in career planning, failure to give nontraditional employees the breadth of experience required for job advancement, and a lonely and unsupportive working environment. The main benefits of inclusive policies at this level include (a) *the opportunity to drive business growth and productivity* by leveraging the many facets of diversity, such as marketing more effectively to minority communities or to senior citizens; (b) *cost savings* due to lower turnover, less absenteeism, and improved productivity and *winning the competition for talent* by being more attractive to women and members of minority groups; and (c) the positive effect that diversity management has on *the company's image and stock price.* The Denny's case provides an opportunity to examine the impact of diversity lawsuits on a company's image and financial stability. It also illustrates some of the practices that make the company more inclusive, as well as the barriers and benefits to implementing such policies.

Note

1. *Bête noire* is French for "black beast" and refers to something or someone dreaded or hated. Note the context of this statement—between World War I and World War II when tensions were mounting between Germany and England and Jews were persecuted in Germany. Einstein's statement is quoted in D. Aczel (1999), *God's Equation: Einstein, Relativity and the Expanding Universe,* p. 121.

CHAPTER 13

The Inclusive Workplace: Level II

*Inclusion Through Corporate-
Community Collaborations*

> *We support the communities where we do business because we draw
> our employees, customers, and suppliers from those communities.*
>
> —A corporate diversity manager
> in a large multinational corporation[1]

The second level of the inclusive workplace, *inclusion and corporate-
community collaborations,* relates to the organization's sense of being a part
of its surrounding community and the reciprocity embedded in this relationship. It reflects the "mezzo" system level of organizations and communities. An
exclusionary workplace sees minimal or no connection to its community. An
inclusive workplace, on the other hand, recognizes the economic and noneconomic consequences of its presence in the community. It acknowledges the
responsibility it has to ameliorate the adverse effects of this presence and to
make a positive contribution to the community's well-being. For example, an
exclusionary organization will view any volunteer work its employees engage in
as a private matter that is part of their after-work activities, whereas an inclusive
workplace will encourage, support, and finance activities such as teaching
computers to elementary school students or mentoring inner-city youth (see
Figure 13.1 for an illustration of the value base for level II of the model).

An emerging construct in the business literature is that of *corporate social
performance* (CSP), currently used as one of the criteria to assess Fortune 500's
most-admired companies. The other commonly used term is *corporate social*

responsibility (CSR). Both terms expand a company's responsibilities beyond its traditional economic shareholders to that of multiple stakeholders, including the community (Greening & Turban, 2000; Rowley & Berman, 2000). Caroll (1979) developed one of the earlier versions of a comprehensive view of corporate social performance and has reiterated his opinion (Caroll, 2000) that social performance review should include a comprehensive assessment of actions related to most social issues and stakeholders.

The most well-known criticism of corporate social responsibility came from the Nobel Prize winner economist Milton Friedman (1970), who proclaimed in his *New York Times Magazine* article on September 13, 1970, that "the social responsibility of business is to increase its profit." It is important to place Friedman's comment in the context of the time in which it was said. Public expectations from corporations were limited and employees and consumers alike were not as socially aware and savvy about their power to influence corporate citizenship behavior as they are today. On close observation, Friedman's comment may not be in such a contradiction to CSR as it may seem. Because of the change in the social context, corporations need to contribute to the welfare of their communities to create goodwill among their customers and to attract talented employees, both are essential for making a profit. It is important to note that both of which corporate social performance and corporate social responsibility focus on a direct business-related role for companies vis-à-vis the community with an emphasis on the strategic and bottom-line implications of socially responsible corporate practices (Heal, 2008; Werther & Chandler, 2006).

The constructs of corporate social performance and corporate social responsibility include more than just the corporate-community collaborations referred to in this level of the inclusive workplace. They apply to a whole host of activities that are socially and environmentally beneficial and, in some respects, are relevant to levels III and IV of the model as well. Both constructs stem from the recognition that economic actions of business entities have noneconomic consequences and that business organizations have an impact on other institutions of society above and beyond their economic sphere.

In the past, when businesses abided by the law and exercised fair and honest practices, they were considered to have integrity. However, this is no longer enough, as the public is aware of businesses' obligation to society and expects them to have a strategy in place to fulfill this obligation. Corporations today do not have the luxury of waiting for government instructions and regulations that would force them into action; the public expects them to be active and proactive in responding to the needs of the community (Schwartz & Gibb, 1999; Werther & Chandler, 2006). In this context, the primary role of the corporation as an economic institution is accepted as a given, and the corporation is expected to engage voluntarily in activities that benefit its community (Johnson, 2009; Greening & Turban, 2000). Clearly, businesses recognize their

Figure 13.1	The Inclusive Workplace: The Value Base for Level II

Inclusion and Corporate-Community Collaborations

Value Frame

System Level	Exclusion	Inclusion
	←	→
Organizations, Communities	Organizational focus is intrinsic with exclusive responsibility to financial stakeholders.	Dual intrinsic and extrinsic focus with recognition of community systems as stakeholders as well.

duty to not only protect their physical and social environment but to also contribute to the welfare of their community. At the same time, there is also accumulating research documenting the connection between a company's social and ethical policies and its financial performance, a connection that has been termed "doing well by doing good" (see, for example, Field, 2007; Benioff & Southwick, 2004).

Inclusive Policies and Practices

Given their economic power, corporations can step in and offer to groups and communities essential resources that would not otherwise be provided by governmental agencies. A wide range of activities falls under the title of corporate social performance, such as supporting educational or cultural institutions in the community, providing mentorship to youth, or tutoring children in local schools (see Box 13.1 for a case example). Snider, Hill, and Martin (2003) explored the community initiatives described on Web sites of 50 U.S. and 43 international companies in a qualitative analysis of corporations' social responsibility (CSR) messages. The companies investigated declared and highlighted a variety of CSR initiatives in both U.S. and global settings. Similarly, a survey of eight multinational corporations revealed that the majority were actively involved with community initiatives aimed at improving the lives of the residents in their communities (Wentling & Palma-Rivas, 2000). These activities included mentor programs for minority students, student internships, sponsorship of local school programs, and participation of company leaders on boards of minority organizations in the community.

For example, the University of Southern California (USC), the largest private employer in the city of Los Angeles, initiated a series of community outreach programs in the early 1990s as part of its strategic plan (Strategic Plan for the University of Southern California, 2004). The university, located in the Los Angeles downtown area that is home to diverse, partly immigrant, and mostly disadvantaged communities, has launched several community-oriented programs. These programs included the Family of Five Schools—a public-private partnership that provides special educational, cultural, and developmental opportunities for approximately 8,000 children who live close to USC's University Park campus; the Joint Educational Project—sending 1,200 mentors, teaching assistants, and mini-teams into the local schools and agencies; and Civic and Community Relations—encouraging more entrepreneurs, and especially minority entrepreneurs, to establish businesses in the immediate vicinity of the university's campuses (USC Civic and Community Relations, n.d.).

Another example is the U.S.-based Shell Youth Training Academy (SYTA) and the similar Nigerian Shell Intensive Training Programme (SITP), both sponsored by the Royal Dutch/Shell Corporation, a global group of energy and petrochemical companies. The academy opened in February 1993 to provide high school students in the Los Angeles Unified School District with postsecondary career opportunities and training. The SYTA's and the SITP's goal is also to provide Shell with access to a larger talent pool of prospective employees in the local community (Shell Youth Training, 2004; Shell Intensive Training Programme, 2009). Two similar programs were opened in Chicago and Oakland with more than a thousand students taking advantage of them since their inception. Once accepted (based on a 2.2 grade point average and teacher recommendations), eleventh- and twelfth-grade students attend half-day classes at the SYTA academy for one semester. The program covers consumer service occupations, career planning, job search skills, assessment of personal interests and aptitude, interpersonal skills, effective communication, and other elements of successful career development.

BOX 13.1
A Company's Community Inclusion Programs
(Level II)—The Case of Nestlé (Switzerland)

Headquartered in Vevey, Switzerland, Nestlé is the largest food and beverage company in the world. The company operates in nearly every country of the world, employing over one quarter of a million individuals and with gross

(Continued)

(Continued)

revenues of over 80 billion Swiss francs annually (Nestlé, 2003). One of *Fortune* magazine's Global Most Admired Companies ("Global Most Admired Companies," 2003), Nestlé declares in its company statement that "for a business to be successful in the long term, it must create value not only for its shareholders but also for society" (Nestlé, 2009). Further, the company notes that investing and trading internationally can create new jobs, raise skill levels, and benefit the local economies. However, some of Nestlé's past business actions have attracted widespread criticism (Yamey, 2000). The most prominent and well-documented controversy concerned the company's methods marketing processed cow's milk or baby formula as a substitute for breastfeeding, to mothers across the world including developing countries. Nestlé's activities attracted worldwide attention during the Nestlé boycott of 1977. The company has since worked hard to improve the public perception of its activities, launching some Fairtrade products and focusing on its corporate social responsibility activities (Nestlé, 2003, p. 2).

To those ends, the Nestlé Foundation, an independent organization, was established in 1966 to promote scientific and technical knowledge transfer to developing countries (Nestlé Foundation, 2003). The foundation sponsors the International Fellowship Program, the purpose of which is to develop nutrition-related research in low-income countries. It also provides research grants on a continuous basis and has recently sponsored research among populations in countries such as China, Senegal, Ethiopia, Vietnam, Pakistan, and Mexico.

Beyond the Nestlé Foundation, the company is involved in numerous other community initiatives and actively encourages employee participation. For example, in Brazil, over half of the Nestlé Brazil employees participate in a program that teaches good nutrition to marginalized families. The program's goal is to reach half a million children. A similar program is under way in Russia. In Morocco, Nestlé provides funding for the Zakoura Foundation's elementary education initiative. The company finances the work of 10 schools, allowing for the education of children who cannot enter the public school system (primarily because of their remote locations). In South Africa, Nestlé is teamed with EcoLink to teach people in remote rural communities the skills needed for such activities as trench gardening or accessing drinkable water. In Nigeria and other African countries where HIV/AIDS is pandemic, Nestlé sponsors the Red Cross and Red Crescent Societies' Africa Health Initiative 2010, focused on reducing the spread of HIV (International Federation of Red Cross and Red Crescent Societies, 2002; Nestlé, 2009).

Barriers and Benefits of Implementing the Inclusive Approach at Level II

BARRIERS AT LEVEL II

The main obstacle for initiating and maintaining activities that benefit the company's social environment is economic pressure to demonstrate profitability on a short-term basis (e.g., quarterly), which makes it difficult to allocate the money necessary for long-term commitments to social goals. When companies are under pressure to demonstrate short-term profitability, it is difficult for managers to justify the allocation of resources necessary for commitments to social causes that may yield results only in the long run. Businesses often perceive the relationship between social responsibility and financial performance as a trade-off. They view the costs incurred from socially responsible actions as an economic disadvantage compared with other business activities (Greening & Turban, 2000; Werther & Chandler, 2006). For example, many suppliers believe that addressing CSR issues makes them less competitive (Vogel, 2005, p. 95). A secondary but important barrier is that of finding the right leaders to be champions of such programs, people who command authority and respect in the organization and who can initiate and maintain these activities. Often, even when a commitment has been made and money allocated for a social cause, there is no steady leadership to sustain such an effort beyond the initial stages of excitement and self-congratulations.

Figure 13.2 provides a summary illustration of the benefits and the obstacles of implementing the inclusive workplace at level II of the model.

BENEFITS

In addition to the moral and ethical value of socially responsible corporate policies and programs, accumulating research provides evidence that companies draw tangible benefits from such activities. Early examinations of corporate social responsibility actions focused on damage control, specifically organizational policies that are aimed at preventing lawsuits (e.g., Frooman, 1997). Research and scholarly articles are typically focused more on tangible benefits such as advantages in recruitment, creating goodwill among consumers, increased employee loyalty, and improved corporate image (e.g., Greening & Turban, 2000; Griffin & Mahon, 1997; Heal, 2008; Martin, 2003; McElhaney, 2008; Orlitzky, Schmidt, & Rynes, 2003; Simpson & Kohers, 2002; Vogel, 2005; Werther & Chandler, 2006).

There is accumulating empirical evidence for the link between corporate social performance and financial performance. For example, in a meta-analysis of 52 quantitative studies over 30 years of research, Orlitzky, Schmidt, and Rynes (2003) found a positive correlation between companies' social performance and

Figure 13.2 The Inclusive Workplace Model: Obstacles and Benefits for Level II

Inclusion and Corporate-Community		
Barriers	**Benefits**	
	Individuals	**Organization**
• Economic pressures to demonstrate profitability • Limited company vision (shortsighted and internally focused) • Lack of leadership to champion and sustain efforts	• Employment, job training • Mentorship • Improved services to the community	• Improved corporate image and reputation • Advantage in recruitment and in labor disputes • Increased employee loyalty • Strong connection between social performance and economic performance

their financial performance. Examining the application of this line of research to the banking industry, Simpson and Kohers's (2002) research supports the link between social and financial performance. They measured corporate social performance using two categories from the rating system mandated by the Community Reinvestment Act[2] (CRA)—indicating high versus low social performance. Their outcome measure of financial performance was the banks' rates of return on assets and loan losses to total loans.[3] The results indicated a strong relationship between social and financial performance. More specifically, the return on assets for the high social performers was almost twice the return on assets of the low social performers, and the loan losses experienced by the high performers was almost half of that experienced by the low social performers.[4] All results were statistically significant.

Social programs generate goodwill from employees and customers alike that may result in fewer labor problems and a more favorable customer view of the company's products. A firm's demonstrated social concern is an important dimension of its reputation in the long run because publics judge a company's concern for the wider society and its ability to achieve mutual relationships with groups in its environment. One of the most interesting theoretical explanations offered for the connection between social and financial performance is that of the "virtuous cycle"—financially successful businesses have slack resources that can be devoted to social performance as a result of their financial performance, which creates a self-perpetuating cycle of simultaneously superior performance in both areas (Waddock & Graves, 1997; Vogel, 2005).

Community-oriented programs may bring additional economic benefits by improving the company's standing with important constituencies such as bankers, investors, and government officials. Reputations have potentially favorable consequences because they enable companies to improve their standing by charging premium prices and by enhancing their access to capital markets. The University of Southern California, mentioned earlier for its community-oriented programs, reaped the benefits of its community collaboration efforts when in 2000 it was named College of the Year by the *Time/Princeton Review College Guide*. The *Time/Princeton* editors noted that the award was given primarily because of the university's comprehensive community outreach program that created an exceptional learning environment for students. This recognition boosted the university's image, and although it is difficult to distinguish between the award's impact and other changes that have affected USC's reputation, its student applications and enrollments have increased in the years since the award. A few years earlier, during the 1992 Los Angeles urban uprising, or riots,[5] many businesses in the university's vicinity were devastated, but the campus itself was spared, presumably because of its good relationships and positive image in the local community. In contrast, Shell, which owns many gas stations in the Los Angeles downtown area, was not so lucky. Most of its stations were burned to the ground. Shell's management realized, after the fact, that their lack of involvement in local programs put them in disfavor with the community. This realization was the impetus for establishing the Shell Youth Academy mentioned earlier. The company reports that most of the program participants find employment upon graduation. Among the company's direct benefits are its improved reputation in the local community and its access to talented and well-trained young people in the local neighborhood who often choose to work at Shell upon graduation (Shell Youth Training, 2004).

Case Illustration: Level II—Inclusion Through Corporate-Community Collaboration—Unilever

Companies have a duty to manage all aspects of business in a responsible and sustainable way.

—Antony Burgmans and Niall FitzGerald, Chairmen, Unilever

Many governments around the world see palm plantations, which produce palm oil, as a cash cow. The demand for palm oil is ever increasing, and its uses are widespread, from food to cosmetics and soap. Faced with heavy foreign debt and poor economies, governments such as Malaysia, Indonesia, and Ghana have introduced palm plantations to improve their economy, but it doesn't always work as planned. In Malaysia, workers have been faced with low wages and poor living conditions (Hassan, 2004; Ramachandran & Shanmugam, 1995). Frequently, running water and electricity, if available at all, are available for only short periods of time during the day. The water is frequently contaminated by the chemicals and effluent found on the plantations. Sanitation facilities are far from satisfactory; commonly, several families share a bucket as their toilet. When the bucket is full, people use the surrounding bushes, and children can be found using open drains around the house as a toilet. If a worker is lucky enough to have a flush toilet, he will frequently find that the waste drains from the septic tank directly into the water supply. Such practices are illegal in Malaysia. The government that promised a better way of life via palm plantations, however, has ignored the plight of the plantation workers. The reason is a matter of definition. Plantations do not fall under any category for which the Malaysian government has planners. As a result, the government has claimed that it is the responsibility of the plantations, not the government, to provide proper working conditions (Ramachandran & Shanmugam, 1995). The plight of the palm oil plantation workers has been documented by global advocacy and conservation organizations (e.g., Hance, 2009).

UNILEVER AND PALM OIL

In 1850, the United Kingdom repealed a tax on soap, which had been previously considered a luxury item. The resultant lower price of soap led to William Lever's entry into the soap business, building a company to mass-produce soap. In 1930, Lever's U.K.-based company known as Lever Brothers merged with Margarine Unie, a Dutch margarine producer, to form the Unilever Group. Unilever has evolved into one of the world's largest consumer goods companies with operations in approximately 100 countries, sales in over 150 countries, and revenue of $45.6 billion in 2002. Unilever specializes in food as well as home and personal care products, owning such widely recognized brand names as Hellmann's, Knorr, Lipton, Bertolli, Slim-Fast, Ben & Jerry's, Dove, Pond's, and Wisk. Despite the 1930 merger, Unilever is still a joint venture between Unilever PLC (U.K.) and Unilever NV (Netherlands), trading separately on the stock market but acting as one company with a single board of directors.

Importance of Palm Oil

Palm oil, derived from the fruit and seeds of the oil palm tree, is one of the more common raw ingredients that Unilever uses throughout its product line. Palm oil is found in soap, margarine, snack foods, cosmetics, cooking oils, and other products. Because of the ubiquitous use of palm oil, Unilever's search for a large, constant supply has a long history. Lever Brothers started looking for palm oil sources in Africa in the early 1900s. In the 1950s, Unilever began operating its own oil palm plantations in Malaysia to complement its African plantations. Today, Unilever each year buys over 1 million tons of palm oil, 6% to 8% of the total world production.

Palm oil offers two major benefits to manufacturers and growers. First, the yield of palm oil is higher than that of any other edible vegetable oil source. Second, the properties of palm oil allow for its use with less processing, saving both time and money.

The Oil Palm Tree Industry

Palm oil is one of the world's most rapidly increasing crops and more palm oil is produced than any other vegetable oil. Global palm oil production is increasing by 9% every year, prompted largely by expanding biofuel markets in the European Union and by food demand in Indonesia, India, and China. Oil palm trees, used to produce palm oil, grow best in wet tropical conditions (Fitzherbert, Struebig, Morel, et al., 2008). Therefore, commercial plantations are usually found in countries within 10 degrees of the equator. Although the palm oil industry originated in Africa, Asia now dominates world production. Malaysia is the world's largest grower of oil palms, producing 50% of the world's supply (over 16 million acres of trees), followed by Indonesia with 30% of the world's production (nearly 10 million acres).

CURRENT TRENDS

Oil palm trees are viewed as a cash crop by governments with large foreign debts or struggling economies. As a result, many governments are encouraging the growth of palm plantations in order to increase the country's income and reduce its debt. The expectation is that plantations will double in acreage within 20 years, primarily in West Africa, South America, and Southeast Asia (Sustainable Agriculture Initiative [SAI], 2002). Some countries, such as Malaysia, are already running out of expansion room.

IMPACT OF PALM PLANTATIONS

People living in oil palm plantation areas have felt the impact of the industry in numerous ways. First, many environmental influences have directly affected the local people. Second, indigenous people have been relocated to make room for plantations. Finally, the local people have been affected economically.

Environmental

The environments that support palm plantations typically support rain forests as well. In many countries, rain forests have been converted into palm plantations. The exact number of converted acres is hard to determine and rather controversial. Some countries, such as Sri Lanka and Ghana, are converting degraded land (such as rubber plantations or mining land) to palm plantations. Malaysian officials claim that no forests have been converted to palm plantations, but the same cannot be said for other countries. For example, in Indonesia, the minister of forests and estate crop development reported that 815,000 acres of forest were being converted to palm plantations annually (Gautam et al., 2000). In 1998, 20,273,789 acres of Indonesian forest were about to be approved for conversion to palm plantations (Manurung, 2002).

The impact of such forest conversion includes a rise in pests, changes in the flow of ground surface water, increased land erosion, and pollution of rivers and drinking water due to the use of fertilizers and pesticides. In Malaysia, the number of polluted rivers had increased from 7 in 1990 to 12 in 2001, with the opening of more land for palm plantations being cited as the reason for the increased pollution ("More Rivers," 2002).

Social

The entry of large plantations has often triggered conflict between local communities and estate investors. In Indonesia, "to secure the vast area needed, estate investors usually use whatever means necessary. It is therefore common knowledge that the estate business is engaged in random forest tree felling and forced control of communal land" (Bider, 2003). For example, according to Cameroonian law, peasants do not have customary rights to land, so expropriation does not require indemnification by the state (World Rainforest Movement, 2001).

Amnesty International reported that in Burma, for at least 13 years prior to their report, there was widespread use of forced labor (Ramachandran & Shanmugam, 1995). Primarily ethnic minorities were forced to work for no pay. In many cases, the army was involved in seizing minorities for work. Unpaid wages are common in other countries, as well. In Mexico, Guatemalan workers have frequently been unpaid for their work, requiring intervention by the Guatemalan government to recover wages.

Economic

Despite governmental desire to encourage palm plantation growth because of the financial opportunities, the benefits rarely make it to the indigenous people. Wages for palm plantation workers are notoriously low (Bhattacharjee, 2003), typically being determined by several factors: world prices for palm oil, weather, size of the fruit, and yields. Unlike some crops, palm plantations are usually fully harvested. Production, then, often exceeds demand, leading to a reduction in palm oil prices. With the increasing acreage of palm plantations, rising supply will likely lead to further price reductions, spurring a higher demand for the product, especially as a substitute for more expensive vegetable oils. As demand increases, governments and plantation investors increase production even further to maintain their necessary income levels. This cycle keeps constant pressure on prices, resulting in consistently low wages for the workers.

Large nonlocal companies are noted for failing to promote the local economy. For example, in Malaysia, nonlocal companies typically pay an oil palm sales tax but little else. The main reason for this is the expatriation of earnings; most of the palm plantations are owned by companies based in Kuala Lumpur. Additionally, many of the companies hire foreign laborers to harvest the palm fruit, denying wages to local workers. Finally, many of the companies import supplies such as food, farm supplies, machinery, chemicals, and fertilizers directly from their home offices in other countries ("Plantation Giants," 2003).

UNILEVER'S SUSTAINABILITY DEVELOPMENT

In 1995, Unilever commissioned two studies on sustainable development. The studies revealed a complex set of criteria for sustainable agriculture. From these criteria, Unilever's Sustainable Agriculture Mission Statement was formally adopted in 1998, which included the following principles:

- Output must be high enough to meet demand.
- Negative environmental impacts on soil, air, water, and biodiversity must be minimized.
- Quality and safety of products must be guaranteed.
- Changing consumer demands must be met.
- Profitability must be competitive with other industry sectors.
- Agriculture must offer an attractive livelihood to workers (Vis & Standish, 2000).

In 1997, two Unilever employees, Jan-Kees Vis and Hans Broekhoff, were working to translate sustainable development into terms that related to Unilever's business. Vis and Broekhoff developed the concept of the triple bottom line to show that Unilever depended on economic, environmental, and social assets. They used this concept to show why Unilever needed to preserve these assets (Standish, Mehalik, Gorman, & Werhane, 1998). Eventually, Vis and Broekhoff developed a set of strategies to preserve the three assets. The strategies now guide Unilever's worldwide operations.

The same philosophy guided Unilever to create an unusual partnership with Oxfam, a global charity organization to fight poverty and injustice, to engage in a research project that explored links between international business and poverty reduction and use Unilever as a case study. The study examined critically Unilever's impact on its environment and demonstrated, among other things, the mutual benefits to the community and to the company that were derived from the company's sponsored community projects. These projects included a donation to UNICEF to reopen 900 health centers that had been closed when public funding was cut for supportive efforts to reduce water pollution in the Brantas River (Clay, 2005).

Unilever's sustainable development plan has led to several honors. Dow Jones ranked Unilever number four on its Sustainability Index (Hartman & SAM Research, 2003), and *Fortune* magazine listed Unilever among *Fortune*'s 50 World's Most Admired Companies ("World's Most Admired Companies," 2009).

SUSTAINABLE AGRICULTURE INITIATIVE

Unilever used its sustainable development commitment and experience to facilitate a broader impact. They were one of the three founding companies of the Sustainable Agriculture Initiative (SAI). SAI was created to actively support the development and communication of sustainable agriculture practices worldwide. Like Unilever's sustainable development plan, SAI's initiatives target the triple bottom line: economics, environment, and society (SAI, 2002).

In addition to SAI, Unilever employees were involved in the formation of the Roundtable on Sustainable Palm Oil designed to address issues specific to the palm oil industry. The organization hosted an industrywide roundtable discussion in Kuala Lumpur in August 2003 to outline the problems of the palm industry for further exploration and improvement.

IMPLEMENTATION OF THE SUSTAINABLE DEVELOPMENT PLAN

Unilever introduced pilot projects to test its sustainable development plan. They started with five of their strategically important crops: palm oil, peas, spinach, tomatoes, and black tea (Vis & Standish, 2000). The pilot program for palm oil was in Malaysia at the Unilever palm plantation (which they have since sold). Unilever (2003b) employed the following sustainable practices:

- Liquid effluent from the mills was used as irrigation and fertilizer for the trees. This reduced the amount of synthetic nutrients needed.
- Leguminous ground cover was grown to prevent soil loss, fix nitrogen, and encourage beneficial insects that are natural predators of tree pests.
- Owls were used to control rats.
- Palm fronds and empty fruit bunches from the mills were left to decompose naturally under the trees. This provided some nutrients (especially potassium) and helped to curb weed growth, restrict beetle pests, and reduce soil loss during

rain. Industry practice had been to burn the empty bunches; using them as mulch helped reduce air pollution.
- Steep hillsides were left as natural forest, which provided a wildlife refuge. Hunting was not permitted.

In addition to Unilever's agricultural programs, the company has undertaken numerous social programs (Unilever, 2003a):

- India: Indian School of Business—Unilever is taking a leading role in developing a world-class business school.
- South Africa: Nelson Mandela Scholarships—The scholarships aim to improve the leadership in South Africa by helping those from disadvantaged backgrounds.
- Sri Lanka: Unilever Cultural Trust Fund—Started in 1979, this fund was designed to protect indigenous work in Sri Lanka.
- Vietnam: Building Partnerships With Suppliers—Unilever offered financial support and education to help develop quality long-term relationships in Vietnam.
- Indonesia: River cleanup—Unilever organized a community-wide effort to clean the badly polluted Brantas River in Java.
- Bangladesh: Improving health care—Lever Brothers Bangladesh provided an initial $135 million to the Friendship Association to convert an old oil tanker into a hospital and provide operating income.

UNILEVER'S CURRENT INVOLVEMENT IN PALM OIL

Divesting of Plantations

Unilever has undertaken a refocusing of its business with the intention of focusing solely on promoting its core brands. As a result, the company is divesting all noncore businesses such as its oil palm plantations. In December 2002, Unilever sold its Malaysian palm plantations that account for over 50,000 acres.

Helping Ghana Grow Oil Palm Plantations

Unilever has a long-standing relationship with Ghana, investing in the country's economy and skills of its employees. Unilever has also been active with numerous community activities such as implementing the Unilever Foundation for Education and Development. The foundation, which launched in 1999, contributes to education to help Ghana reach its goal of being a middle-income economy by 2020.

In addition to the foundation, Unilever recently pledged its expertise to help the Ghana government implement its oil palm tree initiative ("Ghana: Unilever Ready to Assist," 2002). Ghana, like many other countries, sees a large economic benefit in palm plantations. They want to convert 568,000 acres of 1,581,000 acres of degraded mining land into palm plantations ("Ghana: Degraded Mining Lands," 2003).

Questions for Discussion and Further Analysis

1. What was Unilever's motivation to undertake such ambitious programs for sustainability development?

2. What can Unilever do to improve the wages and living conditions of the oil palm workers worldwide? What impact would such actions have on the triple bottom line of Unilever's sustainable development plan?

3. How can Unilever use its influence over the government of Ghana to improve worldwide conditions? Should Unilever encourage or discourage Ghana from entering the oil palm industry?

4. What are the impacts of Unilever's divesting itself of oil palm plantations? Will Unilever still have influence over the triple bottom line of the oil palm industry? Why or why not?

Summary and Conclusion

This chapter describes the second level of the inclusive workplace, *inclusion and corporate-community collaborations,* which relates to the organization's sense of being a part of its surrounding community and to the reciprocity embedded in this relationship. Whereas an exclusionary workplace sees minimal or no connection to its community, an inclusive workplace recognizes the economic and noneconomic consequences of its presence there.

Relevant to level II of the inclusive workplace model is the term "corporate social performance," an emerging construct in the business literature that expands a company's responsibilities beyond its traditional economic shareholders to that of multiple stakeholders, including the community. It stems from the recognition that economic actions of business entities have noneconomic consequences and that business organizations have an impact on other institutions of society above and beyond their economic sphere.

A wide range of activities falls under the title of corporate social performance, such as supporting educational or cultural institutions in the community, providing mentorship to youth, or tutoring children in local schools. The main obstacles for initiating and maintaining activities that benefit the company's social environment are economic pressures to demonstrate profitability on a short-term basis, limited corporate vision, and lack of leaders who could champion and sustain such initiatives. The benefits include advantages in recruitment, goodwill from employees and customers alike, and improved corporate image. In addition to the moral and ethical importance of such actions, recent research provides evidence that companies draw tangible benefits from socially responsible activities. With all this to take into consideration, corporations today do not have the luxury of waiting for government instructions and regulations that would force them into action; the public expects them to be active and proactive in responding to the needs of the community.

Notes

1. The quote is from one of the interviewees for a study of multinational companies. The survey was based on semistructured interviews with company diversity directors (Wentling & Palma-Rivas, 2000, p. 44).

2. The Community Reinvestment Act of 1997 mandated that commercial banks serve their communities by providing private funding for local housing needs and economic development. Under this act, banks are mandated to meet the credit needs of low-income customers.

3. Return on assets (ROA) measures the ability of bank managers to acquire deposits at a reasonable cost, invest these funds in profitable loans and investments, and profitably perform the daily operations of the bank. The ratio of loan losses to loans is another important measure of success because loan losses can be a major expense for banks.

4. The mean return on assets for corporations that were ranked with outstanding social performance was 1.750%, compared with 0.984% of those ranked as needing improvement, and the mean for loan losses was 0.478% compared with 0.812%, respectively.

5. On April 29, 1992, a jury in the Los Angeles suburb of Simi Valley acquitted the four White Los Angeles police officers who had been caught on home video repeatedly clubbing Rodney King, an African American motorist who had led them on a car chase after they tried to stop him for speeding. On the video, the policemen were seen repeatedly beating Rodney King, who was already lying on the ground without any visible signs of resistance. The verdict outraged much of the city, and all hell broke loose on the streets of Los Angeles barely an hour after the jury came back. The riots that began that afternoon became one of the nation's bloodiest, ending 3 days later with 55 people dead, more than 2,300 injured, and 1,100 buildings destroyed. Some scholars use the term "urban uprising" rather than "riots" because the protesters and looters were members of the city's disadvantaged minority communities and their reaction was not only a spontaneous outrage at the unjust verdict but a communal response to a much larger set of social-power issues.

CHAPTER 14

The Inclusive Workplace: Level III

Inclusion Through State/National Collaborations

> Oneness amongst men, the advancement of unity in diversity—this
> has been the core religion of India.
>
> —Rabindranath Tagore (1861–1941),
> Indian freedom fighter, composer of "Jana Gana Mana,"
> India's national anthem, and the first Asian person to be awarded
> the Nobel Prize for Literature (1913)

The third level, *inclusion of disadvantaged groups through state/national collaborations,* refers to the values that drive organizational policies with regard to disadvantaged populations such as welfare recipients, domestic violence victims, and youth in distress. It reflects the "mezzo/macro," national-system level of the state or the federal government where appropriate. The exclusionary workplace views such populations as in the sole domain of welfare agencies or charity organizations. The inclusive workplace perceives welfare recipients seeking work, domestic violence survivors, and youth in distress as a potentially stable and upwardly mobile workforce (e.g., Kossek, Huber-Yoder, Castellino, & Lerner, 1997; Kossek, Huber, & Lerner, 2003). As a result, the inclusive workplace will be more likely to, for example, invest in on-the-job training and evening educational classes for these groups, whereas the exclusionary organization will more readily dispose of these workers or not hire them in the first place.

This third level refers to companies' involvement with programs aimed at helping disadvantaged groups obtain jobs or move on to better jobs. The main focus here is on social class with the confounding issues of gender and race because women and people of color are disproportionately represented in the lower social echelons of society. Populations in need could include former welfare recipients, the working poor, domestic violence survivors, and youth in distress (see Figure 14.1). For example, following the enactment of welfare reform in the United States (the 1996 Personal Responsibility and Work Opportunity Reconciliation Act, P. L. 104–193), which terminated welfare benefits after a maximum of 60 months, more and more individuals with welfare histories have had to enter the labor force. Welfare reform ended 60 years of public assistance programs in which the sole criterion for continued aid was dependency, poverty, age, or disability. New Zealand, a welfare state with universal entitlements to health care and education coverage, underwent a somewhat similar welfare reform in 1996 (Kingfisher & Goldsmith, 2001). The reduction of the Domestic Purposes Benefit, which was designed to support single parents with dependent children, has facilitated and/or forced the entry of poor, single mothers into the workforce. A key component of the program was the expectation that benefit recipients would find jobs by the time their benefits were terminated. Barriers to employment of former welfare recipients (the majority of whom are single mothers) included finding reliable, consistent, and affordable childcare and transportation; family issues such as domestic violence and substance abuse; health problems; education, job skills, and labor market situation; and problems at work such as poor working conditions, low pay, and job location (Blumenberg, 2002; Hildebrandt, 2009; Kossek et al., 1997; Kossek, Huber, & Lerner, 2003; Michalopoulos et al., 2003; Ovwigho et al., 2008; Scein, 1995). Lacking the skill to land stable, high-paying, and benefits-rich jobs, most of the working poor remain at or near poverty level, even when employed full-time.

Traditionally, employers have had very limited involvement or interest in welfare recipients or in other disadvantaged groups and have not viewed the working poor as an element in organizational life worth substantial investment (Kossek et al., 1997; Kossek, Huber, & Lerner, 2003). Corporate sponsorship and support of former welfare recipients could help these disadvantaged groups overcome the difficulties they face in this transition. Therefore, if corporations take appropriate initiative with respect to disadvantaged groups, social and legislative changes such as the welfare-to-work reform could be conceptualized as an opportunity to, on the one hand, make the workplace more inclusive with respect to social class and, on the other hand, give companies access to untapped human resources. Besides the ethical and moral value of such actions, access to potential job seekers may be particularly important in tight job markets like the one experienced in Japan in the 1980s (1.35 advertised jobs for each person seeking work) and in the 1990s in several other countries around the world. It is much more difficult to make the case for hiring workers from disadvantaged groups during periods of economical downturn, such as the global recession of that began in the second half of the first decade in the 21st century. Such periods are characterized by high unemployment and a surplus of skilled workers. One could make the argument, however, that high-skilled workers who may have other options once the recession is over would be less likely to stay with the company compared to workers who may not have other options and would be more likely to stay and provide continuity and stability to the organization.

An inclusive workplace sponsors and supports projects that help former welfare recipients overcome barriers to employment. These programs focus on removing barriers to employment faced by mothers of young children, who constitute the majority of welfare recipients and poor families (Hildebrandt, 2009). They assist former welfare recipients with childcare, transportation, housing, and health care expenses, which are the main barriers to employment faced by this group (Hamersma, 2008; Michalopoulos et al., 2003). They also provide on-the-job training to allow them to improve their job skills and increase their wages and benefits. In Thailand, for example, a group of 14 of the country's successful businesses formed The Plan Group, an umbrella organization that initiates innovative programs to help disadvantaged groups in their country. The four founders of the group were students in the 1970s who saw fellow students killed on the street by the security forces of the country's military government. Once they became successful businessmen, their umbrella organization emerged out of their resolve to make a difference in their country through the implementation of extensive community and national projects (Schwartz & Gibb, 1999).

Employment programs to assist the working poor and other socially disadvantaged groups often require a private public recourse partnership to make

Figure 14.1   The Inclusive Workplace: The Value Base for Level III

Inclusion Through State/National Collaborations		
Value Frame		
System Level	**Exclusion**	**Inclusion**
	◄─────────────────────────────────►	
State, Federal Government	Viewing disadvantaged groups as the domain of welfare agencies and charity organizations and treating them as disposable labor	Treating disadvantaged groups as potentially stable, upwardly mobile employees and investing in their education and training

them successful. In the United States, for example, two forms of public incentives have been offered to private employers to improve employment rates among former welfare recipients. The first is Work Opportunity Tax Credit (WOTC), a subsidy to employers who hire new workers from certain disadvantaged groups, such as welfare recipients, youth food stamp recipients, poor veterans, youth from disadvantaged geographic areas, Supplemental Security Income (SSI) recipients, and low-income ex-felons. The second is the Welfare-to-Work Tax Credit (WtW), a program that applies specifically to long-term welfare recipients (with at least 18 months of continuous welfare receipt at the time of hire) and provides a larger subsidy. Research demonstrated modest success of these two programs. Although these programs assisted former welfare recipients receive and maintain jobs, the author notes that firms' participation in this subsidy program was surprisingly low. The relatively low participation rates could be attributed to lack of information among firms, lack of firms' interest in involvement with government programs, high transaction costs relative to benefits, or difficulty in identifying qualified workers, perhaps because of worker stigma (Hamersma, 2008).

Barriers and Benefits of Implementing the Inclusive Approach at Level III

BARRIERS

The main obstacle to implementing such programs is a limited corporate vision. Companies often focus on only the immediate needs and objectives of the company rather than consider the bigger picture that includes moral and ethical values as well as labor force trends and the larger organizational environment. The other obstacles are stereotypes and prejudices held by management and workers against disadvantaged populations, such as welfare recipients, domestic violence victims, and youth in distress, and against women and people of color in general (Hancock, 2004).

Figure 14.2 provides a summary of barriers and benefits to implementing level III policies and practices.

BENEFITS

Including the working poor, domestic violence survivors, youth in need, and those with welfare histories in human resource planning and policy initiatives of work organizations can benefit companies as well as individuals and their families. Opening up employment and advancement opportunities for these populations may increase their chances of obtaining higher-paying jobs

Figure 14.2   The Inclusive Workplace Model: Obstacles and Benefits for Level III

Inclusion Through State/National Collaborations		
Barriers	**Benefits**	
	Individuals	**Organization**
• Limited company vision (shortsighted and internally focused) • Stereotypes, prejudice, and discrimination against disadvantaged population groups	• Employment, benefits • Job training • Advancement opportunities • Improved job prospects	• Expanded potential employee pool • Increased employee loyalty • Improved customer relations • A more attractive value-based corporate image

with better benefits that will release them from the vicious cycle of low-paying jobs that barely suffice for basic needs. A by-product will be an increase in the pool of consumers with discretionary income. The economic benefits for companies include gaining a more loyal workforce that is committed to the organization (and has lower turnover rates as a result); expanding employee pools; improving customer relations through better treatment of low-wage employees who are often frontline workers; having a more attractive, value-based corporate image that is more appealing to both customers and investors; and increasing the pool of consumers with discretionary income (Kossek et al., 1997; Kossek, Huber, & Lerner, 2003) (see Box 14.1 for the story of a company that partnered with the government to improve the lot of disadvantaged groups).

BOX 14.1
A Company's Collaboration With Governmental Programs for Disadvantaged Populations (Level III): The Case of Hong Yip Service Company Ltd. (Hong Kong)

Hong Yip Service Company Ltd. (Hong Yip), a subsidiary of the Sun Hung Kai Properties Ltd., is one of the largest property management companies in Hong Kong (Hong Yip Service Co. Ltd., 2003). Based in Wanchai, the company manages approximately 100 million sq. ft. of residential and commercial space, including private and public housing, offices, shopping centers, and government properties. Hong Yip is frequently recognized for its commitment to the environment and to social service, having received awards for activities such as its efforts to stop the spread of the SARS virus and its environmentally friendly property management activities (Hong Kong General Chamber of Commerce, 2003). The Hong Kong Council of Social Service recognized Hong Yip as a Caring Company 2002/2003 for demonstrating its willingness to employ individuals from vulnerable groups and for developing partnership projects with the social service sector (Hong Kong Council of Social Services, 2003).

Hong Yip indicates the belief that issues such as environmental protection, youth employment, and employee retraining are ameliorated when companies partner with government and social services (Hong Yip Service Co. Ltd., 2003). To those ends, the company has been involved in ongoing partnerships with the government of Hong Kong to assist in creating more job opportunities for vulnerable populations. One such partnership is with the Employees Retraining Board, whose purpose is to provide retraining to eligible workers so that they can adjust to changes in the economic environment (Employees Retraining Board, 2003). Service recipients include displaced workers, individuals new to Hong Kong, elderly workers, people with disabilities, and industrial accident victims. Hong Yip has also partnered with the Youth Pre-employment Training Programme, designed to provide school leavers aged 15 to 19 with training to enhance their employability (Labour Department, Government of Hong Kong, 2003). After completing training courses offered by the Labour Department, participants receive solid, hands-on experience in the workplace. For Hong Yip, these partnerships constitute a win-win situation: the company is permitted to hire the trainees, should they so choose, upon completion of the program.

Case Illustration: Level III—Inclusion of Disadvantaged Groups at the National/State Level—Eurest

If we are comparing [Australia's record] with arbitrary arrests and executions and having your arms chopped off, the problems in Australia pale in significance.

—Attorney General Daryl Williams, Australia (1996–2003)

For the indignity and degradation thus inflicted on a proud people and a proud culture, we say sorry.

—Australian Prime Minister Kevin Rudd in a long-overdue apology to the Aborigines, February 13, 2008

On October 7, 1830, the "black line" formed in Tasmania. The black line was a human chain of 2,200 soldiers, police, freemen, and convicts stretching across southeastern Tasmania to flush out Aboriginals, Australia's native inhabitants. As a result of massive murderous attacks on Aborigine men, women, and children, by 1835 less than 400 Aborigines remained alive of the estimated 1,500 who lived in Tasmania in 1824 (Madley, 2008).

Prior to the black line incident, settlers would shoot on sight at the 4,000 initial Tasmanian Aboriginals, which caused a decrease of the population to 2,000 by 1820. They would kill the men and take the children from the mothers. Often, the settlers would chase a mother through the bushes until she had to leave her children behind. The children were then used for labor. Though the local government admitted that the aggression originated with the settlers, no settler was ever charged for such crimes. Instead, in 1824 the government permitted Tasmanian settlers to shoot Aboriginals and in 1830 offered a bounty for each captured Aboriginal adult and child (Kiernan, 2000; Madley, 2008).

HISTORY OF THE ABORIGINALS

Britain first colonized Australia in 1788 when the native population of Australia, known as Aboriginals, totaled approximately 750,000. As a result of disease and warfare with the settlers, the Aboriginal population dwindled to fewer than 50,000 by 1901 (Madley, 2008).

Although Britain did not sanction attacks on the Aboriginals, the authorities passed numerous laws that put the native population at a disadvantage. For example, when the island was first colonized, Aboriginals were stripped of their land rights. Additionally, Aboriginals were not considered British subjects. Therefore, the laws, which were written to protect British subjects, did not protect the Aboriginal people from crimes such as murder (Kiernan, 2000).

In 1837, the British House of Commons Select Committee on Aborigines acknowledged some of the killings and further stated that if atonement were to be made to the remaining Aboriginals, it would require no ordinary sacrifice on the part of the British. Since the time of that statement, some British subjects were convicted of murdering Aboriginals. However, injustices continued. For example, by 1856 it was common practice to punish Aboriginals collectively for crimes committed by individuals in their ethnic group, an act that is now considered genocide by international laws (Kiernan, 2000).

The atonement mentioned by the House of Commons began with the passing of several laws ostensibly designed to protect the Aboriginals. The Aboriginal Protection Act of 1869 gave Victoria's governor the right to provide provisions for the Aboriginals. In particular, it gave the governor the right to decide where any Aboriginal could live. It further gave the governor the power to determine the care, custody, and education of Aboriginal children (Kiernan, 2000), a provision that controversially remained in effect until the 1970s.

Building on the 1869 Aboriginal Protection Act, a 1918 Northern Territory ordinance provided for the protection of Aboriginal children. As with the Victorian law, a practice emerged in which children of mixed descent, referred to as half-castes, were removed from their parents and raised by non-Aboriginal "White" parents. This law resulted in the removal of between 50,000 and 100,000 Aboriginal children over the course of the century (Kiernan, 2000).

Despite the controversy surrounding the forced separation of families and the stripping of land rights, the Aborigines were unable to challenge these laws for two reasons: First, they were not citizens. Second, they were non-Christians, who by British definition could not swear an oath. Therefore, the courts rejected any evidence of wrongdoing (Kiernan, 2000; Madley, 2008), essentially leaving no way for the Aborigines to challenge laws or even to testify about crimes committed against them.

The legacy of past injustice persists in the Aboriginal people today. For generations, Aboriginal people were forced to live under segregation, protection, and assimilation policies and were denied the freedom to determine their own future. The extent of intrusion was wide-ranging and included restrictions on movement, relationships and marriage, the control of employment, and the removal of Aboriginal children from parents and family members. These policies created dependence, caused great pain, and had devastating and lasting effects on the Aboriginal population. The destruction and devastation caused by colonization has resulted in the breakdown of social structures and traditional values across many generations. Attempts to improve circumstances have been relatively unsuccessful as there has been little acknowledgement and understanding of the historical context. The fragmentation of family relationships and the learned helplessness has had a crippling effect on successive generations. Deprived of adequate health care, education, and economic independence, many Aboriginal people were left without hope and some have turned to a life of alcohol, drugs, and crime to survive (Cox, Young, & Bairnsfather-Scott, 2009).

AUSTRALIA'S PLAN TO MEND THE INJUSTICES

New Laws

Past laws, which were designed to protect the Aborigines, created more problems than they solved, such as the forced separation of families to protect the children (Cox, Young, & Bairnsfather-Scott, 2009). However, starting in the mid-1900s, tangible progress in the laws began, the most significant of which was Australia's granting citizenship to Aborigines in 1967. Aboriginals were not only granted citizenship, which meant they could now testify in court and challenge laws, but they were also allowed to vote (Zan, 1997).

In 1992, two legal cases led to Australia's reversal of its claim that Australia was *terra nullius,* meaning the land had belonged to no one before settlement. As a result, Australia granted some limited indigenous land rights to the Aboriginal people (Zan, 1997). In addition to the reversal of the land rights, the Australian government enacted a plan to help families that were forcibly separated. The government allotted AU$63 million (US$49 million) to reunite families and provide counseling ("Australian Government," 2001).

Indigenous Employment Policy

As of June 30, 2006, the Aboriginal population had rebounded to 517,200, representing 2.5% of the total Australian population of 20 million people (Australian Bureau of Statistics, 2007). However, the Aborigines represented a significantly higher proportion of the unemployed. According to the Australian Bureau of Statistics (2007), 16% of indigenous people were unemployed, compared with 5% for the general population.

Fueled by the indigenous population's high unemployment rate and higher than average population growth rate, the Australian federal government implemented the Indigenous Employment Policy in 1999, which was composed of several key areas (Australian Employment Services, 2001):

- Corporate Leaders for Indigenous Employment—a partnership between companies and the government with the goal of hiring more indigenous people. The government will fund some of the hiring expenses, such as preemployment training, mentoring, cross-cultural training, and other appropriate expenses.
- Wage assistance—compensates employers up to AU$4,400 (US$3,406) over 26 weeks for providing long-term employment to indigenous workers.
- Structured training and employment projects—compensates employers offering training programs for indigenous people.
- National Indigenous Cadetship Program—supports companies that sponsor indigenous people as cadets. Cadets, similar to interns in other parts of the world, work during vacation breaks from their school and are usually employed by the sponsoring company.
- Indigenous Small Business Fund—funds indigenous organizations that train indigenous people about business practices. It also funds individuals with good business ideas.
- Community Development Employment Projects Placement Incentive—provides a bonus for each placement of an individual into the general workforce.
- Voluntary Service to Indigenous Communities—matches skilled volunteers with the needs of indigenous communities.

An evaluation of the policy showed that progress has been made in increasing opportunities for indigenous job seekers. In the first 2 years of the policy, around 12,000 indigenous people participated in training and were placed in jobs. In line with the policy focus of the program, there has been a strong shift toward private sector companies' participation compared with the level of participation in previous indigenous programs (Department of Employment and Workplace Relations, 2003).

EUREST

Eurest is the largest food service company in Australia, employing 7,050 people at more than 500 sites, as of 2001. Additionally, they have operations in New Zealand and Papua New Guinea. Some of their businesses include catering and managing concession stands and cafeterias across a broad array of industries (e.g., schools, health care facilities, sporting venues, armed forces, and airports).

Eurest was formed in 1997 as a joint venture between Compass Group, the world's leading food service organization, and Accor, the world's largest hotel and tourism service company. Some of the parent company brands include Upper Crust, Harry Ramsden's, Au Bon Pain, Naples 45, Caffe Ritazza, Motel 6, Sofitel, and Red Roof Inns.

Indigenous Training and Employment Program

In 1998, Eurest was one of the first businesses to begin working with the Australian government to promote employment opportunities for Australia's indigenous population (Eurest, 2001). A year later, Australia's Indigenous Employment Policy was born. While the government was busy developing this program, Eurest was busy developing its own—the Indigenous Training and Employment Program (ITEP) (Eurest, 2004). Eurest's ITEP supports the government's goals of indigenous employment. Specifically, ITEP teaches new work skills integrated with consultation and mutual understanding of local communities (Eurest, 2004). The key elements (Northern and Central Land Councils, 2001) that Eurest integrates into the various applications of its plan include the following:

- A dedicated ITEP manager employed by Eurest
- Aboriginal community consultation
- Structured and accredited preemployment training
- A gradual exposure to the workplace
- Mentor support and an on-site buddy system
- Cross-cultural training for non-Aboriginal employees

According to Eurest published figures (2001), Eurest increased its indigenous workforce by 203 people within 18 months of initiating ITEP.

Additionally, Eurest helped a dozen students enhance their employment prospects via a prevocational retail hospitality training course operated by Eurest and Mission Employment (Ellis, 2002).

In addition to increasing indigenous employment within its existing business units, Eurest has worked to develop joint venture projects specifically designed for employment of indigenous people. An example of this is Eurest's joint venture with the Northern and Central Land Councils. The arrangement was to create extensive Aboriginal employment utilizing the Alice to Darwin railway construction project (Northern and Central Land Councils, 2001).

Eurest secured a $10–12 million contract to supply catering, cleaning, retail, canteen, gardening, and general maintenance for construction camps during the railway project, which was expected to last 2 years. The railway project was ideal for Aboriginal people because it ran through remote areas, which is where many Aboriginals live, and required skills that are familiar to them (Northern and Central Land Councils, 2001).

Although exact employment figures for the project were not available, all three partners were dedicated to employing as many indigenous people as possible. In addition to Eurest's ITEP manager, each of the land councils had officers dedicated to maximizing Aboriginal participation in the project (Northern and Central Land Councils, 2001).

Awards

The result of Eurest's efforts is not only greater employment opportunities for Australia's indigenous population, but also the receipt of many accolades for the company (Eurest, 2004): (a) in 1999 (from the Australian National Training Authority) the Australian Training Award (winner in the industry category for hospitality); (from the State Training Board/Department of Training) the Training Excellence Award—Employer of the Year Finalist; (from the Partners in Employment and Training State Summit and Awards) the Aboriginal Programs Industry Excellence Award; (b) in 2000 (from the Department for Employment, Workplace Relations and Small Business) the NAIDOC Award; (from the Compass Group in the Community Award) the Gold Award, Southern Europe and Development Division; (from the Compass Group in the Community Award) the Global Silver Award; and (c) in 2002 (from the Corporate Leaders for Indigenous Employment Awards) Finalist in the Outstanding Organization Category and the 2003 Prime Minister's Employer of the Year Award.

CONTINUING CONTROVERSY

Controversy continues for Australia regarding the government's interactions with the Aboriginal people. For example, the Australian Parliament believed that the money allocated to help separated families was not enough. They recommended compensating families that had been forcibly separated. However, the Australian government formally rejected that recommendation in 2001 ("Australian Government," 2001).

Part of the reason for the controversy surrounding the family-separation issue is a matter of definition. In a 1997 report, Australia's Human Rights and Equal Opportunity Commission called the forced removal of Aboriginal children an act of genocide. Two months after that report was released, however, the High Court of Australia disagreed. They ruled on a suit filed by several Aboriginals who had been separated from their families as children, ruling unanimously that the separations were not an act of genocide (Zan, 1997).

Regardless of the various laws and definitions of events, the Aboriginal people have had one basic request that for many years went unanswered: that the Australian federal government issue an apology. February 13, 2008, their request was finally answered. In a speech to the Australian Parliament and to the nation, Prime Minister Kevin Rudd made a formal apology saying that the Australian government was sorry for the past wrongs caused by successive governments on the indigenous Aboriginal population. The prime minister apologized to all Aborigines for laws and policies that "inflicted profound grief, suffering and loss" (BBC News, 2008).

Questions for Discussion and Further Analysis

1. What impact might the government's subsidization of Aborigines' employment have in the short term? long term?

2. Does the fact that Eurest receives money for training and hiring indigenous employees affect the perceived value of Eurest's action? Why or why not?

3. How might Eurest's Aborigines Employment Plan affect customer perceptions of Eurest? How might it affect employee morale?

4. Eurest's ITEP includes two key elements not specifically addressed in the government's plan: the gradual introduction of indigenous employees to the workplace and a dedicated ITEP manager. Why do you think Eurest added these elements? What benefits might they offer? What problems might they create? If you were consulting for Eurest, would you recommend that they keep or eliminate these two elements? Why?

5. If during a press interview Eurest were asked for their position regarding the continuing Aboriginal controversies, how would you recommend that they respond? What impact might your recommendation have on Eurest's employees, customers, and business and government partners?

Summary and Conclusion

Inclusion of disadvantaged groups through state/national collaborations refers to the values that drive organizational policies with regard to disadvantaged populations such as welfare recipients, domestic violence victims, and youth in distress. Although the exclusionary workplace views disadvantaged populations as in the sole domain of welfare agencies and charity organizations, the inclusive workplace perceives them as a potentially stable and upwardly mobile workforce.

The main obstacle to implementing such programs is a limited corporate vision that is focused on short-term goals. The other obstacles are stereotypes and prejudices held by management and workers against disadvantaged populations. On the other hand, including these population groups in human resource planning and in policy initiatives of work organizations can benefit companies as well as individuals and their families. Opening up employment and advancement opportunities for these populations may increase their chances of obtaining higher-paying jobs with better benefits, which will release them from the vicious cycle of low-paying jobs that barely suffice for basic needs. The economic benefits for companies include gaining a more loyal workforce, expanding employee pools, improving customer relations, and having a more attractive, value-based corporate image.

If corporations take appropriate initiative with respect to disadvantaged groups, social and legislative changes such as the welfare-to-work reform can be conceptualized as an opportunity to, on the one hand, make the workplace more inclusive with respect to social class and, on the other hand, give companies access to untapped human resources. Besides the ethical and moral value of such actions, access to potential job seekers may be particularly important in tight job markets.

CHAPTER 15

The Inclusive Workplace: Level IV

Inclusion Through International Collaborations

> *It is the duty of the corporation to make profits for its shareholders,
> but to earn them in such a way as to make a real and permanent con-
> tribution to the well being of the people and to the development of
> South Africa.*
>
> —Sir Ernest Openheimer, founder of Anglo American in 1917[1]

Level IV, *inclusion through international collaborations*, refers to the organization's positions and practices related to the fair exchange of economic
goods and services and the respectful cultural relationship with individuals
and groups in other countries. It reflects the "macro" system level of international relations. The exclusionary workplace operates from a framework that is
ethnocentric, competition-based, and focused on narrowly defined financial
and national interests (see Figure 15.1). The inclusive workplace sees value in
collaborating across national borders, being pluralistic, and identifying global
mutual interests. The exclusionary organization, for example, will send local
employees on international assignments to strictly enforce a company's values
and norms overseas, whereas the inclusive workplace will hire local managers
and give autonomy to its international branches.

The combination of business internationalization, worker migration, and
workforce diversity creates a challenge for companies engaged in international
business. Multinational companies such as IBM, General Electric, British
Petroleum, Siemens, and Eastman Kodak each do business in more than 50
countries. Of the 1,000 largest industrial companies in the United States, 700
expect their growth abroad to exceed their domestic growth in the next 5 years.

The process through which people, companies, and countries acquire wealth has undergone major changes in recent decades because of the internationalization of capital markets and advances in technology.

The increasingly more open economic markets create opportunities for countries with surplus workforce and underdeveloped economies to come together with countries that can finance economic endeavors and provide jobs. However, these conditions also open up opportunities for exploitation by companies who take advantage of workers' desperation in poor regions by employing them in abhorrent conditions and subminimal payment. In order to compete in this changing environment, companies must develop intelligent systems of human resource management and open up opportunities for a diverse workforce across national boundaries (for a case example of such policies and programs, see Box 15.1). If they wish to survive and succeed in today's changing market conditions, companies need to conduct their business in a fair and ethical way while respecting other cultures.

An interesting example of inclusive practices is that of Hindustan Lever Ltd., the Indian division of Unilever, which, out of business necessity, developed an innovative international initiative. In 1975, the company was almost forced to close its dairy in Etah, not because the villagers did not have enough cows but because, being poverty stricken, they were unable to properly feed their livestock. The management of Hindustan Lever decided to invest efforts and financial resources in its "integrated rural development initiative," helping some 600 villagers reach self-sufficiency. As a result of the program, the health and income

Figure 15.1	The Inclusive Workplace: The Value Base for Level IV Inclusion Through Global Collaborations

Inclusive Policies and Practices: **Inclusion Through Global Collaborations**		
	Value Frame	
System Level	**Exclusion**	**Inclusion**
	←————————————————→	
International, Global	Culture-specific	Pluralistic
	Ethnocentric	Collaboration-based
	Intranational focus	Focus on global mutual interests

levels of the local people have improved considerably, the dairy has been operating at full capacity, and the villagers are now loyal consumers of Hindustan Lever products. Further, the company now requires its managers, who typically live in India's cities, to spend 2 months living and working with the villagers in Etah to get to know them better and to make actual contributions to their community (Jones, 2005, p. 173; Schwartz & Gibb, 1999, pp. 87–88).

BOX 15.1
A Company's International Inclusion Initiatives
(Level IV): The Case of eShopAfrica (Ghana)

eShopAfrica is a fair trade e-commerce business founded in 1999 in Accra, Ghana. The company's founder, Cordelia Salter-Nour, had worked for several years in the technology arm of aid and development organizations in Africa. Despite the increasing use of technology in Africa, Ms. Salter-Nour felt that technology was not benefiting the ordinary person. Further, she realized that small business entrepreneurs in many African countries struggled fiercely to get their businesses off the ground. Hence, she decided that technology could be used to aid the development of small business in Africa (C. Salter-Nour, personal communication, November 25, 2003). The stated aim of eShopAfrica is to use technology to develop a fair trade marketplace for traditional African artisans, allowing them to build sustainable businesses (eShopAfrica, 2009). The company sources its products from tradespeople, many of whom are living in poverty, across an expanding list of African countries including Ghana, Burkina Faso, Ethiopia, Mali, and Zimbabwe. Product offerings include musical instruments, carvings, jewelry, textiles, fashions, and housewares.

Although profitability is as essential to eShopAfrica as it is to any business, the company expresses equal commitment to the businesses and the communities from whom it sources merchandise. The company's fair trade charter, applied to dealings with each supplier, includes payment of fair market prices (as agreed upon with suppliers after establishing product quality guidelines), prompt submission of payment, prohibition of forced labor/organized child labor, and refusal to disturb traditional supply and production lines. Each artisan is featured on the company's Web site, complete with a photo and a biographical sketch. Often information is provided about the artisan's training and the status of his or her small-business venture. For example, Samuel Naah, the carpenter who has gained international recognition for his Ga-culture decorated chests (Hale, 2003; Karlin, 2005; Phillips, 2002), has been able

(Continued)

(Continued)

to pay off his apprenticeship fees and set up his own workshop with the revenues generated by his eShopAfrica sales. To ensure success for the company and the small businesses with whom it works, eShopAfrica has partnered with several NGOs and governmental agencies, including the Ghana Export Promotion Council (the public agency charged with promoting Ghana's non-traditional products in international markets). The company is also included on the World Bank's list of e-commerce businesses that support grassroots entrepreneurs (World Bank Group, 2003).

Another example is the corporate social-responsibility program implemented by Chiquita Brands International, Inc., a producer, distributor, and marketer of fresh and processed foods. Chiquita's banana division accounts for more than half of the company's revenues and employs some 20,000 employees in more than 127 banana farms in five countries in Latin America: Guatemala, Honduras, Costa Rica, Panama, and Colombia (Wicki & Van der Kaaij, 2007). The rural areas from which Chiquita sources bananas struggle to various degrees with poverty, literacy, access to health care, and other basic social and infrastructure needs. The company went through four stages in the process: (1) raising top-management awareness, (2) formulating a vision and core corporate values, (3) changing organizational behavior, and (4) anchoring the change. Through much of its 100-year history, including those as predecessor companies United Fruit and United Brands, the company has been fiercely competitive and suffered from a less than stellar reputation, which was the main impetus for implementing its socially oriented organizational change[2] (Werre, 2003). Lotus Corporation, on the other hand, developed its international inclusive initiative out of ideological conviction. In 1992, although there was not yet a democratically elected government in place, Lotus reversed its previous policy not to do business in South Africa and launched a visionary initiative with the purpose of assisting in the development of the Black business community. The company established its South Africa social investment fund (with an annual budget of about $350,000) and has charged its newly hired manager with a mandate to work directly with Black-run information technology projects. The company created an internship program for Black programming trainees in Johannesburg and brought a group of Black computer instructors to Lotus's Massachusetts headquarters for advanced training, including training Black South Africans to assume managerial positions. In addition to the fund and the training opportunities, Lotus also made efforts to conduct its business dealings in the country in a way that will enhance Black businesses. Specifically, it formed a partnership with the only non-White software distributorship and invested time and resources in providing the technical assistance that was needed to bring the distributorship up to the requisite professional level (Alperson, 1993; Makower, 1995).

Barriers and Benefits to Implementing the Inclusive Approach at Level IV

BARRIERS

There are several obstacles related to applying the principles of the inclusive workplace to international collaborations. The primary barrier is greed, which motivates companies to go beyond a fair economic exchange and take advantage of employees or resources in the host country. Companies exploit uneducated people who live in poor nations with the purpose of gaining economic advantage. The second barrier is discrimination, or inappropriate consideration of age, gender, race, or other personal characteristics with respect to the hiring and employment conditions of both local employees and expatriates (employees who move from one country to the other to do their jobs). And the third is lack of respect for other national cultures, which leads to a forced implementation of the values and norms that are not appropriate for the host country.

BENEFITS

Companies today can reap the benefits of an increasingly global marketplace by employing workers from different nationalities in or outside their native countries. This expansion creates new jobs, including international job opportunities, for these companies' employees. From a business point of view, diversity and nondiscrimination policies applied to international business contacts are crucial. Skill shortages, underutilized customer potential, and improved market understanding are only a few of the more obvious business reasons. Chiquita Brands International (mentioned earlier) counts among its program's employee benefits (a) the adjustment of payment and benefits to many of its employees to make their compensation fairer and (b) the improvement of health and safety conditions in its farms. Among the benefits to the company, Chiquita Brands International credits the program with improved sales in Europe as a result of the company's improved image, reduced health insurance costs because of lower accident rates, improved environmental protection, and improved industrial relations, including reduced work disruptions caused by strikes and stoppages (Werre, 2003; Wicki & Van der Kaaij, 2007).

Another example comes from Bata International, a maker of shoes.[3] When Bata decided to expand its operations in Thailand, it worked with development experts from the Thai Business Initiative in Rural Development to set up small shoe factories in poor villages of the northeastern province of Buri Ram. The company provided the training in manufacturing and business skills, and the village cooperatives owned and managed the factories, investing the profits back into their communities. The company currently provides employment to almost 500 people in Buri Ram, and this investment has boosted the province's economy and helped in the development of many villages in the area. These small rural factories turned out some of the highest-quality shoes of any Bata factory in the world, with very healthy profits for the company (Schwartz & Gibb, 1999).

Although international businesses have existed for centuries, the world has clearly entered an era of unprecedented global economic activity, including worldwide production, distribution, and—in increasingly large numbers—global strategic alliances. With foreign production currently accounting for more than 25% of their domestic production, multinational companies have a great stake in the international scene. These global ventures and international collaborations allow companies to expand their geographical markets and to increase their economic activities. Given that products and services reach a growing number of men and women in countries throughout the world, sales organizations and supplier communities can improve their access to people with talent by increasing the diversity of their workforce. They can also become more aware of specific needs of their internationally based customers, which can enable them to create valued products and services (United Nations Global Compact, 2001; United Nations Global Impact, 2004).

Figure 15.2 provides a summary illustration of the benefits and the barriers of implementing the inclusive workplace at level IV of the model.

Case Illustration: Level IV—Inclusion Through Global Collaborations—The Fair Trade Company

> If fair trade clothes followed the trends and were designed by the right designer, they would sell as well as any others.
>
> —Alice Fisher, commissioning editor at *Vogue*

Opening the newspaper and seeing stories about sweatshops and child labor violations in developing countries has become a common occurrence. In the December 7, 2003, edition of the *New York Times,* Joseph Kahn reported on the sweatshop conditions in one plant, Kin Ki Industrial, a Chinese factory that makes items such as Etch A Sketch, a popular toy in the United States.

Figure 15.2	The Inclusive Workplace Model: Barriers and Benefits for Level IV Inclusion Through Global Collaborations

Inclusion Through State/National Collaborations		
Barriers	**Benefits**	
	Individuals	**Organization**
• Greed–going beyond fair trade and exploiting others • Discrimination • Lack of respect for other nations and cultures	• Job opportunities, both for local residents and for expatriates • Improved health and safety conditions	• Expanded geographic markets • Improved industrial relations and less litigation • Increased economic activities • Better marketing to international customers • Improved corporate image with customers, financial institutions, and stockholders

The story begins by illustrating the "official" working conditions at Kin Ki: good salary, respectable hours without night or weekend work, leisure time, work contracts, pensions, medical benefits, and tasty food provided by the factory cafeteria. It sounds like an ideal situation, one that some workers in industrialized countries might envy. These "official" working conditions are outlined on paper and given to workers just prior to inspections so that they know what to tell inspectors. However, if workers are asked for a copy of their work contract or other documents, the paper instructs them to intentionally waste time and then say that they can't find the paperwork.

The reality of the working conditions, however, is very different. As one Kin Ki official admits, the wages and benefits fall short of legal levels. That may be quite an understatement, if the workers' claims are a fair indication. Workers at the Kin Ki plant claim to earn 24 cents per hour, below the legal minimum of 33 cents per hour. Additionally, the workers are required to work 84-hour weeks (12 hours per day, 7 days per week) without the benefit of overtime pay as required by law. Workers are fed an uninspiring diet of boiled vegetables, beans, and rice, with meat served twice per month. Despite protests by the workers for more pay and more meat, they have received only a few cents extra per day, with no improvements in the food. The employees who led the protests are no longer with the company. One official claimed the "troublemakers" left of their own accord. That may be true because Kin Ki is not a prison, although sometimes it may be hard to tell based on the guarded front entrance, high walls surrounding the factory, and chicken wire on the dormitory windows (Kahn, 2003).

Fair Trade History

There has been a growing movement to eliminate poor working conditions, as experienced at Kin Ki, not only through laws or trade penalties but through positive trading relations, known as fair trade. Fair trade originated in the late 1950s when a U.K. charity, Oxfam, started selling crafts made by Chinese refugees (Aaronson & Zimmerman, 2006; Ram, 2002). This practice helped bolster Oxfam's organizational goal of offering a lasting solution to poverty and suffering around the world.

Since that time, fair trade practices have emerged to ensure that producers, laborers, and farmers are paid a price that not only covers their costs but also allows them to support their families, invest in their businesses, and invest in social and economic improvements (Ram, 2002). Several organizations have formed with the sole focus of promoting and monitoring fair trade practices, including the following:

- The Alternative Trading Organization (U.K.) in 1964
- The International Federation of Alternative Trade (Netherlands) in 1989
- The Fairtrade Foundation (U.K.) in 1992
- Fair Trade Federation (U.S.) in 1994
- Transfair (U.S., Canada, and Japan) in late 1998
- Fair Trade Association of Australia and New Zealand (2003)

Several of the organizations, such as the Fairtrade Foundation and Transfair USA, certify that consumer products meet fair trade guidelines, adding a certification to product packaging such as the Fairtrade Foundation's "fairtrade mark" in the United Kingdom.

PRINCIPLES OF FAIR TRADE

The key principles of fair trade, as defined by the Fair Trade Federation (2008), are as follows:

- The creation of opportunities for economically disadvantaged producers
- Gender equity—particularly making sure that women are properly paid for their work and empowered within their organizations
- Transparency and accountability—including transparent management and open dialogues between importers and producers
- Capacity building—promoting sustainable business practices by producers and providing management-skill development and financial and technical assistance
- Payment of a fair price—as agreed through dialogue between the importer and producer
- Improved working conditions
- Environmental sustainability
- Promoting fairer trade by educating consumers about the importance of purchasing fairly traded products

MARKET EXPANSION

The fair trade market has grown considerably since its start with craft items in the United Kingdom. Consumers can now buy a wide array of fair trade products including produce, coffee, tea, toys, jewelry, furniture, paper products, clothing, chocolate, rugs, and other items (Fair Trade Federation, 2003). The demand for fair trade products has spread across approximately 58 countries as of 2007 including Europe to the United States, Canada, Australia, New Zealand, and Japan (The Fair Trade Foundation, 2008). The number and types of fair trade products, however, varies from country to country.

New fair trade products are regularly introduced around the world. In some cases, the products are new to the world. For example, the world's first fair trade mangoes purchased from farmers in Ecuador became available in Europe in 2002 (Ram, 2002). In 2008, fair trade Austria introduced organic fair trade mangos, pineapples, and avocadoes, which were not previously available. Fair trade flowers were made available in Italy, the United States, and Sweden (The Fair Trade Foundation, 2008). More often the new products are an expansion into a new country. For example, Wild Oats Markets offered fair trade bananas, sold in Europe for years, for the first time in the United States in 2004 (Horovitz, 2004).

More than any other product, coffee is experiencing strong growth worldwide (Fair Trade Federation, 2003), with expected increases ranging from 23% in the United States to 80% in Japan in 2003. Fair trade coffee was introduced in Europe in 1990 and, as of 2001, had grown to $300 million in sales with over 150 brands in over 35,000 supermarkets (Bojarski, 2002). Now in the United States, large-scale food manufacturers are beginning to offer fair trade coffee for the first time. Procter & Gamble has introduced a fair trade coffee line available via the Internet. Kraft is introducing a fair trade coffee line, focusing on distribution via their food service division (Turcsik, 2003).

EXAMPLE OF THE COSTS OF FAIR TRADE GOODS

How much extra do fair trade products cost? That varies by product and company; however, the costs can often be kept relatively close to the price of non–fair trade products, as illustrated by the coffee market. According to TransFair, coffee importers buy directly from growers at $1.31 per pound (10 cents above prevailing market rates), or $1.51 per pound (20 cents above market rates) for organic coffee (TransFair USA, 2007). Although the prices paid by importers are not much more than the prevailing market rates, the monies go directly to the growers instead of to middlemen. As a result, the grower receives a higher price than the 40 cents per pound that they received via middlemen (Bojarski, 2002). How does that translate into cost differentials for the end consumer? Starbucks, one of the largest coffee chains in the United States, offers 1-lb. bags of fair trade coffee beans (mild blend) for $11.45 per pound compared with $9.95 per pound for comparable non–fair trade beans, a 15% difference.

Global Village and the Fair Trade Company

NEED FOR OPTIONS IN JAPAN

In 1990, Safia Minney moved from Britain to Japan because of her husband's work. While there, she became dismayed with her options for organic foods and recycling. Additionally, she found that Japan's culture was filled with excess packaging and a lack of concern for environmental and human rights issues (People Tree, 2001). As a result, Ms. Minney started distributing pamphlets that indicated where it was possible to buy organic foods and to recycle (Davis, 2003). From this effort grew Global Village, a nongovernmental organization with the goal of providing information sources for Japanese consumers to recycle and to purchase environmentally and socially friendly products.

In 1995, Ms. Minney formed Fair Trade Company, a natural outgrowth of Global Village. Whereas Global Village was formed to show consumers where to find socially friendly products, Fair Trade Company was formed to actually provide such products to consumers in Japan.

Fair Trade Company formed relationships with underprivileged people from around the world to use indigenous resources to produce clothing and handicrafts. All of the producers were paid a price—approximately 30% above the prevailing market prices—that would allow them to sustain a living for their families and to invest in their businesses (People Tree, 2001). Fair Trade Company primarily sells clothing, a product in a highly competitive and price-conscious market. The company's solution to keeping their prices down is to "work hard" (Trapp, 2002). That method is a common one among fair trade companies, where lowering workforce costs is viewed as the means to competitive pricing. For example, volunteers make up 68% of the total workforce population (excluding supermarkets) in the United States, Canada, and Japan (Fair Trade Federation, 2003) and 98% in Europe (Krier, 2001).

FORMULA FOR SUCCESS

Naturally, some people may be concerned about the quality of the clothing. As Ms. Minney explains, "If people do have an impression . . . they think they're oatmeal and miserable and made of string. The image isn't really sexy. But the clothing looks and feels great" (Davis, 2003).

Not only did Fair Trade Company have to deal with such negative images of fair trade clothes, but they also had to deal with higher prices. Despite efforts to keep costs down through hard work, Fair Trade Company's T-shirts sell for about 50% more than a consumer would typically pay for a non–fair trade shirt (Davis, 2003).

Regardless of these hurdles, Fair Trade Company experienced 40% to 50% growth per year over their first several years. Soon they launched a small catalog, which by 1999 developed into a 100-page catalog called "People Tree," listing Fair Trade Company's products (People Tree, 2001). By the end of 2002, the catalog had 20,000 customers in Japan, which, combined with sales to about 500 Japanese stores, led Fair Trade Company to annual sales of $7.4 million.

Ms. Minney explains that product quality was the key to her success in Japan. "Japan is very design led. People are not interested unless a product is decently designed and of a certain quality." Ms. Minney added that Japan's customers are only concerned about how something is produced if it looks good first (Trapp, 2002).

After gaining success in Japan, Fair Trade Company branched into the United Kingdom market in September 2000, naming the company People Tree after its catalog. After 2 years of sales in the United Kingdom with little more than word-of-mouth promotion, sales have climbed to $460,000 (Trapp, 2002).

Fair Trade Future

FAIR TRADE PRODUCT CERTIFICATIONS

Certified fair trade products are common in Europe. According to the European Fair Trade Association, nearly 81% of all products sold in Europe feature a certification on the packaging that assures consumers that proper principles were followed (Krier, 2001). Transfair is working to expand their certifications beyond a few labeled products in the United States, Canada, and Japan. There is general agreement that the certifications are having a profound effect on the industry and will become more common in the coming years (Fair Trade Federation, 2003).

FAIR TRADE CITIES

In Europe, a growing trend is to have cities certified as a "fair trade city." The Fairtrade Foundation determines the criteria and awards the designation. To earn this designation, a city must prove that shops and suppliers are committed to selling fair trade products (Hart, 2003). The European Union and the

Fairtrade Foundation have launched an international Fairtrade Town Web site in July of 2009 and there are currently almost 700 Fairtrade Towns/Cities in 18 countries worldwide (The Fairtrade Towns in Europe Project, 2009). Wales is leading the pack in the battle for fair trade city designations and has been declared the first Fairtrade nation in the world (The Fairtrade Towns in Europe Project, 2009). Ammanford became Wales's first fair trade city in July 2002. Since then, Swansea and Cardiff have moved close to the designation (Hart, 2003), and Wrexham is aiming to be the first fair trade county borough in the United Kingdom. With all of the fair trade growth in Wales, some are suggesting that Wales may become the first fair trade country in the world. However, the idea is so new that the Fairtrade Foundation has not yet determined criteria for such a designation ("Wales in the Fast Lane," 2003).

Questions for Discussion and Further Analysis

1. Which method do you think would work better for improving worldwide working conditions: voluntary methods via fair trade products or laws mandating fair working conditions for imports? What would be the benefit and drawbacks of each approach?

2. What impact do you think Fair Trade Company's higher prices have on sales? What might be some of the reasons that Fair Trade Company is paying a higher premium to producers than that paid by importers of fair trade coffee?

3. If you were consulting for People Tree, what would you suggest to help them increase their sales?

4. If you were consulting for another clothing company that wants to implement fair trade practices, how would you use the experience of People Tree to assist this company? How would you tie the company's diversity management practices to its newly initiated fair trade practices? How would you use both to improve the company's image internally (with its employees) and externally (with customers, financial institutions, and stockowners)?

5. Some might claim that the use of a high percentage of volunteers in the fair trade industry is trading one group of low-wage workers for another. What are your opinions on the topic? Is this a fair analogy? Why or why not?

Summary and Conclusion

The fourth level, *inclusion through international collaborations*, refers to the organization's positions and practices related to the fair exchange of economic goods and services and the respectful cultural relationship with individuals and groups in other countries. The exclusionary workplace operates from a framework that is ethnocentric, competition-based, and focused on narrowly defined financial and national interests, but the inclusive workplace sees value in collaborating across national borders, being pluralistic, and identifying global mutual interests.

The combination of business internationalization, worker migration, and workforce diversity creates a challenge for companies engaged in international business. The increasingly more open economic markets create opportunities for the countries with surplus workforce and underdeveloped economies to come together with countries that can finance economic endeavors and provide jobs. These conditions, however, also open up opportunities for exploitation by companies who take advantage of workers' desperation in poor regions by employing them in abhorrent conditions and subminimal payment.

There are several obstacles related to applying the principles of the inclusive workplace to international collaborations. The primary barrier is greed, which motivates companies to go beyond a fair economic exchange and to take advantage of employees or resources of a host country. Other barriers include discrimination in hiring and employment conditions and lack of respect for other national cultures, which leads to a forced implementation of the values and norms that are not appropriate for the host country. On the other hand, implementing inclusive workplace principles can help companies reap the benefits of an increasingly global marketplace by employing workers from different nationalities in their native countries. From a business point of view, diversity and nondiscrimination applied to international business contacts are crucial. Overcoming skill shortages and underutilized customer potential and improving market understanding of foreign markets are only a few of the more obvious business reasons. Finally, applying fair trade principles can improve a company's public image and its standing with customers and stockowners alike.

In order to compete in this changing environment, companies must develop intelligent systems of human resource management and open up opportunities for a diverse workforce across national boundaries. If they wish to survive and succeed in today's changing market conditions, companies need to conduct their business in a fair and ethical way while respecting other cultures.

Notes

1. Anglo American is South Africa's largest company and the world's number one in the mining industry. The quote was provided by Anglo American manager Margie Keeton (Schwartz & Gibb, 1999, p. 88).

2. In 2008, Chiquita Brands International admitted it had paid nearly $2 million in protection money to a murderous paramilitary group in Colombia that has killed or massacred thousands of people. The company said it did so to protect its employees there, but families of civilians killed by paramilitaries have faulted the company for

contributing to their death. The company's admission and the victims' allegations have tarnished the company's image (CBS *60 Minutes,* August 9, 2009. "The Price of Bananas." Retrieved December 5, 2009, from http://www.cbsnews.com/stories/1998/07/08/60minutes/main4080920.shtml).

3. Bata International, founded in 1894 by Tomáš Baťa in Zlim, is in today's Czech Republic. The company is a retailer, manufacturer, and distributor of commercial fashion footwear and accessories. Over the years, the company has grown to over 40,000 employees and over 5,000 stores. It manages a retail presence in over 50 countries and runs 33 production facilities across 22 countries. The Bata shoe organization has traditionally regarded itself as a "multidomestic" rather than a multinational enterprise and makes it a priority to contribute to the economy in any new markets it enters.

CHAPTER 16

Toward a Globally Inclusive Workplace

Putting the Pieces Together

There is only one caste—humanity.

—Pampa, 9th-century Indian poet and writer.

The previous chapters described the value basis, the practice applications, and the barriers and benefits of implementing each system level of the inclusive workplace. From the micro to the macro, these levels begin with inclusion within the organization, proceed through corporate-community relations and collaborations with state/national initiatives, and culminate with international collaborations. In this chapter, we put the different aspects of the inclusive workplace together and examine the implications for a broader vision of managing global diversity.

The Value Base for the Inclusive Workplace

The inclusive workplace is guided by a set of values that propels its policies and practices. An organization's actions, like a person's behavior, are informed by its values, whether explicit or implicit. In order to become inclusive, organizations need to evaluate their current values and norms and initiate new policies and programs that can institute needed change. For the sake of clarity, our discussion in the previous chapters highlighted the values that drive the exclusionary workplace on the one hand, and those that drive the inclusive workplace on the other. In reality, rarely do we find these extreme cases, as most organizations will be somewhere on the continuum. The chart presented in Figure 16.1 provides a summary illustration of the value schemes presented earlier for each of the system levels of the inclusive workplace. The model examines the organization's value frame on each of the four system levels (the vertical *y*-axis) and at the two extremes of the inclusion-exclusion continuum (the horizontal *x*-axis).

The first level, *diversity within work organizations,* relates to the organization's internal relations with its own employees. Whereas an exclusionary workplace is based on the perception that all workers need to conform to pre-established organizational values and norms (determined by its "mainstream"), the inclusive workplace is based on a dynamic, coevolving value frame that relies on mutual respect and equal contributions of different cultural perspectives to the organization's values and norms. The second level, *inclusion and corporate-community collaborations,* relates to the organization's sense of being a part of its surrounding community and the reciprocity embedded in that relationship. An exclusionary workplace sees minimal or no connection to its community. An inclusive workplace, on the other hand, recognizes the economic and noneconomic consequences of its presence in the community. It acknowledges the responsibility it has to ameliorating the adverse effects of this presence and to making a positive contribution to the community's well-being. The third level, *inclusion through state/national collaborations,* refers to the values that drive organizational policies with regard to disadvantaged populations such as welfare recipients, domestic violence victims, and youth in distress. The exclusionary workplace views these populations as being in the sole domain of welfare agencies and charity organizations. The inclusive workplace perceives welfare recipients seeking work, domestic violence survivors, and youth in distress as a potentially stable and upwardly mobile workforce. Finally, the fourth level, *inclusion through global collaborations,* refers to the organization's positions and practices related to the fair exchange of economic goods and services and the respectful cultural relationship with individuals, groups, and organizations in other countries. The exclusionary workplace operates from a framework that is ethnocentric and focused on narrowly defined financial and national interests. The inclusive workplace sees value in collaborating across national borders, being pluralistic, and identifying global mutual interests.

Implementation of the Inclusive Workplace

Implementing the inclusive workplace can have substantial benefits to the organization and to its employees but will present considerable barriers in the process (see Figure 16.2).

Figure 16.1 The Value Base for the Inclusive Workplace

System Level		Value Frame	
		Exclusion ← → **Inclusion**	
		Exclusion	Inclusion
Inclusion and Diversity Within Work Organizations	Individuals, Groups	Conformity to preestablished organizational values and norms that reflect the "majority" or "main-stream."	Pluralistic, coevolving organizational culture that keeps changing to reflect diversity of values and norms.
Inclusion and Corporate-Community Collaborations	Organizations, Communities	Organizational focus is intrinsic with exclusive responsibility to financial stakeholders.	Dual intrinsic and extrinsic focus with recognition of community systems as stakeholders as well.
Inclusion Through State/National Collaborations	State, Federal Government	Viewing disadvantaged groups as the domain of welfare agencies and charity organizations and treating them as disposable labor.	Treating disadvantaged groups as potentially stable, upwardly mobile employees and investing in their education and training.
Inclusion Through Global Collaborations	International, Global	Culture-specific. Ethnocentric. Intranational focus.	Pluralistic. Collaboration-based. Focus on global mutual interests.

Micro ← → Micro

Figure 16.2 Implementing the Inclusive Workplace Model

	Principles	Barriers	Benefits	
			To Individuals	To Organization
Micro				
Inclusion and Diversity Within Work Organizations	Encouraging and facilitating inclusion of employees who are different from the "mainstream"	• Discrimination • Prejudice • Perception of threat to job security	• Access to advancement and job promotions • Improved income and benefits • More decision-making power	• Business growth and productivity • Cost savings (e.g., lower turnover, less absenteeism) • Positive image with employees, customers, and financial institutions
Inclusion and Corporate-Community Collaborations	Recognizing the community as a stakeholder and directly contributing to its welfare	• Economic pressures to demonstrate profitability • Limited company vision • Lack of leadership to champion and sustain efforts	• Employment, job training • Mentorship • Improved services to the community	• Improved corporate image and reputation • Advantage in recruitment and in labor disputes • Increased employee loyalty • Strong connection between social performance and economic performance
Inclusion Through State/National Collaborations	Extending services through programs and policies aimed at assisting disadvantaged groups in society	• Shortsighted and internally focused company vision • Stereotypes, prejudice, and discrimination of disadvantaged population groups	• Employment, benefits • Job training • Advancement opportunities • Improved job prospects	• Expanded potential employee pool • Increased employee loyalty • Improved customer relations • A more attractive value-based corporate image
Inclusion Through Global Collaborations	Conducting business fairly through respecting and accommodating other national cultures	• Greed—going beyond fair trade and exploiting others • Discrimination • Lack of respect for other nations and cultures	• Job opportunities, both for local residents and for expatriates • Improved health and safety conditions	• Expanded geographic markets • Improved industrial relations and preventing litigation • Increased economic activities • Better marketing to international customers • Improved corporate image with customers, financial institutions, and stockowners
Macro				

At level I—inclusion through diversity within work organizations—an inclusive workplace allows, encourages, and facilitates the inclusion of individual employees who are different from the mainstream in the organizational information networks and decision-making processes. The main benefits at this level include better access to promotion and benefits as well as improved job satisfaction and well-being for individual employees. At the organizational level, companies may experience lower turnover and reduced absenteeism as a result of improved job satisfaction among employees, better access to high-potential employees who will be attracted to their organizational culture, and greater appeal to clients of diverse backgrounds. The likely obstacles to implementing inclusive policies and practices at level I include prejudice, overt and covert discrimination, and people's perceptions of group competition for access to power within the organization.

At level II—inclusion through corporate-community relations—an inclusive workplace recognizes the community as a legitimate stakeholder and directly and actively collaborates with community organizations in an effort to contribute to the community's welfare, recognizing that the corporation's own well-being is tied to it. Benefits to individuals in the community include access to opportunities like job training, employment, and additional services that community members would not otherwise have. The organization's tangible rewards include improved corporate image within as well as outside the community, which can translate into advantages in recruitment and avoid or mitigate the potentially negative results of labor disputes. Shortsighted and internally focused corporate vision and economic pressures to demonstrate short-term profitability are among the main barriers to implementing inclusive policies and programs at this level.

At level III—inclusion through state/national collaborations—companies are extending services through programs and policies aimed at assisting disadvantaged groups in society. The focus of the inclusionary policies and programs at this level is on social class—though social class is often related to gender and race/ethnicity group membership. Benefits to individuals often include job training that may lead to employment with the company or improved job prospects with other employers. Work organizations may expand their potential employee pool as a result of these policies, gain a loyal workforce, and improve customer relations, particularly among the disadvantaged groups but also among other clients who care about social issues. The main barriers to implementing inclusive policies at this level include shortsighted and internally focused company vision and stereotyping disadvantaged groups as unstable and disposable labor.

Finally, at level IV—inclusion through international collaborations—a company is inclusive toward its *entire* workforce, both locally and overseas, particularly in developing countries. It avoids the temptation to exploit uneducated employees in poor regions and conducts business in a fair and ethical way that respects and accommodates other cultures. Benefits to individuals in the host countries include access to job training and employment that may otherwise not be available and improved life conditions for individuals, their families, and the communities in which they live. Treating their employees fairly and respectfully also benefits organizations, as they are able to generate goodwill from both their employees and potential customers, gain a loyal and committed workforce, and expand their economic activities. The main barriers related to applying the principles of the inclusive workplace with respect to the international collaborations are greed, cultural and national difficulties in communication, and unfair or inappropriate consideration of diversity in employment conditions of both local employees and expatriates.

Conclusion

The economic, social, and demographic trends described in Part I of the book create an environment that is fertile ground for intergroup conflicts, as explained in Part II of the book. The legislative and social policy initiatives taken by individual countries, and by the international community as a whole, mitigate potential harmful effects and define "the rules of the game" for work organizations. It is important to understand, though, that these trends are not only a backdrop or context for organizations to consider, they also define the *scope* of what companies need to consider as their domain when they design diversity policies and programs. In order to avoid the pitfalls and reap the benefits of a diverse workforce, employers need to adopt a *broader vision of inclusion,* a vision that encompasses not only the organization itself but also its surrounding community and its national and international environment.

An inclusive workplace allows, encourages, and facilitates the inclusion of individual employees who are different from the mainstream in the organizational information networks and decision-making processes at each of the four levels—from the organization, through the community and state, to the international. Full-fledged inclusion as opposed to, for example, sensitivity training initiatives necessitates a radical upending of basic assumptions, patterns, and structures. An organization that does not confront the daunting and complex task of moving toward an inclusive workplace cannot set appropriate diversity-related goals. Valuing diversity goes beyond the golden rule of treating others as you wish to be treated yourself because it involves a higher behavior, one that is receiver-centered rather than self-centered. Sometimes called the "platinum rule," valuing diversity involves treating others as *they* wish to be treated.

This inclusive workplace offers a broad vision for managing diversity in today's global economy, one that contains individuals and groups that have a direct or indirect stake in the organization, such as potential future employees, customers, and investors, all of whom are also increasingly diverse. Although some companies, primarily in North America and Europe, have already introduced diversity initiatives, the inclusive workplace offers a comprehensive and multilevel approach that ensures fair and inclusive treatment of individuals who are different from the mainstream. Changing the organization's culture from merely "diversity tolerant" or "respectful of diversity" to *truly inclusive* can be done through deliberate actions at the four system levels suggested in this book. The limitation of this approach is rooted in its ambitious scope. As demonstrated in the case studies, although some smaller companies can and do adopt inclusive initiatives, it is primarily midsize to large companies with adequate resources that are able to engage in all four levels of inclusion. With the growing number of larger and multinational companies all over the world, however, this model can potentially benefit individual employees, their families and communities, and work organizations.

The goal of diversity management is not to assimilate people of diverse characteristics into the dominant culture but to create a social, legislative, and organizational environment that respects and values individual differences. The conventional assimilation paradigm used the industrial melting pot image—individuals were expected to shed their unique group affiliations and cultural characteristics in order to take on the majority culture's values, norms, and behaviors. In depicting diversity management, I propose an image from the art world—the *painter's palette*. Like colors, when people are forced to blend and give up their unique characteristics, the result is a dull gray. Allowed to display their true colors, they shine brightly and together create an inspiring work of art.

Appendix

Research Measures: Scales of Inclusion and Diversity

The Mor Barak Inclusion-Exclusion Scale

SCALE ITEMS

1	2	3	4	5	6
Strongly Disagree	Moderately Disagree	Slightly Disagree	Slightly Agree	Moderately Agree	Strongly Agree

1. I have influence in decisions taken by my work group regarding our tasks................................. ☐ 1 ☐ 2 ☐ 3 ☐ 4 ☐ 5 ☐ 6

2. My coworkers openly share work-related information with me. .... ☐ 1 ☐ 2 ☐ 3 ☐ 4 ☐ 5 ☐ 6

3. I am typically involved and invited to actively participate in work-related activities of my work group. .... ☐ 1 ☐ 2 ☐ 3 ☐ 4 ☐ 5 ☐ 6

4. I am able to influence decisions that affect my organization. .... ☐ 1 ☐ 2 ☐ 3 ☐ 4 ☐ 5 ☐ 6

5. I am usually among the last to know about important changes in the organization (R). .... ☐ 1 ☐ 2 ☐ 3 ☐ 4 ☐ 5 ☐ 6

6. I am usually invited to important meetings in my organization. .... ☐ 1 ☐ 2 ☐ 3 ☐ 4 ☐ 5 ☐ 6

7. My supervisor often asks for my opinion before making important decisions. .... □ 1 □ 2 □ 3 □ 4 □ 5 □ 6

8. My supervisor does not share information with me (R). .... □ 1 □ 2 □ 3 □ 4 □ 5 □ 6

9. I am invited to actively participate in review and evaluation meetings with my supervisor. .... □ 1 □ 2 □ 3 □ 4 □ 5 □ 6

10. I am often invited to contribute my opinion in meetings with management higher than my immediate supervisor. .... □ 1 □ 2 □ 3 □ 4 □ 5 □ 6

11. I frequently receive communication from management higher than my immediate supervisor (i.e., memos, e-mails). .... □ 1 □ 2 □ 3 □ 4 □ 5 □ 6

12. I am often invited to participate in meetings with management higher than my immediate supervisor. ... □ 1 □ 2 □ 3 □ 4 □ 5 □ 6

13. I am often asked to contribute in planning social activities not directly related to my job function. ...... □ 1 □ 2 □ 3 □ 4 □ 5 □ 6

14. I am always informed about informal social activities and company social events. .... □ 1 □ 2 □ 3 □ 4 □ 5 □ 6

15. I am rarely invited to join my coworkers when they go out for lunch or drinks after work (R). .... □ 1 □ 2 □ 3 □ 4 □ 5 □ 6

OVERVIEW

The Mor Barak Inclusion-Exclusion Scale (2005)[1] measures the degree to which individuals feel a part of critical organizational processes such as access to information, involvement and participation with the organization, and influence in the decision-making process. It uses a matrix system with five system levels (work group, organization, supervisor, higher management, and social/informal) by three inclusion dimensions (decision making, information networks, and participation/involvement). The measure includes 15 items that evaluate a person's sense of inclusion in relation to the following five system levels:

1. work group (questions 1–3)
2. organization (questions 4–6)
3. supervisor (questions 7–9)
4. higher management (questions 10–12)
5. social/informal (questions 13–15)

In each of these levels, the respondents are asked to evaluate their inclusion in the following three dimensions:

a. The decision-making process (questions 1, 4, 7, 10, 13)

b. Information networks (questions 2, 5, 8, 11, 14)

c. Level of participation/involvement (questions 3, 6, 9, 12, 15)

The 15 scale items are summed to create a composite inclusion-exclusion score, with three reverse-scored questions (items 5, 8, 15—noted by the letter R next to them) to prevent response sets in answering the questions. Higher scores on the scale reflect a higher sense of inclusion.

Psychometric Properties and Previous Research Utilizing the Measure

Accumulating research demonstrates both the validity and reliability of the measure across diverse population groups. The measure showed good internal consistency in a sample of 3,400 employees of diverse racial and ethnic backgrounds in a California-based high-tech company with Cronbach's alpha of .88 (Mor Barak & Levin, 2002). Utilizing the inclusion scale in a multivariate model, the study demonstrated that women and members of racial/ethnic minorities were more likely to feel excluded, and that exclusion was linked to job dissatisfaction and a lower sense of well-being. A series of cross-national studies demonstrated the resiliency of the measure across cultures. In a cross-cultural study with samples, of employees from similar high-tech companies in the United States and Israel, the inclusion-exclusion measure again demonstrated good internal consistency with Cronbach's alpha of .90 and .81 for the two national samples, respectively (Mor Barak, Findler, & Wind, 2001). The theoretical factor structure fit both samples well (the Bartlett's Test of Sphericity was 1342.30 and 406.72, both at $p < .001$, and the Kaiser-Meyer-Olkin measure was .87 and .78, respectively, for the two samples). The combined factors accounted for 65% and 67% of the variance in the two samples, respectively. A second study with these samples tested a multivariate model and demonstrated that ethnicity, inclusion/exclusion, perception of fairness, job stress, social support, and job satisfaction were all significant correlates of employee well-being (Mor Barak, Findler, & Wind, 2003). Utilizing only the national sample drawn from a high-tech corporation in Israel, a third study tested a theoretical model using structural equations statistical methodology. The study utilized the 10 items related to decision-making processes and information networks from a 15-item inclusion-exclusion scale and documented the measure's strong internal consistency with a Cronbach's alpha of .81. The findings demonstrated several significant associations between diversity and organizational culture such as fairness and inclusion, employee well-being, job satisfaction, and organizational commitment (Findler, Wind, & Mor Barak, 2007). An earlier version of the scale (Mor Barak & Cherin, 1998) showed strong internal consistency (Cronbach's alpha = .87) and appropriate correlations indicating convergent validity ($r = .63, p < .05$) with Porter and Lawler's (1968) organizational satisfaction, and discriminant validity ($r \cong .32, p < .05$) with Porter's work alienation scale (Price & Mueller, 1986).

Examining perception of inclusion among Korean employees, another international study matched a sample of 381 employees with their 320 supervisors in one of the largest corporations in Korea (Cho & Mor Barak, 2008). The inclusion-exclusion scale again demonstrated good internal consistency with a Cronbach's alpha of .83. Findings from the study indicated that perception of inclusion was strongly related to job satisfaction, organizational commitment, and job performance (as evaluated by the employees' supervisors) among the Korean employees.

Another study examining how perceived inclusion affects teen volunteer's organizational satisfaction illustrated the good internal consistency of the Mor Barak inclusion-exclusion scale (Bortree & Waters, 2008). Cronbach alphas of the three distinct factors ranged from .70 to .82. The finding revealed that inclusion was strongly associated with organizational satisfaction. Acquavita, Pittman, Gibbons, and Castellanos-Brown (2009) again demonstrated high internal consistency of the inclusion-exclusion scale with a Cronbach's alpha of .91. The authors examined the relationship among minority status, workplace racial composition, perceived inclusion, organization diversity, and job satisfaction for social work professionals employed in organizations through the use of a national Internet-based survey. The results showed that perceived inclusion was positively associated with job satisfaction (Acquavita, Pittman, Gibbons, & Castellanos-Brown, 2009).

Findings from a study carried out by Matz-Costa, Pitt-Catosouphes, Besen, and Lynch (2009) suggest that perceived inclusion diminished after the 2007 economic downturn and appeared to be lower among individuals who had decreased job security as a result of the economic crisis. The study utilized 6 of the 15 inclusion-exclusion scale items.

Longitudinal studies conducted in three locations in the United States—California, Massachusetts, and Texas—demonstrated viable relationships between diversity, inclusion, and employee retention in nonprofit public agencies. One of these studies used structural equations modeling to provide empirical support to a comprehensive theory-based model of the relationship between diversity, inclusion, individual well-being, job satisfaction, organizational commitment, and turnover, controlling for stress, perception of fairness, and social support (Mor Barak, Levin, Nissly, & Lane, 2006). Another longitudinal study focused on the relationship between perception of dissimilarity and the inclusion dimension of work group involvement, using the five-item participation/involvement dimension from the original 15-item inclusion measure. The study demonstrated high internal consistency of the scale items with Cronbach's alpha of .89 and .90 for Time 1 and Time 2, respectively. The findings suggested that visible and informational dissimilarity were negatively related to work group involvement. Group openness to diversity was found to moderate the relationship between visible and informational dissimilarity and work group involvement (Hobman, Bordia, & Gallois, 2004).

The Diversity Perceptions Scale

SCALE ITEMS

1	2	3	4	5	6
Strongly Disagree	Moderately Disagree	Slightly Disagree	Slightly Agree	Moderately Agree	Strongly Agree

1. I feel that I have been treated differently here because of my race, gender, sexual orientation, religion, or age (R). .... ☐ 1 ☐ 2 ☐ 3 ☐ 4 ☐ 5 ☐ 6

2. Managers here have a track record of hiring and promoting employees objectively, regardless of their race, gender, sexual orientation, religion, or age. .... ☐ 1 ☐ 2 ☐ 3 ☐ 4 ☐ 5 ☐ 6

3. Managers here give feedback and evaluate employees fairly, regardless of employees' race, gender, sexual orientation, religion, age, or social background. .... ☐ 1 ☐ 2 ☐ 3 ☐ 4 ☐ 5 ☐ 6

4. Managers here make layoff decisions fairly, regardless of factors such as employees' race, gender, age, or social background. .... ☐ 1 ☐ 2 ☐ 3 ☐ 4 ☐ 5 ☐ 6

5. Managers interpret human resource policies (such as sick leave) fairly for all employees.. ☐ 1 ☐ 2 ☐ 3 ☐ 4 ☐ 5 ☐ 6

6. Managers give assignments based on the skills and abilities of employees.. ☐ 1 ☐ 2 ☐ 3 ☐ 4 ☐ 5 ☐ 6

7. Management here encourages the formation of employee network support groups. .... ☐ 1 ☐ 2 ☐ 3 ☐ 4 ☐ 5 ☐ 6

8. There is a mentoring program in use here that identifies and prepares all minority and female employees for promotion. .... ☐ 1 ☐ 2 ☐ 3 ☐ 4 ☐ 5 ☐ 6

9. The "old boys' network" is alive and well here (R)........ ☐ 1 ☐ 2 ☐ 3 ☐ 4 ☐ 5 ☐ 6

10. The company spends enough money and time on
diversity awareness and related training. .... ☐ 1 ☐ 2 ☐ 3 ☐ 4 ☐ 5 ☐ 6

11. Knowing more about cultural norms of diverse groups
would help me be more effective in my job. .... ☐ 1 ☐ 2 ☐ 3 ☐ 4 ☐ 5 ☐ 6

12. I think that diverse viewpoints add value.................... ☐ 1 ☐ 2 ☐ 3 ☐ 4 ☐ 5 ☐ 6

13. I believe diversity is a strategic business issue............. ☐ 1 ☐ 2 ☐ 3 ☐ 4 ☐ 5 ☐ 6

14. I feel at ease with people from backgrounds
different from my own. .... ☐ 1 ☐ 2 ☐ 3 ☐ 4 ☐ 5 ☐ 6

15. I am afraid to disagree with members of other
groups for fear of being called prejudiced (R)............ ☐ 1 ☐ 2 ☐ 3 ☐ 4 ☐ 5 ☐ 6

16. Diversity issues keep some work teams here from
performing to their maximum effectiveness (R). .... ☐ 1 ☐ 2 ☐ 3 ☐ 4 ☐ 5 ☐ 6

OVERVIEW

The diversity perception scale examines employees' views about the diversity climate in the organization (Mor Barak, Cherin, & Berkman, 1998). It includes 16 items with two dimensions: the organizational and the personal, each containing two factors, as follows:

I. Organizational division
   a. Organizational fairness factor (items 1–6)
   b. Organizational inclusion factor (items 7–10)

II. Personal dimension
   c. Personal diversity value factor (items 11–13)
   d. Personal comfort with diversity (items 14–16)

The organizational dimension refers to the perception of management's policies and procedures that affect members of minority groups and women—such as discrimination or preferential treatment in hiring and promotion procedures (factor a). It also refers to management actions that affect inclusion or exclusion of women and members of minority groups—such as mentorship programs or the preservation of the "old boys' network" (factor b). The personal dimension refers to individuals' views of the importance of diversity to work groups and to the organization (factor c) and their level of comfort in interactions with members of other groups (factor d).

The 16 scale items are summed to create a composite diversity perceptions score with four reverse-scored questions (items 1, 9, 15, 16, noted by the letter

R next to them) to prevent response sets in answering the questions. Higher scores on the scale reflect a more positive perception of diversity climate. The dimensions and factors can be summed and analyzed separately to gain more insight into the composition of employees' views of the diversity climate.

Psychometric Properties and Previous Research Utilizing the Measure

The measure focuses on perceptions because it has been documented that behavior is driven by perceptions of reality. For example, Eisenberger, Fasolo, and Davis-LaMastro (1990) found that employees' perceptions of being valued by an organization were associated with their conscientiousness, job involvement, and innovativeness. What people believe is of vital importance, whether or not their beliefs are consistent with reality.

The questionnaire was developed based on a review of the literature, similar surveys used in other companies, and items solicited from various members of the organization reflecting issues that they felt were important to understanding the organizational diversity environment. Items covered the personal dimension (e.g., "I am afraid to disagree with members of other groups for fear of being called prejudiced") and the organizational dimension (e.g., "Management takes seriously the opinions, ideas, and viewpoints of minorities and women"). Item contributors included human resource managers, project managers, midlevel managers, and line workers, both men and women of diverse racial/ethnic background. After the first pool of about 100 items was collected, a pretest of the items was conducted by asking a selected group of workers (again representing various levels of management, occupations, genders, and racial/ethnic backgrounds) to answer the questions and critique the content, wording, and style. A diversity committee of a California-headquartered international company, composed of representatives of ethnic groups, both men and women from different functions in the organization, reviewed the items for face validity. This committee served as a representative liaison group to help develop and conduct an empathic survey (Alderfer, 1980; Alderfer & Brown, 1972). This process was done twice and resulted in a pool of 16 questions with a 6-point Likert-type scale ranging from "strongly agree" to "strongly disagree" with an additional category of "can't answer."

The overall scale, as well as each of its factors, showed strong to adequate internal consistency with Cronbach's alphas of .83, .86, .80, .77, and .71, respectively (Mor Barak, Cherin, & Berkman, 1998). The factor structure was tested on a sample of 2,686 employees in a California-headquartered international high-tech company with a diverse workforce. The factors fit the data well— Bartlett's Test of Sphericity was 4593.15 at $p < .001$, and the Kaiser-Meyer-Olkin measure was .90 (Kaiser, 1970; Norusis, 1993). The four factors had Eigen values between 1.2 and 5.4, explaining 57.1% of the variance (factor I—29.9%; factor II—13.1%; factor III—7.4%; factor IV—6.6%).

The results of the study examining ethnic and gender differences in employee perceptions of organizational diversity climate revealed that, overall, members of the majority group of the organization (White men) had more positive overall perceptions ("Things are good as they are") than women and members of racial and ethnic minority groups ("More needs to be done"). Specifically, White men perceived the organization as more fair and inclusive than did White women or members of racial and ethnic minority groups (both men and women). Conversely, White women and members of racial and ethnic minority groups saw more value in, and felt more comfortable with, diversity than did White men (Mor Barak, Cherin, & Berkman, 1998).

The measure has been used by researchers in various studies in different contexts and with diverse population groups (e.g., testing management skills, examining diversity climate in health care organizations, and testing leadership in a global context).

Caldwell, Mack, Johnson, and Biderman (2002) utilized the Diversity Perception Scale in a sample of 202 African American women employed at a national organization. The study examined the relationships between diversity, affective commitment, job satisfaction, and intention to leave. The measures used in the study included three of the four scale factors with the exception of the personal comfort with diversity factor. The organizational fairness and organizational inclusion factors were found to have good internal consistency, with Cronbach's alpha of .81 and .67, respectively. However, the personal diversity value dimension yielded a very low Cronbach's alpha of .35. The study's findings indicated that there are significant relationships between organizational fairness, inclusion, job satisfaction, affective commitment, and turnover intention. Examining interaction effects, the researchers report that respondents who reported high perceived personal diversity also reported strong associations between perceived organizational fairness and perceived organizational inclusion, as well as between affective commitment and intention to leave (Caldwell, Mack, Johnson, & Biderman, 2002).

Several studies have utilized the Diversity Perception scale as criteria for the development of other scales measuring diversity perception (e.g., McKay, Avery, & Morris, 2008, 2009; McKay, Avery, Tonidandel, Morris, & et al., 2007; Pugh, Dietz, Brief, & Wiley, 2008). For example, McKay et al. (2007) used nine items to assess how managers perceive the value of diversity in organizations and considered the similarity of their scale to the earlier version of this diversity scale. One item utilized by Mackay, Avery and Morris (2008, 2009) was similar to the organizational fairness subscale. The authors reported that the correlation between their measure and the Diversity Perceptions scale provides support for the validity of their scale. Similarly, Pugh, Dietz, Brief, and Wiley (2008) used the Diversity Perceptions scale as a guide to obtain the validity of their scale. Finally, Johnson (2008) suggests using the Diversity Perceptions scale as a self-assessment tool to gauge one's ethical leadership with respect to the moral aspects of diversity and exclusion (pp. 308–311).

Note

1. Revised and expanded from the earlier versions of the Inclusion-Exclusion and Diversity Perceptions Scales (Mor Barak & Cherin, 1998; Mor Barak, Cherin & Berkman, 1998; Mor Barak, Findler, & Wind, 2001; Mor Barak & Levin, 2002).

References

Aaronson, S. A., & Zimmerman, J. M. (2006). Fair trade: How Oxfam presented a systemic approach to poverty, development, human rights, and trade. *Human Rights Quarterly, 28*(4), 998–1030.

Abell, J. P., Havelaar, A. E., & Dankoor, M. M. (1997). *The documentation and evaluation of anti-discrimination training in the Netherlands.* Geneva: International Labour Organization.

About the Firm. (2002–2003). Retrieved December 8, 2003, from www.haynesboone .com/about/about.asp

Abrams, D. (1992). Processes of social identification. In G. M. Breakwell (Ed.), *Social psychology of identity and the self concept* (pp. 57–99). London: Academic/Survey University Press.

Abrams, D., & Hogg, M. A. (1988). Comments on motivational status of self esteem in social identity and intergroup discrimination. *European Journal of Social Psychology, 18,* 317–332.

Abrams, D., Hogg, M. A., & Marques, J. M. (2004). A social psychological framework for understanding social inclusion and exclusion. In D. Abrams (Ed.), *Social Psychology of Inclusion and Exclusion.* UK: Psychology Press.

Acquavita, S. P., Pittman, J., Gibbons, M., & Castellanos-Brown, K. (2009). Personal and organizational diversity factors' impact on social workers' job satisfaction: Results from a national internet-based survey. *Administration in Social Work, 33*(2), 151–166.

Aczel, D. (1999). *God's equation: Einstein, relativity and the expanding universe.* New York: Four Walls Eight Windows.

Adams, J. S. (1965). Inequity in social exchange. In L. Berkowitz (Ed.), *Advances in experimental social psychology* (Vol. 2, pp. 267–299). New York: Academic.

Adamson, J. (2000). *The Denny's story: How a company in crisis resurrected its good name.* New York: Wiley.

Adarand Constructors v. Pena (1995).

Adler, N. J. (1991). *International dimensions of organizational behavior.* Belmont, CA: Wadsworth.

Adler, N. J., & Gundersen, A. (2008). *International dimensions of organizational behavior.* Case Western Reserve University: Thomson.

Ailon, G. (2008). Mirror, mirror on the wall: Culture's consequences in a value test of its own design. *Academy of Management Review, 33*(4), 885–904.

Alba, R., & Silberman, R. (2002). Decolonization immigrations and the social origins of the second generation: The case of North Africans in France. *The International Migration Review, 36*(4), 1169–1193.

Alderfer, C. P. (1980). The methodology of organizational diagnosis. *Professional Psychology, 11*(3), 459–468.

Alderfer, C. P. (1986). An intergroup perspective on group dynamics. In J. W. Lorsch (Ed.), *Handbook of Organizational Behavior* (pp. 190–222). Englewood Cliffs, NJ: Prentice Hall.

Alderfer, C. P., Alderfer, C. J., Tucker, L., & Tucker, R. C. (1980). Diagnosing race relations in management. *Journal of Applied Behavioral Science, 16*, 135–166.

Alderfer, C. P., & Brown, L. D. (1972). Designing an empathic questionnaire for organizational research. *Journal of Applied Psychology, 56*(6), 456–460.

Alderfer, C. P., & Smith, K. K. (1982). Studying intergroup relations embedded in organizations. *Administrative Science Quarterly, 27*(1), 35–65.

Allport, G. W. (1954). *The nature of prejudice.* New York: Doubleday, Anchor.

Allport, G.W. (1979). *The nature of prejudice* (25th anniversary ed.). Reading, MA: Addison-Wesley Publishing Company.

Alperson, M. (1993, May 2). Profile/Mackie McLeod; Helping Lotus do the right thing in South Africa, *The New York Times*. Retrieved December 5, 2009, from http://www.nytimes.com/1993/05/02/business/profile-mackie-mcleod-helping-lotus-do-the-right-thing-in-south-africa.html

Alsop, R. J. (2004). *The 18 immutable laws of corporate reputation: Creating, protecting, and repairing your most valuable asset.* New York: Free Press.

Al-Tuhaih, S. M. (1986). The vicious cycle of manpower in Kuwait. In P. J. Montana & G. S. Roukis (Eds.), *Workforce management in the Arabian peninsula: Forces affecting development.* New York: Greenwood.

Amnesty International. (2003). Criminalizing homosexuality: A licence to torture. Retrieved September 14, 2003, from http://web.amnesty.org/aidoc/ai.nsf/6e57ed407c06502580256d57004ab6c1/dc31f264b72fabf280256a48003c810c/$FILE/ch1.pdf

Anand, S. (2003, May 14). Beat those blues. Retrieved December 3, 2003, from www.hindustantimes.com/2003/May/14/674_248122,00310003.htm

Angel de Prada, M., Pereda, C., & Actis, W. (1997). *Anti-discrimination training activities in Spain.* Geneva: International Labour Organization.

Aparna, J. (2006). The influence of organizational demography on the external networking behavior of teams. *Academy of Management Review, 31*(3), 583–597.

Appelrouth, S., & Desfor Edles, L. (2007). *Classical and contemporary sociological theory* (Ch. 8: George Herbert Mead, pp. 311–347). Thousand Oaks, CA: Pine Forge Press.

Arnold, J. (2003, October 10). Why economists don't fly Concorde. *BBC News*. Retrieved September 12, 2004, from http://news.bbc.co.uk/2/hi/business/2935337.stm

Arnold, W. (2002, October 16). Scandal lets Malaysia prove its mettle. *New York Times.* W1. [An excerpt of the article can be found at http://query.nytimes.com/gst/]

Arrow, K. J. (1998). What has economics to say about racial discrimination? *The Journal of Economic Perspective, 12*(2), 91–100.

Arrow, K. J. (1973). The theory of discrimination. In O. Ashenfelter & A. Rees (Eds.), *Discrimination in labor markets* (pp. 3–33). Princeton, NJ: Princeton University Press.

Ashford, J. B., LeCroy, C. W., & Lortie, K. L. (2009). *Human behavior in the social environment: A multidimensional perspective.* Belmont, CA: Thomson Brooks/Cole.

Ashforth, B. E., & Mael, F. S. (1989). Social identity theory and the organization. *Academy of Management, 14*, 20–39.

Asian Business Coalition on AIDS. (2003). *Case study 2: Haiha-Kotobuki Export Company.* Retrieved December 4, 2003, from www.abconaids.org/asp/view.asp?PageID=47&SiteID= 6&LangID=0&MenuID=108&SponsorID=50

AstraZeneca United Kingdom. (2004). About us. Retrieved May 26, 2004, from www
.astrazeneca.co.uk/azcareers/workinghere/diversity.asp

Athukorala, P. (1986). *Sri Lanka's experience with international contract migration and the reintegration of return migrants* (working papers of the ILO International Migration Programme). Geneva: ILO.

Auclair, M. (1992). Out in Africa: Going where no communicator has gone before. *Communication World, 9*(3), 43–45.

Australian Bureau of Statistics. (2007). Population Distribution, Aboriginal and Torres Strait Islander Australians, 2006. Retrieved December 4, 2009, from http://www
.abs.gov.au/AUSSTATS/abs@.nsf/Latestproducts/4705.0Media%20Release12006?open
document&tabname=Summary&prodno=4705.0&issue=2006&num=&view=

Australian Employment Services. (2001). Indigenous employment policy. Retrieved February 27, 2004, from http://www.workplace.gov.au/Workplace/ESDisplay/
0,1282,a0%3D0%26a1%3D537%26a2%3D524,00.html

Australian Employment Services. (2002, September 5). Eurest—a natural corporate leader. *Corporate Leaders for Indigenous Employment Bulletin.*

Australian government rules out Aboriginal compensation. (2001, June 28). *Agence France Presse.* Retrieved September 13, 2004, from http://web.lexis-nexis.com/
universe/document

Automatic Data Processing [ADP]. (n.d.). *Diversity statement.* Retrieved December 8, 2003, from http://nas.adp.com/about/diversity_statement.html

Award over racism upheld. (2001, October 25). *The Los Angeles Times,* pt. 2, p. 1.

Aycan, Z., Al-Hamadi, A. B., Davis, A., & Budhwar, P. (2007). Cultural orientations and preferences for HRM policies and practices: The case of Oman. *The International Journal of Human Resource Management, 18*(2), 11.

Ayman, R., & Chemers, M. M. (1983). Relationship of supervisory behavior ratings to work group effectiveness and subordinate satisfaction among Iranian managers. *Journal of Applied Psychology, 68,* 338–341.

Baga-Reyes, V. (2003, November 2). Caregiving is Filipinos' new ticket to overseas jobs. *Philippine Daily Inquirer.* Retrieved September 12, 2004, from www.inq7.net/lif/
2003/nov/02/lif_1–1.htm

Baldwin, M. W. (1992). Relational schemas and the processing of social information. *Psychological Bulletin, 112*(3), 461–484.

Baldwin, M. W., & Dandeneau, S. D. (2005). Understanding and modifying the relational schemas underlying insecurity. In M. W. Baldwin (Ed.), *Interpersonal Cognition* (pp. 33–61). New York: Guilford.

Barbosa, I., & Cabral-Cardoso, C. (2008). Managing diversity in academic organizations: A challenge to organizational culture. *Women in Management Review, 22*(4), 274–288.

Barefoot College provides model of self-development at village level. (2003, March 10). *Global Village News and Resources Issue 57.* Retrieved December 11, 2003, from http://gvnr.com/57/1.htm

Barnes, R. (2009). Justices Rule for White Firemen In Bias Lawsuit, *Washington Post,* June 30. Retrieved July 24, 2009, from http://www.washingtonpost.com/wp-dyn/
content/article/2009/06/29/AR2009062901608.html

Bar-Tal, D. (1997). Formation and change of ethnic and national stereotypes: An integrative model. *International Journal of Intercultural Relations, 21*(4), 491–523.

Bar-Tal, D., & Labin, D. (2001). The effect of a major event on stereotyping: Terrorist attacks in Israel and Israeli adolescents' perceptions of Palestinians, Jordanians and Arabs. *European Journal of Social Psychology, 31,* 1–17.

Bartlett, C. A., & Ghoshal, S. (1998). *Managing across borders: The transnational solution.* Boston: Harvard Business School Press.

Bartlett, C.A., & Ghoshal, S. (2002). *Managing across borders: The transnational solution* (2nd ed.). Boston: Harvard Business School Press.

Bartlett, F. C. (1932). *Remembering: An experimental and social study.* Cambridge, UK: Cambridge University Press.

Bartlett, F. C. (1958). *Thinking.* New York: Basic Books.

The Independent [London]. 28 January 2008. Nicholas Birch. "Turkey Divided over Headscarf Ban Decision." <http://www.independent.co.uk/news/europe/turkey-divided-over-headscarf-ban-decision-774865.html> [Accessed July 15th 2009]

Baskerville, R. F. (2003). Hofstede never studied culture. *Accounting, Organizations and Society,* 28: 1–14.

Baugh, J. (1983). *Black street speech: The history, structure, and survival.* Austin: University of Texas Press.

Baumeister, R. F., & Leary, M. R. (1995). The need to belong: Desire for interpersonal attachments as a fundamental human motivation. *Psychological Bulletin, 117,* 497–529.

BBC News. (2008, February 13). Australia apology to Aborigines. Retrieved on December 4, 2009, from: http://news.bbc.co.uk/2/hi/7241965.stm

BBC News., Muslim Veils. Retrieved July 15, 2009, from http://news.bbc.co.uk/2/shared/spl/hi/pop_ups/05/europe_muslim_veils/html/1.stm

Becker, G. (1957). *The economics of discrimination.* Chicago: University of Chicago Press.

Becker, G. S. (1971). *The economics of discrimination* (2nd ed.). Chicago: University of Chicago Press.

Beggs, J. J. (1995). The institutional environment: Implications for race and gender inequality in the U.S. labor market. *American Sociological Review, 60,* 612–633.

Bell, E. (1990). The bicultural life experience of career-oriented Black women. *Journal of Organizational Behavior, 11,* 459–478.

Bell, E., & Nkomo, S. M. (2003). Our separate ways: Black and White women and the struggle for professional identity. *Diversity Factor* (Online). *11*(1), 11–15.

Bell, E. L. (1992). Myths, stereotypes, and realities of Black women: A personal reflection. *Journal of Applied Behavioral Sciences, 28*(3), 363–376.

Bell, E. L. (2004). Myths, stereotypes and realities of Black women. *Journal of Applied Behavioral Science, 40*(2), 146–159.

Bell, E. L. J. E., & Nkomo, S. M. (2001). *Our separate ways: Black and White women and the struggle for professional identity.* Boston: Harvard Business School Press.

Bellah, R. N., Madsen, R., Sullivan, W. M., Swidler, A., & Tipton, S. M. (1985). *Habits of the heart: Individualism and commitment in American life.* New York: Harper & Row.

Benedict, R. (1989). *Patterns of cultures.* Boston: Mariners Books. (Original work published in 1934)

Benioff, M., & Southwick, K. (2004). *Compassionate capitalism: How corporations can make doing good an integral part of doing well.* Franklin Lakes, NJ: Career Press.

Bennington, L., & Wein, R. (2000). Anti-discrimination legislation in Australia: Fair, effective, efficient or irrelevant? *International Journal of Manpower, 21*(1), 21–32.

Benz v. Compania Naviera Hidalgo, S. A., 353 U.S. 138, 147 (1957).

Berlyne, D. E. (1968). American and European psychology. *American Psychologist, 23,* 447–452.

Bernstein, B. (1975). *Class, codes, and control: Theoretical studies toward a sociology of language.* New York: Schoken.

Bernstein, E., & McRae, A. V. (1973). The effects of group membership: The effects of shared threat and prejudice in racially mixed groups. In R. J. Ofsho (Ed.), *Interpersonal behavior in small groups.* Englewood Cliffs, NJ: Prentice Hall.

Bertrand, M., & Mullainathan, S. (2004). Are Emily and Greg more employable than Lakisha and Jamal? *American Economic Review, 94*(4), 991–1013.

Best companies for minorities. (2003, July 7). *Fortune*, 103–120.

Bhagat, R. S. (2002). Book review of *Culture's consequences: Comparing values, behaviors, institutions, and organizations across nations* (2nd ed.). *Academy of Management Review, 27*, 460–462.

Bhargava, A. (1986). The Bhopal incident and Union Carbide: Ramifications of an industrial accident. *Bulletin of Concerned Asian Scholars, 18*(4), 1–18.

Bhattacharjee, A. (2003, May 3). The price of Malaysia's palm oil expansion. Retrieved December 6, 2003, from www.earthisland.org/borneo/news/articles/030502article.html

Bider, B. (2003, November 18). Oil palm estates damage environment. *The Jakarta Post.* Retrieved September 12, 2004, from www.thejakartapost.com/yesterdaydetail.asp?fileid=20031118.Q03

Bilimoria, D., Joy, S., & Liang, X. (2008). Breaking barriers and creating inclusiveness: Lessons of organizational transformation to advance women faculty in academic science and engineering. *Human Resource Management, 47*(3), 423–441.

Billing, M., & Tajfel, H. (1973). Social categorization and similarity in intergroup behavior. *European Journal of Social Psychology, 3*, 27–52.

Bing, J. W. (2004). Hofstede's consequences: The impact of his work on consulting and business practices. *Academy of Management Executive, 18*(1), 80–87.

Birch, N. (2008, January 28). Turkey Divided over Headscarf Ban Decision. *The Independent* [London]. Retrieved July 15, 2009, from http://www.independent.co.uk/news/europe/turkey-divided-over-headscarf-ban-decision-774865.html

Blair, I. V. (2002). The malleability of automatic stereotypes and prejudice. *Personality and Social Psychology Review, 6*(3), 242–261.

Blasovich, J., Wyer, N., Swart, L., & Kibler, J. (1997). Racism and racial categorization. *Journal of Personality and Social Psychology, 72*, 1364–1372.

Blau, P. M. (1977). *Inequality and heterogeneity: A primitive theory of social structure.* New York: Free Press.

Block, R. N., & Roberts, K. (2000). A comparison of labour standards in the United States and Canada. *Relations Industrielles/Industrial Relations, 55*(2), 273–307.

Bloom, D. E., & Brender, A. (1993). Labor and the emerging world economy. *Population Bulletin, 48*(2). Washington, DC: Population Reference Bureau.

Bloom, H. (2002, March/April). Can the United States export diversity. *Across the Board*, 47–51.

Blumenberg, E. (2002). On the way to work: Welfare participants and barriers to employment. *Economic Development Quarterly, 16*(4), 314–325.

Blumiller, E. (2008, October 10). McCain draws line on attacks as crowds cry 'Fight back.' Politics, *New York Times.*

Bojarski, S. (2002, May 1). Do you know where your coffee comes from? *Daily Campus* (Storrs, CT) [www.dailycampus.com].

Bolino, M. C., & Turnley, W. H. (2008). Old faces, new places: Equity theory in cross-cultural contexts. *Journal of Organizational Behavior, 29*(1), 29–50.

Bond, M. A. 2007. *Workplace chemistry: Promoting diversity through organizational change.* Hanover, NH: University Press of New England.

Bortree, D. S., & Waters, R. D. (2008). The value of feeling included: The impact of inclusion on teen volunteers' organizational satisfaction. *International Journal of Volunteer Administration, 25*, 17–26.

Boston, T., & Nair-Reichert, U. (2003). Affirmative action: Perspectives from the United States, India, and Brazil. *Western Journal of Black Studies, 27*(1), 3–14.

Bourhis, R. Y., Sachdev, I., & Gagon, A. (1994). Intergroup research with the Tajfel matrices: Methodological notes. In M. P. Zanna & J. M. Olson (Eds.), *The psychology of prejudices: The Ontario Symposium* (Vol. 7, pp. 209–232). Hillsdale, NJ: Lawrence Erlbaum.

Branscombe, N. R., Schmitt, M. T., & Harvey, R. D. (1999). Perceiving pervasive discrimination among African Americans: Implications for group identification and well-being. *Journal of Personality and Social Psychology, 77,* 135–149.

Brigham, J. C. (1971). Ethnic stereotypes. *Psychological Bulletin, 76,* 15–38.

Brown, P., & Levinson, S. (1978). Universals in language usage: Politeness phenomenon. In E. Goody (Ed.), *Questions and politeness: Strategies in social interaction* (pp. 56–289). Cambridge, UK: Cambridge University Press.

Brown, R. & Hewstone, M. (2005). An integrative theory of intergroup contact. In M.P. Zanna (Ed.), *Advances in Experimental Psychology, Volume 37* (pp. 256–284). Elsevier Academic Press.

Browne, A. (2004, January 19). Belgium next in line as Europe's veil ban spreads. *The Times* (London). Retrieved September 12, 2004, from www.headscarf.net/veil%20ban%20spreads.jpg

Burton, C. (1995). Managing for diversity: Report to Karpin. In E. M. Davis & C. Harris (Eds.), *Making the link: Affirmative action and industrial relations* (pp. 66–71). Sydney, Australia: Affirmative Action Agency and Labour Management Studies Foundation.

Buzinger, M. (2007). Positive action declared unconstitutional. *Indian Journal of Constitutional Law,* 1(1), 198–210.

Byrne D. (1971). *The attraction paradigm.* New York: Academic.

Caldwell, Q. S., Mack, D., Johnson, C. D., & Biderman, M. D. (2002, April). *Value for diversity as a moderator of organizational relationships.* Poster presented at the 17th Annual Meeting of the Society for Industrial and Organizational Psychology, Toronto, Canada.

Campbell, W. K., Krusemark, E. A., Dyckman, K. A., Brunell, A. B., McDowell, J. E., Twenge, J. M., & Clementz, B. A. (2006). A magnetoencephalography investigation of neural correlates for social exclusion and self-control. *Social Neuroscience, 1,* 124–134.

Caroll, A. B. (1979). A three-dimensional model of corporate social performance. *Academy of Management Review, 4,* 497–505.

Caroll, A. B. (2000). A commentary and an overview of key questions on corporate social performance measurement. *Business and Society, 39,* 466–478.

Carrell, M. R., Mann, E. E., & Sigler, T. H. (2006). Defining workforce diversity programs and practices in organizations: A longitudinal study. *Labor Law Journal, 57* (1), 5–12.

Caruso, D. (2003) (Summer). Limits of the classic method: Positive action in the European Union after the new equality directives. *Harvard International Law Journal, 44*(2). Retrieved July 20, 2009, from http://papers.ssrn.com/s013/papers .cfm?abstract_id=437202

Caudron, S. (1993). Employees use diversity-training exercise against Lucky Stores in intentional-discrimination suit. *Personnel Journal, 72*(4), 52.

Chandy, P. R., & Williams, T. G. E. (1994). The impact of journals and authors on international business. *Journal of International Business Studies, 25,* 715–728.

Chartrand, T. L., & Bargh, J. (1999). The chameleon effect: The perception-behavior link and social interaction. *Journal of Personality and Social Psychology, 76*(6), 893–910.

Chater, R. E. J., & Chater, C. V. (1992). Positive action: Towards a strategic approach. *Women in Management Review, 7*(4), 3–14.

Chatman, C. M., & Von Hippel, W. (2001). Attribution Mediation of in-group bias. *Journal of Experimental Social Psychology, 37,* 267–272.

Chatman, J. A., & Flynn, F. J. (2001). The influence of demographic heterogeneity on the emergence and consequences of cooperative norms in work teams. *Academy of Management Journal, 44,* 956–974.

Chesnais, J.-C. (2000, November). The decolonization of Europe. In L. Maurawiec & D. Adamson (Eds.), *Demography and national security: Proceedings of a workshop* (pp. 14–15). Paris: Rand. Retrieved September 12, 2004, from www.rand.org/publications/CF/CF169/CF169.pdf

Chilcote, R. (2003, June 4). Cooler heads prevail in Najaf. Retrieved May 25, 2004, from www.cnn.com/2003/WORLD/meast/04/03/otsc.irq.chilcote.najaf/

Chirac on Secular Society. (2003, December 18). BBC News. Retrieved September 12, 2004, from http://news.bbc.co.uk/2/hi/europe/3330679.stm

Cho, S., & Mor Barak, M. E. (2008). Understanding diversity and inclusion in a percieved homogeneous culture: A study of organizational commitment and job performance among Korean employees. *Administration in Social Work, 32*(4), 100–126.

Choi, J. N. (2007). Group composition and employee creative behavior in a Korean electronics company: Distinct effects of relational demography and group diversity. *Journal of Occupational and Organizational Psychology, 80,* 213–234.

Choi, N. G. (2001). Diversity within diversity: Research and social work practice issues with Asian American Elders. In N. G. Choi (Ed.), *Psychological aspects of the Asian-American experience: Diversity within diversity* (pp. 301–319). New York: The Haworth Press, Inc.

Cholewinski, R. (1997). *Migrant workers in international human rights law: Their protection in countries of employment.* Oxford, UK: Oxford University Press.

Cisneros, S. (1984). *The house on Mango Street.* New York: Vintage Books.

Claringbould, I., & Knoppers, A. (2007). Finding a "normal" woman: Selection processes for board membership. *Sex Roles, 56,* 495–507.

Clark, R. A., & Delia, J. G. (1979). Topoi and rhetorical competence. *Quarterly Journal of Speech, 65,* 165–206.

Clay, J. (2005). *Exploring the links between international business and poverty reduction: A case study of Unilever.* Netherlands: OxfamGB and Unilever.

Coates, T. P. (2007, February 1). Is Obama Black enough? TIME.

Coc, T. H. (1994). *Cultural diversity in organizations.* San Francisco: Berrett-Koehler.

Cohen, C., & Sterba, J. P. (2003). *Affirmative action and racial preference: A debate.* New York: Oxford University Press.

Colgan, F., Creegan, C., McKearney, A., & Wright, T. (2007). Equality and diversity policies and practices at work: Lesbian, gay and bisexual workers. *Equal Opportunities International, 26*(6), 590–609.

Collier, M. J., & Thomas, M. (1988). Cultural identity: An interpretive perspective. In Y. Y. Kim & W. B. Gudykunst (Eds.), *Theories in intercultural communications* (pp. 99–122). Newbury Park, CA: Sage.

Combs, G. M. (2003). The duality of race and gender for managerial African American women: Implications of informal social networks on career advancement. *Human Resource Development Review, 2*(4), 385–405.

Comer, K. (2002, August 8). Black employees to file discrimination lawsuit against Xerox. *The Associated Press State & Local Wire.* Retrieved August 14, 2002, from http://web.lexis-nexis.com/universe/printdoc

Commission for the Study of International Migration and Cooperative Economic Development. (1990). *Unauthorized migration: An economic development response* Washington, DC: U.S. Government Printing Office.

Commission of the European Communities. (1999). Communication from the Commission to the Council, the European Parliament, the Economic and Social Committee and the Committee of the Regions on Certain Community Measures to Combat Discrimination. COM 564 final.

Committee on Asian Women [CAW]. (2000, April). Survey on the legal provisions for protection and prevention of sexual harassment. *Asian Women Workers Newsletter*. Retrieved October 27, 2002, from http://caw.jinbo.net/

Constitution of the Kingdom Saudi Arabia. (n.d.). Retrieved May 15, 2004, from http://www.saudiinstitute.org/const.htm

Constitution of the Republic of South Africa. (1996). Retrieved May 26, 2004, from http://www.polity.org.za/html/govdocs/constitution/saconst.html?rebookmark=1

Cook, J. (2004, February 12). Debate over outsourcing heats up, ignited by election year politics. *Seattle Post-Intelligencer*. Retrieved online September 29, 2004, from http://seattlepi.nwsource.com/business/160281_outsource12.html

Cooke, A. L. (1999). Oppression and the workplace: A framework for understanding. *Diversity Factor, 8*(1), 6.

Corneille, O., Yzerbyt, V. Y., Rogier, A., & Buidin, G. (2001). Threat and the group attribution error: When threat elicits judgments of extremity and homogeneity. *Personality and Social Psychology Bulletin, 27*(4), 437–446.

Cornelissen, J. P., Haslam, S. A., & Balmer, J. M. T. (2007). Social identity, organizational identity and corporate identity: Towards an integrated understanding of processes, patternings and products. *British Journal of Management, 18*(S1), S1–S16.

Corrigan, P. (2004). How stigma interferes with mental health care. *American Psychologist, 59*(7), 614–625.

Council Directive 2000/43/EC of 29 June 2000. *Race Relations (Amendment) Act 2000* and the EC Article 13 Race Directive.

Council of Europe. (2000). *Recent demographic developments in Europe*. Strasbourg Cedex, France: Council of Europe Publishing.

Council of Labor Affairs. Executive Yuan Taiwan R.O.C. (2009).

Council Positive Action Recommendation 84/635/EEC. (1984, December). Retrieved September 12, 2004, from http://forum.europa.eu.int/irc/DownLoad/kVeHAgJ ZmtGIXk ReF0DIMpGk0b6Hv3c-fuJ-hIw46FU5T07cJYCx3N0y2R3McYtJdrhEpj/84_0635.htm

Cowell, A. (2000, October 31). Dublin is a magnet for technology and young people. *New York Times*, p. C1.

Cox, D., Young, M., & Bairnsfather-Scott, A. (2009). No justice without healing: Australian aboriginal people and family violence. *The Australian Feminist Law Journal, 30*, 151–161.

Cox, T. (1994). *Cultural diversity in organizations: Theory, research and practice*. San Francisco: Berrett-Koehler.

Cox, T. (2001). *Creating the multicultural organization: A strategy for capturing the power of diversity*. San Francisco: Jossey-Bass.

Crisp, R.J., Turner, R.N. Rhiannon N. (2009). Can imagined interactions produce positive perceptions? Reducing prejudice through simulated social contact. *American Sociologist, 64*(4): 231–240.

Crosby, F. (1976). A model of egoistical relative deprivation. *Psychological Review, 83*, 85–113.

Cummings, A., Zhou, J., & Oldham, G. R. (1993). *Demographic differences and employee work outcomes: Effects on multiple comparison groups*. Paper presented at the annual meeting of the Academy of Management, Atlanta.

Cunningham, G. B. (2007). Perceptions as reality: The influence of actual and perceived demographic dissimilarity. *Journal of Business and Psychology, 22*(7), 79–89.

Darity, W., Jr. (1999, Fall). Experts speak on G-7 summit. *EarthIsland Journal,* 14.

Darity, W. A., & Deshpande, A. (2000). Tracing the divide: Intergroup disparity across countries. *Eastern Economic Journal, 26*(1), 75–87.

Davies-Netzley, S. A. (1998). Women above the glass ceiling: Perceptions on corporate mobility and strategies for success. *Gender and Society, 12*(3): 339–355

Darwin, C. (1995). *The origin of species.* New York: Gramercy. (Original work published in 1859)

Davis, J. (2003, September 28). Fashion special: Ethics girl. *Independent on Sunday* (London).

Davis, S. (2009, January 29). President's first law: Obama signs Lilly Ledbetter wage bill. *Wall Street Journal.*

DCM Shriram Industries Ltd. (n.d.). Retrieved June 3, 2004, from www.dcmsr.com/

Deaux, K., Reid, A., Martin, D. and Bikman, N. (2006). Ideologies of diversity and inequality: Predicting collective action in groups varying in ethnicity and immigrant status. *Political Psychology 27*(1): 123–146.

De Cieri, H. (2003). *Human resource management in Australia: Strategy, people, performance.* Sydney: McGraw-Hill Australia.

De Meuse, K. P., & Hostager, T. J. (2001). Developing an instrument for measuring attitudes toward and perceptions of workplace diversity: An initial report. *Human Resource Development Quarterly, 12*(1), 33–51.

Dennis, R. S., & Bocarnea, M. (2005). Development of the servant leadership assessment instrument. *Leadership & Organization Development Journal, 26*(8), 600–615

Denny's catches phony discrimination claim on video. (2000, August 28). Retrieved November 3, 2003, from www.newsmax.com/articles/?a=2000/8/26/131812

Denny's named among top performers in Black Enterprise List of the 40 Best Companies for Diversity. (2006, June 12). *Business Wire.* Retrieved December 3, 2009, from http://www.encyclopedia.com/doc/1G1–146914889.html

Denny's promotes diversity leader April Kelly-Drummond. (2008, March 31). *Westside Gazette.* Ft. Lauderdale, Fla.: Jun 12-Jun 18, 2008. Vol. 37, Iss. 17; p. 14A (1 page).

Denzin, N. K. (2007). *Symbolic interationism and cultural studies: The politics of interpretation.* Cambridge, MA: Wiley-Blackwell.

Department of Employment and Workplace Relations. (2003). Indigenous Employment Policy Evaluation Stage Two: Effectiveness Report, Commonwealth of Australia.

Dermott, E. M. (2001). New fatherhood in practice? Parental leave in the U.K. *The International Journal of Sociology and Social Policy, 21*(4–6), 145.

Deshpande, A. (2007). Overlapping identities under liberalization: Gender and caste in India. *Economic Development and Cultural Change, 55,* 735–760.

Devine, P. G. (2001). Implicit prejudice and stereotyping: How automatic are they? Introduction to the special section. *Journal of Personality and Social Psychology, 81*(5), 757–759.

DeVoe, S. E., & Iyengar, S. S. (2004). Managers' theories of subordinates: A crosscultural examination of manager perceptions of motivation and appraisal of performance. *Organizational Behavior and Human Decision Processing, 93*(1), 47–62.

Dew, E. M. (1994). *The trouble in Suriname, 1975–1993.* Westport, CT: Praeger.

Dias, T. (1997, October 1–3). *The disaster and its aftermath: The Hiroshima of the chemical industry.* Paper presented at the Conference on Environmental Justice: Global Ethics for the 21st Century, Melbourne, Australia. Retrieved November 10, 2003, from www.arbld.unimelb.edu.au/envjust/papers/allpapers/dias/home.htm

Diaz-Guerrero, R. (1967). *Psychology of the Mexican.* Austin: University of Texas Press.

Direct and positive impact for farmers. Retrieved August 16, 2009, from http://www
.transfairusa.org/

Directive 2002/73/EC of the European Parliament and of the Council of 23 September
2002 amending Council Directive 76/207/EEC on the implementation of the principle
of equal treatment for men and women as regards access to employment, vocational
training and promotion, and working conditions. Retrieved July 18, 2009, from http://
eur-lex.europa.eu/LexUriServ/LexUriServ.do?uri=CELEX:32002 L0073:EN:HTML

DiTomaso, N., Post, C., & Parks-Yancy, R. (2007). Workforce diversity and inequality:
Power, status, and numbers. *The Annual Review of Sociology,* 33, 473–501.

The Diversity Task Force. (2001). Best practices to achieving workforce diversity. U.S.
Department of Commerce and Vice President Al Gore's National Partnership for
Reinventing Government Benchmarking Study. Retrieved August 22, 2009, from
http://govinfo.library.unt.edu/npr/initiati/benchmk/workforce-diversity.pdf

D'Netto, B., & Sohal, A. S. (1999). Human Resource Practices and Workforce Diversity:
An Empirical Assessment. *International Journal of Manpower, 20*(8), 530–547.

Dobbs, M. F. (1996). Managing diversity: Lessons from the private sector. *Public
Personnel Management, 25*(3), 351.

Donaldson, T., & Preston, L. E. (1995). The stakeholder theory of the corporation:
Concepts, evidence, and implications. *Academy of Management Review, 20*(1), 65–91.

Dothard v. Rawlinson, 433 U.S. 321. (1977).

Dotsch, R., Wigboldus, D. H. J., Langner, O., & van Knippenberg, A. (2008). Ethnic out-
group faces are biased in the prejudiced mind. *Psychological Science, 19*(10), 978–980.

Drajem, M. (2004, January 2). Coming to terms with the logic of outsourcing. *International
Herald Tribune.* Retrieved September 29, 2004, from www.iht.com/articles/123372.html

Dutton, J. E., & Dukerich, J. M. (1991). Keeping an eye on the mirror: Image and identity in organizational adaptation. *Academy of Management Journal, 34,* 517–554.

Earley, P. C. (1997). *Face, harmony, and social structure.* Oxford, UK: Oxford University Press.

Earley, P. C., & Erez, M. (1997). *The transplanted executive: Why you need to understand how
workers in other countries see the world differently.* New York: Oxford University Press.

Eckhardt, G. (2002). Book review of *Culture's consequences: Comparing values, behaviors, institutions, and organizations across nations* (2nd ed.). *Australian Journal of
Management, 27,* 89–94.

Ecuador punctuality. (2003, October 2). Reuters.

Eichenwald, K. (1996, November 1). Texaco to make record payout in bias lawsuit. *The
New York Times,* p. 1.

Eisenberger, R., Fasolo, P., & Davis-LaMastro, V. (1990). Perceived organizational support and employee diligence, commitment, and innovation. *Journal of Applied
Psychology, 75*(1), 51–59.

Eleven tips on getting more efficiency out of women employees. (1943, July). *Mass
Transportation.*

Ellis, G. (2002, September 11). Training increases job hopes. *Illawarra Mercury.*

Elson, D. (1999). Labor markets as gendered institutions. *World Development, 27*(3), 611–627.

Ely, R. (1994). The effects of organizational demographics and social identity on relationships among professional women. *Administrative Science Quarterly, 39,* 203–238.

Ely, R. (1995). The power in demography: Women's social constructions of gender identity at work. *Academy of Management Journal, 38,* 589–634.

Ely, R. J., & Thomas, D. A. (2001). Cultural diversity at work: The effects of diversity perspectives on work group processes and outcomes. *Administrative Science Quarterly,
46*(2), 229–273.

Employees Retraining Board. (2003). About ERB. Retrieved November 26, 2003, from www.erb.org/english/index3.html

Enteman, W. (1996). Stereotyping, prejudice, and discrimination. In P. M. Lester (Ed.), *Images that injure pictorial stereotypes in the media* (pp. 9–14). Westport, CT: Praeger.

Equal Employment Opportunity Commission v. Arabian American Oil Co et al. 499 U.S. 244, 89–1838 (1991).

Erez, M., & Earley, P. C. (1993). *Culture, self-identity and work.* Oxford, UK: Oxford University Press.

Erhardt, N. L., Werbel, J. D., & Shrader, C. B. (2003). Board of director diversity and firm financial performance. *Corporate Governance, 11*(2), 102–111.

eShopAfrica. (2009). eShopAfrica.com: Fair trade direct from Africa. Retrieved August 12, 2009, from www.eShopAfrica.com

Essed, P. (1991). *Understanding everyday racism: An interdisciplinary theory.* Newbury Park, CA: Sage.

Essed, P. (1995). *Understanding everyday racism.* London: Sage.

Essed, P. (1996). *Diversity: Gender, color, and culture.* Amherst: University of Massachusetts Press.

Essed, P. (2001). *Difference, discrimination, and diversity in Dutch work organizations.* Paper presented at International Cross-Cultural Perspectives on Workforce Diversity: The Inclusive Workplace, Bellagio, Italy.

Essed, P. (2002). Cloning cultural homogeneity while talking diversity: Old wine in new bottles in Dutch work organizations? *Transforming Anthropology 11*(1), 1–19.

Essed, P., & de Graaff, M. (2002). The Topicality of Diversity. Municipal Policy in Focus den Haag: E-Quality and Utrecht: Forum, p 149.

Eurest. (2001, April). Media release: Minister backs national indigenous initiative. Rose Bay, NSW, Australia: Author.

Eurest. (2004). Indigenous training and employment project. Retrieved February 27, 2004, from www.eurest.com.au/Second/indigenoustrainingandemploymentprogram.html

Fair Trade Federation. (2003). *2003 Report on fair trade trends in U.S., Canada and the Pacific Rim.*Washington, DC: Author.

Fair Trade Federation. (2008). Fair trade federation interim trends report. Washington, DC: Author.

The Fair Trade Foundation. (2008, May 22). Global fair trade sales increase by 47%. Retrieved August 13, 2009, from www.fairtrade.org.uk/press_releases_and_statements_may_2008.

The Fairtrade Towns in Europe Project. (2009). 3rd European fair-trade towns conference report. Lyon, France. 6–7 February 2009. Retrieved on August 16, 2009, from http://www.fairtradetowns.org/news

Family sues Denny's, alleges bias. (2001, June). Global diversity @ work. Retrieved November 3, 2003, from www.diversityatwork.com/news/sept01/Family.htm

Fassinger, R. E. (2008). Workplace diversity and public policy: Challenges and opportunities for psychology. *American Psychologist, 63*(4), 252–268.

Feagin, J. R., & Feagin, C. B. (1988). Theories of discrimination. In P. S. Rothenberg (Ed.), *Racism and sexism: An integrated study* (pp. 41–48). New York: St. Martin's Press.

Federal Glass Ceiling Commission (FGCC) (1995), *Good for Business: Making Full Use of the Nation's Human Capital. The Environmental Scan. A Fact-Finding Report of the Federal Glass Ceiling Commission,* Government Printing Office, Washington,DC.

Feldman, D. C., & Turnley, W. H. (2004). Contingent employment in academic careers: Relative deprivation among adjunct faculty. *Journal of Vocational Behavior, 64*(2), 284–307.

Fernandez, J. P. (1991). *Managing a diverse workforce.* Lanham, MD: Lexington Books.

Ferner, A., Almond, P., & Colling, T. (2005). Institutional theory and the cross-national transfer of employment policy: The case of 'workforce diversity' in US multinationals. *Journal of International Business Studies, 36*(3), 304–321.

Festinger, L. (1954). A theory of social comparison processes. *Human Relations, 7,* 117–140.

Field, L. (2007). *Business and the Buddha: Doing well by doing good.* Boston, MA: Wisdom Publications.

Figart, D. M. (2005). Rereading Becker: Contextualizing the development of discrimination theory. *Journal of Economic Issues, 39*(2), 475–484.

Fiji Islands Constitution Amendment Act of 1997. (n.d.). Retrieved May 15, 2004, from http://confinder.richmond.edu/fijiislands.htm

Filartiga v. Pena-Irala, 630F.2d 876 (U.S. Court of Appeals, Second Circuit, 1980).

Findler, L. Wind, L., & Mor Barak, M. E. (2007). The challenge of workforce management in a global society: Modeling the relationship between diversity, organizational culture, and employee well-being, job satisfaction and organizational commitment. *Administration in Social Work, 31*(3), 63–94.

Fisher, M. (2006). Wall street women: Navigating gendered networks in the new economy. In Fisher, M. and Downey, G. (Eds), *Frontiers of Capital: Ethnographic Reflections on the New Economy,* Duke University Press: Durham, NC.

Fiske, A. P., & Haslam, N. (1996). Social cognition is thinking about relationships. *Current Directions in Psychological Science, 5*(5), 143–148.

Fitzherbert, E. B., Struebig, M. J., Morel, A., Danielsen, F., Carsten A., Brühl, C. A., Donald, P. F., & and Phalan, B. (2008). How will oil palm expansion affect biodiversity? *Trends in Ecology & Evolution, 23*(10), 538–545.

Fleury, M. T. (1999). The management of culture diversity: Lessons from Brazilian companies. *Industrial Management and Data Systems, 99*(3), 109–117.

Flood, J. (2007). *The original Australians: Story of the Aboriginal People.* Sydney, Australia: Allen and Unwin Academic Press.

Foley Bros., Inc. v. Filardo, 336 U.S. 281, 284–285 (1949).

Foley, S., Linnehan, F., Greenhaus, G. H., & Weer, C. H. (2006). The impact of gender similarity, racial similarity, and work culture on family-supportive supervision. *Group & Organization Management, 31*(4), 420–441.

Fonseca, I. (1996). *Bury me standing: The gypsies and their journey.* New York: Vintage Books.

Ford, A., & Lee, H. H. (1991, March 20). Racial tensions blamed in girl's death shooting: Prolonged distrust, insults and violence between the Korean store owners and their Black neighbors are cited by both sides. *The Los Angeles Times,* p. B1.

Ford Motor Company. (2002). 2002 corporate citizen report (how we did in 2002: employees). Retrieved May 26, 2004, from www.ford.com/en/company/about/corporateCitizenship/principlesProgressPerformance/our-principles/relationships-2002-employees.htm

Forschi, M., Lad, L., & Sigerson, K. (1994). Gender and double standards in the assessment of job applicants. *Social Psychology Quarterly, 57*(4), 326–339.

Foster, D. (1998). Waiting and winning in Indonesia. *Workforce, 3*(5), 28–30.

Fowler, E. (1996). *San'ya blues: Laboring life in contemporary Tokyo.* Ithaca, NY: Cornell University Press.

Frempomaa, Y. Y. (1986). *Migrant workers in West Africa, with special reference to Nigeria and Ghana* (working papers of the ILO International Migration Programme). Geneva: ILO.

Friedman, M. (1970, September 13). The social responsibility of business is to increase its profit. *The New York Times Magazine,*

Friman, H. R. (2001). Informal economies, immigrant entrepreneurship and drug crime in Japan. *Journal of Ethnic and Migration Studies, 27*(2), 313–333.

Frooman, J. (1997). Socially irresponsible and illegal behavior and shareholder wealth. *Business and Society, 36,* 221–249.

Gaertner, S. L., & Dovidio, J. F. (1986). The aversive form of racism. In J. F. Dovidio & S. L. Gaertner (Eds.), *Prejudice, discrimination, and racism.* San Diego, CA: Academic.

García, M. F., Posthuma, R. A., & Colella, A. (2008). Fit perceptions in the employment interview: The role of similarity, liking, and expectations. *Journal of Occupational and Organizational Psychology, 81*(2), 173–189.

Gautam, M., Lele, U., Hyde, W., Kartodihardjo, H., Khan, A., Erwinsyah I., et al. (2000). *The challenges of World Bank involvement in forests: An evaluation of Indonesia's forests and World Bank assistance. Preliminary Report.* Washington, DC: The World Bank Group.

German Courts uphold Muslim headscarf ban in schools, 2008. *Der Spiegel,* March 18 Retrieved July 15, 2009, from http://www.spiegel.de/international/germany/0,1518,542211,00.html

Germany Federal Statistical Office. (2006). Germany's Population by 2050: Results from 11 Coordinated Population Projections. Wiesbaden: Federal Statistical Office.

Ghana: Degraded mining lands to be turned into oil palm plantations. (2003, September 25). *Africa News.* Retrieved from www.allafrica.com/stories/200309250729.html

Ghana: Unilever ready to assist PSI on oil palm. (2002, September 19). *Africa News.* Retrieved from www.allafrica.com

Gilbert, J., Carr-Ruffino, N., Ivancevich, J. M., & Lownes-Jackson, M. (2003). An empirical examination of inter-ethnic stereotypes: Comparing Asian American and African American employees. *Public Personnel Management, 32*(2), 251–266.

Giles, H., & Coupland, N. (1991). *Language: Contexts and consequences.* Bristol, PA: Open University Press.

Giles, W., & Johnson, P. (1986). Perceived threat, ethnic commitment and interethnic language behavior. In Y. Y. Kim (Ed.), *Interethnic communications: Current research* (pp. 91–116). Beverly Hills, CA: Sage.

Glastra F. J., Meerman, M., Schedler, P. E., & de Vries, S. (2000). Broadening the scope of diversity management. Strategic implications in the case of the Netherlands. *Industrial Relations/Relations Industrielles, 50*(4), 698–724.

Glazier, J. A. (2003). Developing cultural fluency: Arab and Jewish students engating in one another's company. *Harvard Educational Review, 73*(2), 141–163.

Global most admired companies. (2003, March 3). *Fortune.*

Goldberg, C., Riordan, C. M., & Zhang, L. (2008). Employees' perception of their leaders: Is being similar always better? *Group Organization Management, 33*(3), 330–355.

Gonzalez, J. A., & Denisi, A. S. (2009). Cross-level effects of demography and diversity climate on organizational attachment and firm effectiveness. *Journal of Organizational Behavior, 30,* 21–40.

The good life in a Bombay call center. (February 3, 2003). *BusinessWeek.* Retrieved October 3, 2004, from www.businessweek.com/magazine/content/03_05/b3818013.htm

Goodman, P. S., & Haisley, E. (2007). Social comparison processes in an organizational context: New directions. *Organizational Behavior and Human Decision Processes, 102,* 109–125.

Gorman, F. (2000). Multinational logistics: Managing diversity. *Air Force Journal of Logistics, 24*(3), 8.

Graham & Whiteside Ltd. (2003). DCM Shriram Industries Ltd. *The Major Companies Database.* Company profile retrieved December 4, 2003, from LexisNexis database.

Grant, B. Z., & Kleiner, B. H. (1997). Managing diversity in the workplace. *Equal Opportunities International, 16*(3), 26–32.

Gratz v. Bollinger, 539 U.S. 244 (2003).

Gray, M., Kurihara, T., Hommen, L., & Feldman, J. (2007). Networks of exclusion: job segmentation and social networks in the knowledge economy. *Equal Opportunities International, 26*(2), 144–161.

Greenberg, J., Ashton-James, C. E., & Ashkanasy, N. M. (2007). Social comparison processes in organizations. *Organizational Behavior and Human Decision Processes, 102,* 22–41.

Greenhaus, J. H., Parasuraman, S., & Wormely, W. (1990). Effects of race on organizational experiences, job performance evaluations and career outcomes. *Academy of Management Journal, 33,* 64–86.

Greening, D. W., & Turban, D. B. (2000). Corporate social performance as a competitive advantage in attracting a quality workforce. *Business and Society, 39*(3), 254–280.

Greenwald, A. G., & Banaji, M. R. (1995). Implicit social cognition: Attitudes, self-esteem, and stereotypes. *Psychological Review, 102*(1), 4–27.

Greer, L. L., Jehn, K. A., & Mannix, E. A. (2008). Conflict transformation: A longitudinal investigation of the relationships between different types of intergroup conflict and the moderating role of conflict resolution. *Small Group Research, 39*(3), 278–302.

Griffin, J. J., & Mahon, J. F. (1997). The corporate social performance and corporate financial performance debate: Twenty-five years of incomparable research. *Business and Society, 36,* 5–31.

Grutter v. Bollinger, 539 U.S. 306 (2003).

Guatam, M., Lele, U., Hyde, W., Kartodihardjo, H., Khan, A., Erwinsyah I., et al. (2000) *Indonesia: The challenges of World Bank involvement in forests.* Washington, DC: World Bank Group.

Gudykunst, W. B., Ting-Toomey, S., & Chua, E. (1988). *Culture and interpersonal communication.* Newbury Park, CA: Sage.

Guerin-Gonzales, C., & Strikwerda, C. (1993). *The politics of immigrant workers: Labor activism and migration in the world economy since 1830.* New York: Homes & Meier.

Guimond, S. (2006). *Social comparison and social psychology: Understanding cognition, intergroup relations, and culture.* Cambridge, UK: Cambridge University Press.

Gutek, B., Larwood, L., & Stromberg, A. (1986). Women at work. In C. L. Cooper & I. Robertson (Eds.), *International review of industrial and organizational psychology* (pp. 217–234). New York: Wiley.

Hai Ha-Kotobuki. (2003). *Company introduction.* Retrieved December 4, 2003, from www.haiha-kotobuki.com.vn/english/introduction.html

Hale, B. (2003, February 3). African crafts go online. BBC News. Retrieved September 12, 2004, from http://news.bbc.co.uk/1/hi/business/2688323.stm

Hall, E. T. (1959). *The silent language of business.* Garden City, NJ: Doubleday.

Hall, E. T. (1976). *Beyond culture.* New York: Anchor Press.

Halliday, M. A. K. (1978). *Language as social semiotic.* Baltimore: University Park Press.

Hamersma, S. (2008). The effects of an employer subsidy on employment outcomes: A study of the work opportunity and welfare-to-work tax credits. *Journal of Policy Analysis and Management, 27*(3), 498–520.

Hampden-Turner, C., & Trompenaars, A. (1993). *The seven cultures of capitalism: Value systems for creating wealth in the United States, Japan, Germany, France, Britain, Sweden, and the Netherlands.* New York: Doubleday.

Hance, J. (2009, November 19). Oil palm workers still below poverty line, despite Minister's statements, mongabay.com. Retrieved December 6, 2009, from http://news .mongabay.com/2009/1119-hance_oilpalmworkers.html

Hancock, A. (2004). *The politics of disgust: The public identity of the welfare queen.* New York: New York University Press.

Harris, D. (2001). *In the eye of the beholder: Observed race and observer characteristics.* (Population Studies Center Research Report 02–522). Ann Arbor: University of Michigan.

Harrison, D. A., & Klein, K. J. (2007). What's the difference? Diversity constructs as separation, variety, or disparity in organizations. *Academy of Management Review, 32,* 1199–1228.

Harrison, D. A., Price, K. H., & Bell, M. P. (1998). Beyond relational demography: Time and the effects of surface and deep-level diversity on work group cohesion. *Academy of Management Journal, 41*(1), 96–107.

Harrison, D. A., & Sin, H. (2006). What is diversity and how should it be measured. In A. M. Konrad, P. Prasad, & J. K. Pringle (Eds.) *Handbook of Workplace Diversity,* 191–216. London: Sage.

Harrison, G. L., & McKinnon, J. L. (1999). Cross-cultural research in management control systems design: A review of the current state. *Accounting, Organizations and Society, 24,* 483–506.

Hart, A. (2003, October 29). Cities playing fair. *South Wales Evening Post,* p. 22.

Hart, W. B. (1999). Interdisciplinary influences in the study of intercultural relations: A citation analysis of the *International Journal of Intercultural Relations. International Journal of Intercultural Relations, 23,* 575–589.

Hartenian, L. S., & Gudmundson, D. E. (2000). Cultural diversity in small business: Implications for firm performance. *Journal of Developmental Entrepreneurship, 5*(3), 209.

Hartmann, G. G., & SAM Research, Inc. (2003, November 20). *Profile of Unilever: Market Sector Leader, DJSI World.* Zurich: SAM Research, Inc.

Harzing, A. (2000). An empirical analysis and extension of the Bartlett and Ghoshal typology of multinational companies. *Journal of International Business Studies, 31*(1), 101–120.

Haslam, S. A., & Ellemers, N. (2005). Social identity in industrial and organizational psychology: Concepts, controversies and contributions. *International Review of Industrial and Organizational Psychology, 20,* 39–118.

Hassan, A. A. G. (2004). *Growth, structural change and regional inequality in Malaysia.* Aldershot, UK: Ashgate Publishing.

Haub, C., & Riche, M. F. (1994). Population by the numbers: Trends in population growth and structure. In L. A. Mazur (Ed.), *Beyond the numbers: A reader on population, consumption, and the environment.* Washington, DC: Island Press.

Hays-Thomas, R. (2004). Why now? A contemporary focus on managing diversity. In M. S. Stockdale & F. J. Crosby, *The psychology and management of workplace diversity* (pp. 3–30). Malden, MA: Blackwell Publishing.

Heal, G. (2008). *When principles pay: Corporate social responsibility and the bottom line.* New York: Columbia University Press.

Heaphy, E., Sanchez-Burks, J., & Ashford, S. (2009). *Cultural impressions of professionalism.* Ross School of Business Paper No. 1041.

Henderson, G. (1994). *Cultural diversity in the workplace.* Westport, CT: Praeger.

Henderson, T. P. (2001, June). Perception that some merchants practice racial profiling generates debate. *Stores Magazine.* Retrieved November 3, 2003, from www.stores .org/archives/jun01edit.asp

Hildebrandt, E. (2009). Impoverished women with children and no welfare benefits: The urgency of researching failures of the temporary assistance for needy families program. *American Journal of Public Health, 99*(5), 793–801.

Hiltzik, M. (2003, October 20). *Silicon valley: Visas down, job exports up. The Los Angeles Times.* Retrieved December 8, 2003, from www.latimes.com/classified/jobs/career/la-fi-golden200ct20,0,7510486.column?coll=la-class-employ-career

History of immigration in France. (n.d.). Retrieved October 27, 2003, from www.fritz-karsen.de/comenius/1999_00/history.html

Hitlan, R. T., Cliffton, R. J., & DeSoto, M. C. (2006). Perceived exclusion in the workplace: The moderating effects of gender on work-related attitudes and psychological health. *North American Journal of Psychology, 8*(2), 217–235.

Hjarnø-Knudsen, L. (2000, July 12–22). *Causes of social exclusion of youths of foreign origin in Denmark: "The Lads of Blaagaards Square."* Paper presented at the conference on Migration and New European Identities: Between Social Integration and Social Exclusion, Cecina, Italy.

Hobman E.V., Bordia, P., & Gallois, C. (2004). Perceived dissimilarity and work group involvement: Moderating effects of group openness to diversity. *Group & Organization Management, 29*(5), 560–587.

Hodges-Aeberhard, J. (1999). Affirmative action in employment: Recent court approaches to a difficult concept. *International Labour Review, 138*(3), 247.

Hofstede, G. (1980). *Culture's consequences: International differences in work related values.* Beverly Hills, CA: Sage.

Hofstede G. (1997). *Cultures and organizations: Software of the mind.* New York: McGraw-Hill.

Hofstede, G. (2001). *Culture's consequences: Comparing values, behaviors, institutions, and organizations across nations* (2nd ed.). Thousand Oaks, CA: Sage.

Hofstede, G. (2007). Asian management in the 21st century. *Asia Pacific Journal of Management, 24,* 411–420.

Hofstede, G., & Bond, M. H. (1988). The Confucius connection: From cultural roots to economic growth. *Organizational Dynamics, 16*(4), 4–21.

Hofstede, G., & Hofstede, G. J. (2004). *Cultures and organizations: Software of the mind* (2nd ed.). NewYork: McGraw-Hill.

Hogg, M. A., & Terry, D. J. (2000). Social identity and self-categorization processes in organizational contexts. *The Academy of Management Review, 25*(1), 121–140

Holtgraves, T. (1997). Styles of language use: Individual and cultural variability in conversational indirectness. *Journal of Personality and Social Psychology, 73*(3), 624–637.

Hong Kong Council of Social Services. (2003). Caring company scheme. Retrieved November 26, 2003, from www.hkcss.org.hk/partnership/caring_com_e.htm

Hong Kong General Chamber of Commerce. (2003, February). *Bulletin.* [http://www.chamber.org.hk/info/the_bulletin/feb2003/ecobiz.asp]

Hong Kong Legal Information Institute, (2009).

Hong Yip Service Co. Ltd. (2003). Company website. Retrieved November 26, 2003, from http://www.hongyip.com.hk/eng/index.htm

Hopkins v. Price Waterhouse, 618 F.Supp. 1109 (D.D.C.1985).

Hopkins v. Price Waterhouse, 825 F.2d 458 (D.C. Cir. 1987).

Hopkins, A. (2006). *Price Waterhouse v. Hopkins:* A personal account of a sexual discrimination plaintiff. *Hofstra Labor & Employment Law Journal, 22, 357–416.*

Hopkins, A. B. (1996). *So ordered: Making partner the hard way.* Amherst: University of Massachusetts Press.

Hookway, J. (2009). Affirmative action spurs Asian debate. *The Wall Street Journal,* July 8, p. A1.

Hordes, M. K., Clancy, J. A., & Baddaley, J. (1995). A primer for global start-ups, *Academy of Management Executive, 9*(2), 7–11.

Horwitz, F. M. (2002). Whither South African management? In N. Warner & P. Joynt (Eds.), *Managing across cultures: Issues and perspectives* (2nd ed., pp. 203–214).

House, R. J., Hangers, P. J., Javidan, M., Dorfman, P. W., & Gupta, V. (2004). *Culture, leadership, and organizations: The GLOBE Study of 62 societies.* Thousand Oaks, CA: Sage.

Howard, J. M., & Rothbart, M. (1980). Social categorization and memory for in-group and out-group behavior. *Journal of Personality and Social Psychology, 38,* 301–310.

Hunt, R. (1998, July). 21.4 oil palm (*elaeis guineensis*). *The Australian New Crops Newsletter* (Issue no. 10). Retrieved September 12, 2004, from http://www.newcrops .uq.edu.au/newslett/ncn10214.htm

Hyun, J. (2006). *Breaking the bamboo ceiling: Career strategies for Asians.* New York, New York: Harper.

Ibarra, H. (1993). Personal networks of women and minorities in management: A conceptual framework. *Academy of Management Review, 18,* 56–87.

Ibarra, H. (1995). Race, opportunity, and diversity of social circles in managerial networks. *Academy of Management Journal, 38,* 673–703.

IBM Web page. Retrieved July 26, 2009, from http://www-03.ibm.com/employment/ us/diverse/50/sp.shtml.

Inkeles, A., & Levinson, D. J. (1969). National character: The study of modal personality and sociocultural systems. In G. Lindzey & E. Aronson (Eds.), *The handbook of social psychology* (2nd ed.). Reading, MA: Addison-Wesley.

Insch, G. S., McIntyre, N., & Napier, N. K. (2008). The expatriate glass ceiling: The second layer of glass. *Journal of Business Ethics, 83,* 19–28.

International Federation of Red Cross and Red Crescent Societies. (2002, November 13). Implementation of the declaration of commitment on HIV/AIDS. Statement delivered by Encho Gospodinov, Head of International Federation Permanent Observer Office to the United Nations in New York, to the United Nations General Assembly, Third Committee, New York. Retrieved September 12, 2004, from http://www.ifrc .org/docs/news/speech02/eg131102.asp

International Gay and Lesbian Human Rights Commission (IGLHRC). (1999, April). Antidiscrimination legislation: A worldwide summary. IGLHRC Fact Sheet. Retrieved October 28, 2002, from www.iglhrc.org/news/factsheets/990604-antidis.html

International Labor Organization. (2005). Retrieved September 7, 2009, from http://www.ilo.org/public/libdoc/ILO-Thesaurus/english/tr2351.htm

International Labour Office. (2000). *World labour report: Income security and social protection in a changing world.* Geneva: Author.

International Labour Office. (2002). *Economically active population, 1950–2010, LABORSTA database.* Retrieved from www.ilo.org

International Labour Office. (2007). *Equality at work: Tackling the challenges. Global Report under the follow-up to the ILO Declaration of fundamental principles and rights at work.* International Labour Conference 96th Session 2007. Retrieved June 26, 2009, from http:// www.ilo.org

International Labour Office. (2009). *Key Indicators of the Labour Market* (6th ed.). Retrieved from www.ilo.org

International Organization for Migration. (2008). *World Migration Report.* Geneva: United Nations.

Jackson, S., Joshi, A., & Erhardt, N. L. (2003). Recent research on team and organizational diversity: SWOT analysis and implications. *Journal of Management, 29,* 801–830.

Jackson, S. E., & Joshi, A. (2010, in press). Work team diversity. To appear in S. Zedeck (Ed.), *APA handbook of industrial and organizational psychology: Volume II.* Washington, DC: APA.

Jackson, S. E., May, K. E., & Whitney, K. (1995). Understanding the dynamics of diversity in decision making teams. In R. A. Guzzo & E. Salas (Eds.), *Team effectiveness and decision making in organizations* (pp. 204–261). San Francisco: Jossey-Bass.

Javidan, M., Dorfman, P., Sully de Luque, M., & House, R. J. (2006). In the eye of the beholder: Cross cultural lessons in leadership from project GLOBE. *Academy of Management Perspective, 20*(1), 67–90.

Javidan, M., & House, R. (2001). Cultural acumen for the global manager: Lessons from Project GLOBE. *Organizational Dynamics, 29*(4), 289–305.

Javidan, M., Stahl, G. K., Brodbeck, F., & Wilderom, C. P. M. (2005). Cross-border transfer of knowledge: Cultural lessons from project GLOBE. *Academy of Management Executive 19*(2), 59–76.

Jehn, K. A., & Bendersky, C. (2004). Intragroup conflict in organizations: A contingency perspective on the conflict-outcome relationship. In. R. Kramer & B. Staw (Eds.), *Research in organizational behavior: An annual series of analytical essays and critical reviews* (Vol. 25, pp. 187–242). San Diego, CA: Elsevier.

Jimenez-Cook, S., & Kleiner, B. H. (2005). Nursing at the cross roads: Increasing workforce diversity and addressing health disparities. *Equal Opportunities International, 24*(7/8), 1–10.

Johnson, C. E. (2008). *Meeting the ethical challenges of leadership: Casting light or shadow.* Thousand Oaks, CA: Sage.

Johnson, H. H. (2009). Corporate social responsibility: Determining your position. In E. Biech (Ed.). *The 2010 Pfeiffer Annual: Consulting* (pp. 141–147).

Johnston, W. B., & Packer, A. E. (1997). *Workforce 2000.* Indianapolis, IN: Hudson Institute.

Joiner, T. A. (2001). The influence of national culture and organizational culture alignment on job stress and performance: Evidence from Greece. *Journal of Managerial Psychology, 16*(3), 229.

Jones, D., Pringle, J., & Shepherd, D. (2000). Managing diversity meets Aotearoa/New Zealand. *Personnel Review, 29*(3), 364–380.

Jones, G. (2005). *Renewing Unilever: Transformation and tradition.* New York: Oxford University Press.

Joplin, J. R. W., & Daus, C. S. (1997). Challenges of leading a diverse workforce. *Academy of Management Executive, 11*(3), 32.

Joshi, A., & Roh, H. (2009). The role of context in work team diversity research: A meta-analytic review. *Academy of Management Journal, 52*(3), 599–627. *Journal of Experimental Social Psychology, 40,* 75–81.

Judd, C. M., Blair, I. V., & Chapleau, K. M. (2004). Automatic stereotypes vs. automatic prejudice: Sorting out the possibilities in the Payne (2001) weapon paradigm.

Judy, R. W., & D'Amico, C. (1997). *Workforce 2020.* Indianapolis, IN: Hudson Institute.

Kabeer, N. (2000). *The power to choose.* London: Verso.

Kacperczyk, A., Sanchez-Burks, J., & Baker, W. (2009). *Social isolation in the workplace: A Cross-cultural and longitudinal analysis.* Manuscript #701, Ross School of Business, University of Michigan.

Kahn, J. (2003, December 7). Ruse in toyland: Chinese workers' hidden woe. *New York Times,* p. 1.

Kaiser, H. F. (1970). A second generation little Jiffy. *Psychometrika, 35,* 401–415.

Kaiser, R., & Prange, H. (2004). Managing diversity in a system of multi-level governance: The open method of co-ordination in innovation policy, *Journal of European Public Policy,11 (2),* 249–266

Kalev, A., (2009). Cracking the glass cages? Restructuring and ascriptive inequality at work, *American Journal of Sociology, 114*(6), 1591–643

Kalev, A., Dobbin, F., & Kelly, E. (2006). Best practices or best guesses? Assessing the efficacy of corporate affirmative action and diversity policies. *American Sociological Review, 71*(4), 589–617.

Kamen, A. (1992, June 22). Myth of "model minority" haunts Asian American; Stereotype eclipses diverse group's problems. *The Washington Post,* A1.

Kamenou, N., & Fearfull, A. (2006). Ethnic minority women: A lost voice in HRM. *Human Resource Management Journal, 16*(2), 154–172.

Kang, H. H., & Tran, L. C. (2003, December 29). Filipino workers in Taiwan: A status report. *BusinessWorld,* 22–26.

Kanter, R. M. (1992). Power failure in management circuits. In J. M. Shafritz & J. S. Ott (Eds.), *Classics of organization theory* (3rd ed., pp. ix, 534). Pacific Grove, CA: Brooks/Cole.

Karlin, S. (2005, February 1). Coffins to die for. Fortune Small Business Magazine. Retrieved December 5, 2009, from http://money.cnn.com/magazines/fsb/fsb_archive/2005/02/01/8250629/index.htm

Kashima, Y., Yamaguchi, S., Kim, U., Choi, S.C, Gelfand, M.J., & Yuki, M. (1995). Culture, gender, and self: A perspective from individualism-collectivism research. *Journal of Personality and Social Psychology,* 925–937.

Katz, D., & Braly, K. (1935). Racial prejudice and racial stereotypes. *Journal of Abnormal and Social Psychology, 30,* 175–193.

Kearney, E., & Gerbert, D. (2009). Managing diversity and enhancing team outcomes: The promise of transformational leadership. *Journal of Applied Psychology 94*(1), 77–89.

Kearney, E., Gerbert, D., & Voelpel, S. (2009). When and how diversity benefits teams: The importance of team members' need for cognition. *Academy of Management Journal, 52,* 581–598.

Kellough, E. J. (2006). *Understanding affirmative action: Politics, discrimination, and the search for justice.* Washington, D.C.: Georgetown University Press.

Kennedy, S., Schrier, J., & Rogers, S. (1984). The price of our success: Our monocultural science. *American Psychologist, 39,* 996–997.

Kennedy Dubourdieu, E. (2007). From positive discrimination to equality of opportunity: Building cohesion in Britain another way? *Revue Francaise de Civilisation Britannique,* 51–64.

Kiernan, B. (2000, September 10). Australia's Aboriginal genocides. *Bangkok Post.*

Kim, S. U. (1988). The role of social values and competitiveness in economic growth: With special reference to Korea. In D. Sinha & H. S. R. Kao (Eds.), *Social values and development: Asian perspectives* (pp. 76–92). New Delhi: Sage.

Kim, Y. Y. (1988). On theorizing intercultural communication. In Y. Y. Kim & W. B. Gudykunst (Eds.), *Theories in intercultural communication* (pp. 11–21). Newbury Park, CA: Sage.

King, R. B. (1999). Time spent in parenthood status among adults in the United States. *Demography, 36,* 377–385.

Kingfisher, C., & Goldsmith, M. (2001). Reforming women in the United States and Aotearoa/New Zealand: A comparative ethnography of welfare reform in global context. *American Anthropologist, 103*(3), 714–732.

Kirkman, B. L., Lowe, K. B., & Gibson, C. B. (2006). A quarter century of *Culture's consequences:* A review of empirical research incorporating Hofstede's cultural values framework. *Journal of International Business Studies, 37,* 285–320.

Kirkpatrick, D., Phillips, J. J., & Phillips, P. P. (2003, October). Getting results from diversity training—in dollars and cents. *HR Focus, 80*(10), 3–4.

Kitayama, S. (2002). Culture and basic psychological processes—Toward a system view of culture: Comment on Oyserman et al. *Psychological Bulletin, 128,* 89–96.

Klasen, S. (1999). Does gender inequality reduce growth and development? Evidence from cross-country regressions. World Bank. Retrieved September 12, 2004, from www.worldbank.org/gender/prr/wp7.pdf

Knight, N., & Nisbett, R. E. (2007). Culture, class and cognition: Evidence from Italy. *Journal of Cognition and Culture, 7,* 283–291

Kochan, T., Bezrukova, K., Ely, R., Jackson, S., & Joshi, A. (2003). The effects of diversity on business performance: Report of the diversity research network. *Human Resource Management, 42*(1), 3–21.

Konrad, A. M. (2003b). Special issue introduction: Defining the domain of workplace diversity scholarship. *Group & Organization Management, 28*(4), 4–17.

Konrad, A. M. & Hartmann, L. (2001). Gender differences in attitudes toward affirmative action programs in Australia: Effects of beliefs, interests, and attitudes toward women. *Sex Roles, 45*(5/6), 415–432.

Kossek, E. E., Huber, M. S. Q., & Lerner, J. V. (2003). Sustaining work force inclusion and well-being of mothers on public assistance: Individual deficit and social ecology perspectives. *Journal of Vocational Behavior, 62*(1), 155–175.

Kossek, E. E., Huber-Yoder, M., Castellino, D., & Lerner, J. (1997). The working poor: Locked out of careers and the organizational mainstream? *Academy of Management Executive, 11*(1), 76–92.

Kossek, E. E., & Lobel, S. A. (1996). Introduction: Transforming human resource systems to manage diversity: An introduction and orienting framework. In E. E. Kossek & S. A. Lobel (Eds.), *Managing diversity: Human resource strategies for transforming the workplace.* Cambridge, MA: Blackwell.

Kossek, E.E., Lobel, S.A., & Brown, J. (2006). Human resource strategies to manage workforce diversity: Examining "the business case." In A. M. Konrad, P. Prasad, & J. K. Pringle. *Handbook of workplaced diversity.* Thousand Oaks, CA: Sage.

Kossek, E. E., & Zonia, S. C. (1993). Assessing diversity climate: A field study of reactions to employer efforts to promote diversity. *Journal of Organizational Behavior, 14,* 61–81.

Kramar, R. (1998). Managing diversity: Beyond affirmative action in Australia. *Women in Management Review, 13*(4), 133–146.

Krautil, F. (1995). Managing diversity in Esso Australia. In E. M. Davis & C. Harris (Eds.), *Making the link: Affirmative action and industrial relations.* Sydney, Australia: Affirmative Action Agency and Labour Management Studies Foundation.

Kreitz, P.A. (2008). Best practices for managing organizational diversity. *The Journal of Academic Librarianship, 34*(2), 101–120.

Krier, J. M. (2001). *Fair trade in Europe 2001: Facts and figures on the fair trade sector in 18 European countries.* Maastricht, Netherlands: EFTA (European Fair Trade Association).

Kroeber, A. L., & Kluckhohn, C. (1952). *Culture: A critical review of concepts and definitions.* Cambridge, MA: Harvard University Press.

Kurowski, L. (2002). Cloaked culture and veiled diversity: Why theorists ignored early US workforce diversity. *Management Decision, 40*(2), 183–191.

Labour Department Government of Hong Kong. (2003). Youth pre-employment training program. Retrieved November 20, 2003, from www.yptp.com.hk/

Lai, Y., & Kleiner, B. H. (2001). How to conduct diversity training effectively. *Equal Opportunities International, 20*(5/6/7), 14–18.

Larkey, L. K. (1996). Toward a theory of communicative interactions in culturally diverse workgroups. *Academy of Management Review, 21*(2), 463–491.

La Siembra Co-op. (2003). Welcome to La Siembra Co-op. Retrieved December 9, 2003, from www.lasiembra.com/home.htm

Lau, D. C., Lam, L. W., & Deutsch Salamon, S. (2008). The impact of relational demographics on perceived managerial trustworthiness: Similarity or norms? *The Journal of Social Psychology, 148*(2), 187–209.

Lau, D. C., & Murnighan, J. K. (1998). Demographic diversity and faultiness: The compositional dynamics of organizational groups. *Academy of Management Review, 23*(2), 325.

Laurent, A. (1984). The cultural diversity of Western conceptions of management. *International Studies of Management and Organizations, 13*, 75–96.

Lawler, E. E. (1992). *The ultimate advantage: Creating the high-involvement organization.* San Francisco: Jossey-Bass.

Lawler, E. E., III. (2008). *Talent: Making people your competitive advantage.* San Francisco: Jossey-Bass.

Leary, M. R., & Baumeister, R. F. (2000). The nature and function of self-esteem: Sociometer theory. In M. P. Zanna (Ed.), *Advances in experimental social psychology* (Vol. 32, pp. 2–51). San Diego, CA: Academic Press.

Leary, M. R., & Downs, D. L. (1995). Interpersonal functions of the self-esteem motive: The self-esteem system as a sociometer. In M. H. Kernis (Ed.), *Efficacy, agency, and self-esteem.* New York: Plenum.

Leary, M. R., Schreindorfer, L. S., & Haupt, A. L. (1995). The role of low self-esteem in emotional and behavioral problems: Why is low self-esteem dysfunctional? *Journal of Social and Clinical Psychology, 14*(3), 297–314.

Lee, C. M., & Gudykunst, W. B. (2001). Attraction to interethnic interactions. *International Journal of Intercultural Relations, 25*, 373–387.

Lee, M. (1997). Why do some women participate in the labor force while others stay at home? *Korea Journal of Population and Development, 26*(2), 33–54.

Lent, R. (1970). Binocular resolution and perception of race in the United States. *British Journal of Psychology, 61*, 521–533.

Levy, S. R. (1999). Reducing prejudice: Lessons from social-cognitive factors underlying perceiver differences in prejudice. *Journal of Social Issues, 55*(4), 745–765.

Libertella, A., Sora, A., & Natale, S. (2007). Affirmative action policy and changing views. *Journal of Business Ethics, 74*, 65–71.

Linder, M. (1992). *Migrant workers and minimum wages: Regulating the exploitation of agricultural labor in the United States.* Boulder, CO: Westview Press.

Linnehan, F., & Konrad, A. M. (1999). Diluting diversity: Implications for intergroup inequality in organizations. *Journal of Management Inquiry, 8*(4), 399–414.

Linnehan, F., Konrad, A., Reitman, F., Greenhalgh, A., & London, M. (2003). Behavioral goals for a diverse organization: The effects of attitudes, social norms, and racial identity for Asian Americans and Whites. *Journal of Applied Social Psychology, 33*(7), 1331–1359.

Linville, P. W., Fischer, G. W., & Salovey, P. (1989). Perceived distributions of characteristics of ingroup and outgroup members: Empirical evidence and a computer simulation. *Journal of Personality and Social Psychology, 57*(2), 165–188.

Littrell, R. F., & Nkomo, S. M. (2005). Gender and race differences in leader behavior preferences in South Africa. *Women in Management Review, 20*(8), 562–580.

Locksley, A., Ortiz, V., & Hepburn, C. (1980). Social categorization and discriminatory behavior: Extinguishing the minimal intergroup discrimination effect. *Journal of Personality and Social Psychology, 39*, 773–783.

Lock up gays, says Ugandan president. (1999, September 29). BBC News. Retrieved September 14, 2003, from http://news.bbc.co.uk/1/hi/world/africa/460893.stm

Loden, M., & Rosener, J. B. (1991). *Workforce America: Managing employee diversity as a vital resource.* Homewood, IL: Business One Irwin.

Lopez, S.H., Hodson, R., & Roscigno, V. (2009). Power, status and abuse at work: General and sexual harassment compared. *The Sociological Quarterly, 50*(1), 3–27.

Lowery, B. S., Hardin, C. D., & Sinclair, S. (2001). Social influence effects on automatic racial prejudice. *Journal of Personality and Social Psychology, 81*(5), 842–855.

Lutz, W., & Goujon, A. (2001). The world's changing human capital stock. *Population and Development Review, 27*(2), 323–339.

Lutz, W., & Gui, Y. C. (2000). *China's unfolding educational revolution.* International Institute for Applied Systems Analysis, POPNET, No. 33.

Lynch, F. R. (2001). *The diversity machine: The drive to change the white male workplace.* New Brunswick, N.J.: Transaction Publishers.

Maatman, G. L. (2000, September 11). Harassment, discrimination laws go global. *National Underwriter*, 34–35.

MacDonald, G., & Leary, M. R. (2005). Why does social exclusion hurt? The relationship between social and physical pain. *Psychological Bulletin, 131*(2), 202–223.

MacPherson, K. (2004). Legislatures consider ban on "outsourcing" government business. *Pittsburgh Post Gazette.* Retrieved on line October 3, 2004, from www.postgazette.com/pg/04095/295972.stm

Madley, B. (2008). From terror to genocide: Britain's Tasmanian penal colony and Australia's history wars. *Journal of British Studies, 47*, 77–106.

Makower, J. (1995). *Beyond the bottom line: Putting social responsibility to work for your business and the world.* New York: Simon & Schuster.

Mangaliso, M. P. (2001). Building competitive advantage from Ubuntu: Management lessons from South Africa. *Academy of Management Executive, 15*(3), 23–33.

Mann, S. (1999). *Hiding what we feel, faking what we don't.* London: HarperCollins.

Manton, K. G., Corder, L., & Stallard, E. (1997, March 18). Chronic disability trends in elderly United States populations: 1982–1994. *Proceedings of the National Academy of Sciences, USA, 94*(6), 2593–2598.

Manton, K. G. & Gu, X. (2001). Changes in the prevalence of chronic disability in the United States black and nonblack population above age 65 from 1982 to 1999. *PNAS 98*(11), 6354–6359.

Manurung, E. G. T. (2002, October 9). Loss from oil palm estates. *Jakarta Post.* Retrieved August 31, 2009, from http://www.thejakartapost.com/search/news/loss+from+oil+palm+estates

Markus, H., & Kitayama, S. (1991). Culture and the self: Implications for cognition, emotion, and motivation. *Psychological Review, 98*(2), 224–253.

Marquis, J. P., Lim, N., Scott, L. M., Harrell, M. C., & Kavanagh, J. (2008). Managing diversity in corporate America: An exploratory analysis. *Occasional Paper, Labor and Population.* RAND.

Martin, P. L. (1994). Germany: Reluctant land of immigration. In W. A. Cornelius, J. F. Hollifield, & P. L. Martin (Eds.), *Controlling immigration: A global perspective.* Stanford, CA: Stanford University Press.

Martin, R. L. (2003). The virtue matrix: Calculating the return on corporate social responsibility. In *Harvard Business Review on Corporate Responsibility.* Boston: Harvard Business School Press.

Massey, D. S., Arango, J., Hugo, G., Kouaouci, A., Pellegrino, A., & Taylor, J. E. (2005). *Worlds in motion: Understanding international migration at the end of the millennium.* New York: Oxford University Press.

Matz-Costa, C., Pitt-Catosouphes, M., Besen, E., & Lynch, K. (2009). The difference of downturn can make: Assessing the early effects of the economic crisis on the employment experiences of workers. *The Sloan Center on Aging and Work at Boston college, Issue brief, 22,* 1–23.

McCall, G. J. (2006). Symbolic interaction. In Peter J. Burke (Ed.), *Contemporary Social Psychological Theories* (pp. 1–23). Stanford, CA: Stanford University Press.

McDonald, F., & Potton, M. (1997). The nascent European policy towards older workers: Can the European Union help the older worker? *Personnel Review, 26*(4), 293–306.

McDonald, S., Lin, N., & Ao, D. (2009). Networks of opportunity: Gender, race and job leads. *Social Problems, 56*(3), 385–402.

McElhaney, K. A. (2008). *Just good business: The strategic guide to aligning corporate responsibility and brand.* San Francisco Berrett-Koehler Publishers.

McGoldrick, D. (2006). *Human rights and religion: The Islamic headscarf in Europe.* London: Hart Publishing.

McGregor, J. (2006). The pervasive power of man-made news. *Pacific Journalism Review, 12*(1), 21–34.

McGregor, J., & Gray, L. (2002). Stereotypes and older workers: The New Zealand experience. *Social Policy Journal of New Zealand, 18,* 163–177.

McGuire, G. M. (2000), Gender, race, ethnicity, and networks: The factors affecting the status of employee's network members. *Work and Occupation, 27*(4), 501–523.

McKay, P. F, Avery, D. R., & Morris, M. A. (2008). Mean racial-ethnic differences in employee sales performance: The moderating role of diversity climate. *Personnel Psychology, 61*(2), 349–374.

McKay, P. F., Avery, D. R., & Morris, M. A. (2009). A tale of two climates: Diversity climate from subordinates' and managers' perspectives and their role in store unit sales performance. *Personnel Psychology, 62*(4), 767–791.

McKay, P. F., Avery, D. R., Tonidandel, S., Morris, M. A., Herandez, M., & Hebl, M. R. (2007). Racial differences in employee retention: Are diversity climate perceptions the key? *Personnel Psychology, 60*(1), 35–62.

McPherson, M., Smith-Lovin, L., & Cook, J. M. (2001). Birds of a feather: Homophily in social networks. *Annual Review of Sociology, 27,* 415–444.

McSweeney, B. (2002). Hofstede's model of national cultural differences and their consequences: A triumph of faith—a failure of analysis. *Human Relations, 55*(1), 89–118.

Mead, G. H. (1982). *The individual and the social self: Unpublished works of George Herbert Mead* (D. Miller, Ed.). Chicago: University of Chicago Press.

Mead, M. (2001). *Sex and temperament in three primitive societies.* New York: HarperCollins. (Originally published in 1935)

Michalopoulos, C., Edin, K., Fink, B., et al. (2003). *Welfare reform in Philadelphia: Implementation, effects, experiences of poor families and neighborhoods.* New York: Manpower Demonstration and Research Corporation.

Milliken, F. J., & Martins L. L. (1996). Searching for common threads: Understanding the multiple effects of diversity in organizational groups. *Academy of Management Review, 21*(2), 402–433.

Ministry of Interior in Taiwan. (2009).

Mississippi University for Women v. Hogan, 458 U.S. 718 (1982).

Molinsky, A. L. (2005). Language fluency and the evaluation of cultural faux pa: Russians interviewing for jobs in the United States. *Social Psychology Quarterly, 68*(2), 103–120.

Moore, S. (1999). Understanding and managing diversity among groups at work: Key issues for organisational training and development. *Journal of European Industrial Training, 23*(4/5), 208.

Mor Barak, M. E. (2000a). Beyond affirmative action: Toward a model of organizational inclusion. In M. E. Mor Barak & D. Bargal (Eds.), *Social services in the workplace.* New York: Haworth.

Mor Barak, M. E. (2000b). The inclusive workplace: An eco-systems approach to diversity management. *Social Work, 45*(4), 339–354.

Mor Barak, M. E. (2005). *Managing diversity: Toward a globally inclusive workplace.* Thousand Oaks, CA: Sage.

Mor Barak, M. E., & Cherin, D. A. (1998). A tool to expand organizational understanding of workforce diversity: Exploring a measure of inclusion-exclusion. *Administration in Social Work, 22*(1), 47–65.

Mor Barak, M. E., Cherin, D. A., & Berkman, S. (1998). Ethnic and gender differences in employee diversity perceptions: Organizational and personal dimensions. *Journal of Applied Behavioral Sciences, 34*(1), 82–104.

Mor Barak, M. E., Findler, L., & Wind, L. (2001). International dimensions of diversity, inclusion, and commitment in work organizations. *Journal of Behavioral and Applied Management, 2*(2), 72–91.

Mor Barak, M. E., Findler, L., & Wind, L. (2003). Cross-cultural aspects of diversity and well-being in the workplace: An international perspective. *Journal of Social Work Research and Evaluation, 4*(2), 49–73.

Mor Barak, M. E., & Levin, A. (2002). Outside of the corporate mainstream and excluded from the work community: A study of diversity, job satisfaction and well-being. *Community, Work & Family, 5*(2), 133–157.

Mor Barak, M. E., Levin, A., Nissly, J. A., & Lane, C. J. (2006). Why do they leave? Modeling child welfare workers' turnover intentions. *Children and Youth Service Review, 28,* 548–577.

More rivers in the country are polluted, says law. (2002, July 20). Bernama: The Malaysian National News Agency.

Morris, M.W., Podolny, J., & Sullivan, B. N. (2008, July-August). *Organization Science, 19*(4), 517–532.

Morrison, A. H. (1992). *The new leaders: Guidelines on leadership diversity in America.* San Francisco: Jossey-Bass.

Morrison, A. M., & Von Glinow, M. A. (1990). Women and minorities in management. *American Psychologist, 45*, 200–208.

Moscovici, S. (1972). Society and theory in social psychology. In J. Israel & H. Tajfel (Eds.), *The context of social psychology* (pp. 17–68). London: Academic.

MSNBC News. (2009, November 26). Obama's bow in Japan sparks some criticism. Conservative commentators accuse president of groveling to foreign leader. Retrieved November 30, 2009, from: http://www.msnbc.msn.com/id/33978533/ns/politics-white_house/

Mullen, B., & Goethals, G. R. (1987). *Theories of group behavior.* New York: Springer-Verlag.

Muller, H. J., & Parham, P. A. (1998). Integrating workforce diversity into the business school curriculum: An experiment. *Journal of Management Education, 22*(2), 122.

Mussweiler, T. Ruter, K., & Epstude, K. (2006). The why, who and how of social comparison: A social-cognition perspective. In S. Guimond (Ed.), *Social comparison and social psychology: Understanding cognition, intergroup relations and culture.* New York: Cambridge University Press.

Nath, D. (2000). Gently shattering the glass ceiling: Experiences of Indian women managers. *Women in Management Review, 15*(1), 44–55.

National Public Radio. (2009, November 16). The presidential bow. Retrieved November 30, 2009, from: http://minnesota.publicradio.org/collections/special/columns/news_cut/archive/2009/11/the_presidential_bow.shtml?refid=0

NATLEX. International Labour Organization. (n.d.). Retrieved April 30, 2004, from www.ilo.org/dyn/natlex/natlex_browse.home

Nazario, S. (2002, September 29). Enrique's Journey. *The Los Angeles Times,* pp. A1–A10.

Nazario, S. (2007). *Enrique's journey: A story of a boy's dangerous odyssey to reunite with his mother.* New York: Random House.

Nelson, S. S. (2003, December 10). Turkish women fighting head-scarf ban. *Knight Ridder/Tribune News Service.*

Nestlé, S. A. (2003). *Nestlé: People Development Review.* Retrieved September 12, 2004, from www.nestle.com/html/npd/

Nestlé Foundation. (2003). Nestlé Foundation for the study of problems of nutrition in the world: Foundation website. Retrieved October 30, 2003, from www.nestlefoundation.org

Nestlé. (2009). *Creating shared values—The role of business in society.* Retrieved December 6, 2009, from http://www.nestle.com/SharedValueCSR/Overview.htm

Neuliep, J. W. (2008). *Intercultural communication: A contextual approach* (4th ed.). Thousand Oaks, CA: Sage.

Neuman, E., Sanchez-Burks, J., Goh, K., & Ybarra, O. (2004). *Cultural theories about conflict and team performance among European Americans* (working paper). Ann Arbor: University of Michigan.

Nigeria—Watchdog goes back to school. (2002, October 8). *AllAfrica, Inc. Africa News.* LexisNexis Academic, http://web.lexis-nexis.com/universe

Nisbett, R. E., & Miyamoto, Y. (2005). The influence of culture: Holistic versus analytic perception. *Trends in Cognitive Sciences, 9*(10), 467–473.

Nisbett, R. E., Peng, K., Choi, I., & Norenzayan, A. (2001). Culture and systems of thought: Holistic versus analytic cognition. *Psychological Review, 108*(2), 291–310.

Nixon, J. C., & West, J. F. (2000). American addresses work force diversity. *Business Forum, 25*(1/2), 4.

Nkomo, S. (2001, July). *Much to do about diversity: The muting of race, gender and class in managing diversity practice.* Paper presented at the International Cross-Cultural Perspectives on Workforce Diversity: The Inclusive Workplace, Bellagio, Italy.

Nkomo, S., & Cox, T., Jr. (1996). Diverse identities in organizations. In S. R Clegg, C. Hardy, & W. R. Nord (Eds.), *Handbook of organizations studies* (pp. 338–356). London: Sage.

Nkomo, S., & Kossek, E. (2000). Managing diversity: Human resource issues. In E. Kossek & R. Block (Eds.), *Managing human resources in the 21st century: From core concepts to strategic choice.* Cincinnati, OH: South-West College Publishing, module 9.

Northern and Central Land Councils. (2001, January 19). *Media release: Land Councils and Eurest in benchmark agreement for Aboriginal employment on the railway project.* Casuarina and Alice Springs, NT, Australia: Authors. Retrieved February 27, 2004, from www.nlc.org.au/html/files/01_01_railway.pdf

Norusis, M. J. (1993). SPSS for *Windows, release 6.0.* Chicago: SPSS.

Nurden, R. (1997, October 30). Teaching tailored for business people's every demand. *The European,* p. 9.

Nyambegera, S. M. (2002). Ethnicity and human resource management practice in sub-Saharan Africa: The relevance of the managing diversity discourse. *The International Journal of Human Resource Management, 13*(7), 1077–1090.

Ocholla, D. N. (2002). Diversity in the library and information workplace: A South African perspective. *Library Management, 23*(1/2), 59.

Organization for Economic Co-operation and Development [OECD]. (1998). *Trends in international migration* (Annual Report of the Continuous Reporting System on Migration, SOPEMI). Paris: Author.

OECD. (2009). *International migration: The human face of globalisation.* OECD Publishing.

Office of the United Nations High Commissioner for Human Rights. (2003, November). Status of ratifications of the principal international human rights treaties. Retrieved May 15, 2004, from www.unhchr.ch/pdf/report.pdf

O'Leary, V. E., & Ickovics, J. R. (1992). Cracking the glass ceiling: Overcoming isolation and discrimination. In U. Sekeran & F. Leong (Eds.), *Womanpower: Managing in times of demographic turbulence* (pp. 7–30). Newbury Park, CA: Sage.

Olson, W. (1997, February). Framing Texaco: How lawyers and the *New York Times* concocted a scam. *The American Spectator.* Retrieved May 26, 2004, from http://walterolson.com/articles/texacotp.html

Ontario Co-operative Association. (2003, October 20). *Press release: Sweet victory for fair trade chocolate.* Retrieved December 9, 2003, from www.fairtradetoronto.com/news/news_main.cfm?category=3&newsid=29

Organization for Economic Co-operation and Development (OECD). (2000). *Trends in international migration* (Annual Report of the Continuous Reporting System on Migration, SOPEMI). Paris: Author.

Organization for Economic Co-operation and Development (OECD). (2009). *International Migration Outlook* (2008 ed.). Paris: Author.

Orlando, R. C. (2000). Racial diversity, business strategy, and firm performance: A resource-based view. *Academy of Management Journal, 43*(2), 164–177.

Orlitzky, M., Schmidt, F. L., & Rynes, S. L. (2003). Corporate social and financial performance: A meta-analysis. *Organization Studies, 24*(3), 403–431.

O'Rourke, R. (1997). Member states fail to agree on key issues. *International Financial Law Review, 16*(8), 51–52.

Osborne, B. (2005). *Fair employment in Northern Ireland: A generation on.* Belfast: Blackstaff Press.

Oslo push for women directors. (2003, June 13). BBC News. Retrieved May, 2004, from http://news.bbc.co.uk/1/hi/business/2988992.stm

Ovwigho, P. C., Saunders, C., & Born, C. E. (2008). Barriers to independence among TANF recipients: Comparing caseworker records and client surveys. *Administration in Social Work, 32*(3), 84–110.

Ozbilgin, M., & Tatli, A. (2008). *Global diversity management: An evidence based approach.* London Palgrave Macmillan.

Palmer, G. (2003). Diversity management, past, present and future. *Asia Pacific Journal of Human Resources, 41*(1), 13–24.

Palmi, P. (2001). The management of diversity in public administration: The European approach. *Economic Research, 14*(1), 49–58.

Paluck, E. L. (2006). Diversity training and intergroup contact: A call to action research. *Journal of Social Issues, 62*(3), 577–595.

Parham, P. A., & Muller, H. J. (2008). Review of workplace diversity content in organizational behavior texts. *Academy of Management Learning and Education, 7*(3), 424–428.

Park, K. 2008. "I can provide for my children": Korean immigrant women's changing perspectives on work outside the home. *Gender Issues, 25*(1), 26–42.

Pekerti, A. A., & Thomas, D. C. (2003). Communication in intercultural interaction: An empirical investigation of indicentric and sociocentric communication styles. *Journal of Cross-Cultural Psychology, 34*(2), 139–154.

People Tree. (2001, July). *Company Newsletter,* 1 (London).

Perez-Floriano, L. R, & Gonzalez, J. A. (2007). Risk, safety and culture in Brazil and Argentina: The case of TransInc Corporation. *International Journal of Manpower, 28*(5), 403–417.

Perraton, J., Goldblatt, D., Held, D., & McGrew, A. (2000). Economic activity in a globalizing world. In D. H. A. McGrew (Ed.), *The global transformations reader.* Cambridge, UK: Polity Press.

Perry, B. A. (2007). *The Michigan affirmative action cases.* Lawrence, KS: University Press of Kansas.

Petersen, P., Saporta, I., & Seidel, M. L. (2000). Offering a job: Meritocracy and social networks. *American Journal of Sociology, 106*(3), 763–816.

Pettigrew, T. F. (1986). The intergroup contact hypothesis reconsidered. In M. Hewstone & R. Brown (Eds.), *Contact and conflict in intergroup encounters.* New York: Blackwell.

Pettigrew, T. F. (1998). Reactions toward the new minorities of western Europe. *Annual Review of Sociology, 24,* 77–103.

Pettigrew T. F., Allport, G. W., & Barnett, E. O. (1958). Binocular resolution and perception of race in South Africa. *British Journal of Psychology, 49,* 265–278.

Pettigrew, T. F., & Martin, J. (1989). Organizational inclusion of minority groups: A social psychological analysis. In J. P. Van Oudenhoven & T. M. Willemsen (Eds.), *Ethnic minorities: Social psychological perspectives.* Berwyn, PA: Swets North America.

Pettigrew, T. F., & Tropp, L. R. (2006). A meta-analytic test of intergroup contact theory. *Journal of Personality and Social Psychology, 90,* 751–783.

Pfeffer, J. (1989). A political perspective on careers: Interests, networks, and environments. In M. B. Arthur, D. T. Hall, & B. S. Lawrence (Eds.), *Handbook of career theory* (pp. 380–396). Cambridge, UK: Cambridge University Press.

Phillips, M. (2002, May 22). Ghana's tech frontier, internet start-up flourishes. *The Wall Street Journal.* Retrieved September 13, 2004, from www.busyinternet.com/site/about/pr/wsj/WSJ_com%20-%20Technology.htm

Pitts, D. (2009). Diversity management, job satisfaction and performance: Evidence from U.S. federal agencies. *Public Administration Review, 69*(2), 328–338.

Plantation giants should plough back earnings, says PBS. (2003, July 13). *Bernama: The Malaysian National News Agency.* Retrieved September 13, 2004, from www.pbs-sabah.org/pbs3/html/news/2003/130703bernama.html

Point, S., & Singh, V., (2003). Defining and dimensionalising diversity: Evidence from corporate websites across Europe. *European Management Journal, 21*(6), 750–761.

Ponterotto, J. G., Utsey, S. O., & Pedersen, P. (2006). *Preventing prejudice: A guide for counselors, educators, and parents.* Thousand Oaks, CA: Sage.

Population Reference Bureau. (2009a). Italy Statistics: Demographic and Health Highlights. Retrieved December 9, 2009, from http://www.prb.org/Countries/Italy.aspx

Population Reference Bureau. (2009b). *2009 World Population Data Sheet.* Washington, DC.

Port Authority. (2000). Port Authority to enhance social services it provides for homeless. Retrieved December 15, 2003, from www.panynj.gov/pr/113–00.html

Port Authority of New York and New Jersey. (2004, April 13). Port Authority renews partnership with urban pathways. Press Release Number: 43–2004.

Porter, L., & Lawler, E. E., III. (1968). *Managerial attitudes and performance.* Homewood, IL: Irwin.

Powell, G. N. & Graves, L. M. (2003). Women and men in management (3rd ed.). Thousand Oaks, CA: Sage.

Pradhan, A. (1989, November 6). Ethnic markets: Sales niche of the future. *National Underwriter,* 18.

Pramualratana, A., & Rau, B. (2001). *HIV/AIDS programs in private sector businesses.* Bangkok: Thailand Business Coalition on AIDS.

Prasad, P., Pringle, J. K., & Konrad, A. M. (2006). Examining the contours of workplace diversity: Concepts, contexts and chanllenges. In A. M. Konrad, P. Prasad, & J. K. Pringle (Eds.), *Handbook of workplace diversity* (pp. 1–22) London: Sage.

Price, J. L., & Mueller, C. W. (1986). *Handbook of organizational measurement.* Marshfield, MA: Pittman.

Price Waterhouse v. Hopkins, 490 U.S. 228 (1989).

Pugh, S. D., Dietz, J., Brief, A. P., & Wiley, J. W. (2008). Looking inside and out: The impact of employee and community demographic composition on organizational diversity climate. *Journal of Applied Psychology, 93*(6), 1422–1428.

Pyke, J. (2007). *Productive diversity in Australia—How and why companies make the most of diversity.* Saarbrucken, Germany: VDM Verlag Dr. Muller.

Quinn, N., & Holland, D. (1987). *Cultural models of language and thought.* New York: Cambridge University Press.

Ram, H. (2002, March 9). The a-z of fair trade: Harry Ram explains why the decision to make the switch to fair trade produce should be as easy as abc. *Independent* (London).

Ramachandran, S., & Shanmugam, B. (1995). Plight of plantation workers in Malaysia: Defeated by definitions. *Asian Survey, 35*(4), 394–407.

Rea, D., & Eastwood, J. (1992). Legislating for Northern Ireland's fair employment problem. *International Journal of Manpower, 13*(6–7), 31–39.

Read, J. G. (2002). Challenging myths of Muslim women: The influence of Islam on Arab-American women's labor force participation. *Muslim World, 96,* 19–39.

Reardon, K. K. (1995). *They don't get it, do they? Communication in the workplace: Closing the gap between women and men* (pp. 183–191). New York: Little, Brown.

Redfield, R. (1941). *The folk culture of Yucatan.* Chicago: University of Chicago Press.

Regev, D. (2007, August 25). The Department of Commerce "harassment project": Inspectors will visit work organizations starting next month. Yediot Aharonot (Hebrew).

Ricci v. DeStefano (2009).

Richard, O. C. (2000). Racial diversity, business strategy, and firm performance: A recourse-based view. *Academy of Management Journal, 43*(2), 164–177.

Richburg, K. (2004, March 4). French senate approves ban on religious attire. *The Washington Post,* A14.

Richmond v. J. A. Croson Co., 488 U.S. 469 (1989).

Ridgeway, C. L. (1988). Gender differences in task groups: A status and legitimacy account. In M. Webster & M. Forschi (Eds.), *Status generalization: New theory and research* (pp. 188–206). Stanford, CA: Stanford University Press.

Riesch, C., & Kleiner, B. H. (2005). Discrimination towards customers in the restaurant industry. *Equal Opportunities International, 24*(7/8), 29–37.

Roberts, L., & White, J. (2000). DaimlerChrysler to cut thousands of jobs in North America. World Socialist Website, International Committee of the Fourth International. Retrieved September 12, 2004, from www.wsws.org/articles/2000/ nov2000/chry-n28.shtml

Robertson, C. J., Al-Khatib, J. A., & Al-Habib, M. (2002). The relationship between Arab values and work beliefs: An exploratory examination. *Thunderbird International Business Review, 44*(5), 583.

Robinson, G., & Dechant, K. (1997). Building a business case for diversity. *Academy of Management Executive, 11*(3), 21–31.

Robinson, R. V. (1983). Book review of *Culture's consequences: International differences in work-related values. Work and Occupations, 10,* 110–115.

Roemer, J. E. (2002). Equality of opportunity: A progress report. *Social Choice Welfare, 19,* 455–471.

Ross, L., & Ward, A. (1996). Naive realism: Implications for social conflict and misunderstanding. In T. Brown, E. Reed, & E. Turiel (Eds.), *Values and knowledge* (pp. 103–105). Hillsdale, NJ: Lawrence Erlbaum.

Rowley, T., & Berman, S. (2000). A brand new brand of corporate social performance. *Business & Society, 39*(4), 397–418.

Rubin, M., & Badea, C. (2007). Why do people perceive ingroup homogeneity on ingroup traits and outgroup homogeneity on outgroup traits? *Personality and Social Psychology Bulletin, 33*(1), 31–42.

Sahin v. Turkey (2004, 2005). application no 44774/98, Chamber judgment of 29 June 2004, Grand Chamber judgment of 10 November 2005.

Sanchez-Burks, J. (1999). *Ascetic Protestantism and cultural schemas for relational sensitivity in the workplace.* Unpublished doctoral dissertation, Department of Psychology, University of Michigan, Ann Arbor.

Sanchez-Burks, J. (2002). Protestant relational ideology and (in)attention to relational cues in work settings. *Journal of Personality and Social Psychology, 83*(4), 919–929.

Sanchez-Burks, J. (2005). Protestant relational ideology: The cognitive underpinnings andorganizational implications of an American anomaly. *Research in Organizational Behavior* (R. Kramer & B. Staw, Eds), *26,* 265–305.

Sanchez-Burks, J., Bartel, C., & Blount, S. (2009). Performance in intercultural interactions at work. *Journal of Applied Psychology, 94*(1), 216–229.

Sanchez-Burks, J., Choi, I., Nisbett, R., Zhao, S., & Jasook, K. (2003). Conversing across cultures: East-west communication styles in work and nonwork contexts. *Journal of Personality and Social Psychology, 85*(2), 263–372.

Sanchez-Burks, J., & Lee, F. (2007). Culture and workways. In S. Kitayama & D. Cohen (Eds.), *Handbook of cultural psychology* (Vol. 1, pp. 346–369). New York: Guilford.

Sanchez-Burks, J., Nisbett, R. E., & Ybarra, O. (2000). Cultural styles, relational schemas and prejudice against outgroups. *Journal of Personality and Social Psychology, 79*(2), 174–189.

Sardar, Z. (2001, July 30). More hackney than Hollywood. *New Statesman, 14*(667), 14–16.

Sassen, S. (1988). *The mobility of labor and capital: A study in international investment and labor flow.* Cambridge, UK: Cambridge University Press.

Sassen, S. (1994). Economic internationalization: The new migration in Japan and the United States. *Social Justice, 21*(2), 62–82.

Sassen, S. (1999). *Guests and aliens.* New York: New Press.

Sassenberg, K., Moskowitz, G. B., Jacoby, J., & Hansen, N. (2007). The carry-over effect of competition: The impact of competition on prejudice towards uninvolved outgroups. *Journal of Experimental Social Psychology, 43*(4), 529–538.

Savage, C. (2009, June 10). Videos shed new light on Sotomayor's positions. *New York Times.* Retrieved on http://www.nytimes.com/2009/06/11/us/politics/ 11judge.html?_r=1

Scandal lets malaysia prove its mettle. (2002, October 16). *The New York Times, p.* W1. [An exerpt of the article can be found at http://query.nytimes.com/gst/abstract .html?res=FB0C12F6345E0C758DDDA90994DA404482]

Scein, V. (1995). *Working from the margins: Voices of mothers in poverty.* New York: Russell Sage.

Schiffman, R., & Wicklund, R. A. (1992). The minimal group paradigm and its minimal group psychology: On equating social identity with arbitrary group membership. *Theory and Psychology, 2*(1), 29–50.

Schmitt, M. T., Branscombe, N. R., Silvia, P. J., Garcia, D. M., & Spears, R. (2006). Categorizing at the group-level in response to intragroup social comparisons: A self-categorization theory integration of self-evaluation and social identity motives. *European Journal of Social Psychology, 36,* 297–314.

Schmitt, M. T., Spears, R., & Branscombe, N. R. (2003). Constructing a minority group identity out of a shared rejection: The case of international students. *European Journal of Social Psychology, 33,* 1–12.

Schneider, B. (1987). The people make the place. *Personnel Psychology, 40,* 437–453.

Schneider, B. D., Smith, B., & Paul, M. C. (2001). P-E fit and the attraction-selection-attrition model of organizaitonal functioning; Introduction and overview. In M. Erez, U. Kleinbeck, & H. Thierry, (Eds.), *Work motivation in the context of a globalizing economy.* Mahwah, NJ: Lawrence Erlbaum.

Schoeff, M., Jr. (2009). Diversity's strategic role. *Workforce Management.* Retrieved on July 26, 2009, from http://www.workforce.com/section/06/feature/25/37/81/index.html

Schwartz, P., & Gibb, B. (1999). *When good companies do bad things.* New York: Wiley.

Scott, J. C. (1999, January/February). Developing cultural fluency: The goal of international business communication instruction in the 21st century. *Journal of Education for Business,* 140–143.

Scriven, J. (1984). Women at work in Sweden. In M. J. Davidson & C. L. Cook (Eds.), *Working women: An international survey.* London: Wiley.

Seol, D. H. (1999). *Foreign labor and Korean society.* Seoul: Seoul National University.

Sexton, V. S., & Misiak, H. (1984). American psychology and psychology abroad. *American Psychologist, 39,* 1026–1031.

Shackelford, W. G. (2003). The changing definition of workplace diversity. *Black Collegian, 33*(2), 53.

Shell Intensive Training Programme. (2009). Retrieved December 6, 2009, from http://www .shell.com/home/content/nigeria/society_environment/youth/sitp.html

Shell Youth Training. (2004). Retrieved May 31, 2004, from www.countonshell.com/community/involvement/shell_youth_training.html

Sherif, M. (1966). *Group conflict and co-operation: Their social psychology.* London: Routledge & Kegan Paul.

Sherif, M., & Sherif, C. W. (1953). *Groups in harmony and tension.* New York: Harper.

Shinnar, R. S. (2008). Coping with negative social identity: The case of Mexican immigrants. *The Journal of Social Psychology, 148*(5), 553–575.

Shorter-Gooden, K. (2004). Multiple resistance strategies: How African American women cope with racism and sexism. *Journal of Black Psychology, 30*(3), 406–425.

Simpson, G. W., & Kohers, T. (2002). The link between corporate social and financial performance: Evidence from the banking industry. *Journal of Business Ethics, 35,* 97–109.

Singh, J. P. (1990). Managerial culture and work-related values in India. *Organization Studies, 11,* 75–101.

Slabbert, A. (2001). Cross-cultural racism in South Africa—dead or alive? *Social Behavior and Personality, 29*(2), 125–132.

Smeesters, B., Arrijn, P., Feld, S., & Nayer, A. (2000). The occurrence of discrimination in Belgium. In Zegers de Beijl (Ed.), *Documenting discrimination against migrant workers in the labour market.* Geneva: International Labour Office.

Smith, P. B., & Fischer, R. (2003). Reward allocation and culture. *Journal of Cross-Cultural Psychology, 34*(3), 251–268.

Smith, P. M. (2008). Culturally conscious organizations: A conceptual framework. *Libraries and the Academy,* 8(2), 141–155.

Smith, R. K. M. (2007). Religion and education: A human rights dilemma illustrated by the recent "headscarf case." *Globalisation, Societies and Education, 5*(3), 303–314.

Snider, J., Hill, R. P., & Martin, D. (2003). Corporate social responsibility in the 21st century: A view from the world's most successful firms. *Journal of Business Ethics, 48*(2), 175.

Social Accountability International. (2003). *2003 CCA Winner Profiles.* Retrieved December 8, 2003, from www.cepaa.org/programs/CCAWinnerProfiles03 .htm#novadelta

Søndergaard, M. (1994). Research note: Hofstede's consequences: A study of reviews, citations and replications. *Organization Studies, 15,* 447–456.

Sowell, T. (1996). *Migrations and cultures: A world view.* New York: Basic Books.

Sowell, T. (2004). *Affirmative action around the world: An empirical study.* New Haven: Yale University Press.

Standish, M., Mehalik, M. M., Gorman, M. E., & Werhane, P. H. (1998). General dilemma: Should Unilever and Vis pursue sustainable agriculture? Retrieved December 1, 2003, from http://repo-nt.tcc.virginia.edu/ethics/Cases/unilever/ UnileverC.doc

Stanecki, K. (2002). *The AIDS pandemic in the 21st century* (draft report prepared for the XIV International Conference on AIDS). Washington, DC: U.S. Census Bureau.

State of California Constitution, article I, section 31.

Stephan, W. G., Ybarra, O., & Martinez, C. (1998). Prejudice toward immigrants to Spain and Israel: An integrated threat theory analysis. *Journal of Cross-Cultural Psychology, 29,* 4, 559–576.

Stevens, F. G., Plaut, V. C., & Sanchez-Burks, J. (2008). Unlocking the benefits of diversity: All-inclusive multiculturalism and positive organizational change. *Journal of Applied Behavioral Science, 44*(1), 116–133.

Stone, B. (2004, April 19). Should I stay or should I go? *Newsweek.* Retrieved September 29, 2004, from www.msnbc.msn.com/id/4710299/

Stouffer, S. A., Suchman, E. A., DeVinney, L. C., Star, S. A., & Williams, R. M. (1949). *The American soldier: Adjustment during army life* (Vol. 1). Princeton, NJ: Princeton University Press.

Strachan, G., & Jamieson, S. (1999). Equal opportunity in Australia in the 1990s. *New Zealand Journal of Industrial Relations, 24*(3), 319–341.

Strategic Plan for the University of Southern California. (2004). Retrieved May 31, 2004, from March 26,2010, www.usc.edu/about/mission/strategic_plan94.html

The Sunday Times. (2007). Sri Lanka, No to sexual harassment. Retrieved March 26,2010, from http://communicatinglabourrights.wordpress.com/2007/12/17/sri-lanka-no-to-sexual-harassment/

Sunstein, C. R. (1999). Affirmative action, caste, and cultural comparisons. *Michigan Law Review I, 97,* 1311–1320.

Sustainable Agriculture Initiative [SAI]. (2002). *High-level pan-European conference on agriculture and biodiversity: Towards integrating biological and landscape diversity for sustainable agriculture in Europe.* Strasbourg, France: Council of Europe Press.

Svehla, T. (1994). Diversity management: Key to future success. *Frontiers of Health Services Management, 11*(2), 3.

Syed, J., & Murray, P. A. (2008). A cultural feminist approach towards managing diversity in top management teams. *Equal Opportunities International, 27*(5), 413–432.

Tajfel, H. (1957). Values and perceptual judgment of magnitude. *Psychological Review, 64,* 192–204.

Tajfel, H. (1959). Quantitative judgment in social perception. *British Journal of Psychology, 50,* 16–29.

Tajfel, H. (1978). *Differentiation between social groups.* New York: Academic.

Tajfel, H. (1982). *Social identity and intergroup relations.* Cambridge, UK: Cambridge University Press.

Tajfel, H., Flament, C., Billing, M. G., & Bundy, R. F. (1971). Social categorization and intergroup behaviour. *European Journal of Social Psychology, 1,* 149–177.

Tajfel, H., & Turner, J. C. (1979). An integrative theory of intergourp conflict. In W. G. Austin & S. Worchel (Eds.), *The social psychology of intergroup relations* (pp. 33–47). Monterey, CA: Brooks/Cole.

Tajfel, H., & Turner, J. C. (1986). The social identity theory of intergroup behavior. In S. Worchel & W. G. Austin (Eds.), *Psychology of intergroup relations* (pp. 7–24). Chicago: Nelson-Hall.

Tajfel H., & Wilkes, A. L. (1963). Classification and quantitative judgment. *British Journal of Psychology, 54,* 101–113.

Talaski, K. (2002, January 23). New chief could be Kmart's savior. Retrieved November 3, 2003, from http://www.usatoday.com/money/retail/2002–01–23-kmart-adamson.htm

Tannen, D. (1990). *You just don't understand: Women and men in conversation.* New York: Morrow.

Tarlo, E. (1996). *Clothing matters: Dress and identity in India.* Chicago: University of Chicago Press.

Tavris, C., & Aronson, E. (2007). *Mistakes were made (but not by me): Why we justify foolish beliefs, bad decisions, and hurtful acts.* Orlando, FL: Harcourt.

Taylor, D. M., & Moghaddam, F. M. (1994). *Theories of intergroup relations.* Westport, CT: Praeger.

Taylor, P. (1986). Structural factors in women's work patterns: Women in organizations. In A. Stromberg & S. Harkess (Eds.), *Women working: Theories and facts in perspective* (2nd ed., pp. 167–182). Palo Alto, CA: Mayfield.

Taylor, P., Powell, D., & Wrench, J. (1997). *The evaluation of anti-discrimination training activities in the United Kingdom.* Geneva: International Labour Organization.

Telestra Corporation Limited. (n.d.). *Telestra: Multicultural Service Centres.* Retrieved December 8, 2003, from www.diversityaustralia.gov.au/_inc/doc_pdf/case/telstra.pdf

Texaco independent investigator's report. (1996, November 11). Court TV Online. Retrieved May 26, 2004, from www.courttv.com/archive/legaldocs/business/texaco/report.html

Texaco investigator: Tape analysis shows no racial slur. (1996, November 11). Retrieved September 13, 2004, from www.cnn.com/US/9611/11/texaco/

Texas Civil Rights Project. (1999, October 12). TCRP files 4th lawsuit in campaign against local restaurants for racial discrimination (2nd suit against a Denny's restaurant). Retrieved November 3, 2003, from www.texascivilrightsproject.org/Press_Releases/1999/2nd_Denny's_lawsuit.htm

Theological students fail their classes because of headscarf ban. (2002, May 28). *Turkish Daily News.* Retrieved September 13, 2004, from www.turkishdailynews.com/

Thiederman, S. (2008). *Making diversity work: 7 steps for defeating bias in the workplace.* New York: New York Kaplan Publishing.

Thomas, R. R., Jr. (1991). *Beyond race and gender: Unleashing the power of your total work force by managing diversity.* New York: American Management Association.

Thomas, R. R., Jr. (1996). A diversity framework. In M. M. Chemers, S. Oskamp, & M. A. Costanzo (Eds.), *Diversity in organizations: New perspectives for a changing workplace* (pp. 245–263). Thousand Oaks, CA: Sage.

Thomas, R. R., Jr. (1999). *Building a house for diversity.* New York: American Management Association.

Thomas, R. R., Jr. (2005). *Building on the promise of diversity: How we can move to the next level in our workplaces, our communities, and our society.* New York: AMACOM.

Thomas, R. T., Thomas, D. A., Ely, R. J., Boston, MA: Meyerson, D. (2002). *Harvard Business Review on managing diversity.* Harvard Business School Press.

Ting-Toomey, S. (1988). Intercultural conflict styles. In Y. Y. Kim & W. B. Gudykunst (Eds.), *Theories in intercultural communication* (pp. 22–38). Newbury Park, CA: Sage.

Ting-Toomey, S. (2007). Intercultural conflict training: Theory-practice approaches and research challenges. *Journal of Intercultural Communication Research, 36*(3), 255–271.

Tolbert, K. (1999, December 14). Japan officials cited for harassment. *Washington Post Foreign Service,* p. A31.

Tomaskovic-Devey, D. (1993). *Gender and racial inequality at work: The sources and consequences of job segregation.* Ithaca, NY: ILR Press.

Tomei, M. (2003). Discrimination and equality at work: A review of the concepts. *International Labour Review, 42,* 401–417.

TransFair Canada. (2003). TransFair Canada: Organization information. Retrieved December 9, 2003, from www.transfair.ca/tfc/index.html

TransFair USA. (2007, June 14). Social and organic premium increase for Fair Trade Certified coffee: Direct and Positive Impact for Farmers. Retrieved March 26, 2010, from http://www.transfairusa.org/pdfs/certification/FTC_price.pdf

Trapp, R. (2002, December 7). The commercial challenge of fair trade: More people are buying ethical goods—and not just because they feel they should, says Roger Trapp. *Independent* (London).

Triandis, H. C. (1996). *Individualism and collectivism.* Boulder, CO: Westview Press.

Triandis, H. C. (2003). The future of workforce diversity in international organisations: A commentary. *Applied Psychology: An International Review, 52*(3), 486–495.

Triandis, H. C. (2004). The many dimensions of culture. *Academy of Management Executive, 18*(1), 88–93.

Triandis, H. C., Marin, G., Lisansky, J., & Betancourt, H. (1984). Simpatia as a cultural script of Hispanics. *Journal of Personality and Social Psychology, 47,* 1363–1375.

Trooper sues, claims bias in Ocala Denny's. (2003, June 19). *Star-Banner.* Retrieved September 13, 2004, from www.sptimes.com/2003/06/21/news_pf/State/Trooper_sues__claims_.shtml

Tse, D. K., Francis, J., & Walls, J. F. (1994). Cultural differences in conducting intra- and inter-cultural negotiations: A Sino-Canadian comparison. *Journal of International Business Studies, 25,* 537–555.

Tsogas, G., & Subeliani, D. (2005). Managing diversity in the Netherlands: A case study of Rabobank. *International Journal of Human Resource Management, 16*(5), 831–851.

Tsui, A. S., Egan, T. D., & O'Reilly, C. A. (1992). Being different: Relational demography and organizational attachment. *Administrative Science Quarterly, 37,* 549–579.

Tsui, A. S., & Farh, J. L. (1997). Where gunaxi matters: Relational demography and gunaxi in the Chinese context. *Work and Occupations, 24*(1), 56–79.

Tsui, A. S., & Gutek, B. (1999). *Demographic differences in organizations.* Lanham, MD: Lexington Books.

Tsui, A. S., & O'Reilly, C. A. (1989). Beyond simple demographic effects: The importance of relational demography in superior-subordinate dyads. *Academy of Management Journal, 32,* 402–423.

Tsui, A. S., Porter, L. W., & Egan, T. D. (2002). When both similarities and dissimilarities matter: Extending the concept of relational demography. *Human Relations, 55*(8), 899–929.

Tu, W. M. (1985). Selfhood and otherness in Confucian thought. In A. Marsella, G. DeVos, & F. Hsu (Eds.), *Culture and self: Asian and western perspectives* (pp. 231–251). New York: Tavistock.

Tuchman, G. (1997, September 4). DA: Denny's didn't discriminate against Asian Americans. The Associated Press. Retrieved November 3, 2003, from www.cnn.com/ US/9709/04/dennys.dropped

Tummala, K. K. (1999). Policy of preference: Lessons from India, the United States and South Africa. *Public Administration Review, 59*(6), 495–508.

Tung, C. (2000). The cost of caring: The social reproductive labor of Filipina live-in home health caregivers. *Frontiers, 21*(1), 61–82.

Turban, D. B., & Greening, D. W. (1996). Corporate social performance and organizational attractiveness to prospective employees. *Academy of Management Journal, 40*(3), 658–672.

Turcsik, R. (2003, December 1). Supermarket grocery business: Full steam ahead. *Progressive Grocer: The Publication of Strategic Management.*

Turner, J. C. (1987). *Rediscovering the social group: A self-categorization theory.* Oxford, UK: Basil Blackwell.

Turner, J. C., & Giles, H. (1981). *Intergroup behavior.* New York: Basil Blackwell.

Turner, W., & Kleiner, B. H. (2001). What managers must know to conduct business in Brazil. *Management Research News, 24*(3/4), 72–75.

25 years, 25 success stories. (2009). La Ciemba. Retrieved December 15, 2009, from http://www.caic.ca/25stories.html

2004 Tyler Laureates: Barefoot College. (2004). Retrieved May 5, 2004, from www.usc.edu/dept/LAS/tylerprize/04tyler.html

Twyman, C. M. (2002). Finding justice in South African labor law: The use of arbitration to evaluate affirmative action. *Case Western Reserve Journal of International Law, 33,* 307–342.

Umiker, W. (1995). Workplace loyalty in the 1990s. *The Health Care Supervisor, 13*(3), 30–35.

Unilever. (2003a). Environment and society. Retrieved December 3, 2003, from www.unilever.com/environmentsociety

Unilever. (2003b). Malaysia: Improving biodiversity at our palm oil plantations. Retrieved December 3, 2003, from www.unilever.com/environmentsociety/environ mentalcasestudies/biodiversity/Malaysia_PalmOil.asp

United Nations. (1999a). *Demographic yearbook, 1999.* New York: Author.

United Nations. (1999b). *Maternity protection at work* (Report V (1), International Labor Conference, 87th Session). Geneva: International Labour Organization.

United Nations. (2000a). *Replacement migration* (ESA/P/WP.160). New York: Author. Retrieved September 13, 2004, from http://www.un.org/esa/population/publications/ migration/cover-preface.pdf

United Nations. (2000b). *The World's Women 2000.* New York: Author.

United Nations. (2001). *World population prospects* (2000 Revision, Vol. 1. ST/ESA/SER.A/198). New York: Author.

United Nations. (2002), *World investment report 2002* (UNCTAD/WIR/). Retrieved September 13, 2004, from www.unctad.org/en/docs/wir2003light_en.pdf.

United Nations. (2009a). *World population prospects* (2008 Revision). Retrieved September 13, 2009, from http://esa.un.org/unpp/p2k0data.asp

United Nations. (2009b). *World investment report 2009.* Retrieved September 13, 2009, from www.unctad.org/

United Nations Discrimination (Employment and Occupation) Convention, 1958 (No. 111). Retrieved July 20, 2009, from http://www.unhchr.ch/html/menu3/b/d_i10111.htm

United Nations Economic and Social Commission for Asia and the Pacific. (2003). *Saving our futures: Multiminiterial Action Guide HIV/AIDS in Asia and the Pacific.* United Nations, ST/ESCAP/2250 No. E.03.II.F.26.

United Nations Educational, Scientific, and Cultural Organization (UNESCO). (2009). *Key Statistical Tables on Education.* Consulted on 9/29/09 at www.uis.unesco.org/

United Nations Environment Programme, International Fund for Agricultural Development. (2004). The Barefoot College Project, Tilonia, Rajasthan, India. Retrieved May 5, 2004, from www.unep.org/unep/envpolimp/techcoop/19.htm

United Nations Fact Sheet No. 2 (Rev. 1)., The International Bill of Human Rights (1996, June). Office of the United Nations High Commissioner for Human Rights. Retrieved September 29, 2002, from www.unhchr.ch/html/menu6/2/fs2.htm

United Nations Global Compact. (2001). Discrimination is everybody's business: From discrimination to diversity. New York: Volvo Cars in collaboration with the U.N High Commissioner on Human Rights. Retrieved May 27, 2004, from http://research .dnv.com/csr/PW_Tools/PWD/1/00/L/1–00-L-2001–01–0/lib2001/Diversity_report.pdf

United Nations Global Impact. (2004, March 30). Corporate Social Responsilbity and Diversity Management. Keynote address at the MIA Award Ceremony, Copenhagen, by George Kell, United Nations. Retrieved December 5, 2009, from http:// www.unglobalcompact.org/WebsiteInfo/search_global_compact.html?cx=0178676 15180777054248%3Arbjhpb8rvpy&cof=FORID%3A11&q=Discrimination+is+eve rybodys+business#1311

United Nations, Treaty Collections, Chapter IV Human Rights, 3. International Covenant on Economic, Social and Cultural Rights. Retrieved July 18, 2009, from http://treaties.un.org/Pages/ViewDetails.aspx?src=TREATY&mtdsg_no=IV-3& chapter=4&lang=en

Universal Declaration of Human Rights. (1948, December 10). United Nations. Retrieved September 26, 2002, from www.unhchr.ch/udhr/index.htm

The U.N. Refugee Agency. (2008). Turkey: Situation of women who wear headscarves Retrieved July 15, 2009, http://www.unhcr.org/refworld/type,QUERYRESPONSE,, TUR,4885a91a8,0.html

USA Today (2009, January 2). Women CEOs Slowly Gain on Corporate America. Retrieved August 31, 2009, from http://www.usatoday.com/money/companies/management/2009–01–01-women-ceos-increase_N.htm

U.S. Bureau of Labor Statistics. (2009). Employment status of the civilian noninstitutional population by age, sex, and race. Retrieved September 29, 2008, from www.bls.gov/cps/

U.S. Census Bureau. (2000). Projection of the total resident population by 5-year age groups, and sex with special age categories middle series, 2050-2070. Retrieved August 16, 2009, from http://www.census.gov/population/projections/nation/summary/np-t3-g.txt

USC Civic and Community Relations. (2010). *Our communities*. Retrieved April 2010, http://communities.usc.edu/programs/#21

U.S. Department of Justice. (1993). *United States of America v. Flagstar Corporation and Denny's, Inc.,* No. 93–20208-JW, consolidated with *Ridgeway v. Flagstar Corporation and Denny's, Inc.,* No. 93–20202-JW. Retrieved November 3, 2003, from www.usdoj.gov/crt/housing/documents/dennysettle2.htm

U.S. Equal Employment Opportunity Commission. (2002, October 30). EEOC settles sexual harassment lawsuit against Denny's. Retrieved November 5, 2003, from www.eeoc.gov/press/10–30–02.html

Vakulenko, A. (2007). Islamic headscarves' and the European Convention: An intersectional perspective. *Social and Legal Studies, 16,* 183–199.

Van Dijk, T. A. (1987). *Communicating racism.* Newbury Park, CA: Sage.

Van Dijk, T. A. (2006). *Racism and the European press.* Presentation prepared for the European Commission against Racism and Intolerance (ECRI), November 16–17, 2006.

Van Dijk, T. A. (2007). *Racism, the press and freedom of expression: A summary of ten theses.* Presentation made in the ECRI meeting of November 16–17, 2006, in Strasbourg. To be published by the European Commission against Racism and Intolerance (ECRI).

Van Knippenberg, D., & Schippers, M. C. (2007). Work group diversity. *Annual Review of Psychology, 58,* 515–541.

Van Swol, L. (2003). The effects of nonverbal mirroring on perceived persuasiveness, agreement with an imitator, and reciprocity in a group discussion. *Communication Research, 30,* 46–56.

Vaupel, J. W. (2001). Demographic insights into longevity. *Population, 13*(1), 245–260.

Vaupel, J. W., Carey, J. R., Christensen, K., Johnson T. E., Yashin A. I., Holm, N.V., et al. (1998), Biodemographic trajectories of longevity. *Science, 280,* 5365, 855–860.

Velasquez, M. G. (1992). *Business ethics: Concepts and cases* (pp. 23–36). New Delhi: Englewood Cliffs, NJ: Prentice Hall.

Velasquez, M. G. (2005). Business ethics: Concepts and cases, (6th ed.). New Delhi: Prentice Hall of India.

Velasquez, M. G. (2006). *Business ethics: Concepts and cases (6th Economy ed.).* Upper Saddle River, NJ: Prentice Hall.

Verdicchio, P. (1999). *Bound by distance: Rethinking nationalism through the Italian diaspora.* Madison, NJ: Farleigh Dickson University Press.

Vibhuti Patel (2005). A brief history of the battle against sexual harassment at the workplace. Retrieved July 26, 2009, from http://infochangeindia.org/20051101160/Women/ Analysis/A-brief-history-of-the-battle-against-sexual-harassment-at-the-workplace.html

Virgin Group. (2003). *The Virgin story.* Retrieved December 15, 2003, from www .virgin.com/aboutus/

Virgin Group. (2009). Company Overview. Retrieved December 7, 2009, from http://www.gbcimpact.org/virgin

Vis, J. K., & Standish, M. (2000). How to make agri-food supply chains sustainable: Unilever's perspective. *Sustainable Development International, 3,* 111–117.

Vishaka guidelines against sexual harassment in the workplace. (2009). Retrieved July 26, 2009, from http://peoplefriendlypolice.wordpress.com/supreme-court-guidelines-against-sexual-harassment/

Vogel, D. (2005). *The market for virtue: The potential and limits of corporate social responsibility.* Washington, DC: Brookings Institution Press.

Vonk, R., & Van Knippenberg, A. (1995). Processing attitude statements from in-group and out-group members: Effects of within-group and within-person inconsistencies on reading times. *Journal of Personality and Social Psychology, 68*(2), 215–227.

Waddock, S., & Graves, S. M..(1997). The corporate social performance -financial performance link. *Strategic Management Journal, 18*(4), 303–319.

Wagner, J. A. (2002). Utilitarian and ontological variation in individualism-collectivism. In B. M. Staw & R. M. Kramer (Eds.), *Research in organizational behavior.* Oxford, UK: JAI /Elsevier Science.

Wales in the fast lane to sign up to idea of fair trade. (2003, March 6). *Western Mail* (Cardiff,Wales).

Walker, S. (2002, May/June). Africanity vs. Blackness: Race, class and culture in Brazil. *NACLA Report on the Americas, 35*(6), 16–20, 50.

The Wall Street Journal. (2009, July 1). Why companies invest in rural India. Retrieved December 3, 2009, from: http://online.wsj.com/article/SB124643327175778655.html

Walster, E., Walster, G. W., & Berscheid, E. (1978). *Equity: Theory and research.* Boston: Allyn & Bacon.

The Washington Post. (2009, July 4). Transcript: President Obama's Cairo address to the Muslim world. Retrieved July 15, 2009, from http://www.washingtonpost .com/wpdyn/content/article/2009/06/04/AR2009060401117.html

Webster's New World Dictionary (p. 403) (1984). New York: Simon & Schuster.

Webster's New World Dictionary (p. 188) (2003). Discrimination. New York: Simon & Schuster.

Wei, L. Q., Lau, C. M.,Young, M. N., & Wang, Z. (2005). The impact of top management team demography on firm performance in China. *Asian Business & Management, 4,* 227–250.

Weiss, S. (1992). Inland Steel Industries California. *The Business Enterprise Trust,* 1–21. More information and the abstract can be found at www.caseplace.org/cases3117/ cases_show.htm?doc_id=81989

Wentling, R. M. (2004). Factors that assist and barriers that hinder the success of diversity initiatives in multinational corporations. *Human Resource Development International, 7*(2), 165–180.

Wentling, R. M., & Palma-Rivas, N. (2000). Current status of diversity initiatives in selected multinational corporations. *Human Resource Development Quarterly, 11*(1), 35–60.

Were, M. (2003). Implementing corporate responsibility: The Chiquita case. *Journal of Business Ethics, 44*(2–3), 247–260.

Werther, W. B., & Chandler, D. (2006). *Strategic corporate social responsibility.* Thousand Oaks, CA: Sage.

What "model minority" doesn't tell? (1998, January 3). *The Chicago Tribune,* p. 18.

White, C. M. (2001). Affirmative action and education in Fiji: Legislation, contestation, and colonial discourse. *Harvard Educational Review, 71*(2), 240–268.

White, K. M., & Preston, S. H. (1996). How many Americans are alive because of twentieth century improvements in mortality? *Population and Development Review, 22,* 415–429.

Wicki, S., & Van der Kaaij, J. (2007). Is it true love between the octopus and the frog? How to avoid the authenticity gap. *Corporate Reputation Review, 10*(4), 312–318.

Williamson, J. G. (1998). Globalization and the labor market: Using history to inform policy. In P. Aghion & J. G. Williamson (Eds.), *Growth, inequality, and globalization: Theory, history, and policy.* Cambridge, UK: Cambridge University Press.

Winfeld, L. (2005). *Straight talk about gays in the workplace: Creating an inclusive, productive environment for everyone in your organization* (3rd ed.).New York: Harrington Park.

Wong, S. (2008). Diversity—Making space for everyone at NASA/GODDARD space flight center using dialogue to break through barriers. *Human Resource Management, 47*(2), 389–399.

Wood, G. (2008). Gender stereotypical attitudes: Past, present and future influences on women's career development. *Equal Opportunities International, 27*(7), 613–628.

Woolworths Holdings Limited. (2004). Corporate governance. Retrieved May 26, 2004, from www.woolworthsholdings.co.za/commentary/corporate_governance.html

World Bank. (1995). *Workers in an integrating world* (World Development Report 1995). Washington, DC: Author.

World Bank. (2001). *Engendering development.* New York: Oxford University Press.

World Bank. (2009). Data Finder, Population Total: Italy. Retrieved December 8, 2009, from: http://datafinder.worldbank.org/population-total

World Bank Group. (2003). Global coalitions for voices of the poor web guide: E-commerce to support grassroots entrepreneurs. Retrieved October 31, 2003, from www.worldbank.org/wbp/voices/globcoal/webguide/ecom.htm

World Bank Group. (2009). Global coalitions for voices of the poor Web guide: E-commerce to support grassroots entrepreneurs. Retrieved August 12, 2009, from http://go.worldbank.org/HUJ7SC8GK0

World Business Council for Sustainable Development. (2003). Sonae: Delta Cafés socially responsible coffees. Retrieved December 8, 2003, from www.wbcsd.org/templates/TemplateWBCSD4/layout.asp?MenuID=1

World Business Council for Sustainable Development. (2009). Sonae: Delta cafes socially responsible coffees. Retrieved December 17, 2009, from http://www.wbcsd.org/plugins/docsearch/details.asp?DocTypeId=-1&ObjectId=MjQ1Ng&URLBack= result.asp%3FDocTypeId%3D-1%26SortOrder%3D%26CurPage%3D349

World Rainforest Movement. (2001). *The bitter fruit of oil palm.* Montevideo, Uruguay: Author.

World's most admired companies. (2009). *Fortune.* http://money.cnn.com/magazines/fortune/mostadmired/2009/snapshots/6127.html

Wrench, J. (2001, July 23–27). *Diversity management in the European context: A critical examination of organisational strategies for combating ethnic discrimination and exclusion.* Paper presented at the International Cross-cultural Perspectives on Workforce Diversity, Bellagio, Italy.

Wrench, J. (2007). *Diversity management and discrimination.* Burlington, VT: Ashgate Publishers.

Wright, P., Ferris, S. P., Hiller, J. S., & Kroll, M. (1995). Competitiveness through management of diversity: Effects on stock price valuation. *Academy of Management Journal, 38*(1), 272–287.

Wright, S. C. & Tropp, R. (2002). Collective action in response to disadvantage: Intergroup perceptions, social identification, and social change. Relative deprivation: Specification, development, and integration. In I.Walker, and H. Smith, J. (Eds). *Relative deprivation: Specification, development, and integration.* pp. 200–236. New York: Cambridge University Press.

Yamey, G. (2000, July 1). Nestlé violates international marketing code, says audit, *BMJ 2000, 321*(8).

Yang, C., D'Souza, G., C., Bapat, A. S., & Colarelli, S. M. (2006). A cross-national analysis of affirmative action: An evolutionary psychological perspective. *Managerial and Decision Economics, 27,* 203–216.

Yarhouse, M. A. (2000). Review of social cognition research on stereotyping: Application to psychologists working with older adults. *Journal of Clinical Geropsychology, 6*(2), 121–131.

Zan, M. (1997, August 22). Aborigines fight for justice. *Jakarta Post.*

Zegers de Beijl, R. (Ed.). (1999). *Documenting discrimination against migrant workers in the labour market.* Geneva: International Labour Office.

Zegers, de Beijl, R. (2000). *Documenting discrimination against migrant workers in the labour market : A comparative study of four European countries.* Geneva: International Labour Office.

Zhong, C. B., & Leonardelli, G. J. (2008). Cold and lonely: Does social exclusion literally feel cold? *Psychological Science, 19,* 838–842.

Zinn, D. L. (1994). The Senegalese immigrants in Bari: What happens when the Africans peer back. In R. Benmayor & A. Skotnes (Eds.), *Migration and identity* (pp. 53–68). Oxford, UK: Oxford University Press.

Zlotnick, H. (1994). International migration: Causes and effects. In L. A. Mazur (Ed.), *Beyond the number: A reader on population, consumption, and the environment.* Washington, DC: Island Press.

Zlotnick, H. (1996). Migration to and from developing regions: A review of past trends. In W. Lutz (Ed.), *The future population of the world: What can we assume today?* (2nd ed., pp. 299–335). London: Earthscan.

Index

Page numbers followed by "n" indicate notes.

Abayas (Muslim attire), 208, 211 (n7), 212 (n8)
Ability/disability diversity, 103–104, 120–121
Aboriginals (Australia), 295–301
Active life expectancy, 86
Adamson, Jim, 265, 267–268, 269
Adarand Constructors v. Pena (1995), 76
ADP. *See* Automatic Data Processing
Affirmative/positive action:
  debate over, 75–76, 76–78 (box), 78–80
  enforcement, 74
  goals, 63–64
  legislation, 65–66, 66–68 (table), 68–69
  policies and programs, 71–72, 72–74 (box)
  as positive social policy, 59–60
  principles, 69–72, 72–74 (box), 74
  specific goals and target population, 70–71
Africa:
  educational trends, 125
  gender diversity in workplace, 96, 100
  HIV/AIDS, 89, 91, 105 (n2)
  intercultural encounters, 186
  life expectancy, 86
  migration and migrants, 111, 112
  population trends, 85–86, 89, 91
  slavery, 156–157
  See also specific countries
African Americans:
  Denny's, Inc. and, 265–272
  exclusion of, 171

  prejudices about, 154
  Texaco and, 243 (box)
  Xerox Corporation and, 62–63, 63 (box)
Age discrimination, 147
Age diversity, 84–87, 88, 100–101, 105 (n4)
Agriculture, 114
AIDS, 9 (box), 89, 91, 105 (n2)
Ailon, G., 199
Alabama Board of Corrections, 57 (n14)
Albert, Isaac Olawale, 186
Albright, Madeleine, 208
Allport, Gordon W., 153, 177, 178 (box)
America Online (AOL), 238
Anglo American (firm), 303, 315 (n1)
Anglo-Americans, relational mental models of, 219–220
Anglo-European New Zealanders, 209 (box)
Anguilla, 55
Antidiscrimination legislation, 26–27, 51–56, 162 (n3)
  See also Discrimination
Anti-sexual harassment legislation, 30, 34–36, 37–41 (table)
AOL. *See* America Online
Apartheid, 156
Arabian American Oil Company (Aramco), 42–43
A-S-A (attraction-selection-attrition) cycle, 240–241

Asia:
   anti-sexual harassment legislation, 36,
      37–41 (table)
   educational trends, 124, 125
   face orientation, 227
   gender diversity in workplace, 96, 98,
      100, 120
   harmony orientation, 227
   long-term orientation, 197, 198
   migration and migrants, 111, 112
   population trends, 85, 86, 91
   relational mental models, 219
   See also specific countries
Asian, as term, 150 (box), 182
Asian Americans, 149–150
Asian New Zealanders, 209 (box)
Assertiveness, 200
AstraZeneca, 248
Attraction-selection-attrition (A-S-A)
      cycle, 240–241
Attributes, 149
Australia:
   Aboriginals, 295–301
   affirmative/positive action legislation,
      66 (table), 74
   antidiscrimination/equal rights
      legislation, 23, 51
   diversity management development,
      238, 251 (n3)
   Indigenous Employment Policy,
      298–299
   sexual orientation legislation,
      32 (table)
Austria, 51, 110
Automatic Data Processing (ADP), 247
Autostereotypes, 154
Avoidance of uncertainty, 191,
      193 (table), 196–197, 201

Bangladesh, 108, 127 (n8), 287
Banking industry, 280
Barefoot College, 123, 123–124 (box)
Barnett, E. O., 177, 178 (box)
Bartlett, F. C., 215
Bata International, 308, 316 (n3)
Baumeister, R. F., 169
BE. *See* Black Enterprise
Belarus, 51

Belgium, 24–25 (box), 72, 108,
      159–160 (box)
Belize, 51
Bell, Ella L. J. Edmondson, 171
Benin, 113
Berlin, Germany, 205
Bermuda, 55
Bhopal, India, explosion, 119,
      119–120 (box)
Black Enterprise (BE), 270
Black line incident, 296
Blacks, in Netherlands, 156
   See also African Americans
Botswana, 89, 91
Boureslan, Mr., 42–43
Bowing, 206–207
Bradley, Joseph P., 158
Brandt, Willy, 205
Brazil:
   community inclusion programs,
      278 (box)
   diversity management, 240, 251 (n6)
   life expectancy, 86
   racial and ethnic differences, 134
   sexual orientation legislation,
      32 (table)
Britain. *See* United Kingdom
Broekhoff, Hans, 285
Burkina Faso, 113
Burma, 91, 284
Burqahs (Muslim attire),
      208, 211 (n7)
Burundi, 100
Business card exchange,
      227–228 (box)

California Proposition 209, 78
Cambodia, 91
Cambodians, 206
Cameroon, 284
Canada:
   affirmative/positive action legislation,
      66 (table)
   antidiscrimination/equal rights
      legislation, 26, 51
   cross-cultural communication, 205
   international inclusion programs,
      11–12 (box)

migration and migrants, 94, 95 (box),
    109, 251 (n8)
sexual orientation legislation,
    32 (table)
Caribbean, 100, 112
    See also specific countries
Caste system, 24, 102–103 (box)
Catholics, in Northern Ireland,
    72–74 (box)
CAW. *See* Committee on Asian Women
Central America, 93–94 (box), 96, 112
    See also specific countries
Chaebol, 216
Chicano movement, 186
China:
    age diversity, 106 (n13)
    antidiscrimination/equal rights
        legislation, 51
    business card exchange, 228 (box)
    classes of people, traditional, 1–2
    conflict and harmony, 222
    educational trends, 125
    eye contact, 154–155
    foreign direct investment in, 119
    international collaborations, 308–309
    life expectancy, 86
    migration and migrants, 112, 114,
        251 (n8)
    monolithic organizations, 244
    nonverbal communication, 207 (box)
    regional differences, 131
    relational mental models, 216, 221,
        228–229
    women employees, 244
    workforce diversity, as term, 132
Chinese New Zealanders, 209 (box)
Chinese Value Survey (CVS), 192, 197
Chiquita Brands International, Inc., 306,
    307, 315 (n2)
Chirac, Jacques, 20–21 (box)
Chrysler, 117
Cisneros, Sandra, 164
Citibank, 221
Civil Rights Act (1964). *See* Title VII of
    the Civil Rights Act of 1964
Civil Rights Act (1991), 29–30
Clinton, Bill, 78, 205
Clothing, as nonverbal communication,
    207–208

Cocoa products, fair trade, 11–12 (box)
Coffee industry, 10–11 (box), 311–312
Collaborations, 11, 11–12 (box)
    See also Corporate-community
        collaborations; International
        collaborations; State/national
        collaborations
Collectivist *versus* individualist cultures,
    191, 192 (table), 194–195, 200,
    225–226
Colombia, 66 (table)
Combined *versus* differentiated
    relational mental models,
    219–222, 220 (figure),
    227–228 (box), 227–229
Committee on Asian Women (CAW),
    36, 58 (n19)
Committee on Elimination of
    Discrimination Against Women,
    23–24
Committee on Elimination of Racial
    Discrimination, 23, 24,
    24 (box)
Communication:
    defined, 203
    direct *versus* indirect, 229,
        230 (figure)
    nonverbal, 201, 202 (box), 206–208,
        207 (box)
    verbal, 203–205
    See also Cross-cultural
        communication
Community Reinvestment Act (1997),
    280, 289 (n2)
Compass Group, 298, 299
Compensatory justice, 247
Concorde project, 204, 211 (n4)
Conflict, 222–223, 224 (figure)
Congo, 51
Corporate-community collaborations,
    274–289
    barriers to, 279, 280 (figure)
    benefits of, 279–281, 280 (figure)
    case illustration, 281–288
    implementation, 320 (figure), 321
    inclusive policies and practices,
        276–277, 277–278 (box)
    value base, 276 (figure), 318,
        319 (figure)

Corporate social performance, 274–275
   See also Corporate-community
     collaborations
Corporate social responsibility, 274–275
   See also Corporate-community
     collaborations
Costa Rica, 32 (table), 66 (table)
Covert discrimination, 60, 63, 63 (box)
Cox, T., 136 (table), 244–246
Cross-cultural communication, 201–210
   barriers to, 203, 204 (figure)
   cultural fluency, 206
   direct *versus* indirect communication,
     229, 230 (figure)
   face and harmony orientation, 226–227
   importance of, 201–203, 202 (box)
   interpersonal, 223–229, 230 (figure)
   language fluency, 206
   nonverbal communication, 201,
     202 (box), 206–208, 207 (box)
   relationship *versus* task orientation,
     227–228 (box), 227–229
   styles, 208–210, 209 (box)
   theoretical perspectives, 225–229,
     226 (table), 230 (figure)
   verbal communication, 203–205
Cross-national diversity management, 236
Cultural audit, 242 (table), 243, 257
Cultural fluency, 206
Cultural styles, 215–218, 216 (box),
   217 (box)
Cultural value dimensions (GLOBE
   study), 200–201
Cultural value dimensions (Hofstede),
   191–199
   critique of Hofstede's framework,
     198–199
   individualism *versus* collectivism,
     191, 192 (table), 194–195
   long- *versus* short-term orientation,
     192, 193 (table), 197–198
   masculinity *versus* femininity,
     191, 192 (table), 196
   overview, 191–192, 192–193 (table), 193
   power distance, 191, 192 (table), 194
   uncertainty, avoidance of, 191,
     193 (table), 196–197
Culture, defined, 190
Culture's Consequences (Hofstede), 191, 199

CVS. *See* Chinese Value Survey
Cyprus, 51
Czech Republic, 51, 111

DaimlerChrysler, 117
Darwin, Charles, 162 (n2)
DCM Shriram Industries Ltd.,
   259–260 (box)
Dehumanization, 155–158
Delta Cafés Group, 10–11 (box)
Demographic trends, 83–106
   ability/disability diversity, 103–104
   about, 4–5
   age diversity, 100–101
   gender diversity, 96–100, 97 (table),
     99 (table)
   international population trends,
     84–95
   migration trends, 91–94, 92 (table),
     93–94 (box), 93 (figure), 95 (box)
   national trends, 95–105
   racial and ethnic diversity, 101–103,
     102–103 (box)
   sexual orientation diversity, 104–105
   working-age population trends, 87,
     89, 89–90 (table)
Denmark, 32 (table), 52, 168, 196
Denny's, Inc., 264–272
Denny's Single Parent Student
   Scholarship, 269
Developed countries:
   ability/disability diversity, 104
   age composition of population, 87, 88
   life expectancy, 83
Developing countries:
   ability/disability diversity, 104
   age composition of population, 4, 87, 88
   educational trends, 125
   foreign direct investment in, 118–119
   worker migration, 111–112
De Vries, S., 137 (table)
Direct *versus* indirect communication,
   229, 230 (figure)
Disability diversity, 103–104, 120–121
Disadvantaged groups, 10–11 (box)
   See also specific groups
Discrimination:
   age, 147
   covert, 60, 63, 63 (box)

defined, 60, 149, 158
employment-related, 42–43, 60,
    64–65, 158–159, 159–160 (box)
exclusion and, 169
"fair," 57 (n13)
gender, 28–29, 30, 158–159, 163 (n10)
individual, 60
institutional, 60–61, 61–62 (box), 63,
    63 (box)
intentional, 61–62 (box), 63, 63 (box)
overt, 60, 61–62 (box)
racial, 27–28, 42
religious, 72, 72–74 (box)
social categorization and, 180–182 (box)
unintentional, 61
See also Affirmative/positive action;
    Antidiscrimination legislation
Discriminatory impact, 58 (n15)
Disparate-impact theory, 58 (n15)
Distinction categories, 132, 147–149
See also Diversity
DiTomaso, N., 136 (table)
Diversity:
    adverse implications of, 130–131
    age, 84–87, 88, 100–101, 105 (n4)
    invisible, 135, 145
    jelly bean metaphor, 236–237
    occupational, 112–115
    social identity theory and, 183–186
    as term, 162 (n2)
    toward global definition of, 146–149
    visible, 135, 145
    See also Workforce diversity; Work
        organization diversity
Diversity enlargement approach, 241,
    242 (table)
Diversity legislation:
    about, 16–17
    antidiscrimination legislation, 26–27,
        51–56, 162 (n3)
    anti-sexual harassment legislation, 30,
        34–36, 37–41 (table)
    implementation, 23–24,
        24–25 (box), 25
    International Bill of Human Rights,
        17, 18 (figure)
    International Covenant on Economic,
        Social, and Cultural Rights, 22–23

as negative social policy, 59
noncompliance with, 42–43
practical implications, 36, 42–43
sexual orientation legislation, 30,
    31 (figure), 32–34 (table)
See also Affirmative/positive action;
    Universal Declaration of Human
    Rights; specific laws
Diversity management, 234–251
    characteristics, 248–250
    cross-national, 236
    defined, 235
    development of, 237–240
    human resource paradigm, 240–241,
        242–243 (box), 242 (table),
        243–244
    impetus for implementing,
        246–248 (table)
    intranational, 236
    limitations, 249–250
    multicultural organization paradigm,
        244–246
Diversity maturity, 259
Diversity Perceptions Scale, 328–332
Diversity sensitivity approach, 241,
    242–243 (box), 242 (table)
Diversity statements, 132–133, 248, 258
Diversity Task Force, 136 (table)
Diversity training, 154–155, 258
Dobbs, M., 136 (table)
Dothard v. Rawlinson (1977), 29, 57 (n14)
Duke Power Company, 58 (n15)
Durkheim, Émile, 36, 42

East Timor, 10–11 (box)
Economic self-interest, 169
Ecuador, 32 (table), 111, 216 (box)
Educational trends, 121–125, 122 (table),
    123–124 (box), 124 (table)
EEOC. See Equal Employment
    Opportunity Commission
Egypt, 52, 208
"Eleven Tips on Getting More
    Efficiency Out Of Women
    Employees," 61–62 (box)
Emotional detachment versus emotional
    involvement, 218–222, 220 (figure)
Emotional overcoat theory, 220–221

Employer migration, 115, 116–117 (box),
    117–119, 119–120 (box)
Employment-related discrimination,
    42–43, 64–65, 158–159,
    159–160 (box)
England, 108, 204, 208, 211 (n4)
    See also United Kingdom
Enrique (immigrant), 94 (box)
Equal Employment Opportunity
    Commission (EEOC), 35,
    42–43, 63
Equal Employment Opportunity
    Commission v. Arabian American
    Oil Co. (1991), 42–43
Equal opportunities theorists, 64–65
Equal remuneration legislation, 29–30
Equity theory, 175
eShopAfrica, 305–306 (box)
Ethiopia, 66 (table)
Ethnic groups. See Racial and ethnic
    groups
EU. See European Union
Eurest, 299–300
Europe:
    affirmative/positive action
        legislation, 70
    age diversity, 86, 87, 88
    business card exchange,
        227–228 (box)
    diversity, as term, 133, 162 (n2)
    diversity concept in, 132–133
    educational trends, 124
    gender diversity in workplace, 96, 98
    migration and migrants, 91,
        108–109, 112
    theory development, 173–174
    workforce diversity research, 7
    See also European Union; specific
        countries
European Americans:
    conflict and harmony, 222
    relational mental models, 215–216,
        217–218, 217 (box), 220–221
    time/punctuality, 215–216
European Union (EU):
    affirmative/positive action
        legislation, 69
    antidiscrimination legislation, 27

anti-sexual harassment legislation,
    35–36
diversity management development,
    238–239, 251 (n5)
migration and migrants, 91, 110–111,
    115
    See also Europe; specific countries
Exclusion:
    as critical workforce problem, 6–8,
        165–167
    discrimination and, 169
    economic self-interest and, 169
    organizational demography research
        documenting, 170–173
    of racial/ethnic minorities, 165–166,
        172–173
    social identity theory and, 183–186
    stereotypes and, 169–170
    of women, 165–166, 166–167,
        171–173
    See also Inclusion-exclusion
        continuum; Social identity
        theory
Executive Order 10925, 69
Executive Order 11246, 69, 238
Exemplary Voluntary Efforts Award, 264
Eye contact, 154–155

Face concept, 226–227, 231n
"Fair discrimination," 57 (n13)
Fair trade, 11–12 (box), 305–306 (box),
    310–314
Fair Trade Company, 312–313
Fairtrade Foundation, 310, 313–314
Falkland Islands, 54–55
FDI. See Foreign direct investment
Feminine versus masculine cultures, 191,
    192 (table), 196
Festinger, L., 167–168
Fifth Amendment, 76
Fiji, 27, 32 (table), 52
Filartiga v. Pena-Irala (1980), 23,
    57 (n2)
Finland:
    affirmative/positive action legislation,
        67 (table)
    antidiscrimination/equal rights
        legislation, 52

diversity statements, 132–133
as feminine society, 196
migration and migrants, 111
sexual orientation legislation,
  32 (table)
Flagstar, 266, 267
Fleury, M. T., 137 (table)
Ford Australia, 249
Ford Motor Company, 243
Foreign direct investment (FDI),
  117–119, 127 (n7)
Fortune magazine, 265, 270, 286
France:
  affirmative/positive action legislation,
    67 (table)
  Concorde project, 204, 211 (n4)
  diversity statements, 132–133
  diversity statistics, 251 (n5)
  Iraq conflict, 154
  life expectancy, 83
  migration and migrants, 108, 109,
    110, 111
  religious attire in workplace ban,
    20–21 (box)
  sexual orientation legislation,
    32 (table)
Friedman, Milton, 275
Future orientation, 200

Gandhi, Mahatma, 208
Gays. *See* Sexual orientation diversity;
  Sexual orientation legislation
Gender discrimination:
  Japan, 28–29, 158–159
  United States, 29, 30, 158, 163 (n10)
Gender diversity, 96–100, 97 (table),
  99 (table), 120–121
Gender egalitarianism, 200
Gender roles, 19
Gender stereotypes, 152–153
Generalizations, in diversity training,
  154–155
Germany:
  antidiscrimination/equal rights
    legislation, 52
  diversity statements, 132–133
  headscarf ban, 20 (box)
  migration and migrants, 94, 109, 110,
    111, 159–160 (box), 251 (n8)

Nazi genocide, 157
population projections, 4
relational mental models, 221
working-age population trends, 87
Gestures, 206–207, 217–218
Ghana:
  gender diversity in workplace, 100
  international collaborations,
    305–306 (box)
  migration and migrants, 112, 113
  palm oil/plantations, 281–282, 284, 287
  racial and ethnic diversity, 103
Gibraltar, 55
Ginsburg, Ruth Bader, 77 (box)
Glastra, F., 137 (table)
Global collaborations. *See* International
  collaborations
Global companies, 3
Global Leadership and Organizational
  Behavior Effectiveness (GLOBE),
  200–201
Global Village, 312
Gonzales Construction, 76
Gordon, Tiane Mitchell, 238
Gorman, F., 137 (table)
Grant, B., 137 (table)
Gratz v. Bolinger (2003), 79
Great Britain. *See* United Kingdom
Greece, 110, 115, 194
Griggs v. Duke Power Company (1971),
  58 (n15)
Group distinction categories, 132, 147–149
  See also Diversity
Group mobility through social creativity
  strategy, 185–186
Guinea, 205, 225
Gutierrez, Lucio, 216 (box)
Guyana, 52

Hai Ha-Kotobuki Joint Venture Co.,
  Ltd., 9 (box)
Harex, 14n
Harmony, 222–223, 224 (figure), 226–227
Harris, D., 180
Harrison, D. A., 137 (table), 139 (table)
Headscarves *(hijabs)*, 19–20 (box), 208,
  211 (n7)
Healthy life expectancy, 86
Heterostereotypes, 154

High-tech industry, 121 (box), 251 (n8)
Hijabs (headscarves), 19–20 (box), 208, 211 (n7)
Hindustan Lever Ltd., 304–305
HIV/AIDS, 9 (box), 89, 91, 105 (n2)
Hofstede, Geert, 190–191, 198–199
   See also Cultural value dimensions (Hofstede)
Homelessness, 10 (box)
Homosexuality. See Sexual orientation diversity; Sexual orientation legislation
Honduras, 94 (box)
Hong Kong:
   antidiscrimination/equal rights legislation, 51
   anti-sexual harassment legislation, 35, 36, 39 (table)
   migration and migrants, 95 (box)
   state/national collaborations, 294–295 (box)
Hong Yip Service Company Ltd., 294–295 (box)
Hood-Phillips, Rachelle, 264, 267–268, 270, 272
Hopkins, Ann Branigar, 152–153
House, Robert J., 200
House on Mango Street, The (Cisneros), 164
Hudson Institute, 246
Human orientation, 200
Human resource paradigm, 240–241, 242–243 (box), 242 (table), 243–244
Hungary, 52, 67 (table), 101, 111

IBM, 191, 237–238, 263
Iceland, 32 (table), 52
IGLHRC. *See* International Gay and Lesbian Human Rights Commission
ILO. *See* International Labour Organization
Immigrants. *See* Migrants; Migration
Inclusion-exclusion continuum, 166, 167–170
Inclusive workplace:
   benefits of, 12, 14
   characteristics, 8–12, 9 (box), 10–11 (box), 11–12 (box)
   defined, 8, 253 (box)

Inclusive workplace model:
   implementation of, 318, 320 (figure), 321–322
   overview, 8–12, 9 (box), 10–11 (box), 11–12 (box), 252–255
   value base for, 317–318, 319 (figure)
Inclusive workplace model: level I. *See* Work organization diversity
Inclusive workplace model: level II. *See* Corporate-community collaborations
Inclusive workplace model: level III. *See* State/national collaborations
Inclusive workplace model: level IV. *See* International collaborations
India:
   affirmative/positive action legislation, 67 (table), 69, 70, 71
   antidiscrimination/equal rights legislation, 52
   anti-sexual harassment legislation, 35, 40 (table)
   caste system, 102–103 (box)
   corporate-community collaborations, 287
   educational trends, 123, 123–124 (box)
   international collaborations, 304–305
   migration and migrants, 94, 112, 114, 251 (n8)
   outsourcing to, 116–117 (box)
   sexual harassment, 121 (box)
   women's status in, 185
   work organization diversity, 259–260 (box)
Indian, as term, 150 (box)
Indigenous Employment Policy (Australia), 298–299
Indigenous Training and Employment Program (ITEP), 299
Indirect *versus* direct communication, 229, 230 (figure)
Individual discrimination, 60
Individualist *versus* collectivist cultures, 191, 192 (table), 194–195, 200, 225–226
Individual mobility strategy, 184–185

Indonesia:
  antidiscrimination/equal rights
    legislation, 52
  anti-sexual harassment legislation,
    40 (table)
  corporate-community
    collaborations, 287
  face orientation, 227
  migration and migrants, 112
  palm oil/plantations, 281–282, 284
Infosys Technologies Limited, 121 (box)
In-group collectivism, 200
In-groups, 154, 170
Institutional collectivism, 200
Institutional discrimination, 60–61,
  61–62 (box), 63, 63 (box)
Intentional discrimination, 61–62 (box),
  63, 63 (box)
Intergroup contact theory, 175
Intergroup differences, 9, 9 (box)
Intergroup relations theories, 174–175
  See also Social identity theory
International Bill of Human Rights, 17,
  18 (figure), 22–23
  See also Universal Declaration of
    Human Rights
International collaborations, 303–316,
  305–306 (box)
  barriers to, 307, 309 (figure)
  benefits of, 307–308, 309 (figure)
  case illustration, 308–314
  implementation, 320 (figure),
    321–322
  value base, 304 (figure), 318,
    319 (figure)
International corporations, 3
International Covenant on Economic,
  Social, and Cultural Rights, 22–23
International Gay and Lesbian Human
  Rights Commission (IGLHRC),
  58 (n16)
International Labour Organization
  (ILO):
  discrimination definition, 60, 158
  diversity definition, 139 (table)
  diversity management studies, 239
  employment discrimination studies,
    24–25 (box), 159–160 (box)
  NATLEX database, 57 (n9)

International population trends, 84–95
International student identity group,
  185–186
Interpersonal relationships, 213–231
  cross-cultural communication and,
    223–229, 226 (table),
    227–228 (box), 230 (figure)
  cultural styles and relational mental
    models, 215–218, 216 (box),
    217 (box)
  diversity in, 218–223, 220 (figure),
    224 (figure)
Intranational diversity management, 236
Intrinsic motivation, 218
Invisible diversity, 135, 145
Iraq, 52
Iraq conflict (2003), 154, 201, 202 (box)
Ireland:
  antidiscrimination/equal rights
    legislation, 52
  migration and migrants, 111, 115
  sexual orientation legislation,
    32 (table)
  transnational firms' sales and support
    call centers, 126
Islam. See Muslims
Israel:
  antidiscrimination/equal rights
    legislation, 52
  anti-sexual harassment legislation,
    40 (table)
  collectivism, 195
  cross-cultural communication, 205
  relational mental models, 221
  sexual orientation legislation,
    33 (table)
Italy:
  affirmative/positive action
    legislation, 72
  migration and migrants, 94, 108, 110,
    111, 115
  population projections, 4
  regional differences, 131
  working-age population trends, 87
ITEP. See Indigenous Training and
  Employment Program

J. A. Croson Company, 76
Jackson, S. E., 138 (table)

Jamaica, 52
Japan:
    age diversity, 106 (n13)
    antidiscrimination/equal rights
        legislation, 28–29, 52
    anti-sexual harassment legislation, 36,
        41 (table)
    diversity in, 132
    gender discrimination, 158–159
    international inclusion initiatives,
        312–313
    life expectancy, 86
    as masculine society, 196
    migration and migrants, 95 (box),
        112, 114
    nonverbal communication, 206–207
    relational mental models, 218, 220
    sexual harassment lawsuits, 42
    working-age population trends, 87
Jelly bean jar incident at Texaco,
    242–243 (box)
Jelly bean metaphor for diversity, 236–237
Jews, Nazi genocide of, 157
Jimenez-Cook, S., 139 (table)
Joshi, A., 138 (table), 140 (table)

Kennedy, Anthony, 77 (box)
Kennedy, J. F., 205
Kenya, 67 (table)
King, Rodney, 289 (n5)
Kin Ki Industrial, 308–309
Klein, K. J., 137 (table)
Kleiner, B. H., 137 (table), 139 (table),
    140 (table)
Kluckhohn, C., 190
Konrad, A. M., 142 (table)
Korea:
    antidiscrimination/equal rights
        legislation, 53
    business card exchange, 228 (box)
    collectivism, 195
    conflict and harmony, 222, 223
    diversity, 132
    migration and migrants, 94, 112
    relational mental models, 216
Korean Americans, 153, 163 (n9)
Kossek, E. E., 140 (table), 241,
    242 (table), 243–244
Kreitz, P. A., 140 (table)

Kroeber, A. L., 190
Kuwait, 109, 195

Lai, Y., 140 (table)
Langevin, Jim, 212 (n8)
Language diversity, 204–205
Language fluency, 206
Larkey, Linda, 145
La Siembra Co-op, 11–12 (box)
Latin America:
    gender diversity in workplace, 96, 100
    population age 39 or under, 86
    time/punctuality, 215, 216
    See also specific countries
Latinos, relational mental models of,
    217–218, 219–220
Lau, D., 140 (table)
Leary, M. R., 169
Legislation:
    antidiscrimination, 26–27, 51–56,
        162 (n3)
    anti-sexual harassment, 30, 34–36,
        37–41 (table)
    equal remuneration, 29–30
    global trends, 5
    sexual orientation, 30, 31 (figure),
        32–34 (table)
    See also Diversity legislation; specific laws
Lesbians. See Sexual orientation
    diversity; Sexual orientation
    legislation
Lesotho, 89, 91
Levy, Barbara, 271
Life expectancy, 83, 86
Lifetime Fitness, 117 (box)
Lilly Ledbetter Fair Pay Act (2009), 29
Linguistic diversity, 204–205
Lithuania, 23, 53
Loan losses to total loans ratio, 280,
    289 (n3)
Lobel, S. A., 140 (table), 241, 242 (table),
    243–244
Local communities, 9, 10 (box)
    See also Corporate-community
        collaborations
Long- versus short-term orientation,
    192, 193 (table), 197–198
Los Angeles urban uprising/riots (1992),
    281, 289 (n5)

Lotus Corporation, 306–307
Low-context to high-context cultures
    continuum, 225, 226, 226 (table)
Lucky Stores, 155
Luxembourg, 33 (table)

Malawi, 53
Malaysia:
    affirmative/positive action
        legislation, 79
    anti-sexual harassment legislation,
        34–35, 36, 37 (table)
    ethnic diversity, 102 (box), 103
    migration and migrants, 112
    palm oil/plantations, 281–282, 283,
        284, 285, 286–287
Malta, 53
Malvinas, 54–55
Masculine *versus* feminine cultures, 191,
    192 (table), 196
Mass Transportation, 61–62 (box)
McKee, Bill, 63
McSally, Martha, 212 (n8)
Mead, G. H., 168
Meerman, M., 137 (table)
Mexican Americans, 186, 217 (box),
    219–220
Mexico:
    foreign direct investment in, 119
    harmony orientation, 227
    migration and migrants, 93–94 (box),
        94, 112
    palm oil/plantations, 284
    relational mental models, 216,
        217 (box), 218, 219–220
    time/punctuality, 216
    workforce diversity, as term, 132
    young-adult population, 4
Michelangelo, 205
Middle East, 109, 112, 125, 195
    See also specific countries
Migrants, 5, 108–109, 112–115, 206
Migration:
    of employers, 115, 116–117 (box),
        117–119, 119–120 (box)
    global demographic trends, 91–94,
        92 (table), 93–94 (box),
        93 (figure), 95 (box)
    of workers, 110–112, 159–160 (box)

Minimal group experiments, 180–182 (box)
Minney, Safia, 312
Mission statements, 247–248
*Mississippi University for Women v.
    Hogan* (1982), 30
Mitsubishi, 118
Model minority myth, 149–150
Monolithic organizations, 244–245
Moore, S., 141 (table)
Mor-Barak inclusion-exclusion scale,
    324–328
Moroccans, 24–25 (box), 179
Morocco, 111, 278 (box)
Motivation, intrinsic, 218
Mountain Gravel and Construction
    Company, 76
Mozambique, 89, 91, 100
Muller, H. J., 141 (table), 142 (table)
Multicultural organization paradigm,
    244–246
Multicultural organizations, 245
Multinational companies, 3
Murnighan, J., 140 (table)
Museveni, Yoweri, 162 (n5)
Muslims:
    attire, 208, 211 (n7), 212 (n8)
    Denny's, Inc. and, 271
    stereotypes of, 150–151 (box), 153

NAACP. *See* National Association for the
    Advancement of Colored People
Naah, Samuel, 305–306 (box)
Naïve realism, 215
Najad, Iraq, 201, 202 (box)
Namibia, 53, 67 (table), 68
National Association for the
    Advancement of Colored People
    (NAACP), 270
National demographic trends, 95–105
NATLEX database, 57 (n9)
Nazi genocide, 157
Neoclassical economists, 64
Nepal, 24, 34, 37 (table)
Nestlé, 277–278 (box)
Nestlé Foundation, 278 (box)
Netherlands:
    antidiscrimination/equal rights
        legislation, 53
    Blacks in, 156

diversity, as term, 133
diversity concept in, 132
diversity statements, 132–133
homogenous workforce in, 239
migration and migrants, 108, 110,
   111, 159–160 (box)
Moroccans in, 179
sexual orientation legislation,
   33 (table)
New Haven, Conn., firefighters,
   76–77 (box)
New Zealand:
   antidiscrimination/equal rights
      legislation, 53
   communication styles, 209 (box)
   older worker stereotypes, 152
   racial and ethnic differences, 134–135
   sexual orientation legislation,
      33 (table)
   welfare reform, 291
   women in media, 152
Nextel Communications, 263
Niger, 113
Nigeria:
   antidiscrimination/equal rights
      legislation, 53
   corporate-community collaborations,
      277, 278 (box)
   migration and migrants, 112, 113
   women's rights, 23–24
Nixon, J., 141 (table)
Nkomo, Stella, 146–147, 171
Nonverbal communication, 201,
   202 (box), 206–208, 207 (box)
North America:
   gender diversity in workplace, 98
   migration and migrants, 112
   population age 39 or under, 85
   theory development, 173–174
   See also specific countries
Northern Ireland, 55, 67 (table), 72,
   72–74 (box)
   See also United Kingdom
Norway:
   affirmative/positive action legislation,
      68 (table), 70–71
   antidiscrimination/equal rights
      legislation, 53
   diversity management, 241

diversity statements, 132–133
sexual orientation legislation,
   33 (table)

Obama, Barack, 21 (box), 29, 179,
   206–207
Occupational diversity, 112–115
Ocholla, D., 142 (table)
Older workers, 152
Oman, 195
Oppression, 155–158
Organizational demography research,
   170–173
Organizational outcomes, strategy for
   achieving, 242 (table), 243–244
Our Separate Ways (Bell & Nkomo), 171
Out-groups, 154, 170
Outsourcing, 116–117 (box)
Overt discrimination, 60, 61–62 (box)
Oxfam, 285–286, 310

Pakeha, 209 (box)
Pakistan, 35, 36, 101
Palmisano, Sam, 237–238
Palm oil/plantations, 281–288
Parham, P. A., 141 (table), 142 (table)
Park, Kyung-Young, 1–2
Parks-Yancy, R., 136 (table)
Paternity leave, 196
Perception of Inclusion-Exclusion Scale,
   324–328
Performance orientation, 200
Petra, S., 137 (table)
Pettigrew, T. F., 177, 178 (box)
Philippines:
   antidiscrimination/equal rights
      legislation, 53
   migration and migrants, 93, 94,
      95 (box), 112
Plan Group, The, 292
Plural organizations, 245
Poland, 53, 111
Population:
   age 14 or under, 86, 90 (table)
   age 39 or under, 85–86
   international trends, 84–95
   working-age, 87, 89, 89–90 (table)
   world, 84–85
   young-adult, 4

Port Authority of New York and New Jersey, 10 (box)
Portugal, 10–11 (box), 110, 111, 115
Positive action. *See* Affirmative/positive action
Post, C., 136 (table)
Power distance, 191, 192 (table), 194, 201
Prasad, P., 142 (table)
Prejudice, 151, 153–154
Price Waterhouse v. Hopkins (1989), 152–153
Pringle, J. K., 142 (table)
Proposition 209 (California), 78
Protestant relational ideology, 216
Punctuality, 215–216, 216 (box)
Punitive damages awards, 57 (n11), 58 (n18)

Quanxi, 216
Quotas, 65, 71, 79

Racial and ethnic groups:
    exclusion of minorities, 165–166, 172–173
    global demographic trends, 101–103, 102–103 (box)
    photograph categorization study, 180
Racial categorization experiments, 177, 178 (box)
Racial discrimination, 27–28, 42
Racial stereotypes, 152
Realistic conflict theory, 174–175
Regional differences, 131
Rejection-identification model, 186
Relational mental models, 215–218, 216 (box), 217 (box), 219–222, 220 (figure), 227–228 (box), 227–229
Relationship *versus* task orientation, 227–228 (box), 227–229
Relative deprivation theory, 175
Religious attire/symbols in workplace, 19–21 (box), 21
Religious discrimination, 72, 72–74 (box)
Republic of Korea. *See* South Korea
Research:
    Diversity Perceptions Scale, 328–332
    organizational demography, 170–173

Perception of Inclusion-Exclusion Scale, 324–328
workforce diversity, 7
Return on assets (ROA), 280, 289 (n3), 289 (n4)
Rhodesia, 156
Ricci v. DeStefano (2009), 76–77 (box)
Richardson, Jerry, 266
Richmond v. J. A. Croson Co. (1989), 76
ROA. *See* Return on assets
Roh, H., 140 (table)
Roma, 23, 130
Roman Catholics, in Northern Ireland, 72–74 (box)
Roundtable on Sustainable Palm Oil, 286
Roy, Bunker, 123–124 (box)
Royal Dutch/Shell Corporation, 277, 280
Rudd, Kevin, 295, 301
Russian Federation, 53–54, 87
Rwanda, 100

SAI. *See* Sustainable Agriculture Initiative
Saint Lucia, 54
Saint Vincent and Grenadines, 54
Salter-Nour, Cordelia, 305 (box)
Sanctions, 74
Sanlam, 261–262
Sardar, Ziauddin, 150, 150–151 (box)
Saudi Arabia:
    antidiscrimination/equal rights legislation, 54
    clothing as nonverbal communication, 208, 212 (n8)
    collectivism, 195
    constitution, 22
    diversity management, 236
    migration and migrants, 95 (box), 112
Scales of inclusion and diversity:
    Diversity Perceptions Scale, 328–332
    Perception of Inclusion-Exclusion Scale, 324–328
Schippers, M. C., 144 (table)
Schrempp, Juergen, 117
Scientists, 115
Self-esteem, sociometer model of, 168–169
Seuss, Dr., 234–235
Sexual harassment, 30, 34–36, 37–41 (table), 42, 121 (box)

Sexual orientation diversity:
    global demographic trends, 104–105
    global differences in treatment of,
        147–148, 162 (n5)
    as invisible diversity, 135, 145
    migration and, 120–121
Sexual orientation legislation, 30,
    31 (figure), 32–34 (table)
Shackelford, W., 143 (table)
Shell Intensive Training Programme, 277
Shell Youth Training Academy, 277, 280
Shiba Shinyo Kinko Bank, 28
Short- *versus* long-term orientation,
    192, 193 (table), 197–198
Sierra Leone, 100
Simpatia, 216, 227
Sin, H., 139 (table)
Slavery, 156–157, 158
Slovak Republic, 79–80
Slovenia, 33 (table)
Sneetches and Other Stories, The (Seuss),
    234–235
Social categorization, 177–180,
    180–182 (box)
Social comparison, 167–168, 183
Social competition, 186
Social creativity, 185–186
Social-emotional mental models, 219–220
Social identity theory, 175–186
    about, 175–176
    implications for diversity and
        exclusion, 183–186
    limitation in understanding diversity
        and exclusion, 183
    origin, 176
    significance, 176–177
    social categorization and intergroup
        discrimination, 177–182
    social identity and social comparison,
        182–183
Socioeconomic transitions, 107–127
    educational trends and workforce
        diversity, 121–125, 122 (table),
        123–124 (box), 124 (table)
    implications for diversity of gender,
        disability, and sexual orientation,
        120–121, 121 (box)
    migration of employers, 115,
        116–117 (box), 117–119,
        119–120 (box)

    occupational diversity of migrants,
        112–115
    worker migration, 110–112
Sociometer model of self-esteem,
    168–169
Sotomayor, Sonia, 77–78 (box)
South Africa:
    affirmative/positive action legislation,
        68, 68 (table), 70, 74, 75–76, 81
    antidiscrimination/equal rights
        legislation, 27–28, 53
    apartheid, 156
    communication between
        management and labor, 209–210
    corporate-community collaborations,
        278 (box), 287
    diversity management, 236, 239–240
    diversity statements, 248
    employment equity policies,
        261–262
    foreign direct investment in, 119
    international collaborations,
        306–307
    linguistic diversity, 205
    population growth, 89, 91
    race and socioeconomics, 145
    racial categorization experiments,
        177, 178 (box)
    racial discrimination, 27–28
    racial stereotypes, 152
    sexual orientation legislation,
        33 (table)
South America, 96
    See also specific countries
South Korea:
    age diversity, 101
    anti-sexual harassment legislation, 35,
        36, 38 (table)
    diversity management, 236
    as masculine society, 196
    migration and migrants, 112, 113
Spain:
    diversity management, 239
    migration and migrants, 111, 115,
        159–160 (box)
    relational mental models, 221
    sexual orientation legislation, 33
        (table)
Sri Lanka, 38 (table), 287
St. Helena, 55

State/national collaborations, 290–302
    barriers to, 293, 294 (figure)
    benefits of, 293–294, 294–295 (box),
        294 (figure)
    case illustration, 295–301
    implementation, 320 (figure), 321
    value base, 292 (figure), 318, 319 (figure)
Stereotypes:
    defined, 149, 151
    described, 149–150
    exclusion and, 169–170
    gender, 152–153
    generalizations and, 155, 157 (figure)
    as morally wrong, 151–152
    of Muslims, 150–151 (box), 153
    of older workers in New Zealand, 152
    positive and negative, 152
    racial, 152
    types, 154
    of women in workplace, 65
Suriname, 111
Sustainable Agriculture Initiative
    (SAI), 286
Sustainable development, 285–287
Svehla, T., 143 (table)
Swaziland, 91
Sweden:
    affirmative/positive action legislation,
        68 (table)
    antidiscrimination/equal rights
        legislation, 54
    diversity statements, 132–133
    as feminine society, 196
    migration and migrants, 94, 108, 111
    sexual orientation legislation,
        33–34 (table)
Switzerland, 132–133, 215–216,
    277–278 (box)
Symbolic interaction theory, 168

Tables, rectangular *versus* round,
    207 (box)
Taiwan, 34 (table), 39 (table), 95 (box)
Tajifel, Henri, 176, 180–181 (box)
Task-focused mental models, 219
Task *versus* relationship orientation,
    227–228 (box), 227–229
Tasmanian Aboriginals, 296
Telstra Corporation Limited, 249

Texaco, 242–243 (box)
Thailand:
    antidiscrimination/equal rights
        legislation, 54
    anti-sexual harassment legislation,
        38 (table)
    international collaborations, 308
    migration and migrants, 112
    population growth, 91
    state/national collaborations, 292
Thomas, R. R., Jr., 143 (table),
    144 (table), 146, 259
Thompson, Rachel, 265, 266
Time/punctuality, relational mental
    models about, 215–216, 216 (box)
Title VII of the Civil Rights Act of 1964:
    antidiscrimination legislation,
        162 (n3)
    employment discrimination, 43
    equal employment opportunity, 238
    race discrimination, 58 (n15)
    sex discrimination, 29, 58 (n14)
Togo, 113
Transfair USA, 310, 311, 313
Trinidad and Tobago, 54
Tunisia, 20 (box), 54
Turkey, 19–20 (box), 110, 111

Ubuntu, 210
Uganda, 162 (n5)
UK. *See* United Kingdom
Ukraine, 54
UN. *See* United Nations
Uncertainty avoidance, 191, 193 (table),
    196–197, 201
Unilever, 282–283, 285–288
Unilever Foundation for Education and
    Development, 287
Unintentional discrimination, 61
Union Carbide Corporation, 119,
    119–120 (box)
United Arab Emirates, 95 (box)
United Kingdom (UK):
    affirmative/positive action legislation,
        71–72
    age diversity, 101
    antidiscrimination/equal rights
        legislation, 27, 54–55
    anti-sexual harassment legislation, 35

Australian Aboriginals and, 296–297
diversity management, 239
diversity statements, 132–133, 248
fair trade, 313, 314
as masculine society, 196
migration and migrants, 94, 108, 110,
    111, 251 (n8)
United Nations (UN), 17, 23–24, 24
    (box), 207 (box)
    See also International Bill of Human
        Rights; International Labour
        Organization; Universal
        Declaration of Human Rights
United States:
    affirmative/positive action legislation,
        68 (table), 69, 70, 71
    affirmative/positive action legislation
        court challenges, 76,
        76–78 (box), 78–79
    age diversity, 87, 88, 100, 105 (n4)
    antidiscrimination/equal rights
        legislation, 55, 162 (n3)
    anti-sexual harassment legislation, 35
    business card exchange, 227–228 (box)
    civil rights legislation, 26
    conflict and harmony, 222, 223
    corporate social responsibility, 277
    diversity, as term, 133, 162 (n2)
    diversity definitions, narrow
        category-based, 134–135
    diversity management, 236, 238
    diversity training, 258
    employment discrimination overseas,
        42–43
    employment discrimination study, 25
    equal remuneration legislation, 29–30
    "fair discrimination" in
        gender-related employment,
        57 (n13)
    foreign direct investment in, 117–118,
        127 (n7)
    gender discrimination, 29, 30, 158,
        163(n10)
    gender diversity in workplace, 98–99
    gender stereotyping and workplace
        discrimination, 152–153
    homelessness, 10 (box)
    individualism, 195
    Iraq conflict, 154, 201, 202 (box)

life expectancy, 83, 86
migration and migrants, 109, 112,
    114, 153, 163 (n9)
migration trends, 91, 93–94 (box), 94,
    95 (box)
mission statements, 247
nonverbal communication, 206–207
outsourcing, 116–117 (box)
plural organizations, 245
punitive damages awards, 57 (n11)
racial and ethnic differences, 134
racial discrimination, 42
relational mental models, 220–221,
    228–229
religious freedom, 21 (box)
sexual harassment, 121 (box)
sexual orientation legislation,
    34 (table)
slavery, 156–157
welfare reform, 291, 293
workforce diversity research, 7
working-age population trends, 87
young-adult population, 4
Universal Declaration of Human Rights:
    about, 17
    as customary international law,
        57 (n2)
    employment rights, 18–19
    equality and nondiscrimination, 18,
        21, 45
    freedom of thought, conscience, and
        religion, 21, 48
    text, 44–50
    underlying philosophy, 16, 18, 45
    universal scope of, 21
    See also Diversity legislation
University of Michigan, 78–79
University of Southern California,
    277, 280

Van Knippenberg, D., 144 (table)
Vanuatu, 56
Venezuela, 36, 58 (n18)
Verbal communication, 203–205
Vietnam, 9 (box), 68 (table), 112, 287
Virgin Company, 3
Virtuous cycle, 280
Vis, Jan-Kees, 285
Visible diversity, 135, 145

Wales, 314
  See also United Kingdom
Walker, Sheila, 134
Wards Cove v. Antonio (1989), 58 (n15)
Watchmark-Comnitel, 116 (box)
Welfare reform, 291, 292, 293
Welfare-to-Work Tax Credit, 293
West, J., 141 (table)
"White man's burden," 156
Women:
  exclusion of, 165–166, 166–167,
    171–173
  gender discrimination in workplace,
    158–159, 163 (n10)
  India, 185
  in media, 152
  as migrants, 5
  New Zealand, 152
  Nigeria, 23–24
  relational mental models, 220
  rights of, 23–24
  status of, 185
  stereotypes of, 65
  in workplace, 4–5, 65, 158–159,
    163 (n10), 244
Woolworths Holdings, 248
Worker migration, 110–112,
  159–160 (box)
Workforce diversity:
  defined, 148
  definitions, based on conceptual
    rules, 136–144 (table), 145–146

definitions, broad category-based,
  135, 136–144 (table), 145
definitions, narrow category-based,
  134–135, 136–144 (table)
educational trends and, 121–125,
  122 (table), 123–124 (box),
  124 (table)
research, 7
  See also Diversity
Working-age population trends, 87, 89,
  89–90 (table)
Work-life balance, 258
Work Opportunity Tax Credit, 293
Work organization diversity, 256–273
  barriers to, 261–262, 261 (figure)
  benefits of, 261 (figure), 262–264
  case illustration, 264–272
  implementation, 320 (figure), 321
  inclusive policies and practices,
    257–259, 259–260 (box)
  value base, 257 (figure), 318,
    319 (figure)

Xerox Corporation, 62–63, 63 (box)

Yokoyama, Knock, 42
Young-adult population, 4
Yugoslavia, 110, 111

Zambia, 55
Zetsche, Dieter, 117
Zimbabwe, 55, 156